The State of Southern Illinois

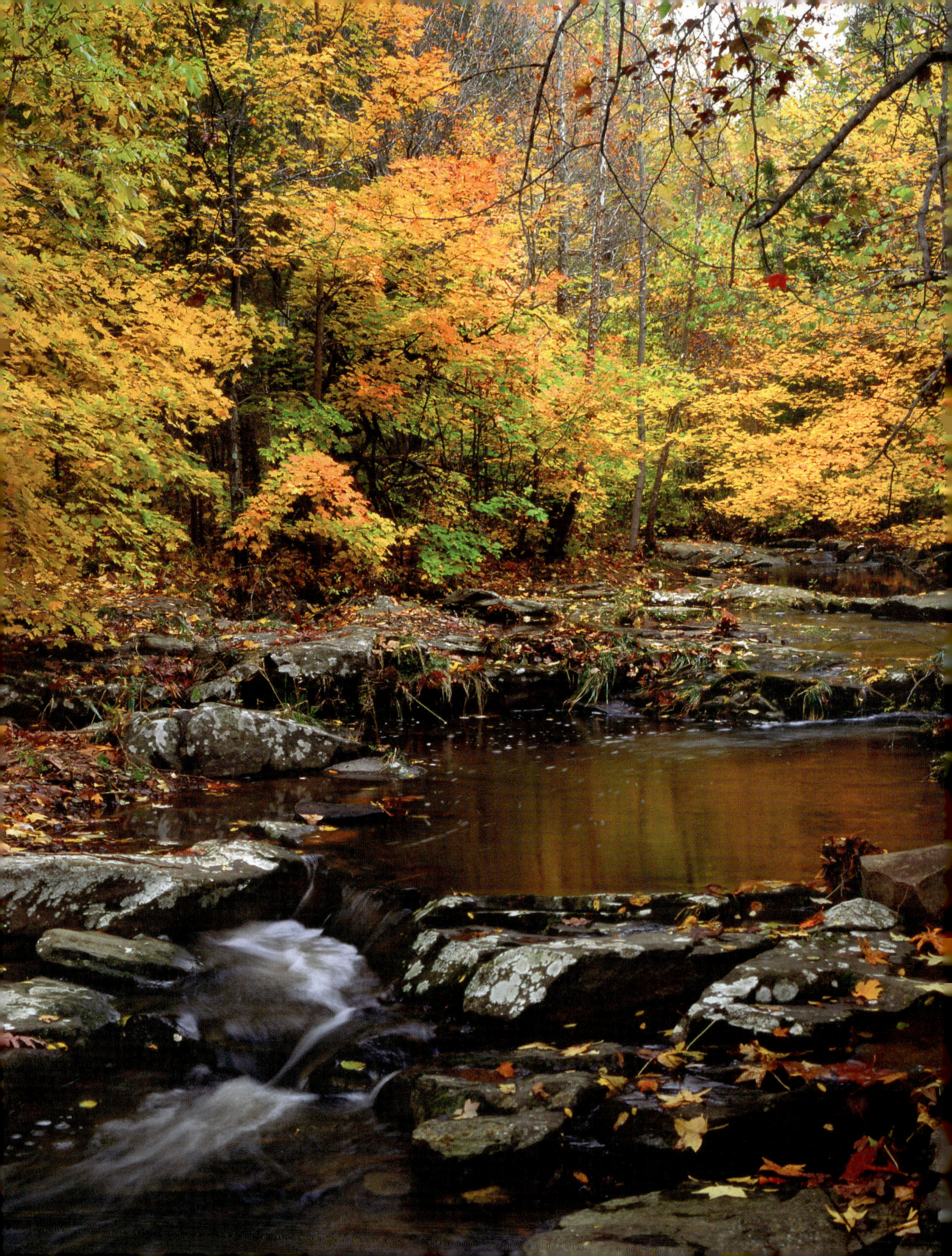

The State of Southern Illinois

An Illustrated History

Herbert K. Russell

Southern Illinois University Press
Carbondale

Printed in the United States of America

27 26 25 24 5 4 3 2

Frontispiece: Bucks Creek, Johnson County, Illinois (cropped); © David Hammond

Library of Congress Cataloging-in-Publication Data
Russell, Herbert K., [date]
The state of southern Illinois : an illustrated history / Herbert K. Russell.
p. cm.
Includes bibliographical references and index.
ISBN-13: 978-0-8093-3056-0 (cloth : alk. paper)
ISBN-10: 0-8093-3056-3 (cloth : alk. paper)
ISBN-13: 978-0-8093-9072-4 (ebook)
ISBN-10: 0-8093-9072-8 (ebook)
1. Illinois—Pictorial works. 2. Illinois—History—Pictorial works. I. Title.
F542.R874 2012
977.3—dc22 2011015557

Printed on recycled paper ♻

SIU
Southern Illinois University System

Table of Contents

Acknowledgments

Several people contributed in different ways to the making of this book: former marketing and editorial director James D. Simmons of the Southern Illinois University Press, whose suggestion that I work with Southern Illinois materials resulted in earlier books; former Press director John F. Stetter, who suggested that I write this book; and the Press' current editor-in-chief, Karl Kageff, who served as acquisitions editor and improved it. The Press' editing, design, and production manager, Barb Martin, shaped the volume, which was edited by Wayne Larsen; Lola Starck produced the maps.

I have been helped also by resources and personnel from Southern Illinois University's Morris Library and by its Special Collections Research Center. I am grateful also to Professor Daniel Overturf for helping me locate several of his former photography students and their photos; to Professor Carole Lawson for translating various French phrases; to family friend Emily Williams for her computer expertise; and especially to my wife, Thyra Russell, who helped throughout.

I am grateful also to Professor Henry Dan Piper, whose 1973 book *Land between the Rivers: The Southern Illinois Country* served as precedent. Piper recognized the uniqueness of the region, even to the point of capitalizing the *S* on *Southern Illinois*, a practice I have continued in the pages that follow.

Introduction

The title of this book refers both to the current state, or condition, of Southern Illinois and to the historical antecedents that make it so different from the rest of Illinois that it sometimes seems like a separate state. The book focuses primarily on the region south of U.S. Route 50, from Salem south to Cairo, and describes the underlying geology, the role a glacier played in shaping Southern Illinois, the presence of prehistoric and later Indians, the settlement by southerners, the region's colorful twentieth-century history, and life at the beginning of the twenty-first century. Parts of the book are revisionist: they offer new details about old assumptions and provide new ways of looking at things. A good many revisions concern the Civil War era.

The story of Southern Illinois wishing to secede at the beginning of the Civil War is easily its most exaggerated stereotype—but is arrived at only by ignoring how most Southern Illinoisans actually behaved. The southern third of Illinois was settled predominantly by southerners, the majority of whom were fleeing poverty. Many had lived by hunting and on "hog, hominy, and honey" on small farms in the Appalachian hills and uplands. Others were too poor to own land but might work as laborers or sharecroppers on farms owned by others. Contrary to what is sometimes written and taught, southern settlers did not introduce slavery to Illinois. France was the first European nation to control large parts of Illinois, and it was the French who introduced black slavery. Those who are unaware of this have naturally assumed that the region's southern settlers brought slaves with them. This is partly true, for some southern settlers did bring slaves, but small farmers and those too poor to own land were generally too poor to own slaves, and in any event, many landowners from Kentucky, Virginia, and elsewhere came to Southern Illinois to free their slaves.

Because most early settlers in Southern Illinois left behind few or no financial assets in the South, they had little reason to return and fight for the Confederate States of America. Relatedly, the aristocratic plantation society of the South often regarded poor whites as little more than "white trash" and treated them accordingly. Southern Illinois' settlers remained in the region because it offered them a better life than they had known elsewhere. This commitment to a new life in the North helps to explain an important phenomenon that occurred during the first sixteen months of the Civil War: Southern Illinoisans in the sixteen southernmost counties, from Benton south to Cairo, enlisted in the Union Army at a far greater rate (about 40 percent of eligible men) than did residents of the remainder of the state (about 28 percent). This detail was generally overlooked by northern newspapers in the 1860s and has seldom been mentioned since. To put it another way, some facts about

Southern Illinois have been ignored for so long by so many as to create a fictional history of the region.

There was, for example, no "army" of Southern Illinoisans that rushed south to enlist in the Confederate Army at the start of the Civil War, although this story has been repeated many times. The largest group to leave for the South consisted of only thirty-four men, most of whom departed from Marion on May 25, 1861. Thirty of the thirty-four had been born or raised in the South; only one had been born in Southern Illinois. They were placed in the 15th Tennessee Volunteer Infantry, and some fought and died at Shiloh and elsewhere. Others deserted or returned home to protect their families from Civil War passions manifested by their neighbors.

The popular story that John A. Logan saved Southern Illinois from secession with an August 19, 1861, speech on the Marion square is more folklore than fact. Logan did make an effective recruiting speech that contributed to the region's high enlistment rate, but by the time he made it, Captain (later General) Ulysses S. Grant had already mustered in a Union Army regiment of Southern Illinoisans at Anna; the thirty-four hotheads who wished to secede had been gone for eighty-six days; and for nearly four months thousands of Union troops had controlled or occupied strategic parts of Southern Illinois, including the Illinois Central Railroad, the East St. Louis waterfront and rail lines, the city of Cairo, some of the area's bridges, and parts of the Ohio and Mississippi Rivers.

The politician who did the most to counter secessionist talk in Illinois was Democrat Stephen A. Douglas, who made speeches in Springfield and Chicago urging loyalty to the Union soon after the war began. A similar task was performed in Carbondale by businessman Daniel H. Brush. He made public speeches urging loyalty to the Union on April 23 and 25, nearly four months before Logan's Marion speech. Stephen A. Douglas and Daniel Brush were both from the Northeast, a fact that anticipates a good many others herein: Southern Illinois is not nearly so southern as it has been painted, is less southern than some wish it to be, and has borrowed repeatedly from the East and the North. With regard to African Americans, for example, the Illinois legislature often followed practices popularized in the East and North to prolong slavery, keep blacks in their place, and make it difficult for them to settle in the state.

At the same time, some actions attributed to easterners belong instead to transplanted southerners. The first organized antislavery impulse in Southern Illinois churches came not from eastern ministers Elijah Lovejoy and John Mason Peck, as is sometimes reported, but from a former Virginian named James Lemen. Lemen was promoting the goals of "Emancipation Baptists" in 1809 at New Design, near Waterloo in Monroe County, thirteen years before Peck arrived in Illinois and twenty-seven years before Lovejoy did. Lemen and his five sons worked with other Emancipation Baptists and with Illinois governor Edward Coles during the years 1822–24 and helped prevent Illinois from becoming a slave state.

This book also provides useful information about pre–Civil War free blacks in Southern Illinois. We have heard so little of these that some readers may not know that Southern Illinois had any free African Americans. This book offers the first sustained discussion of twelve pre–Civil War black communities in the region, locates these settlements on a map, updates the story of how African Americans came to be in Southern Illinois, and touches on their involvement in the Civil War.

The book briefly notes why Southern Illinois had no major Indian wars and offers information about the Cherokee migration through Southern Illinois on the Trail of Tears. A good many Southern Illinoisans claim a Cherokee ancestor and usually assume that he or she slipped away from the Trail of Tears between Golconda and Jonesboro in the winter of 1838–39; marriage and family followed. This scenario could have occurred, for we know that at least 182 Cherokee left the trail during the march, but it is useful to recall that Cherokee and whites often intermarried in the Appalachian hills, and the Cherokee ancestor may have joined the family years before.

The State of Southern Illinois also shows how the railroads created dozens of towns that still exist, and notes the roles of coal, labor violence, gangsters, race relations, and the media in fashioning Southern Illinois' earlier image. Finally, the book updates history by marking the end of the "old" Southern Illinois that existed through the late 1960s and shows how education and changing times brought a new Southern Illinois into existence. The volume ends on a positive note, as it should, for Southern Illinois is a wonderful place to live, work, and visit. Photographs from some of the region's best photographers illustrate this, and maps keep readers on the right track. Southern Illinois retains its regional identity and probably always will. It is, after all, unique and in many ways a state of its own.

The State of Southern Illinois

The beauty of Southern Illinois is easily explained: nature has spent ages making it perfect, or nearly so. But it was not always this way. Millions of years ago, Illinois had a rocky and barren landscape, and some scientists think it had volcanoes. Volcanic rubble has been found far under the land's surface, buried by the glaciers that once covered most of the state. The glaciers may have leveled existing Illinois volcanoes before burying them, or perhaps the glaciers carried volcanic stones down from what is now Canada and then covered them.

What is known is that volcanic activity occurred some 170 million years ago in the Ohio River counties of Hardin and Pope south of Harrisburg. In several places the underground heat was so intense that it melted minerals and forced them upward, preparing the way for the fluorspar and lead industries that later flourished near the town of Rosiclare. The volcano best known to geologists is nearby Hicks Dome, an upward bulge in the earth caused by a sudden volcanic explosion. It is not well known to the public because it is on private property and because it is a "cryptovolcano," a volcano with limited signs of above-ground activity.

But Hicks Dome is a youngster compared with the ancient oceans that covered Illinois 600 million years ago. These receded and returned for some 300 million years, leaving behind sand, which became sandstone, and the remains of tiny sea organisms, which became limestone. The organic material trapped in the limestone is spread on fields and gardens to neutralize Southern Illinois' naturally acidic soils. The lighter and softer

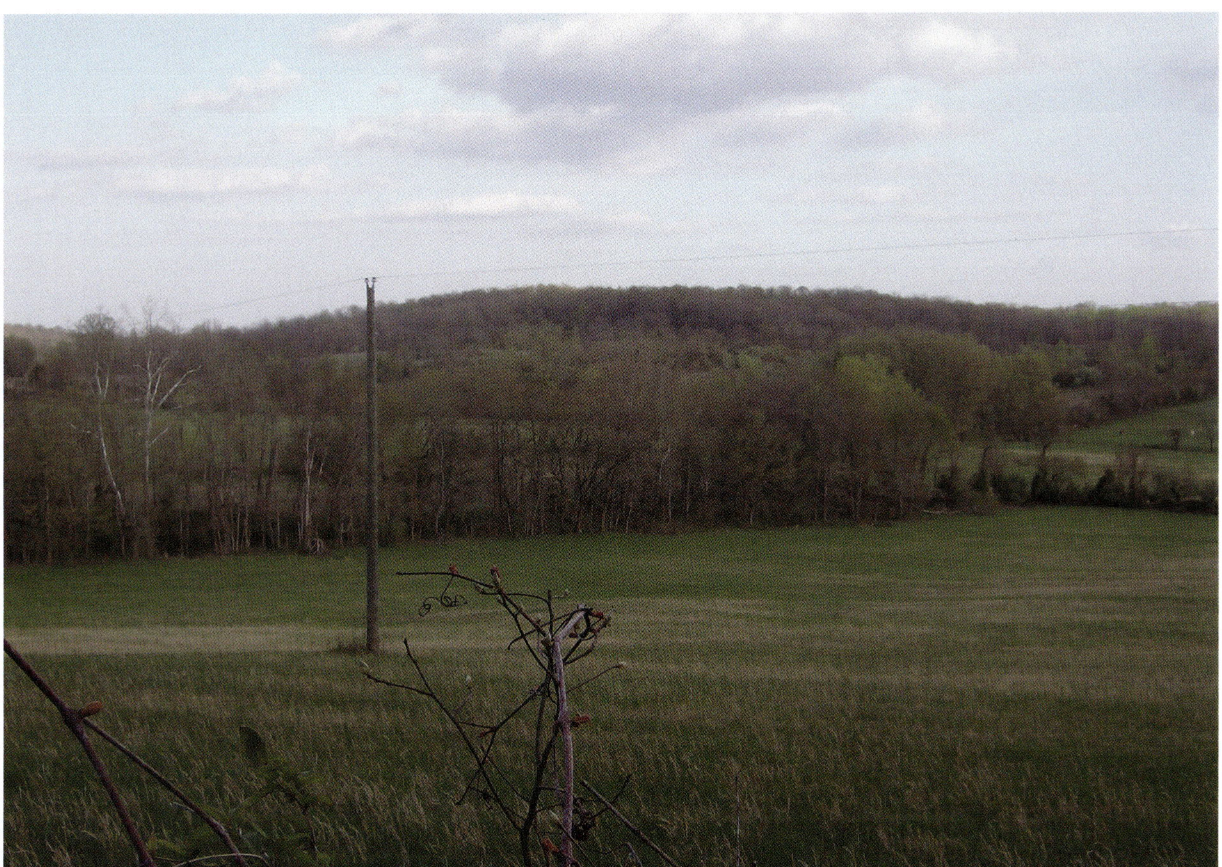

Relic from the age of fire and ice, Hicks Dome appears as a low hill in the center of the photo. The dome was created by a now extinct volcano that pushed rocks upward during an explosion. Hardin County. Photo courtesy of Brian DeNeal

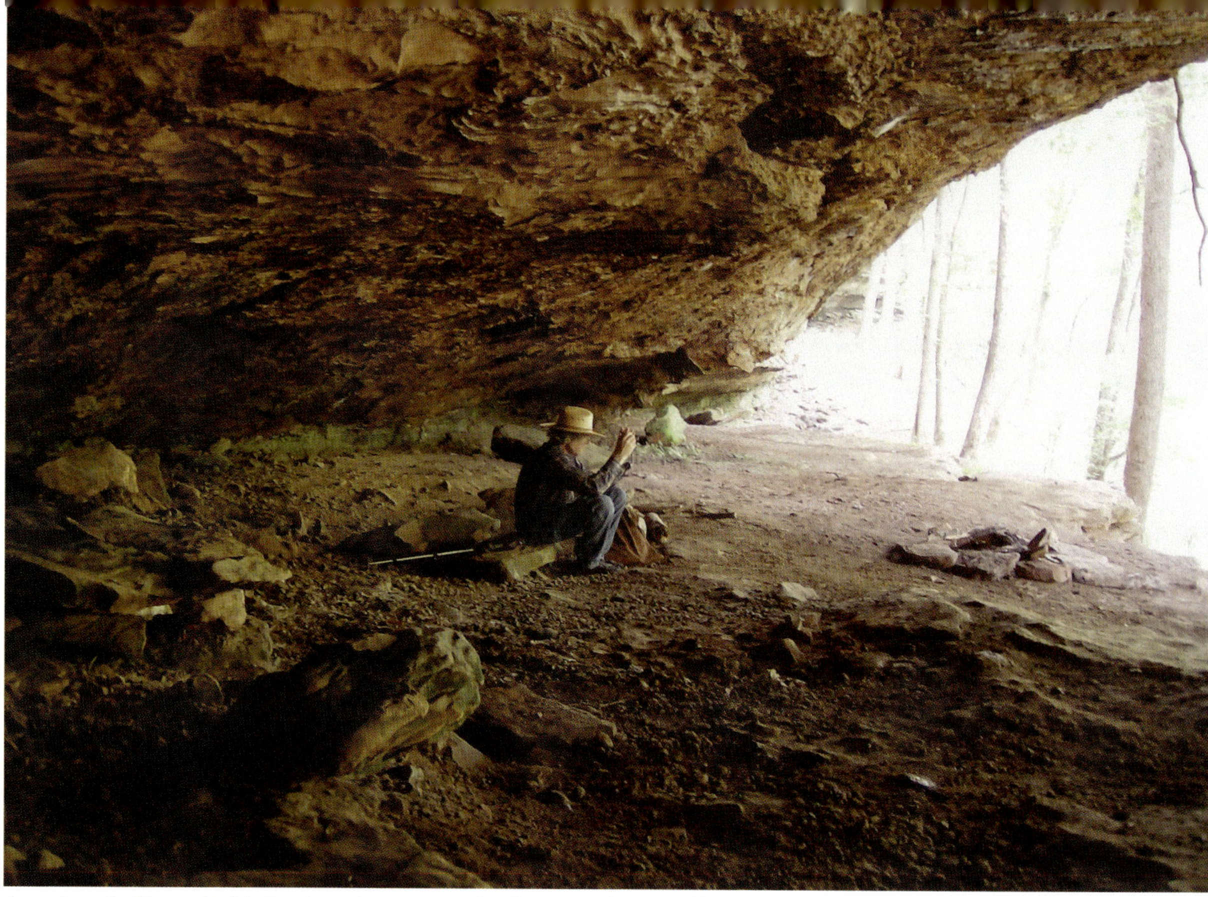

American Indians, the Native Americans, were the first to make use of limestone and sandstone ledges—as ready-made shelters known as "overhangs." Overhangs are still used, here to adjust a camera in a shady nook. Lusk Creek Wilderness Area. Photo courtesy of Brian DeNeal

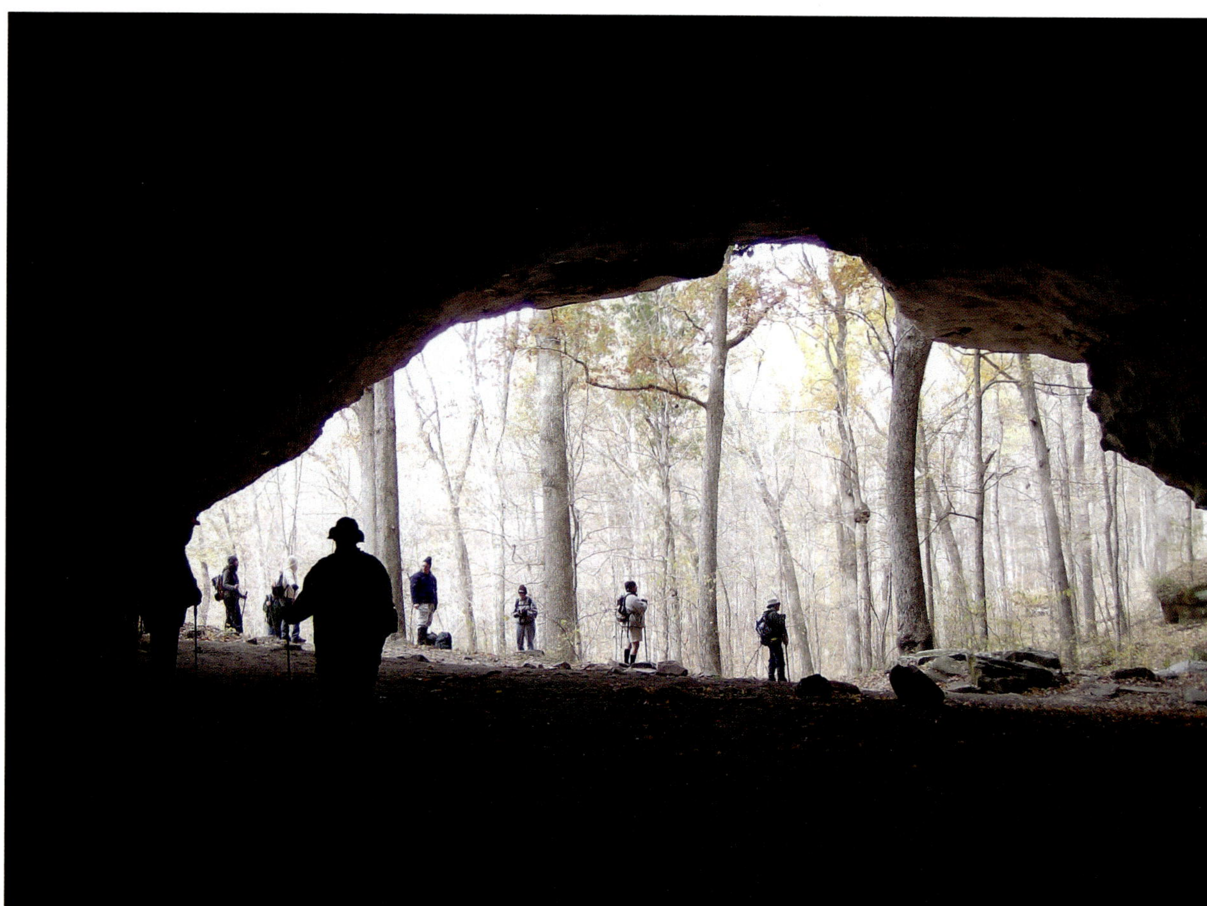

The view from inside a rock shelter suggests something of its security. Sand Cave, Pope County. Photo courtesy of Brian DeNeal

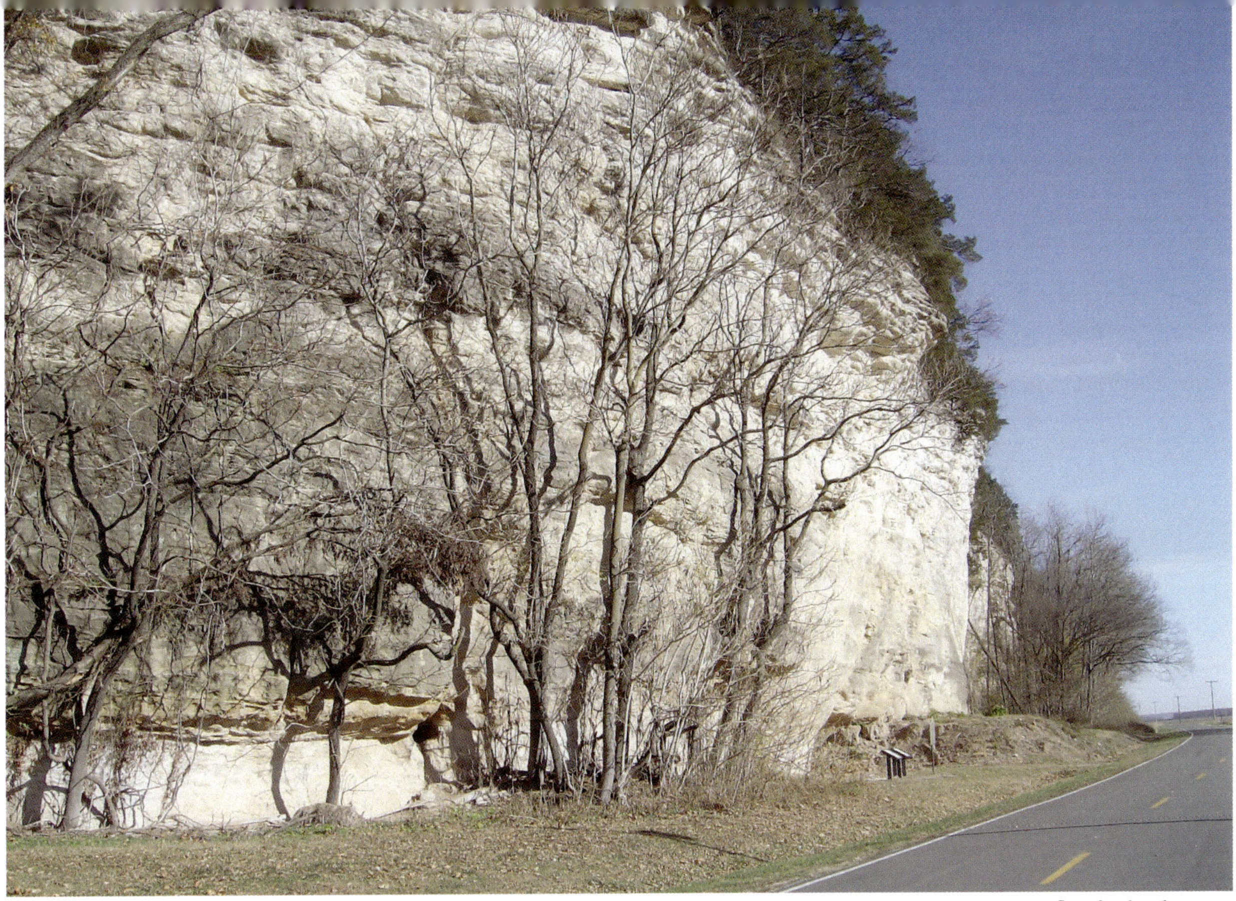

The Modoc Rock Shelter near Prairie du Rocher was used by humans for 10,000 years as Mississippi River floods slowly added sediment that filled the shelter to its ceiling and left the site as it appears today. Signs at the lower right interpret archaeological findings. Randolph County. Photo courtesy of Brian DeNeal

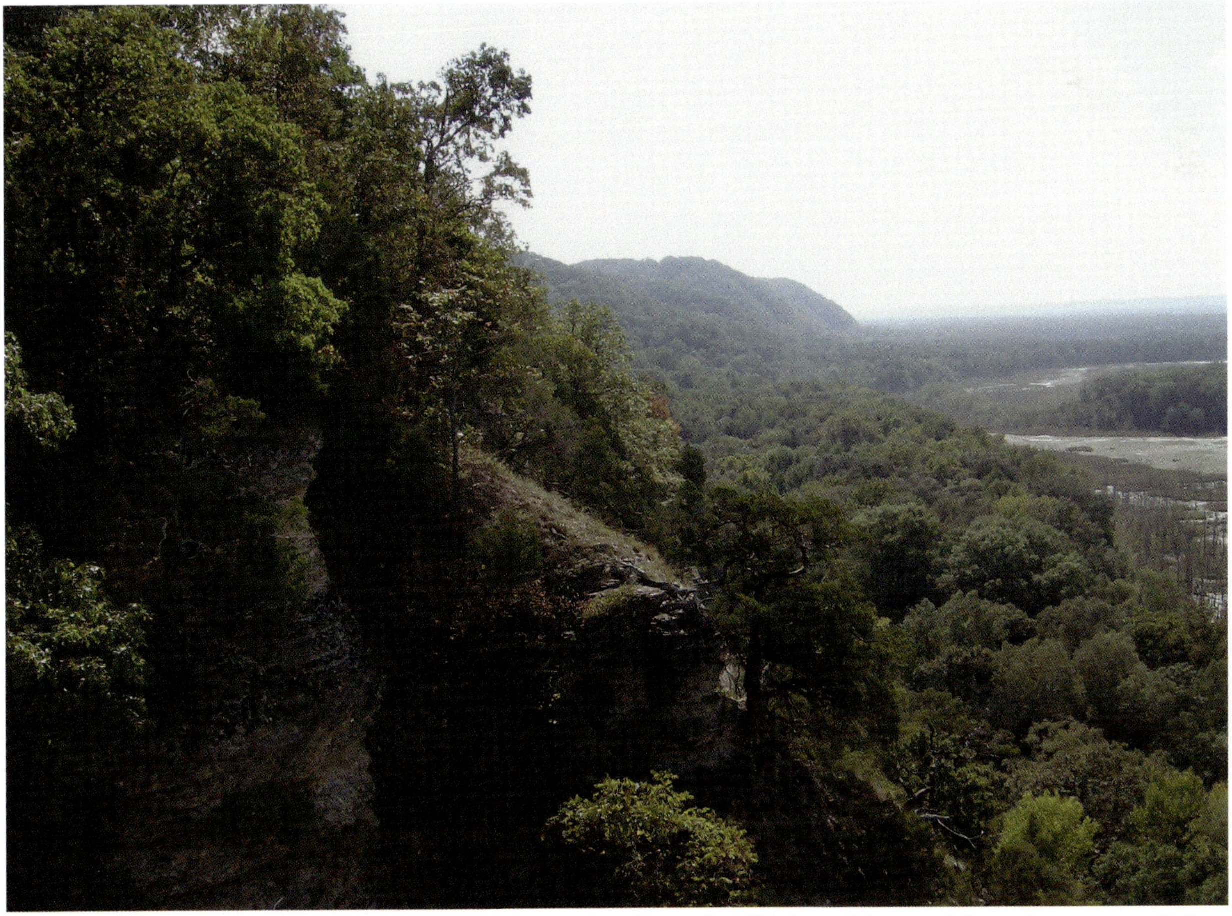

Limestone bluffs meet the Mississippi River bottoms near the village of Wolf Lake and Route 3. Missouri appears as a light blue line on the horizon at right. Photo courtesy of Brian DeNeal

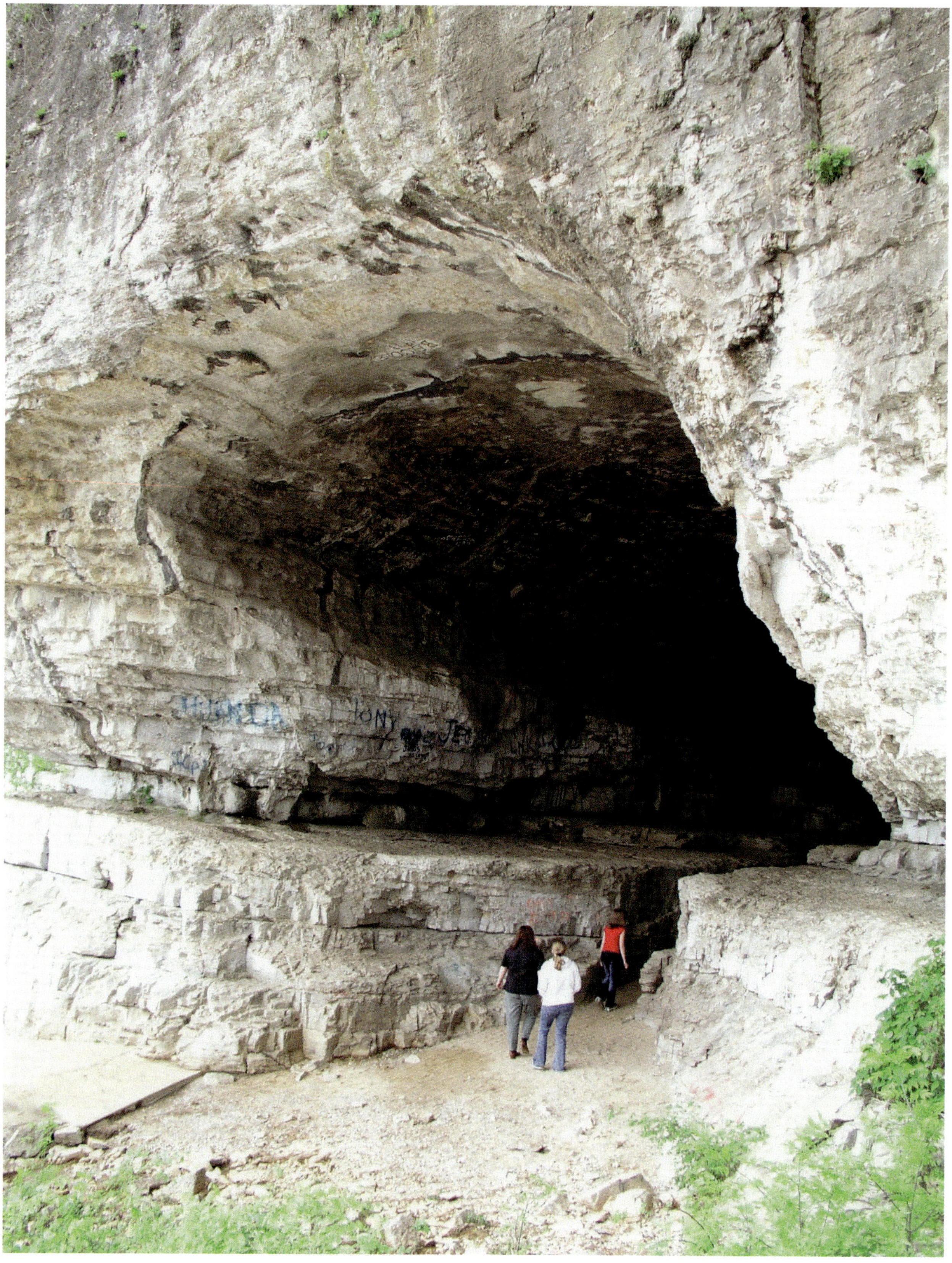

Limestone forms the best-known landmark on the Ohio River, Cave in Rock. Photo courtesy of Shannon Woodworth

sandstone yields readily to chisels and was used by early Southern Illinoisans for markers such as tombstones. Both stones have served extensively as building materials and are seen throughout the region.

Some 300 million years ago, the land that is now Southern Illinois was a tropical swamp in which heat and moisture caused prodigious growth of trees and other plants. These matured, fell over, and were covered by others until heat and the weight of partially decayed vegetation, sediment, and water compressed the vegetable matter into coal. The presence of coal's most troublesome contaminant, sulfur, was determined at this time: coal that was covered by salty sea water while it was forming or afterward has a higher sulfur content than coal that was protected from sea water by a layer of impermeable stone or covered by fresh water.

Another important geologic phenomenon occurred some 500 million years ago when nature laid the foundations for earthquakes in the New Madrid Fault. Twenty to twenty-five miles below the earth's surface, this 150-mile system of rock fractures zigzags from Cairo to New Madrid, Missouri, and into and out of Kentucky and Tennessee to the Arkansas town of Marked Tree. Some scientists think that pressures within the earth nearly tore the continent apart along this line, leaving a group of rock fractures, or faults, known collectively as the New Madrid Fault. The fault has been subsiding for millions of years, and when rocks on or near it experience stress beyond their limits, they shift and produce earthquakes. Quakes in the Wabash River area of southeastern Illinois may also be related to this fault.

About 60 million years ago, subsidence along the New Madrid Fault encouraged the Gulf of Mexico to extend northward into Southern Illinois and cover much of what is now the counties of Alexander, Pulaski, and Massac, and parts of Pope and Johnson Counties. The eventual locations of such villages as Belknap and Karnak were on the north shore of this ancient gulf, which brought with it a southern ecosystem of wetlands, sloughs, and swamps that still prevails. Complementing these are Horseshoe Lake, a U-shaped cutoff left by an early channel of the Mississippi River, and an ancient channel of the Ohio, which ran through the four southernmost counties some twenty miles north of the Ohio's present course.

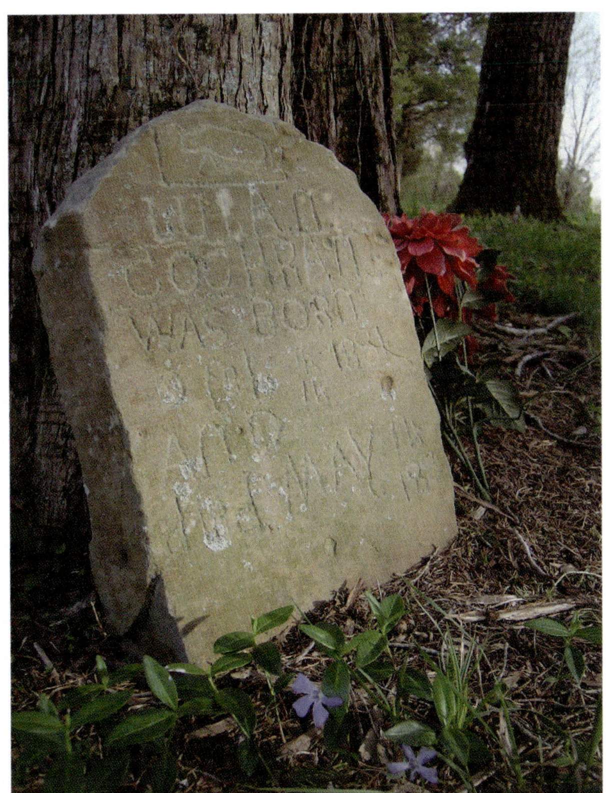

A tombstone made from local rock. Pope County. Photo courtesy of Brian DeNeal

The bayous, wetlands, and Louisiana-like ecology of Southern Illinois' lower counties stand in contrast to the rest of the state, which has a far different geologic past. For thousands of years, erosive forces of wind and rain raked the rocky surfaces of ancient Illinois and shaped hills of limestone and sandstone while wearing down the valleys. Nearly all of these would be obliterated by nature's next important shaping force, the glaciers.

Scientists do not agree on why snow fell so thickly about 2 million years ago, or why it continued so long as to create the Ice Age and glaciers that inched down out of the Arctic and Canada to affect Illinois. These advanced and receded in repetitive cycles of warming and cooling until they pulverized mineral-laden rocks and helped create soil. The glacier of greatest magnitude is called the "Illinoian" because it covered nearly all the state. A sheet of ice that stood over a mile high, it started from the north some 300,000 years ago and moved slowly south before parking itself 150,000 years ago near Illinois Route 13, slightly south of Carbondale and Marion and north of Harrisburg.

The Illinoian glacier was responsible for shaping most of the terrain of Southern Illinois. Land south of Interstate 70 (Effingham) to Route 13 (Carbondale, Marion, and Harrisburg) is generally flat to rolling with

(Right hand page) Great blue herons begin their day at Crab Orchard Lake, Williamson County. Photo courtesy of David Hammond

The extension of the Gulf of Mexico into the lower counties of Southern Illinois helped create a Deep South ecology that remains to this day. A Cache River observation area offers an excellent view of surrounding swamps and wetlands. Photo courtesy of David Hammond

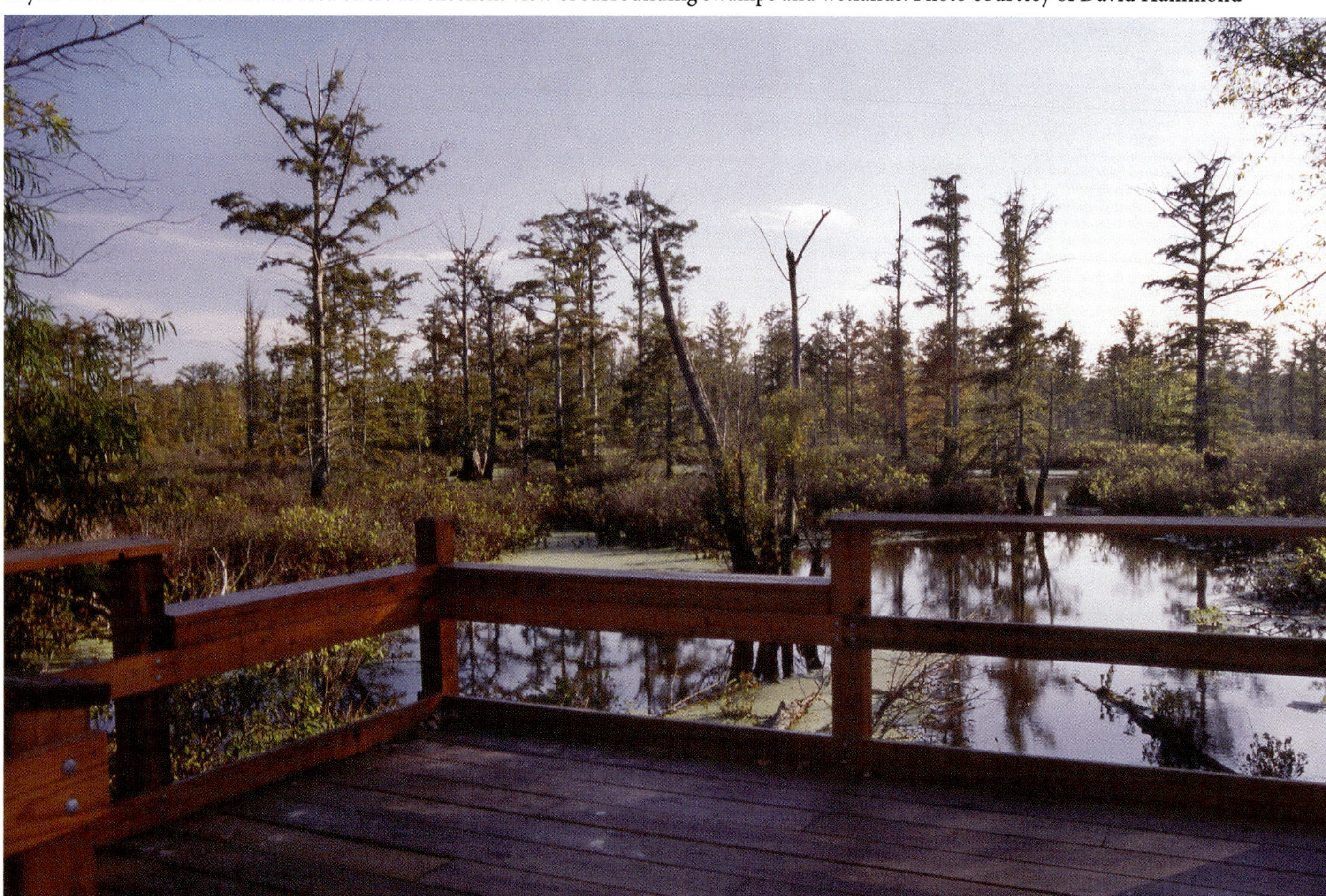

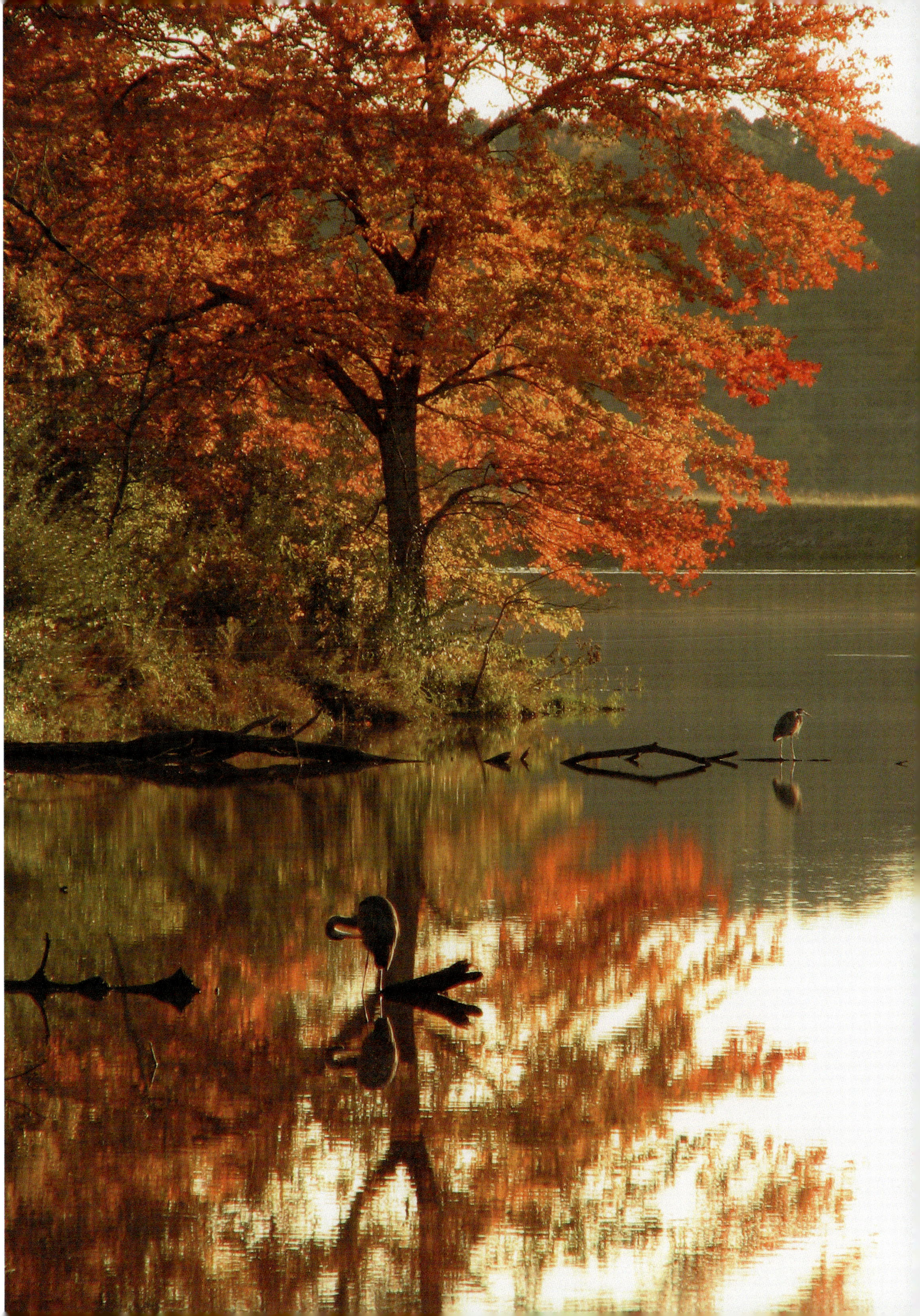

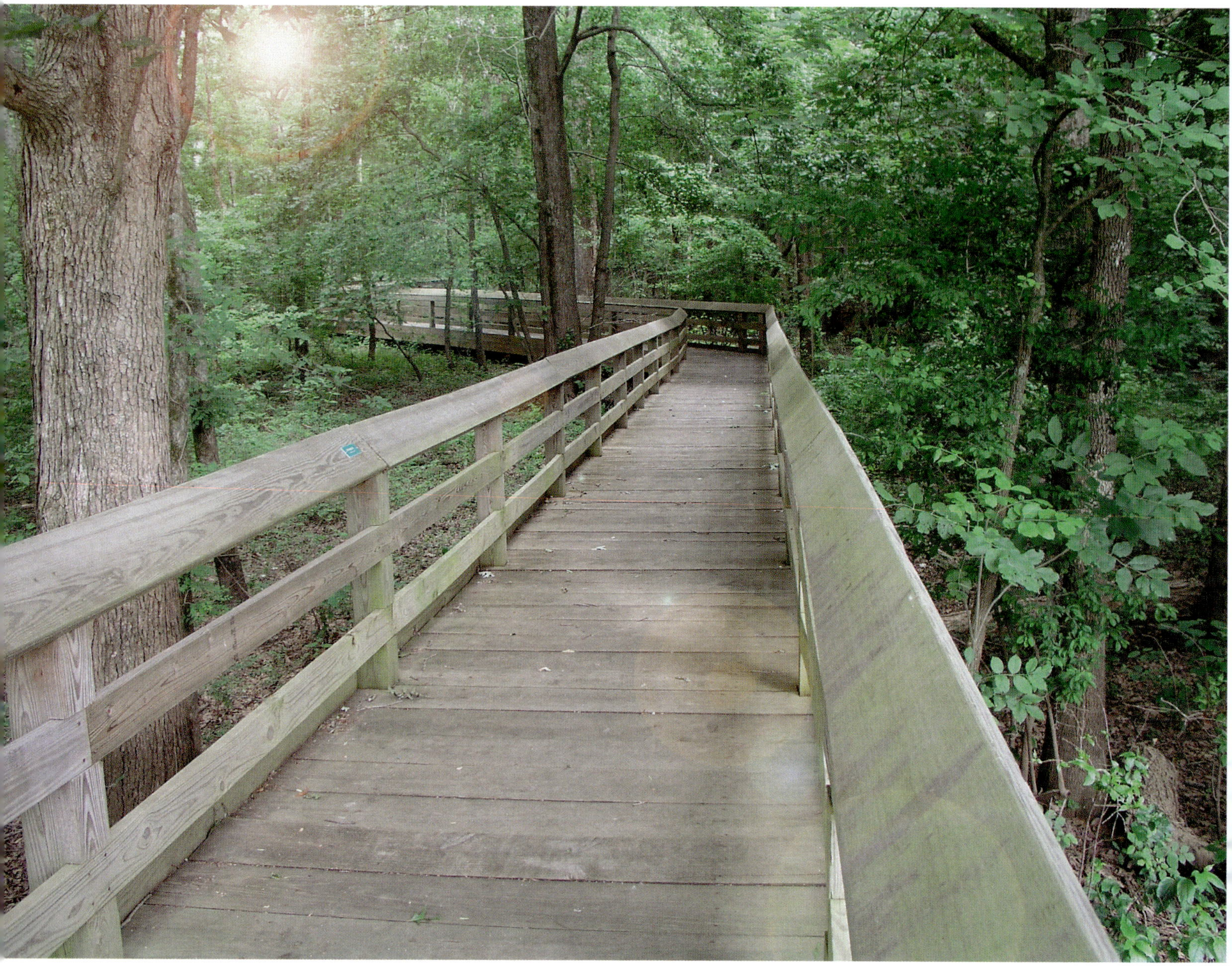

This elevated boardwalk in the Cache River State Natural Area is handicap accessible and leads visitors to swamp and bottomland trees that are identified by type. Many Southern Illinois trees hold state records for size. Section 8 Nature Preserve, Route 37 north of New Grand Chain. Photo courtesy of Shannon Woodworth

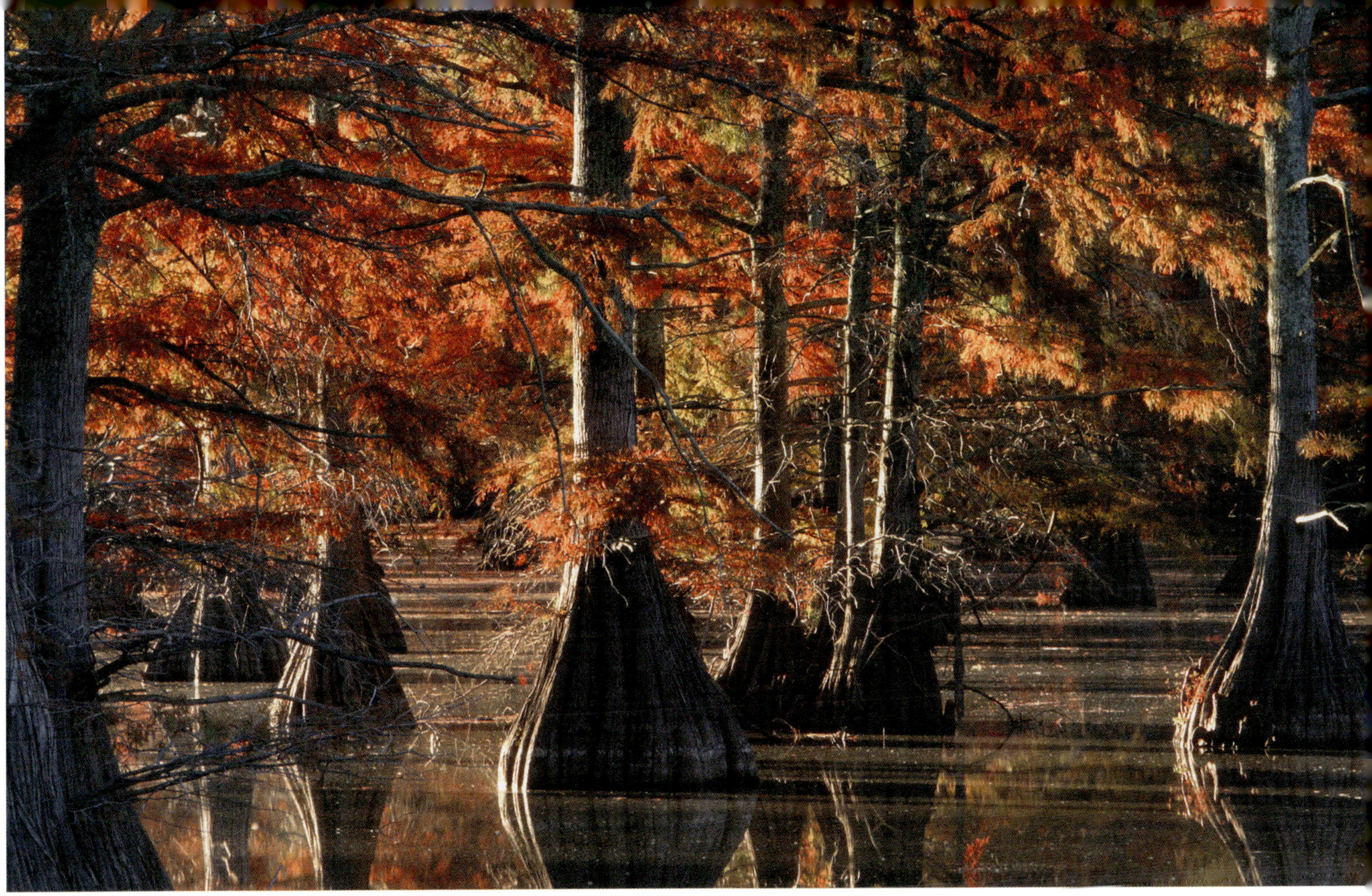

A bald cypress swamp assumes fall colors at Horseshoe Lake in Alexander County. Photo courtesy of Susan Day/Daybreak Imagery

Canoeists paddle among shrubs in a Cache River swamp. Photo courtesy of David Hammond

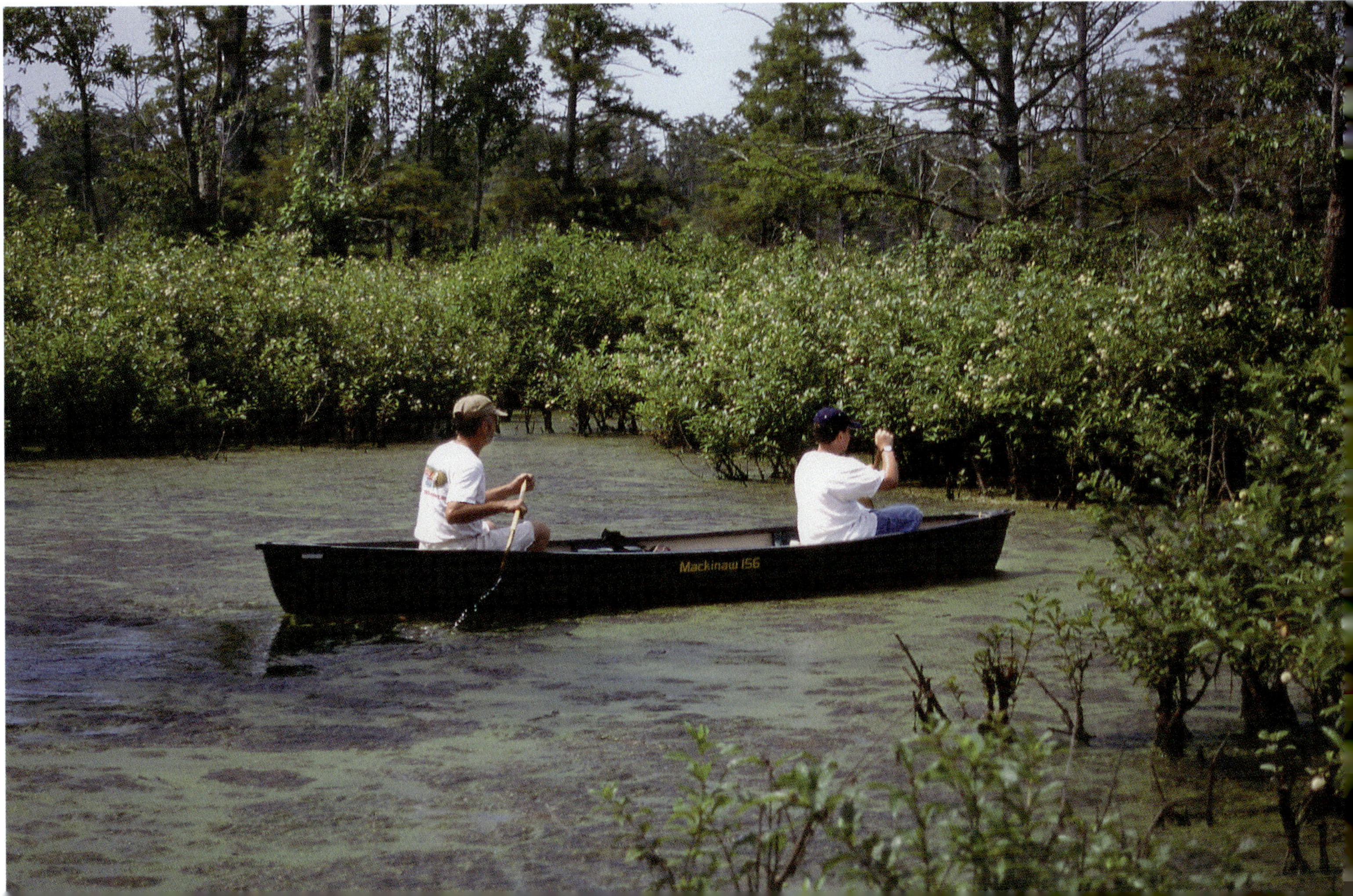

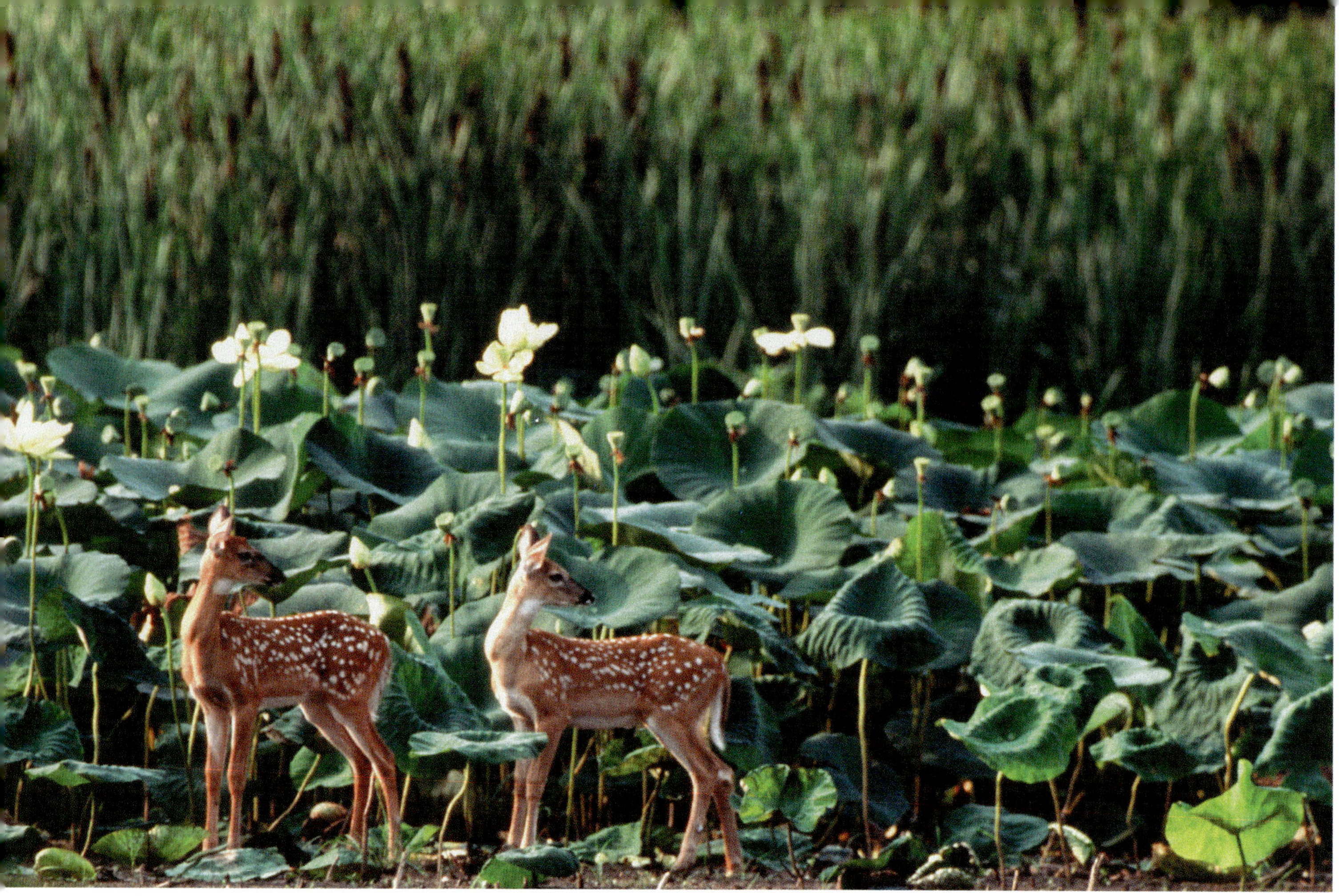

Twin fawns pause on a Southern Illinois lake bed among lotus flowers taller than they are. Photo courtesy of Richard Day/Daybreak Imagery

Geese on a chilly morning. Southern Illinois swamps and lakes are resting, nesting, and feeding areas for birds on or near the Mississippi Flyway, a route for migratory birds. Photo courtesy of David Hammond

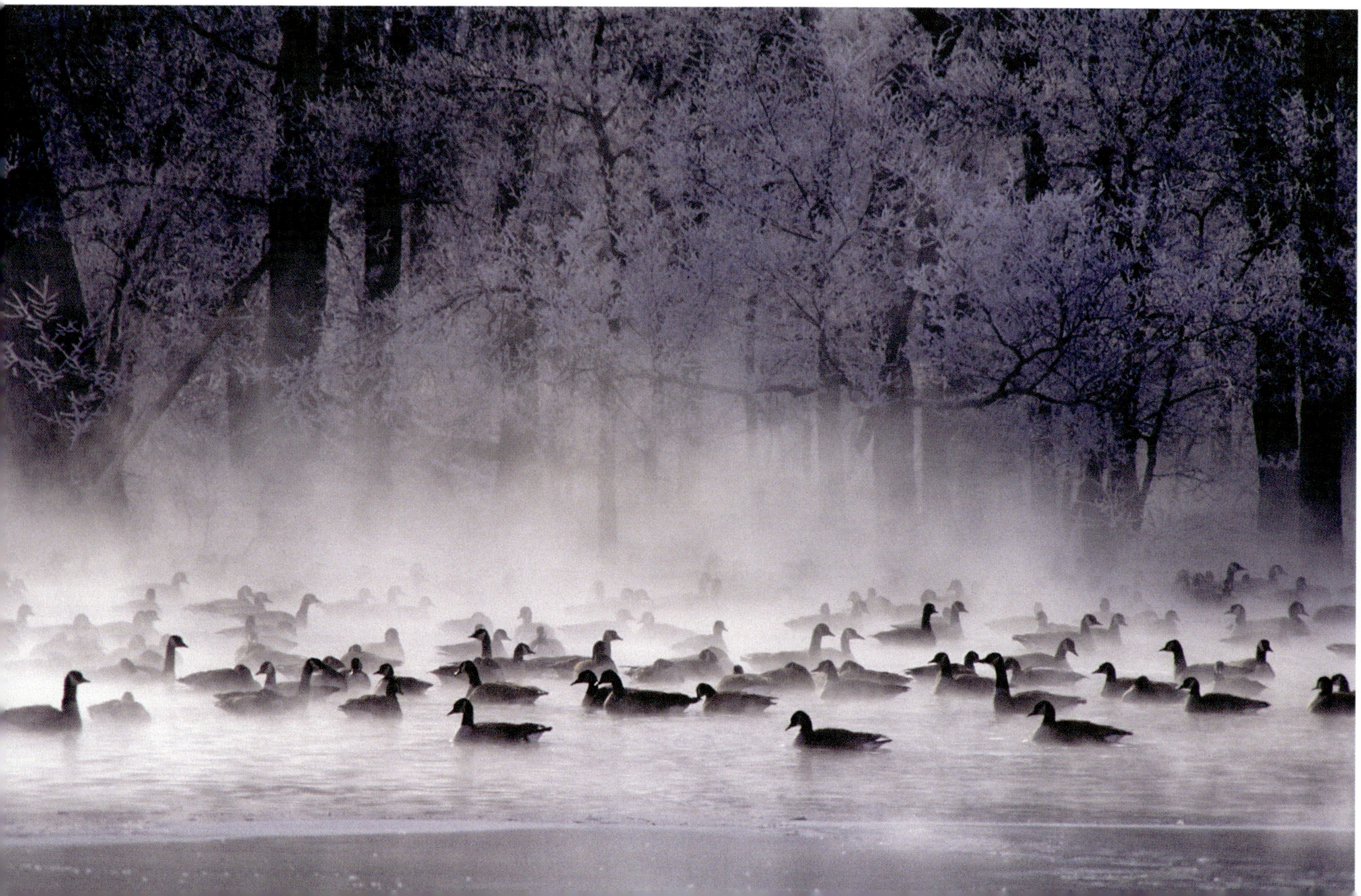

dozens of small prairies smoothed by the Illinoian glacier; unglaciated areas south of Route 13 are hilly except near rivers. One of the prettiest of these unglaciated areas is the Shawnee Hills, an east-west mountain range stretching from Cave in Rock and Golconda on the Ohio River west to Anna, Cobden, Alto Pass, and Pomona in a band fifteen to forty miles wide. Except for the effects of wind, water, and erosion, the Shawnee Hills are largely as nature left them some 300 million years ago. The most spectacular examples of this ancient landscape are found south of Harrisburg. Here layers of hard and soft stone have weathered at different rates and produced named rock structures such as Camel Rock in the Garden of the Gods and Old Stone Face, unsmiling guardian of Eagle Mountain.

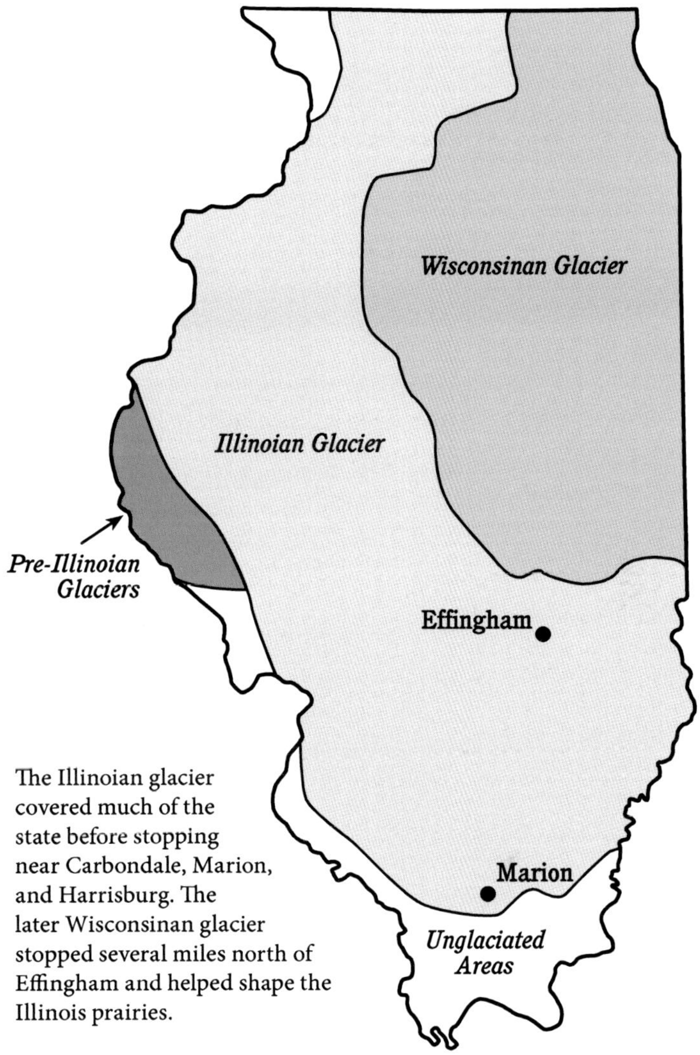

The Illinoian glacier covered much of the state before stopping near Carbondale, Marion, and Harrisburg. The later Wisconsinan glacier stopped several miles north of Effingham and helped shape the Illinois prairies.

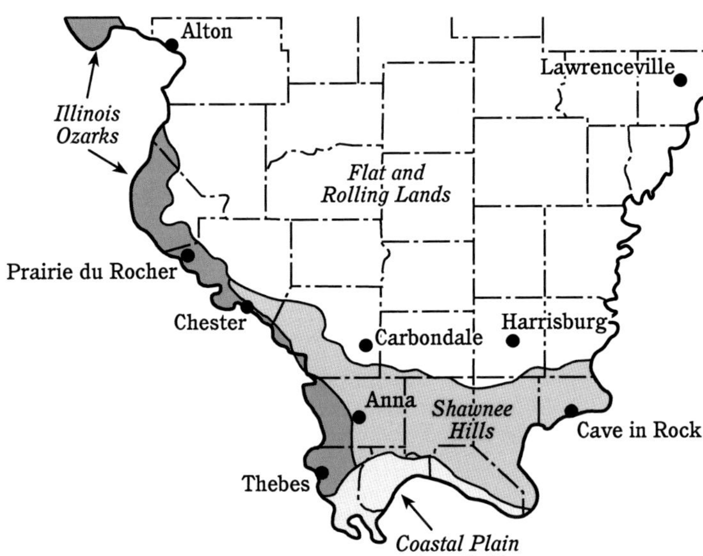

These hills impound archaic silence
Much as misers with their gold.
They do not waste it on the world
But keep it, hug it, and grow old.

—From *Blue Hills, Blue Shadows*
by Gary DeNeal

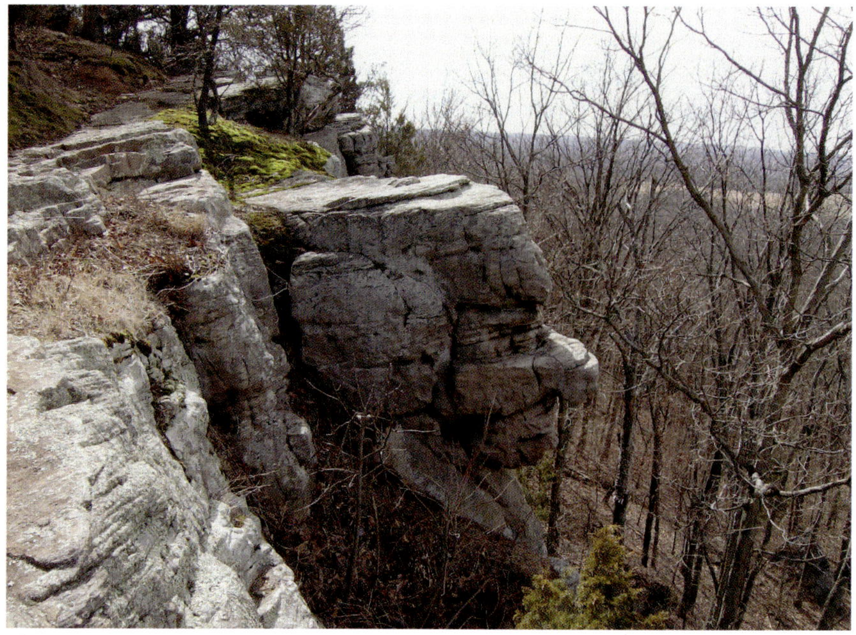

The profile of Old Stone Face in Saline County was sculpted by eons of wind and rain and saved for posterity when glaciers stopped before reaching it. Photo courtesy of Brian DeNeal

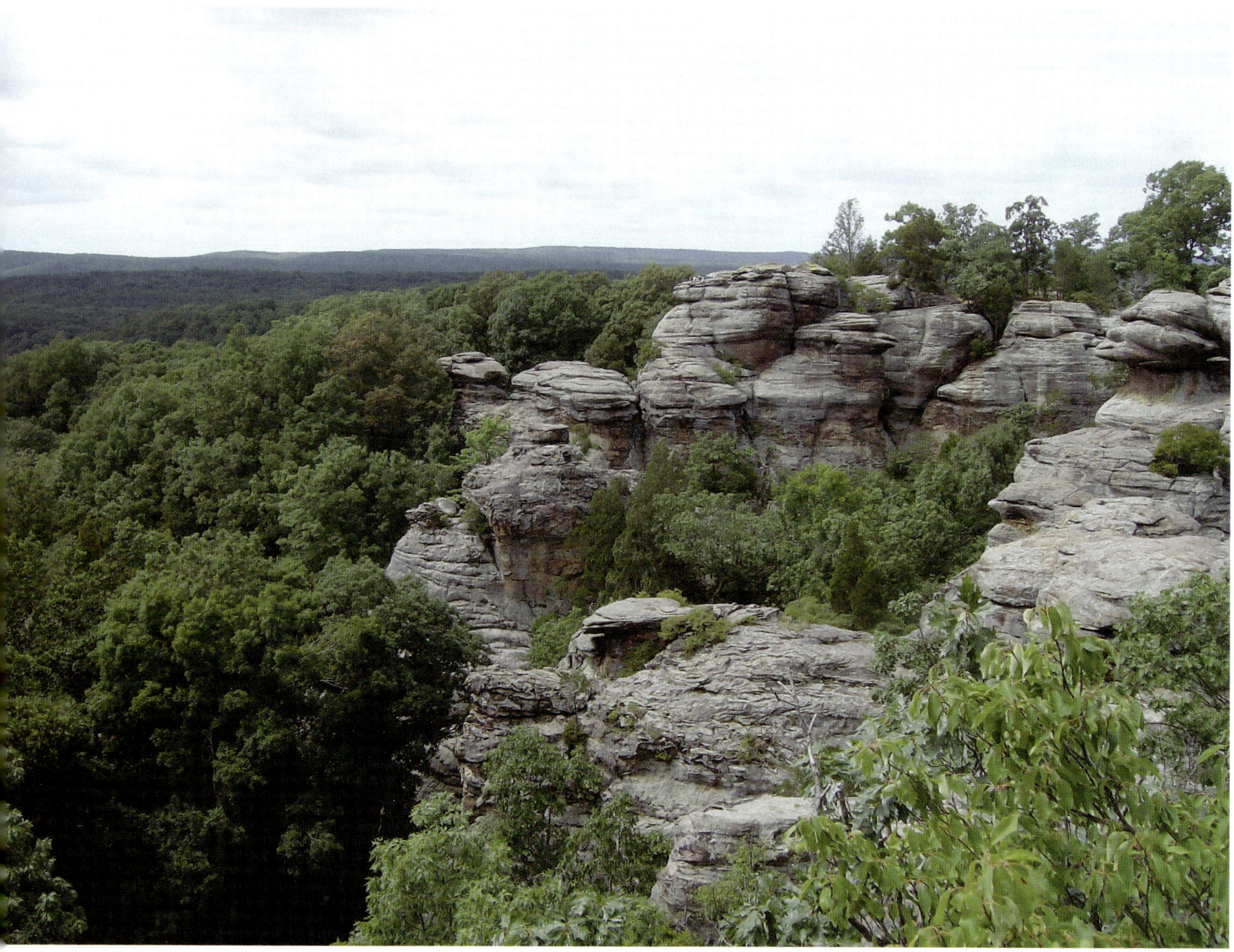

Camel Rock is one of the region's most recognizable geologic formations. Garden of the Gods, Saline County. Photo courtesy of Brian DeNeal

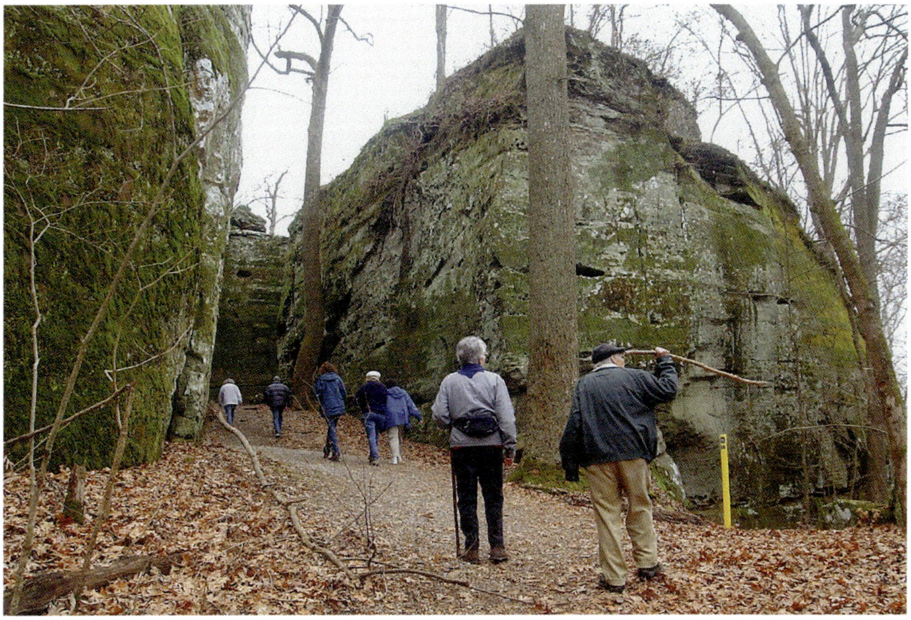

Hotel-sized boulders at Giant City State Park near Makanda show the rugged topography of areas untouched by glaciers. Photo by Steve Jahnke; courtesy of the *Southern Illinoisan*

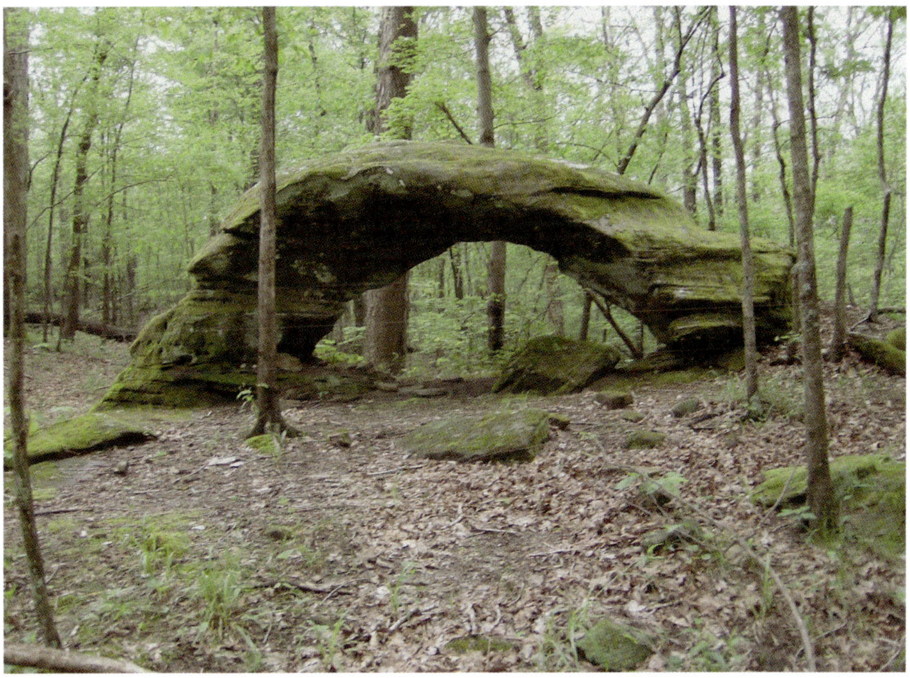

A moss-covered natural bridge in the Shawnee Hills. Johnson County. Photo courtesy of Brian DeNeal

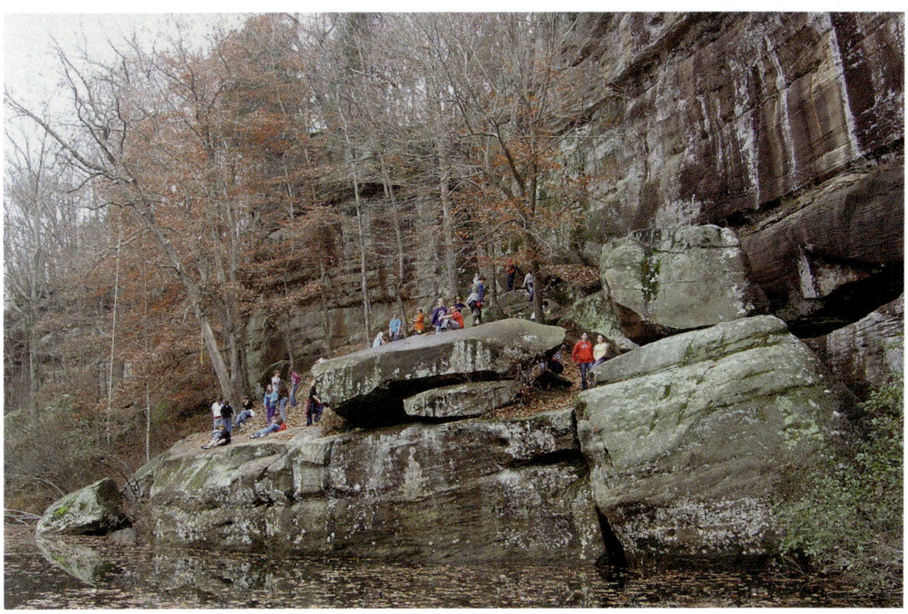

Older than dirt and then some, the Shawnee Hills are thought to be 300 million years old and offer a pretty outing for school children. Bell Smith Springs. Photo courtesy of Brian DeNeal

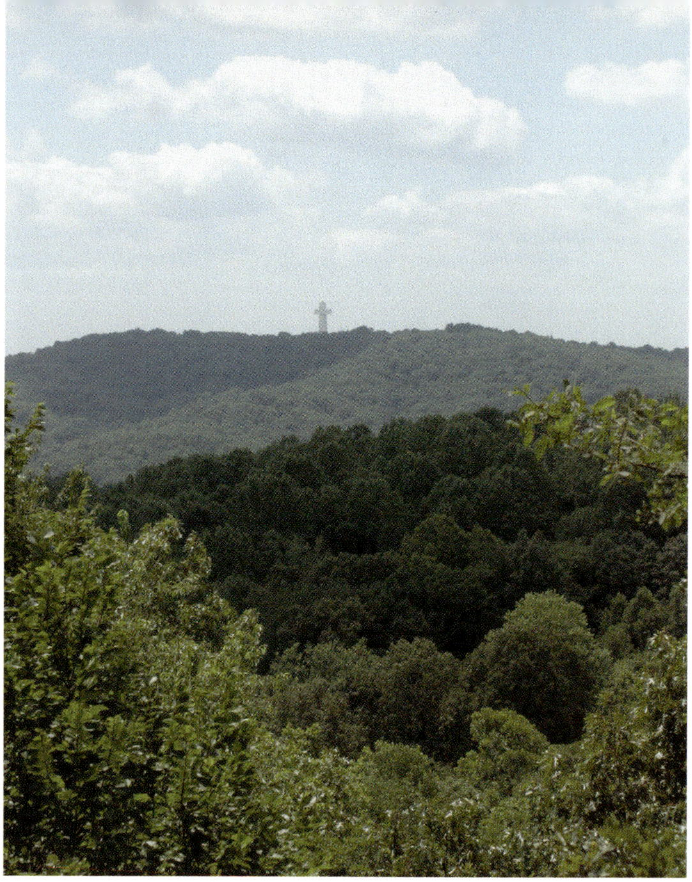

The rocky hilltop of Bald Knob is the site of a cross visible for miles. Union County. Photo courtesy of Shannon Woodworth

A second area spared by the glacier flanks the Mississippi River for 100 miles and is known as the Illinois Ozarks. These immense bluffs of limestone and sandstone run north from Thebes to Anna and curve northwest to Chester before heading past Prairie du Rocher ("prairie by the rock") to Alton. The best-known mountain in the Illinois Ozarks is Bald Knob, site of a Christian cross that rises 111 feet. One of the most important wetlands is LaRue Swamp, which abuts the Pine Hills portion of the Illinois Ozarks in Union County where it provides habitat for a wide assortment of rare plant and animal species.

The Shawnee Hills and the Illinois Ozarks look somewhat alike but have different names because they were formed during two different geologic periods. The Shawnee Hills are an ancient gift from Kentucky, an extension of one of its mountain ranges. The Illinois Ozarks are 50 million to 100 million years older and are related to the Missouri Ozarks, which crossed into Illinois before the Mississippi River assumed its present channel. Both sets of hills received modern shaping from the New Madrid Fault during the earthquakes of 1811–12, as settler Thomas Gore remarked of disruptions near the Johnson-Union County line: "Great blocks of stone, large as a house, were torn from the bluff . . . in a terrifying earthquake."

The last of the Illinois glaciers arrived about 75,000 years ago and gave much of central Illinois its flat prairie lands and rich, black dirt. It is called the "Wisconsinan" glacier, but like the Illinoian it probably came from the northeast through what is now Michigan and Lake Michigan. It moved south through the sites of towns such as Kankakee, Bloomington, Champaign, and Mattoon before the main part of the glacier neared its southern limit a dozen or so miles north of Effingham. When the Wisconsinan glacier melted 10,000–12,000 years ago, it left behind finely ground soil and minerals on a large, flat prairie and helped lay the foundations for agricultural differences between Southern Illinois and the rest of the state. The thin, acidic topsoil of Southern Illinois between Effingham and Carbondale measures several inches in depth because it is older and eroded and because only one soil-enriching glacier passed through the region. The black soil in much of northern and central Illinois enjoys the benefits of several glaciers and centuries of soil-building prairie plants such as big bluestem. These soils often measure several feet in depth and are perfect for crops. Both glaciers delivered northern plant species to their respective regions, most visibly in the lower

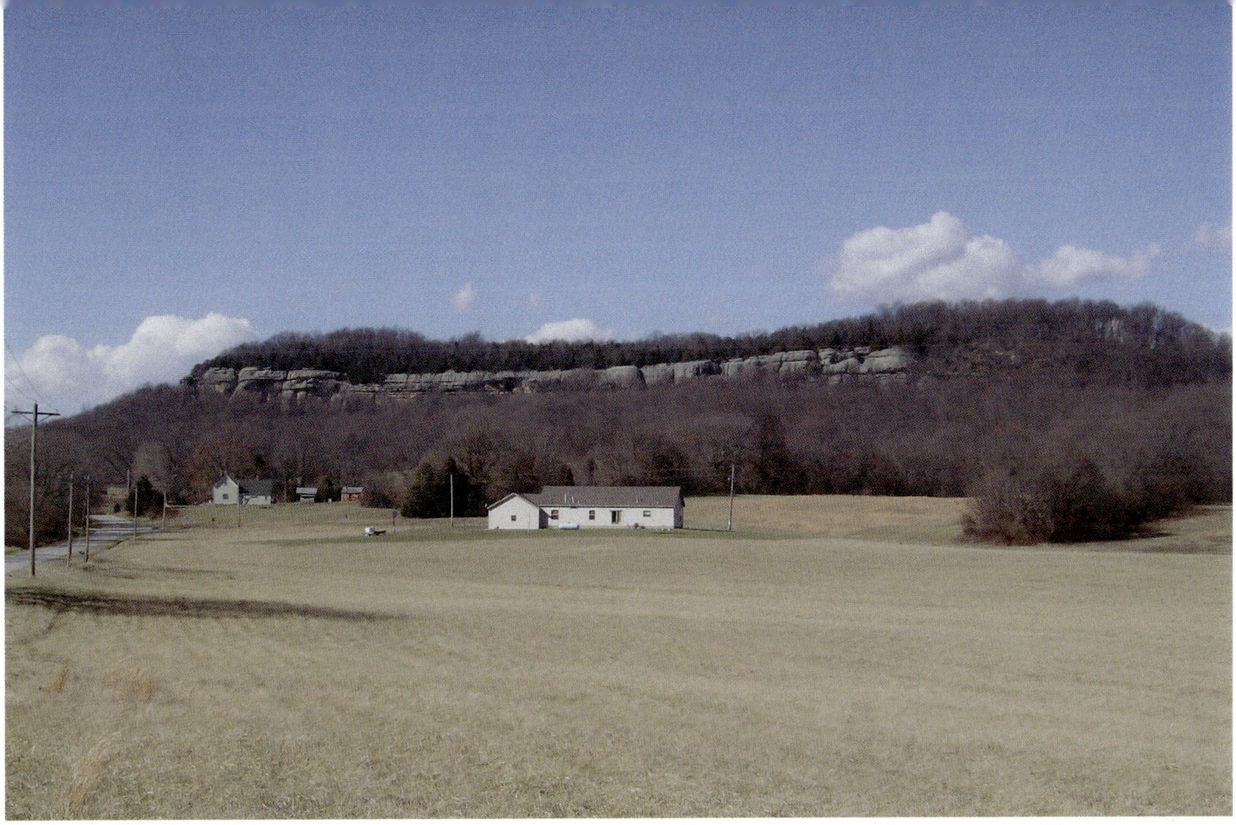

One of the region's most impressive rock formations is Drapers Bluff, here seen towering above houses in Union County. Photo courtesy of Brian DeNeal

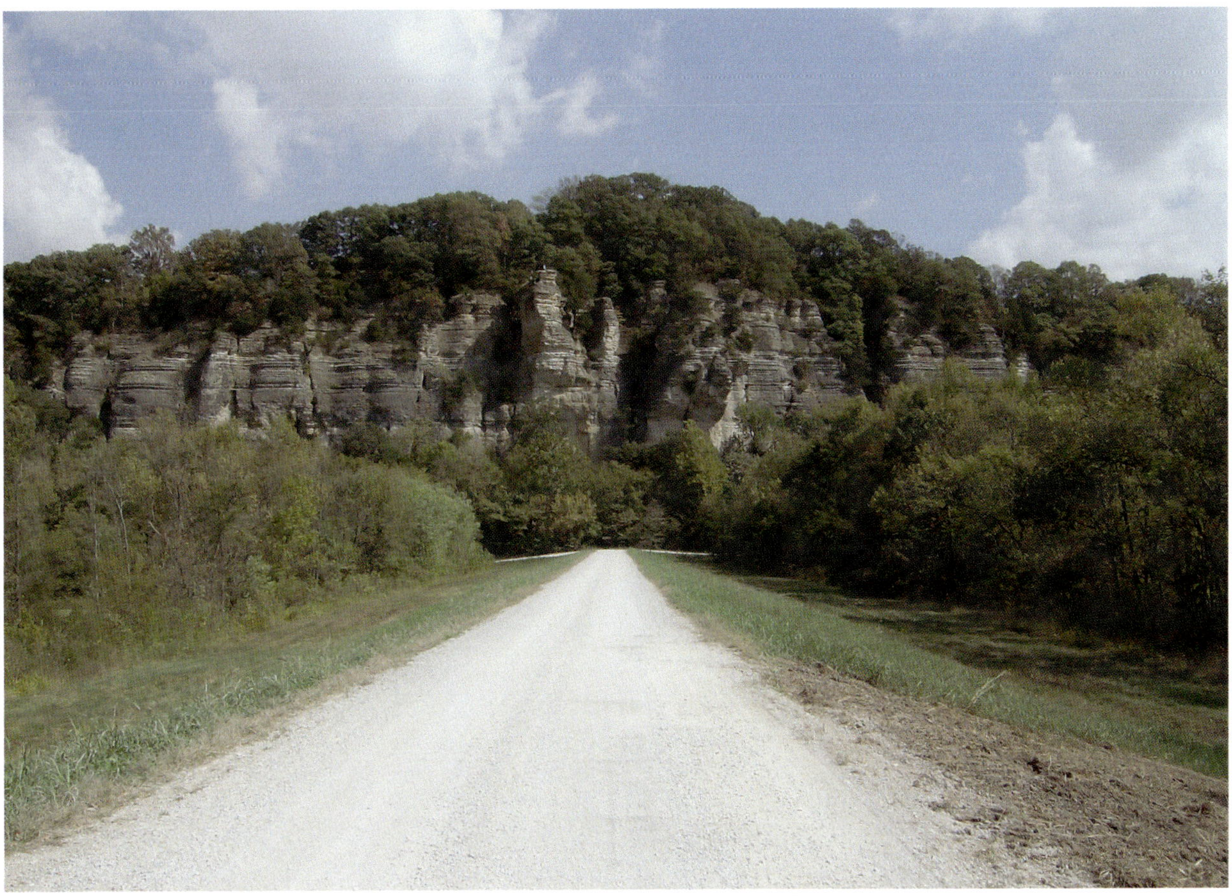

The cliffs of Pine Hills rise 300 feet above old river bottoms and LaRue Swamp. A tiny human figure in white is visible at the top of the bluff. Near Route 3, Union County. Photo courtesy of Brian DeNeal

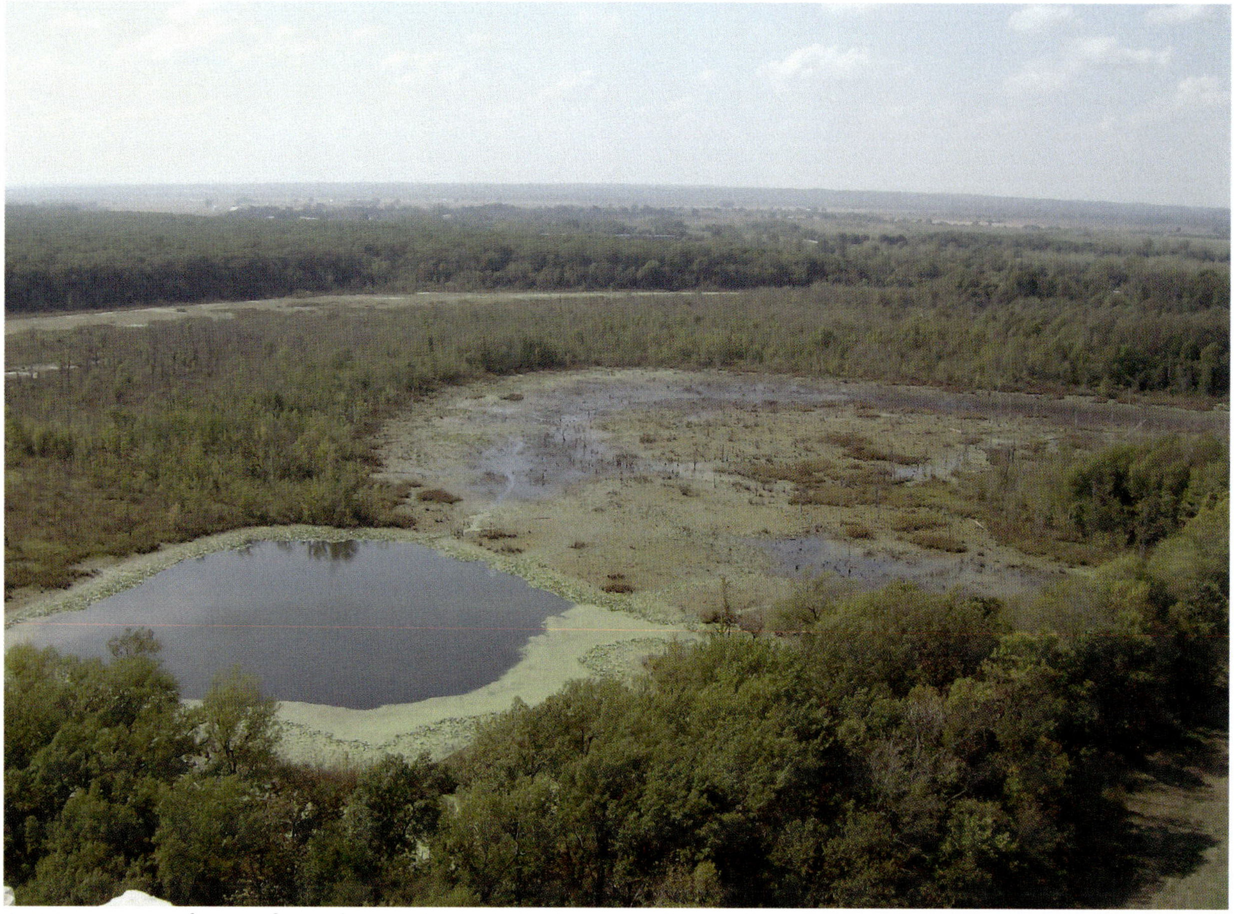

At LaRue Swamp, dozens of rare plants and animals live in or near the winding oxbows of these old channels of an ancient river. Near Route 3, Union County. Photo courtesy of Brian DeNeal

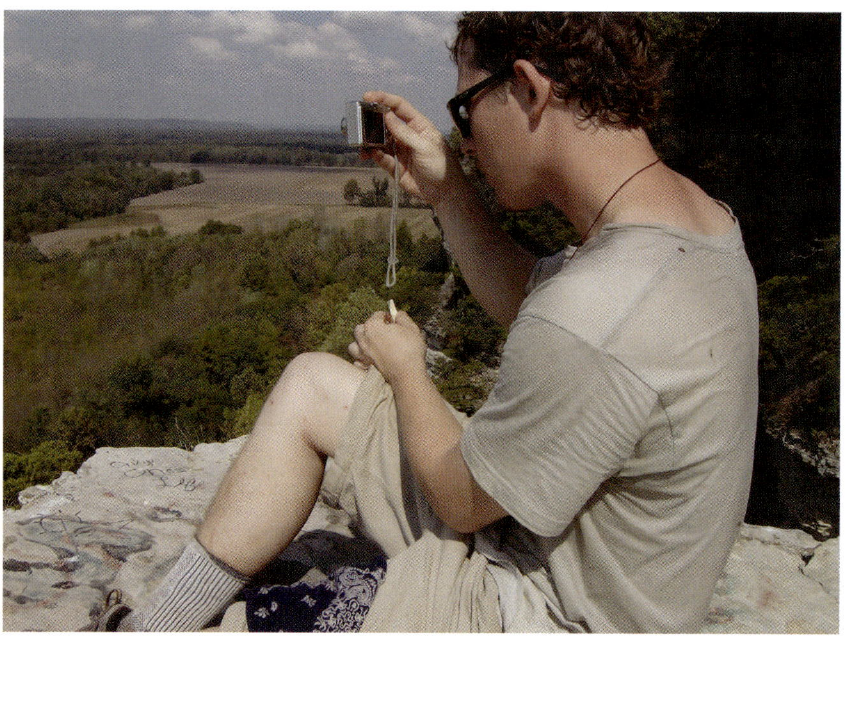

A hiker records the final leg of his eleven-day walk across the Southern Illinois hills from the Ohio River to the Mississippi. Inspiration Point, Pine Hills Recreation Area. Photo courtesy of Brian DeNeal

eleven counties of Southern Illinois, which enjoy the most diverse assortment of plants in the Midwest. In a final act of generosity, Mother Nature lifted layers of windblown topsoil from the West and from the floodplains left by glaciers and sifted them over much of Illinois.

Early southern emigrants from the wooded hills of Kentucky and Tennessee did not usually settle on prairies because they assumed that land that would not grow trees would not grow crops—an assumption that was given misleading validity when they reached the Williamson County prairies. Poor Prairie, near Marion, was "poor" because its heavy clay would not readily allow water or plant roots to penetrate it. Nearby Herrin's Prairie was characterized by a layer of clay so unyielding that people said it would grow only buckhorn sumac. This condition in which a hard "claypan" hinders root growth and water absorption is found under much of Southern Illinois, but settlers accepted it and showed little interest in prairie lands unless woods and water were nearby. Many of the later-arriving easterners, New England Yankees, and European immigrants settled north of Effingham on what was once thought to be inferior land, but it was these nonsoutherners who ended

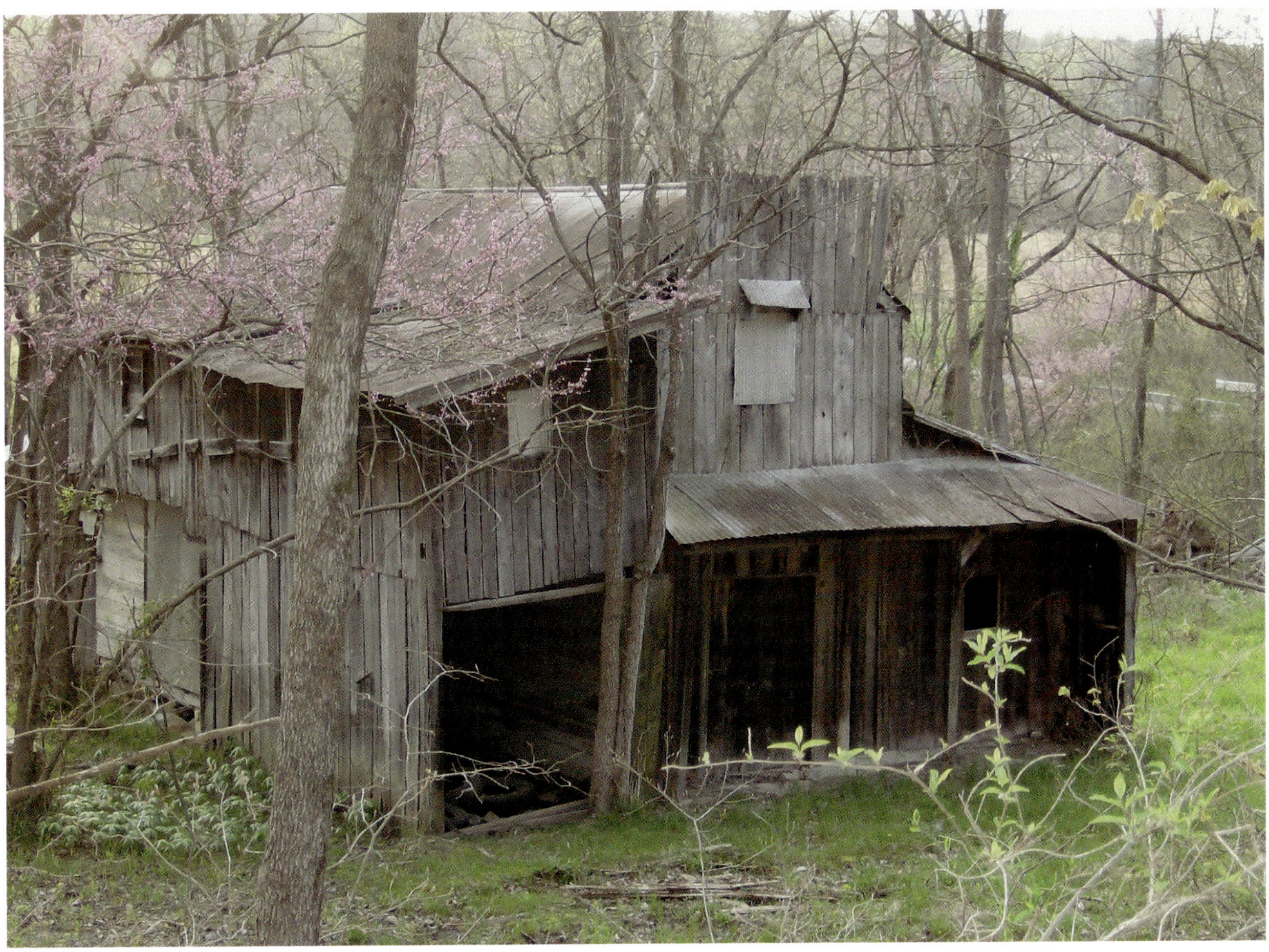

Spring woods overtake a hillside grain mill from an earlier era of farming. Photo courtesy of Brian DeNeal

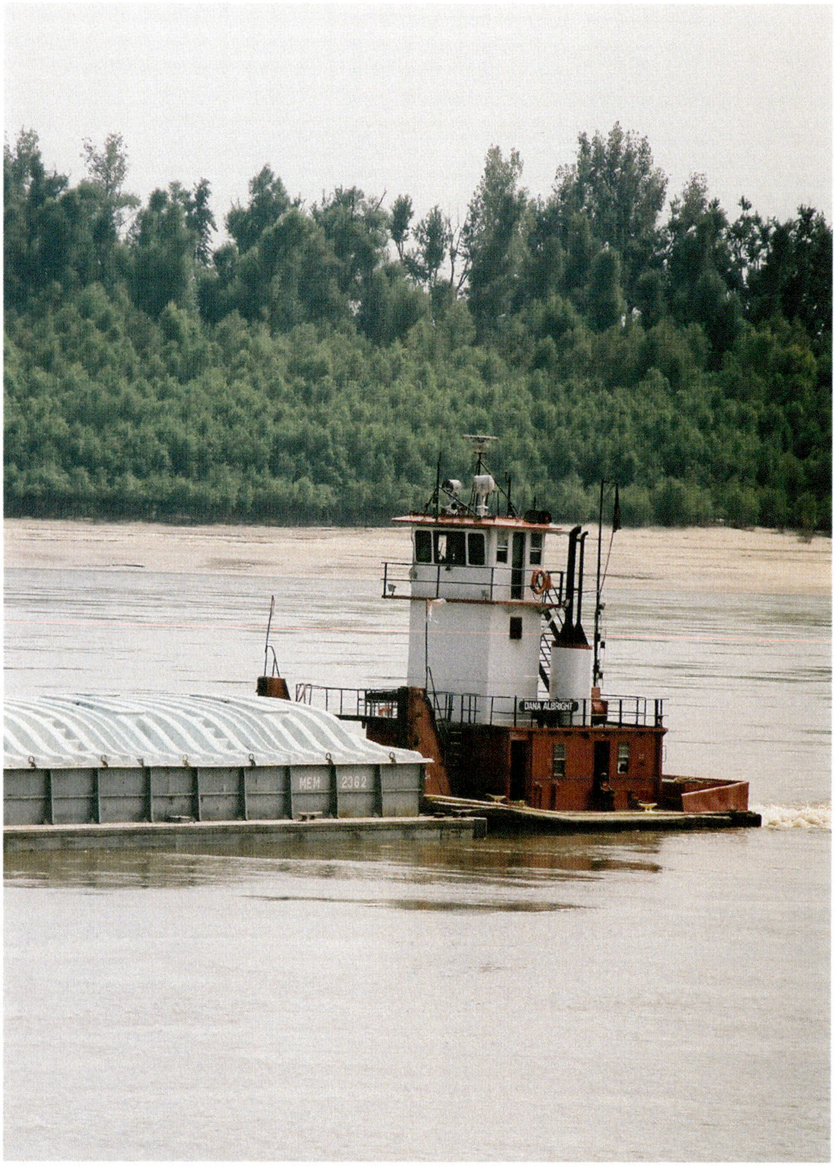

Rounding the horn at Cairo, a towboat leaves the Mississippi and turns upstream on the Ohio. Southern Illinois—"the land between the rivers"—is framed by these two great rivers and the Wabash. Photo by Herbert K. Russell

up with the state's superior farm land and with proportionately greater incomes.

From the very beginning, then, Southern Illinois was different from the ground up and from the ground down. It was beautiful country, but the erosion that helped shape its rolling hills and streams had carried off part of the thin topsoil left by the region's only glacier. Most of northern Illinois enjoyed the soil-making benefits of several glaciers and, in the case of the central Illinois prairie, the very rich nutrients associated with the recent Wisconsinan glacier and fertility from 10,000 years of soil-enriching prairie plants.

The glaciers also helped shape the five Great Lakes. Called "great" because of their surface areas and their depths (two are over 1,000 feet deep), the lakes can accommodate all but the largest of ships. The five lakes are connected and drain naturally to the east, toward New York State and the Atlantic Ocean—and this too would help determine the future of Southern Illinois and the rest of the state.

Only one thing remained to complete the Southern Illinois "land between the rivers," and that was the rivers themselves. When the glaciers melted, the water that was released (meltwater) filled the Great Lakes and scoured out river channels that were miles wide in order to accommodate the uncountable trillions of gallons of water that suddenly rushed southward. As these immense floods passed through Southern Illinois, they carved out many of the watercourses that would later shape state and county boundaries. The state's four major rivers—the Ohio, Mississippi, Wabash, and Illinois—were all defined by meltwater from the glaciers. Three major rivers in Southern

Illinois' interior—the Kaskaskia, Embarras (usually pronounced "Ambraw"), and Little Wabash—were shaped when the last ice sheet, the Wisconsinan, began to melt north of Effingham. The Big Muddy and Saline Rivers were also shaped by glacial waters. When the great flow of glacial meltwater had passed, all the rivers receded to smaller channels but left behind thousands of acres of fertile bottomlands. One of the richest bottoms is east of St. Louis on the Illinois side, which benefited from water-borne silt and nutrients from three major rivers, the Missouri, the Illinois, and the Mississippi. It was in these flat bottomlands (really the former bed of the Mississippi itself) that the first humans arrived about 9500 B.C.—at which point the geologic record is engaged by a human one.

The ancestors of the first humans to reach Illinois may have come out of northern Asia by boat or on a bridge of land to Alaska that melting glaciers or other natural phenomena later obscured or obliterated. It was these far easterners whose descendants became the American Indians—the Native Americans—and whose wanderings led them out of Alaska through Canada and several future American states to the Illinois bottoms across the river from St. Louis. By A.D. 1000 they had established one of the most illustrious civilizations in the world. The site is known worldwide as Cahokia Mounds, and is recognized by the international community through the United Nations as a World Heritage Site. Something of its sophistication is suggested in the nearby artist's rendering.

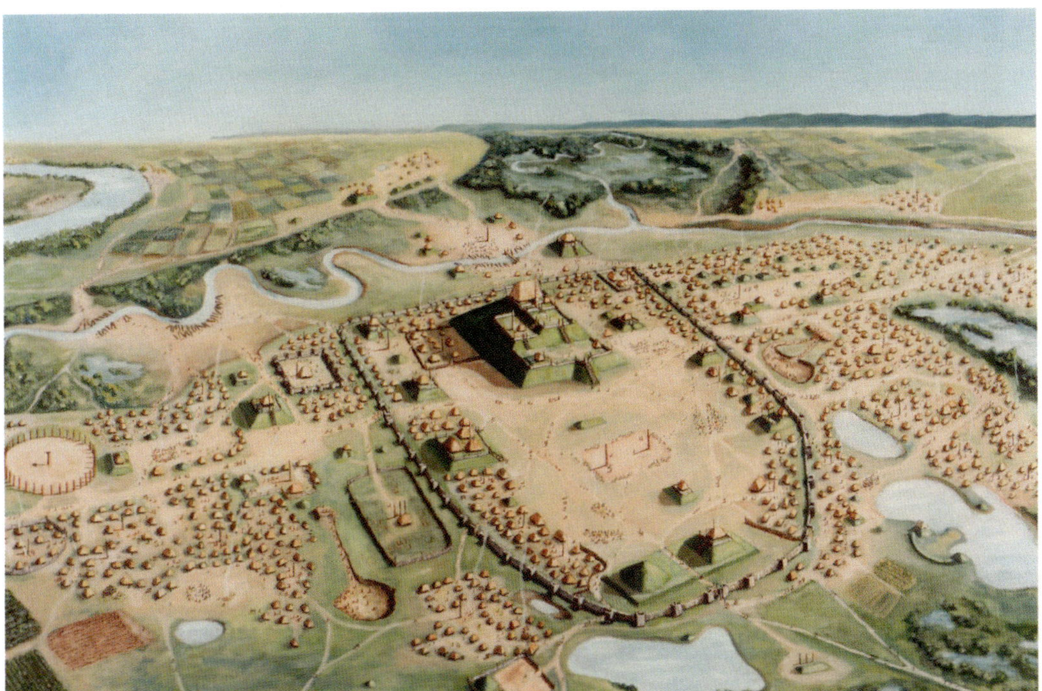

Cahokia Mounds circa A.D. 1150–1200, by William R. Iseminger. Monks Mound (*center*) was headquarters for a Native American civilization that flourished near the Mississippi and several southern rivers for 400 years before dying out about A.D. 1350. Collinsville. Courtesy of Cahokia Mounds State Historic Site

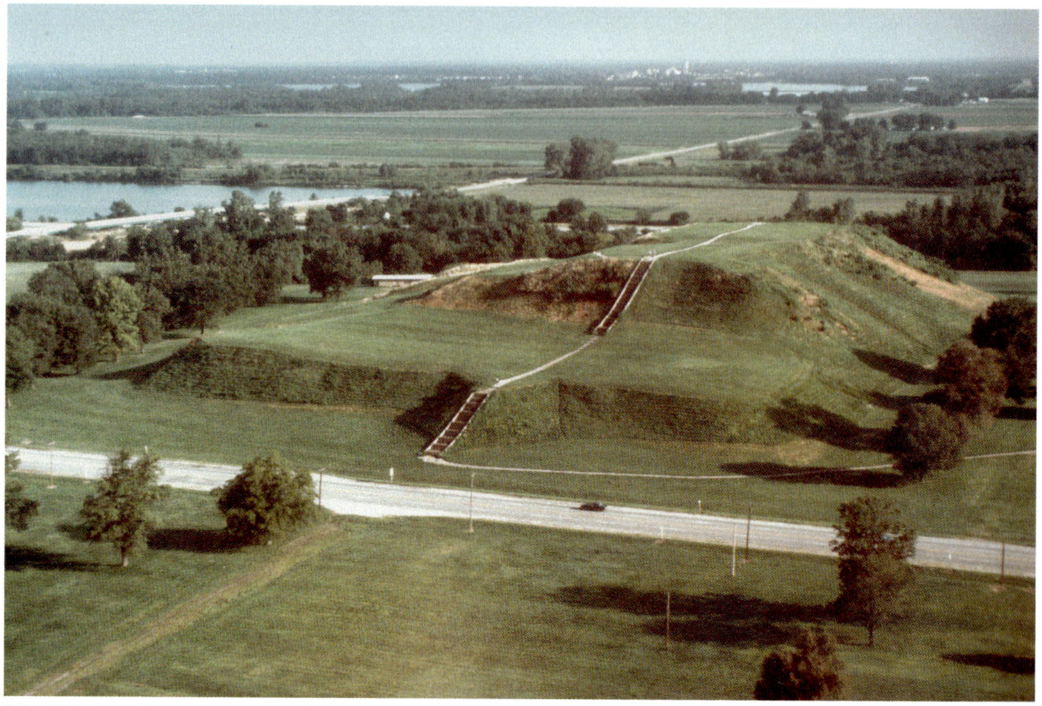

Monks Mound as it appears today. Collinsville. Courtesy of Cahokia Mounds State Historic Site

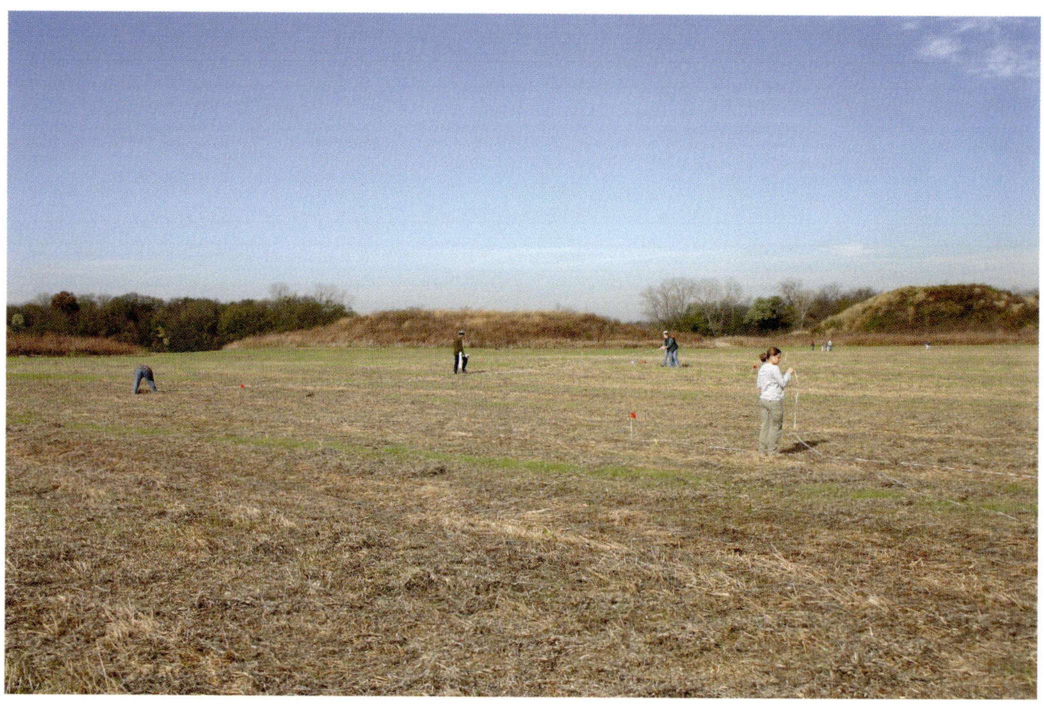

At Kincaid Mounds in Massac County, archaeology faculty and students from Southern Illinois University Carbondale assist with geophysical survey work near two mounds constructed circa A.D. 1000 to 1100. The field in the foreground may have served as a plaza or commons area for the 150-acre site. Photo courtesy of Brian M. Butler

The city of Cahokia Mounds grew to perhaps 20,000 inhabitants or more, an immense, ancient metropolis, larger even than London at the time. The people established a vast trading network throughout the central United States. In unglaciated areas such as Union County's Mill Creek and elsewhere, they found chert, a flint-like material easily shaped into hoes and spades. About A.D. 900 they began building mounds, and Monks Mound (named for some later inhabitants) is among the great archaeological treasures of the world. Standing over 100 feet high and occupying about sixteen acres at its base, it is North America's largest man-made, prehistoric (before written records) structure. It is also one of the largest man-made structures anywhere, exceeding Egypt's Great Pyramid (which measures a scant thirteen acres at its base). Cahokia's 120 or so smaller mounds had social, religious, and calendar purposes. Unfortunately, Cahokia's Native American inhabitants left no written records, and sometime before 1350 their civilization came to a close.

Similar but smaller mounds were constructed about A.D. 1000–1100 near the Ohio River between Unionville and New Liberty in southern Massac and Pope Counties. Known as Kincaid Mounds (after a former landowner), the settlement there was similar to Cahokia Mounds in that the people enjoyed an abundance of wildlife and fertile soil, left no written records, and disappeared from the site before 1350. Who they were or where they went remains guesswork, in part because Illinois was largely uninhabited during the century or so that followed their departure. Modern research has weakened the hypothesis that Old World diseases from early European explorers destroyed the people of Kincaid and Cahokia Mounds. One supposition among many is that the inhabitants exhausted their soil, game, and fuel and had to move on. Floods, wars, drought, plagues, internal dissent, and earthquakes may have provided other incentives to leave.

Some of these early Illinoisans left behind images that may someday yield a part of their story. Carved and painted artworks are to be found at dozens of Southern Illinois sites on the inside walls of rock shelters and on boulders, rocks, and bluffs. Early white travelers on the Mississippi near Alton told of seeing a large painted image called the "Piasa Bird" on a bluff later destroyed by modern construction. Some frequent images include a cross in a circle, human and birdlike creatures, human hands and feet, snakes, turtles, water monsters, deer, wolves, and buffalo. A statuette of a man, woman, or animal is occasionally found, but there is little that casts light on the artists. One scholarly assumption is that the pictographs (painted images) and petroglyphs (carved or "pecked" images) may be religious in nature and offer a Native American view of heaven, earth, and an underworld. Southern Illinois researcher Irvin Peithmann, discoverer of the Modoc Rock Shelter, correctly observed that such artifacts bring us to within a stone's throw of the Stone Age but, alas, no closer.

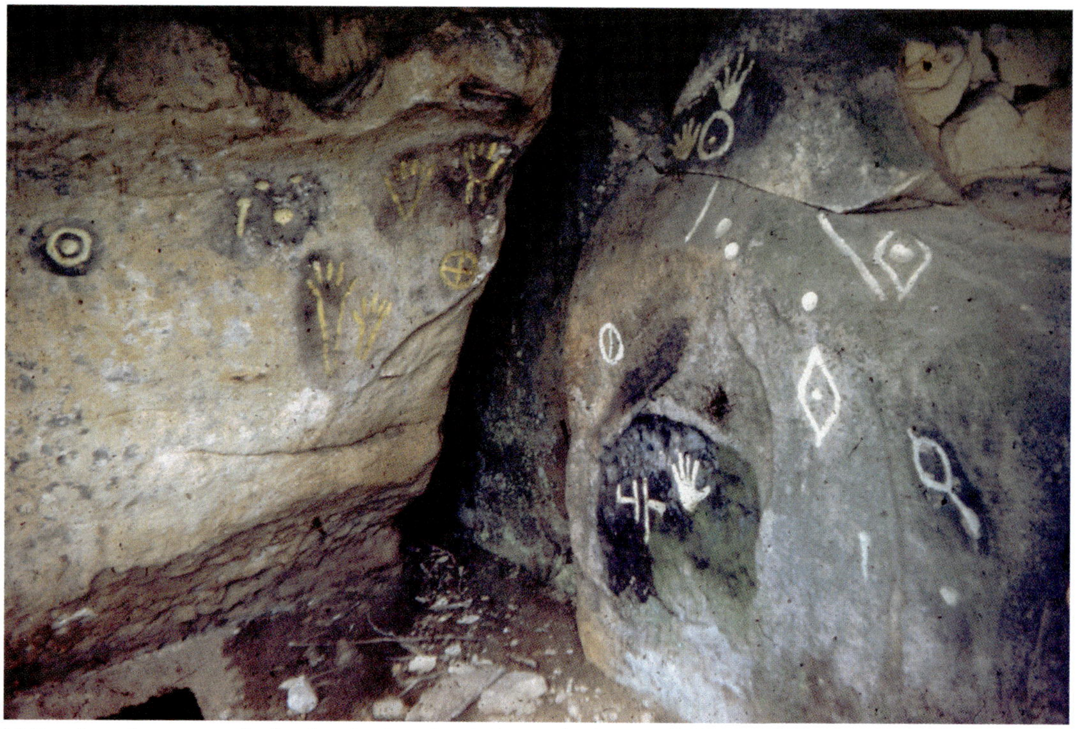

Native American petroglyphs showing hands, circles, and other symbols were "pecked" into the stone with a rock hammer or "hammer stone." Archaeologists discourage the use of chalk to highlight rock art (as shown in this old photo) because it degrades the images. John W. Allen Collection, Special Collections Research Center, Morris Library, Southern Illinois University Carbondale

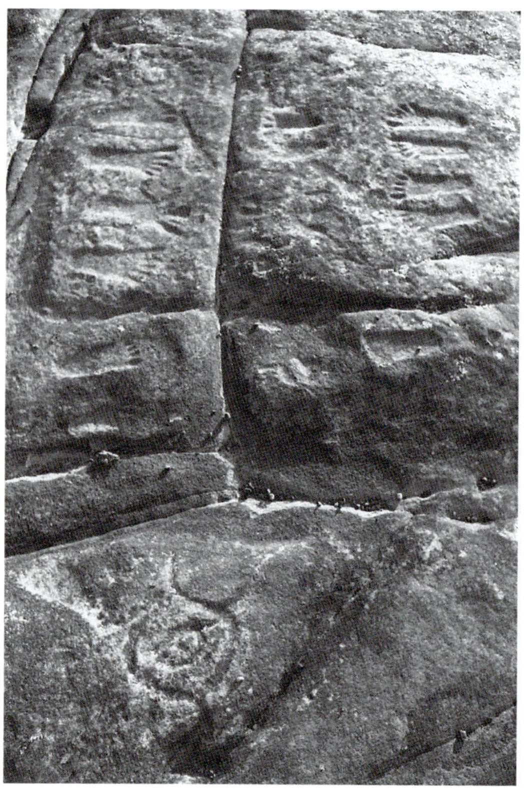

Pecked out of stone by Native Americans, Footprint Rock in Johnson County is appropriately named. Photo courtesy of Charles Hammond

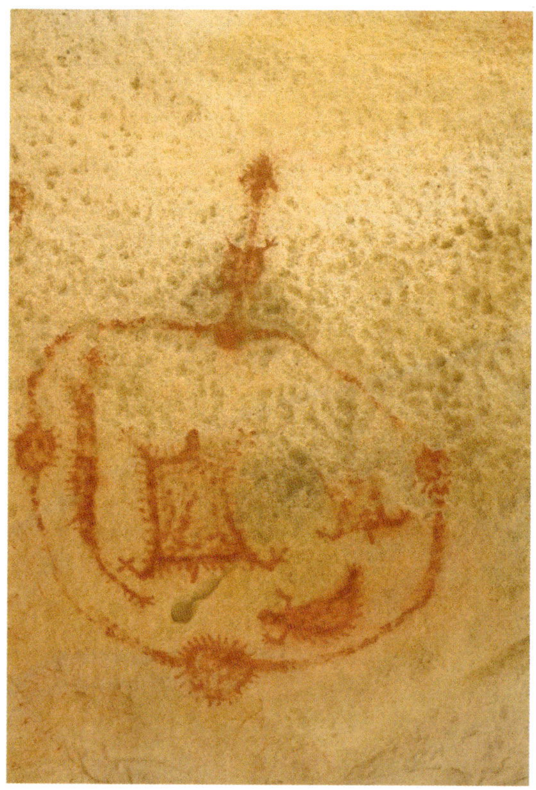

This cave-top pictograph painted by an American Indian artist shows stretched bison hides and an arrow emerging from a circle with four suns. Pope County. Photo courtesy of Charles Hammond

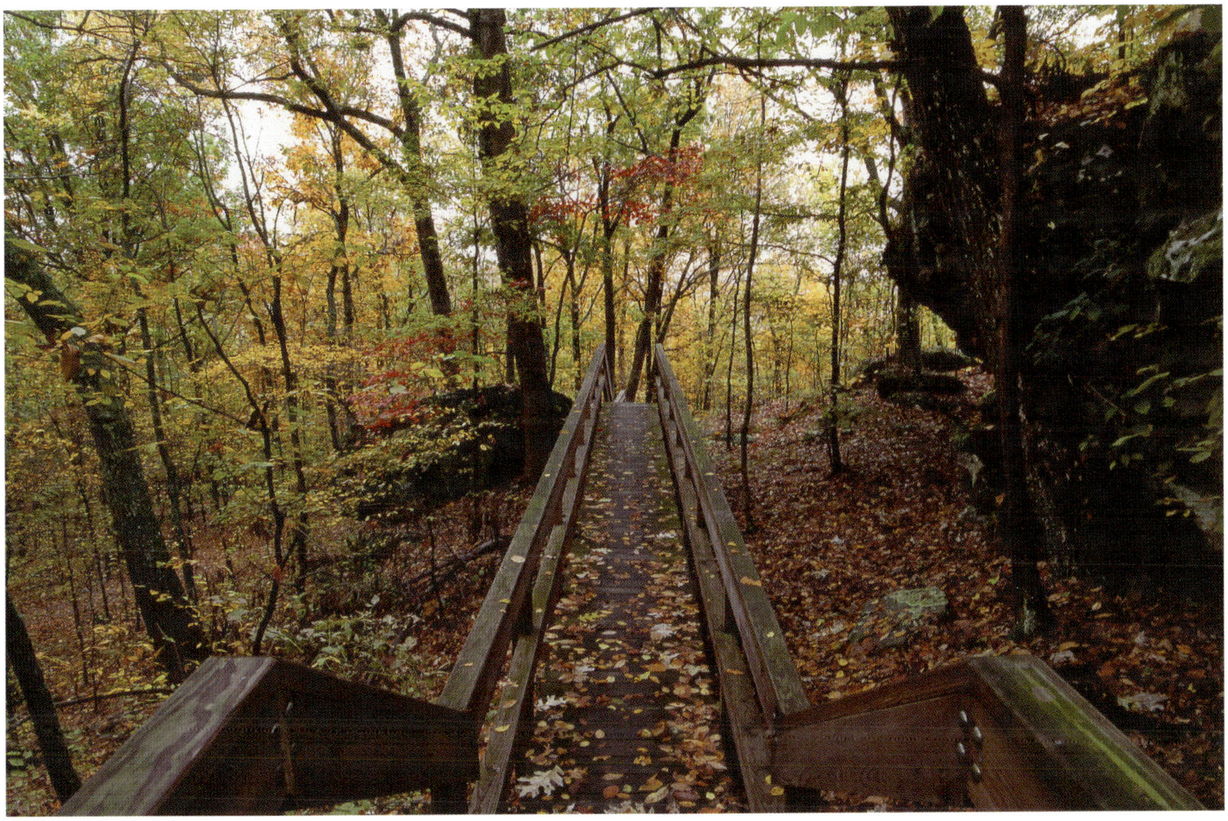

The top of Millstone Bluff was the site of an ancient Indian settlement from A.D. 500 to 1500. White pioneers shaped the rock into millstones to grind grain. Pope County. Photo courtesy of David Hammond

The Indians from the Far East and the glaciers from the far north illustrate two of Southern Illinois' most enduring contradictions: although the region was settled in modern times by southerners and is invariably thought of as "southern," much of the region's history has been shaped by people and phenomena arriving from the east and north. Prominent among these were the first Europeans, the French.

In 1608, just a year after the English established their first colony in Virginia, the French arrived in Canada. They would spend the next century and a half exploring the North American wilderness, exploiting the lucrative trade in furs, and occasionally fighting with the British. But while the British settled up and down the Atlantic coast and as far west as the Appalachian Mountains, the French went west and southwest, from the St. Lawrence River to the Great Lakes and on to the Mississippi. In 1673 they decided to explore the Mississippi River north to south and drifted into Southern Illinois.

The French traveled only as far south as the mouth of the Arkansas River on this first trip but would soon claim much of eastern Canada and the central United States as "New France." In the 1680s and '90s fur traders and Catholic churchmen established settlements near the Mississippi River in Southern Illinois. By 1703 they had occupied Cahokia (a dozen miles southwest of Cahokia Mounds) and Kaskaskia and would soon establish Prairie du Rocher (1722) and St. Philippe as well as Ste. Genevieve, Missouri. Fort de Chartres helped protect these and other French villages and their most important town, Kaskaskia. The French finally had over a dozen important outposts in the Midwest, including those in modern-day St. Louis, Peoria, Chicago, and Detroit. The Illinois River and the Great Lakes were among their primary highways, but branching trails offered overland passage. One of the lengthiest French trails started at Kaskaskia, passed by Walnut Hill (near

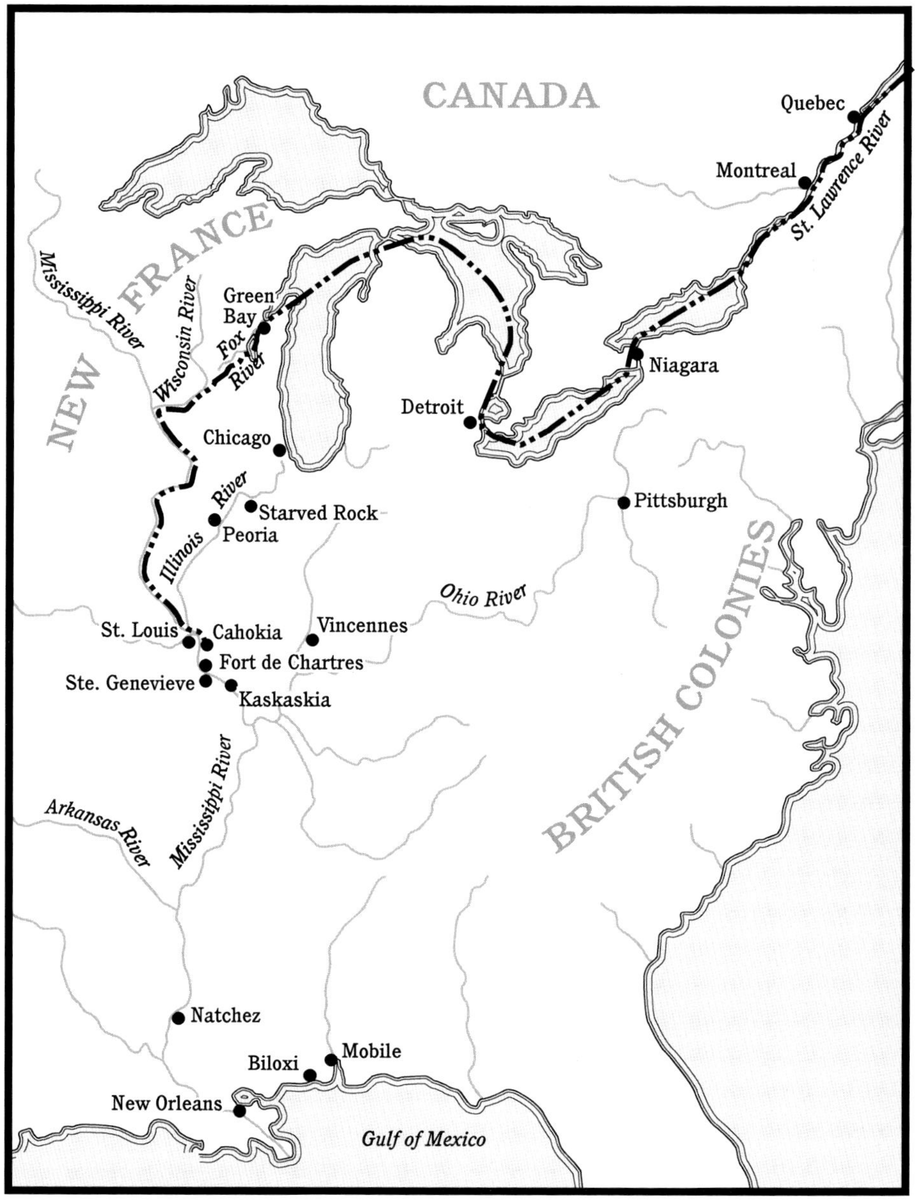

The French were the first Europeans to settle in Southern Illinois. They came by way of the St. Lawrence River and Quebec (*upper right*) and through the Great Lakes to Green Bay. There they took the Fox River south and carried their canoes to the Wisconsin River, which flowed into the Mississippi. Dots mark some of the places important to the French.

Centralia) and Salem, and then branched: one path proceeded east to Vincennes, Indiana, on the Wabash River; another path angled northeast toward Effingham and on to Danville and Detroit, a major French settlement.

The French labored on Fort de Chartres for decades, moving it, rebuilding it, retreating from floods, and finally fashioning the stone structure that stands restored today. Its massive walls were made of local limestone, but its strength was never tested in battle. There were no coordinated Indian uprisings against Fort de Chartres, and no armies attacked it during France's occupancy of Southern Illinois. Today it is the site of colorful reenactments.

By the 1720s New France stretched from Canada to Louisiana, and Kaskaskia had become the most important commercial center between the Great Lakes and the Gulf of Mexico. Furs and animal skins—beaver, bear, wildcat, and deer—offered the most reliable income, followed by agricultural products. The French farms between Cahokia and Kaskaskia became the breadbasket for much of the French presence in North America, and persistent rumors of gold and silver fueled continued interest. Fur traders, farmers, and French soldiers married Native American women or had children by them, and the two cultures blended.

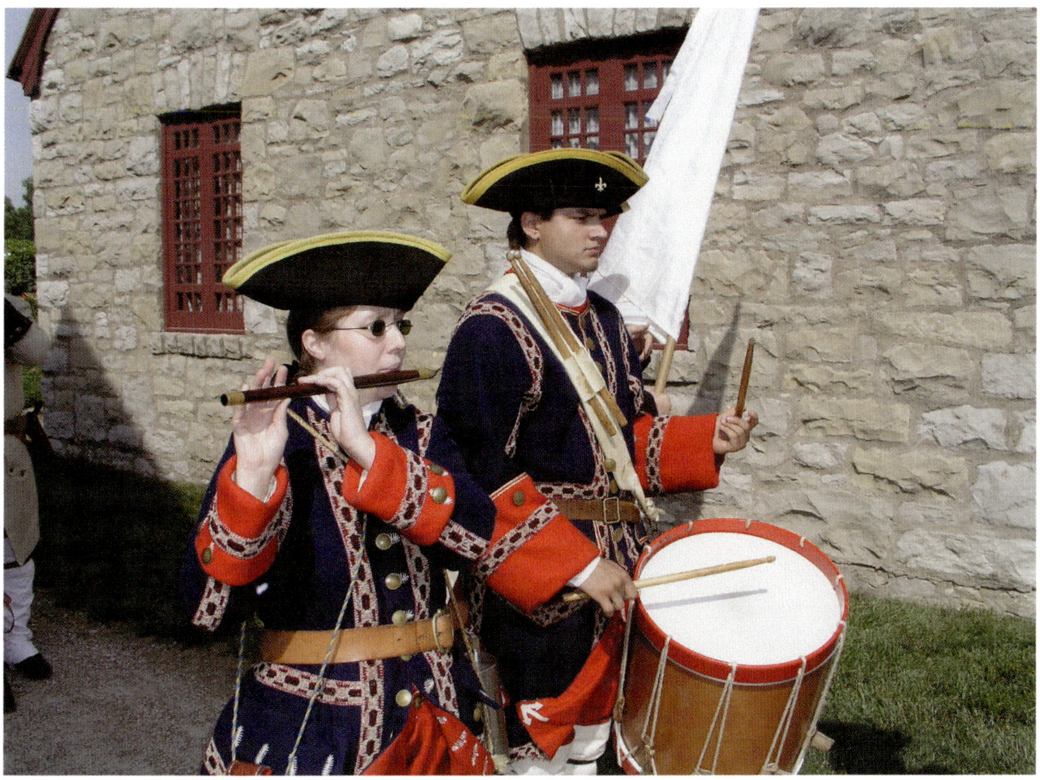

Reenactors at Fort de Chartres perform a military number. Randolph County. Photo courtesy of Shannon Woodworth

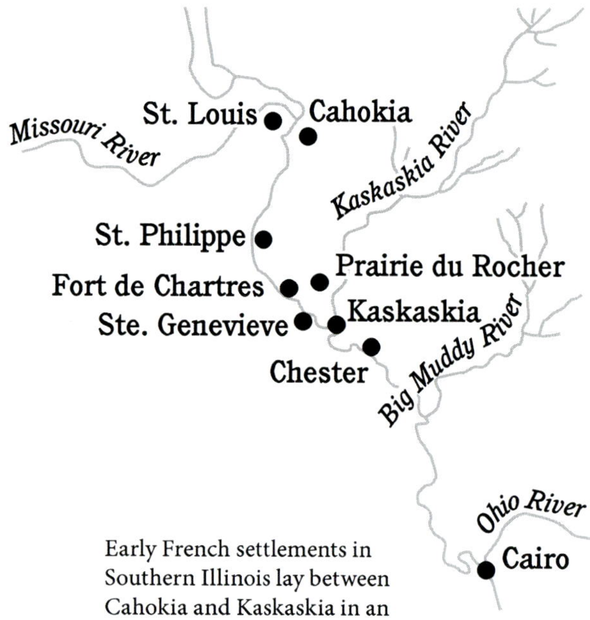

Early French settlements in Southern Illinois lay between Cahokia and Kaskaskia in an area later known as the "American Bottom." These fertile bottomlands border the Mississippi and extend east from the river to the nearby bluffs of the Illinois Ozarks.

French farmers usually lived in town and traveled to and from their farms as needed. Individual farms were laid out in the long-lot fashion, narrow belts of land 64 or 128 yards wide that began at the edge of the Mississippi and proceeded eastward toward the bluffs of the Illinois Ozarks. These "ribbon farms" were practical in that many farms could enjoy river frontage. Wheat, corn, and oats were the most important crops, although lead discovered near Ste. Genevieve contributed to the economy, as did various salt springs. Boatmen with flour, cured ham and venison, cheese, or lumber drifted southward on the Mississippi through this nearly silent Eden to a recently opened port with yet another French name, New Orleans. Furs might be shipped northward toward Detroit and Canada if there was a danger of spoilage in the heat and high humidity of the South.

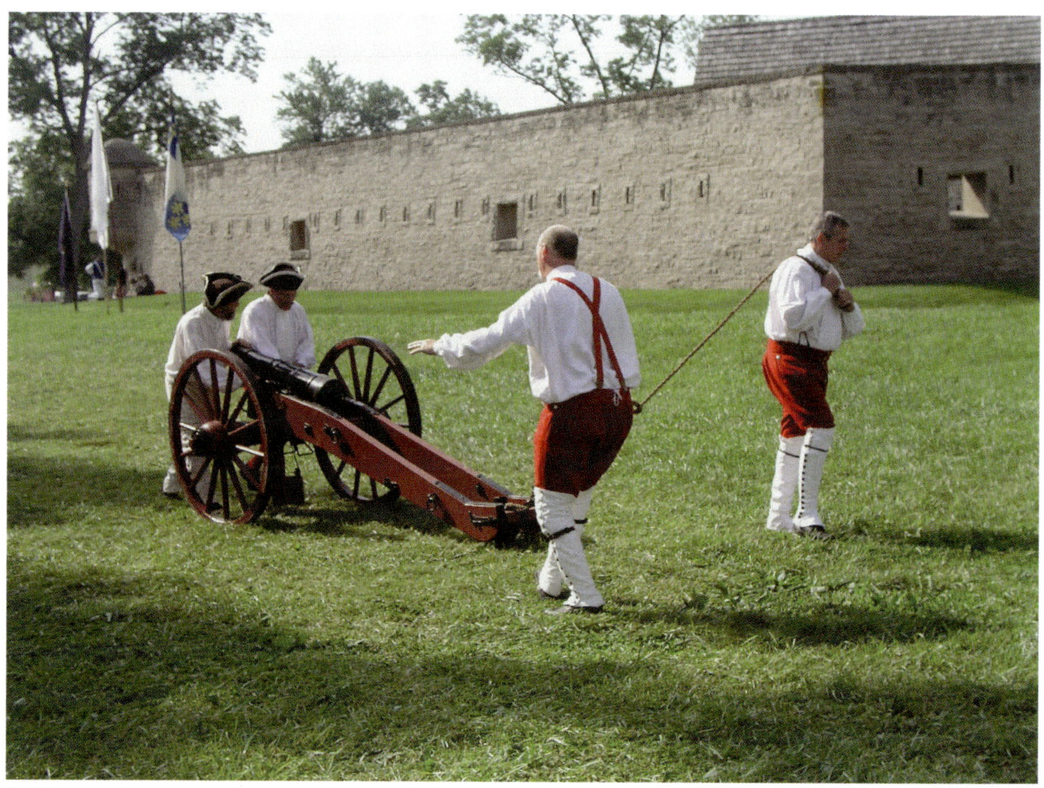

Soldiers position a cannon near the French fort. Photo courtesy of Shannon Woodworth

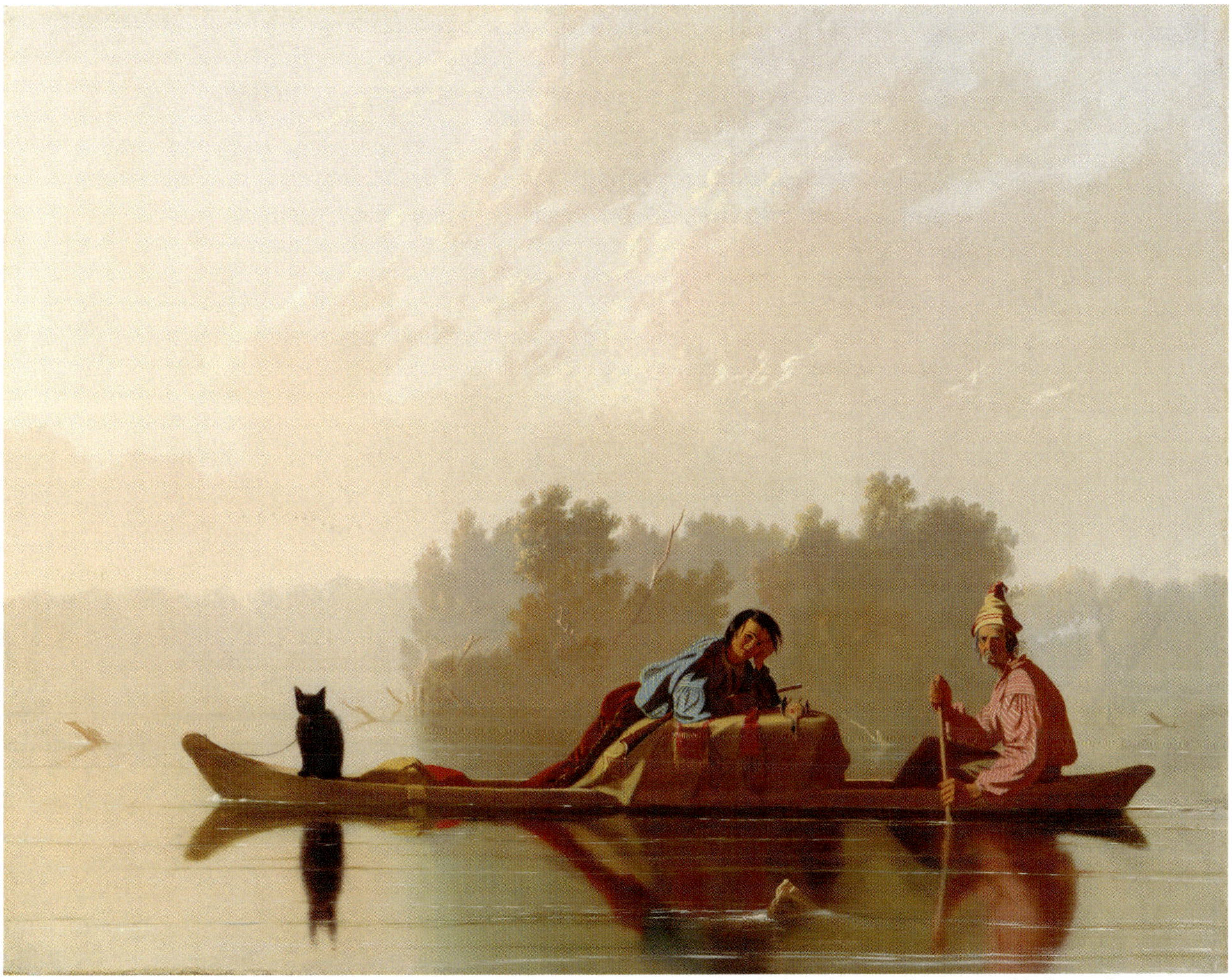

George Caleb Bingham's *Fur Traders Descending the Missouri* was completed after the French army yielded North America to the British, but it captures perfectly the indolence and tranquility associated with the French period in Southern Illinois. Bingham, George Caleb (1811–1879); *Fur Traders Descending the Missouri.* 1845. Oil on canvas, 29 × 36½ in. (73.7 × 92.7 cm.). Morris K. Jessup Fund, 1933 (33.61); The Metropolitan Museum of Art, New York, NY, U.S.A.; Image copyright © The Metropolitan Museum of Art / Art Resource, NY

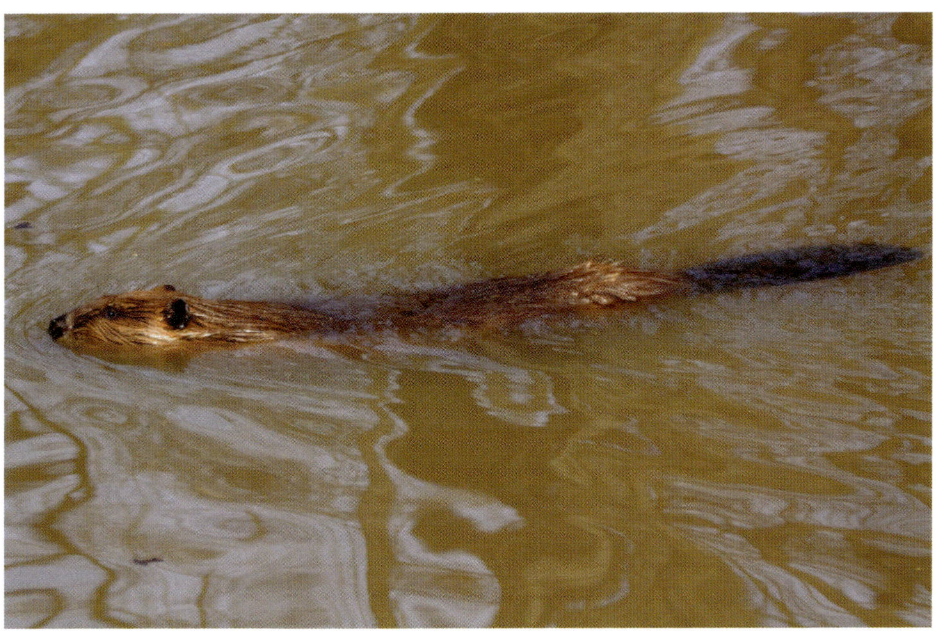

Trappers and traders sought beaver pelts, prized in Europe for the making of felt. Union County Refuge. Photo courtesy of David Hammond

French influence on the Ohio River was far less pronounced because of a disaster at Juchereau's Tannery near what is now Mound City, in Pulaski County. Established in 1702 to process and ship animal skins, the tannery ceased operations in 1704 following an outbreak of disease or an Indian attack, or perhaps both. The French subsequently gave the area a wide berth until 1757, when the threat of English troops near Southern Illinois forced the French to construct a fort on the Ohio River near Metropolis. Named Fort Massiac (but pronounced "Massac" by the English and Americans), it stood within several days' march north to Vincennes, a French settlement on the east bank of the Wabash River in Indiana.

Established as a fur-trading post in the early 1730s, Vincennes offered trappers an alternate route to markets by sending furs up Indiana's Wabash and Maumee Rivers toward Lake Erie. An ancient buffalo and Indian trail connected Vincennes to Cahokia, thus providing an overland link between the settlements—as well as etching the first outline of what would become U.S. Route 50. By 1757 the French were in control of the Southern Illinois triangle later known as "Egypt."

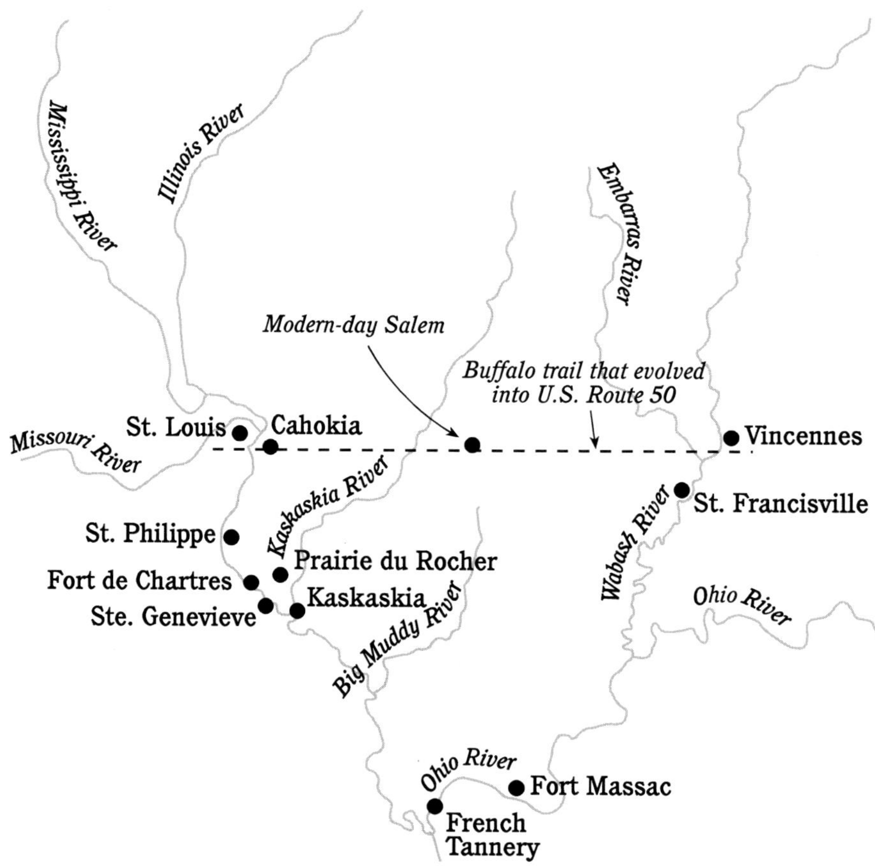

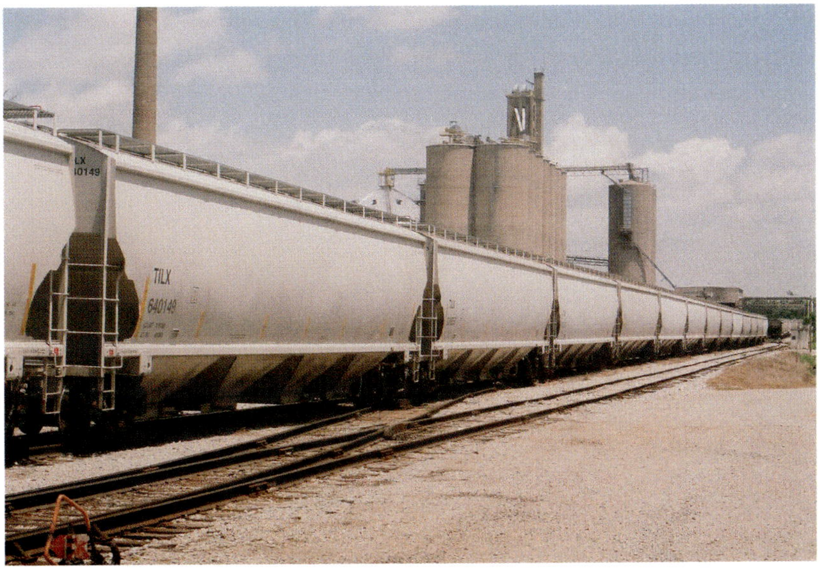

Near the site of a French tannery established in 1702, a Mound City grain terminal loads railcars. Photo by Herbert K. Russell

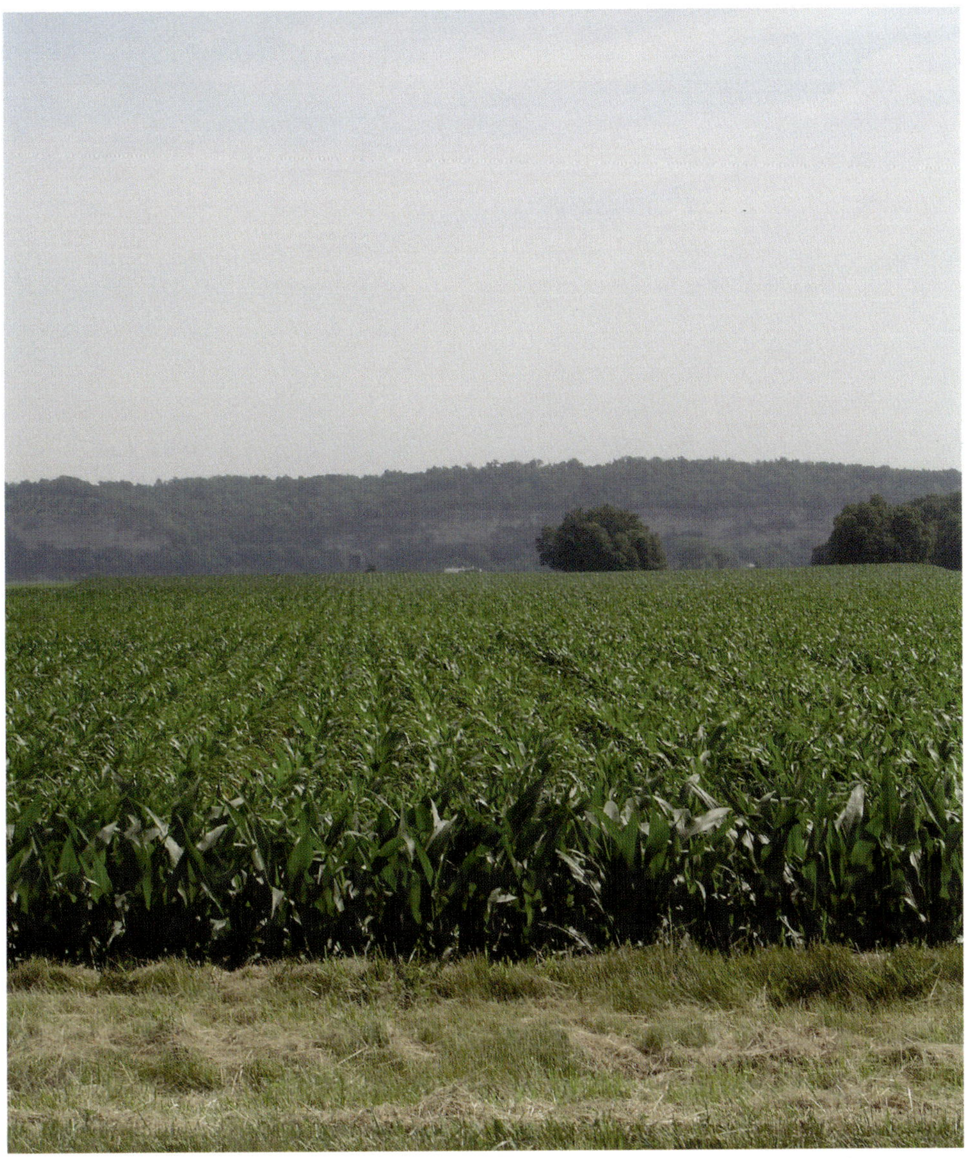

Endless rows of corn have replaced the French favorite of wheat in fields near the vanished village of St. Philippe, Monroe County. High humidity obscures the limestone bluffs of the Illinois Ozarks in the background. Photo courtesy of Shannon Woodworth

Perhaps some of the French farms were difficult to bring into production, perhaps a manpower shortage existed, or perhaps rumors of gold and silver mines were revived; for whatever reason, the French brought African slaves into Southern Illinois in the early 1720s. Africans were generally sold into slavery by their fellow Africans after being kidnapped by rival tribes or captured by enemies during battle, after displeasing a local chief, or as punishment for crimes. The new slaves were walked or boated to markets on rivers, the coast, or the Mediterranean Sea, where they were generally sold to an African middleman or to slave buyers from India, Asia, and Europe. African slavery was established long before Europeans arrived, and when they did appear, most simply adapted to local practices. African royalty and black port authorities often shared in the profits by receiving a tax or other monies on sales that sent slaves all over the globe. Between 1500 and 1800, for example, about as many black slaves were purchased by Muslim slavers for resale in north Africa, the Mideast, India, and elsewhere as would be purchased for use in the New World. Of the slaves exported to the New World, 95 percent went to Central or South America and to the Caribbean islands to labor in sugar and coffee plantations or in mines, while the remaining 5 percent went to North America. Some of the slaves brought to Southern Illinois came from what is now the Republic of Haiti, on the Caribbean island of Hispaniola, near Cuba, from whence they had been taken to French-controlled New Orleans and upstream to Kaskaskia. Others came directly from West Africa to French-controlled Biloxi on the Gulf Coast and then to Kaskaskia.

Once in Illinois, the black slaves joined French-owned red slaves, for Native Americans sometimes made slaves of other Indians and traded them. Because war was a constant among most Illinois tribes, there was usually a supply of slaves from Illinois and elsewhere. Both red and black slaves could attend Catholic Church services, but the New Testament's Golden Rule was offset by the Old Testament's twenty-fifth chapter of Leviticus. This text sanctioned enslavement of "bondmen" and "bondmaids," providing they were "heathens" from a nation other than the enslavers. By 1732 French Kaskaskia had 102 black slaves; St. Philippe, 22; Cahokia, 4; and New Chartres (the village that grew up beside Fort de Chartres), 37.

> Monsieur Beauvais rode out of the village at a slow canter. . . . That he prospered was more on account of his being a part of the times than any effort put forth by him.
>
> —From Elizabeth Holbrook's novel *Old 'Kaskia Days*

Those visiting French towns often found a more relaxed society than they expected and reported that some French devoted all their time to hunting and fishing while others danced away their evenings with Indian girls. Only a few youth pursued an education, offered at Kaskaskia by a Catholic religious order, the Jesuits, who opened the first college in Illinois. Some visitors also asserted that the French drank too much (wine, of course, and bourbon) and were lazy. The French extended the same laxity to some of their slaves, several of whom they freed.

In the 1750s events to the distant north and east began to change everything. Chronic friction between the French and English in North America ignited the French and Indian War and led to the French surrender of Montreal to the British. Peace came in 1763, after which the lightly populated French empire in North America disintegrated, the final act coming in 1765, when the few French soldiers remaining at Fort de Chartres formally surrendered it to Great Britain's Black Watch Regiment, the 42nd Highlanders of Scotland.

The French presence remains embedded in Southern Illinois in the names of creeks such as the Beaucoup ("much water") and the Bonpas ("easy passage") and in rivers such as the Cache ("a hiding place") and the Embarras (an "obstruction"). *Illinois* itself derives from the French pronunciation of *Illiniwek* or *Illini*, a prominent Native American group. French influence also colors village names such as Belle Rive (named for Bellerive, a French official), as well as Dupo, formerly Prairie du Pont, and hamlets such as Renault and others. One of the region's major cities also derives from the French: in 1764 fur trader Pierre Laclede sensed that changing times and hostilities between the British and Native Americans would be bad for business and settled west of the Mississippi, where he founded St. Louis.

And of course the French presence continues with Southern Illinois families who trace their ancestry to the French. A few

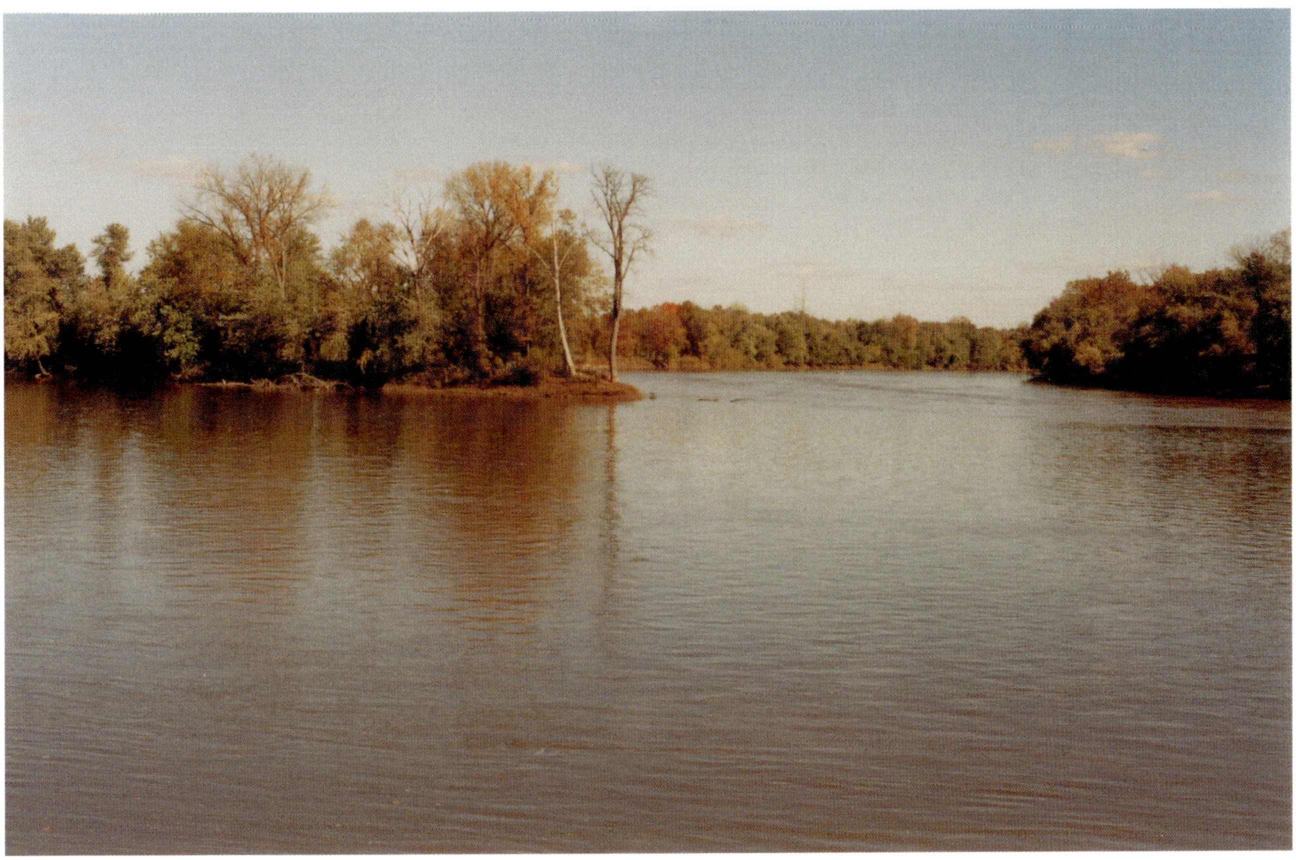

A site familiar to French fur traders and trappers, the Wabash River (*foreground*) is joined by Indiana's White River at Mt. Carmel. Photo by Herbert K. Russell

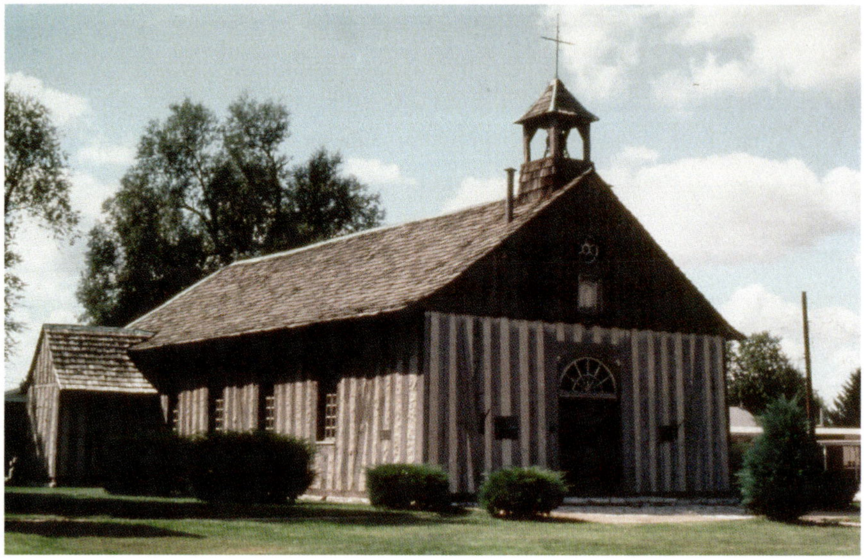

An eighteenth-century French church in Cahokia, site of the first French settlement in Illinois. The restored church shows the distinctive upright posts used by the French during the years when France claimed Southern Illinois, from 1673 to 1763. Ned Trovillion Collection, Special Collections Research Center, Morris Library, Southern Illinois University Carbondale

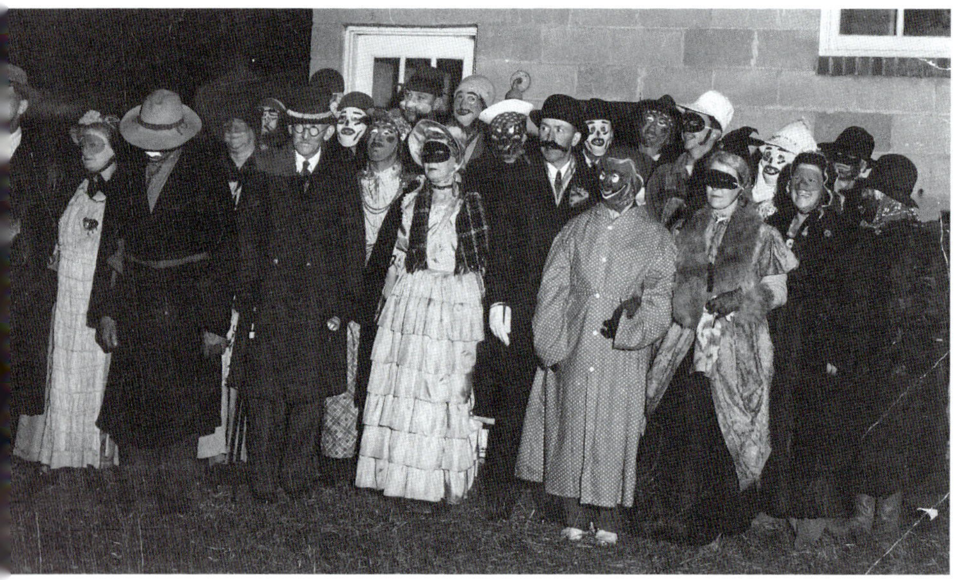

Participants in a centuries-old tradition, residents of Prairie du Rocher observe the New Year's Eve celebration of La Guiannée, circa 1950. Randolph County. John W. Allen Collection, Special Collections Research Center, Morris Library, Southern Illinois University Carbondale

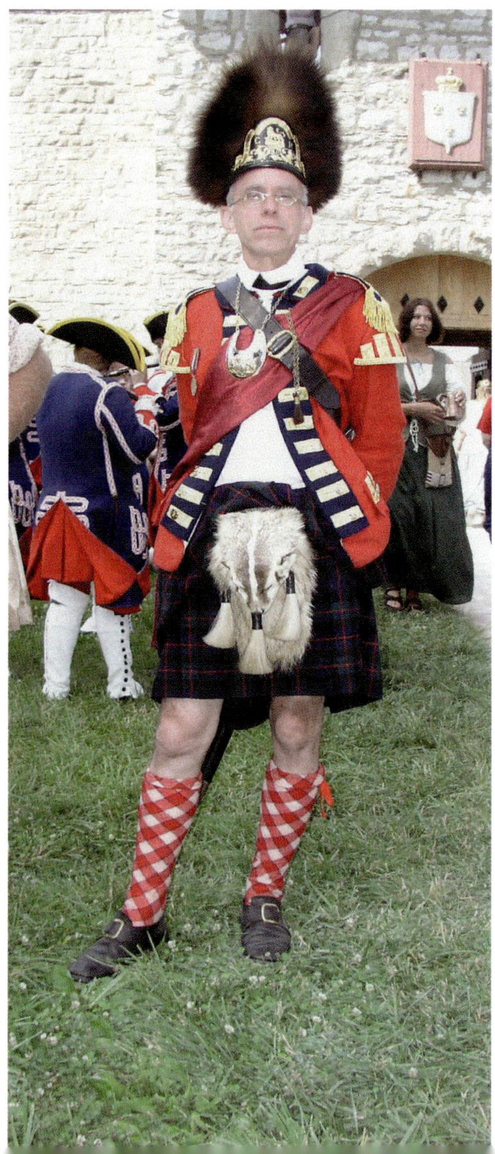

A Scottish Highlander prepares to perform his role in a reenactment in which British forces assume control of Fort de Chartres. French surrender of the fort in 1765 was colorful, serious, and anticlimactic: after years of preparing for battle, the fort was surrendered to the English without a shot. Photo courtesy of Shannon Woodworth

miles back from the Mississippi, French descendants and their friends at Prairie du Rocher keep alive the old practice of La Guiannée, a mobile songfest in which singers travel from house to house spreading and receiving holiday cheer and food to welcome the New Year. Families descended from the French are not numerous along the Ohio River, but the Wabash Valley has several French families remaining from the days when Vincennes was an important trading post. A descendant of one of these, Glenn Poshard, would serve as president of Southern Illinois University (SIU).

The British army's control of Southern Illinois lasted barely a dozen years and left such a faint impression that many people are unaware it was ever in the area. The British tried to avoid clashes with French civilians—traders, trappers, farmers, shopkeepers, and the clergy—and allowed the French to keep their religion, lands, and personal property. This seemingly innocent gesture of goodwill also allowed the French to keep their slaves, who were regarded as property, and so the institution of slavery became well established before the state of Illinois or even the United States existed.

Britain had multiple claims on Southern Illinois, one by defeating the French, another by a 1609 land claim made by King James I after the English established Jamestown, Virginia, and named it for him. Exercising a prerogative common to kings, James used this Virginia foothold to claim all lands west of it from sea to sea. When the British defeated the French a century and a half later in 1763, a new English king, George III, became the owner of Southern Illinois.

England's ownership of Illinois was soon put in dispute by the Revolutionary War and by a young Virginian named George Rogers Clark. A natural leader, Clark asked Virginia governor Patrick Henry to support a secret mission to attack British outposts in what is now the Midwest. After securing an officer's rank for himself and supplies for his journey, Clark started down the Ohio River with 175 men and in June 1778 landed near present-day Metropolis and Fort Massac, which the British had abandoned after receiving it from the French.

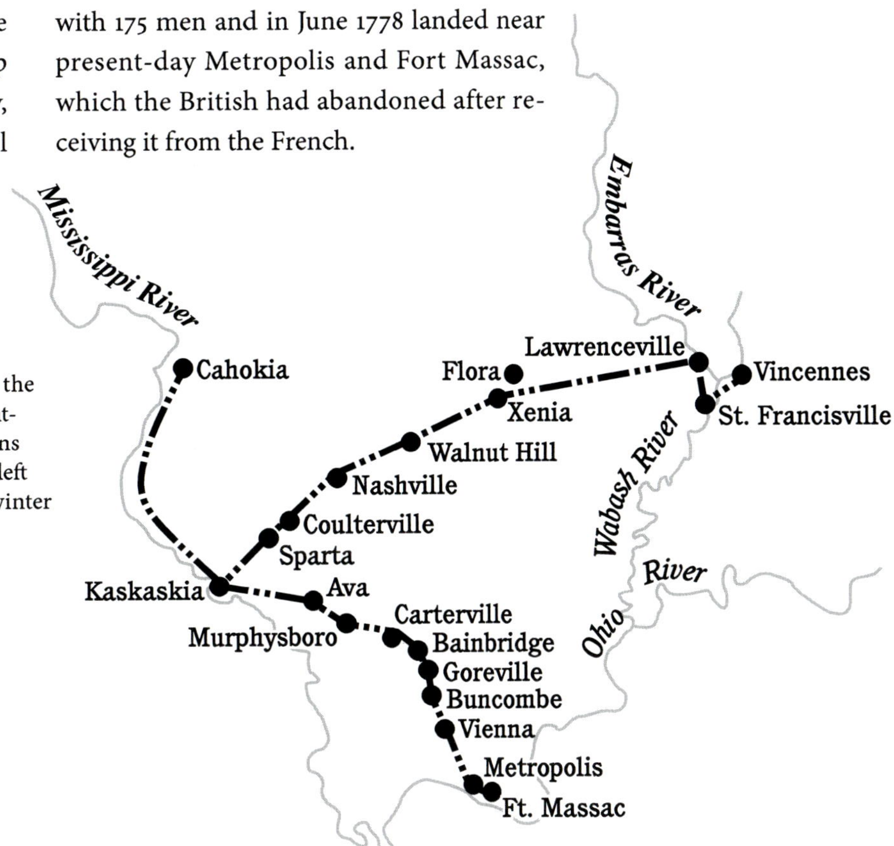

George Rogers Clark's July 1778 route to the British fort at Kaskaskia began at present-day Fort Massac. After neutralizing towns between Kaskaskia and Cahokia, Clark left Kaskaskia in February 1779 for his midwinter assault on Vincennes.

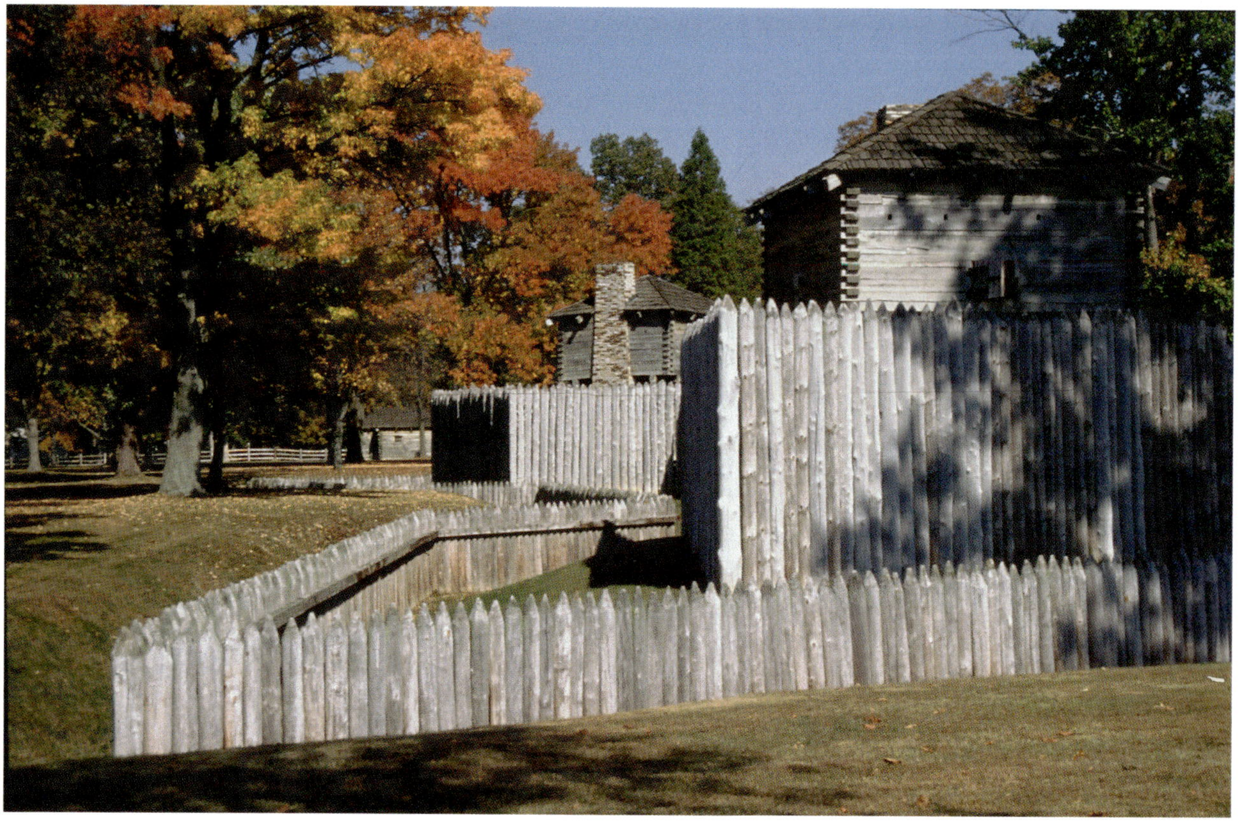

Fort Massiac was built by the French, burned by the Indians, and ceded to the British—who pronounced the fort's name "Massac." The reconstructed Fort Massac, built by the Americans, is shown here. Ned Trovillion Collection, Special Collections Research Center, Morris Library, Southern Illinois University Carbondale

Clark decided to surprise the British at Kaskaskia by coming in overland from the east instead of going up the Mississippi River. Following a trail made by buffalo, Indians, or the French, Clark went through or near the sites of modern-day Vienna, Buncombe, and Goreville to the future hamlet of Bainbridge west of Marion; there he turned northwest, passing near Carterville, Murphysboro, and Ava before arriving in Kaskaskia. Because the British knew nothing of Clark's plans, they had moved their troops elsewhere, leaving a single agent in charge of the settlement at Kaskaskia. French citizens who had earlier pledged loyalty to the British were easily induced to change their allegiance to Clark's home state of Virginia. Clark's men secured nearby towns as far north as Cahokia, and he made plans to capture British-held Vincennes just over the Wabash River in Indiana.

Vincennes had peacefully surrendered to one of Clark's men in mid-1778, but the British had recaptured it, and Clark saw that he must seize and hold the fort before British reinforcements arrived. Because the British would not expect an attack in midwinter, Clark set off in February 1779 with 130 men to walk the 180 miles from Kaskaskia to Vincennes. He followed a French path through or near the present towns of Sparta, Coulterville, Nashville, and Walnut Hill and then took a buffalo and fur traders trail through

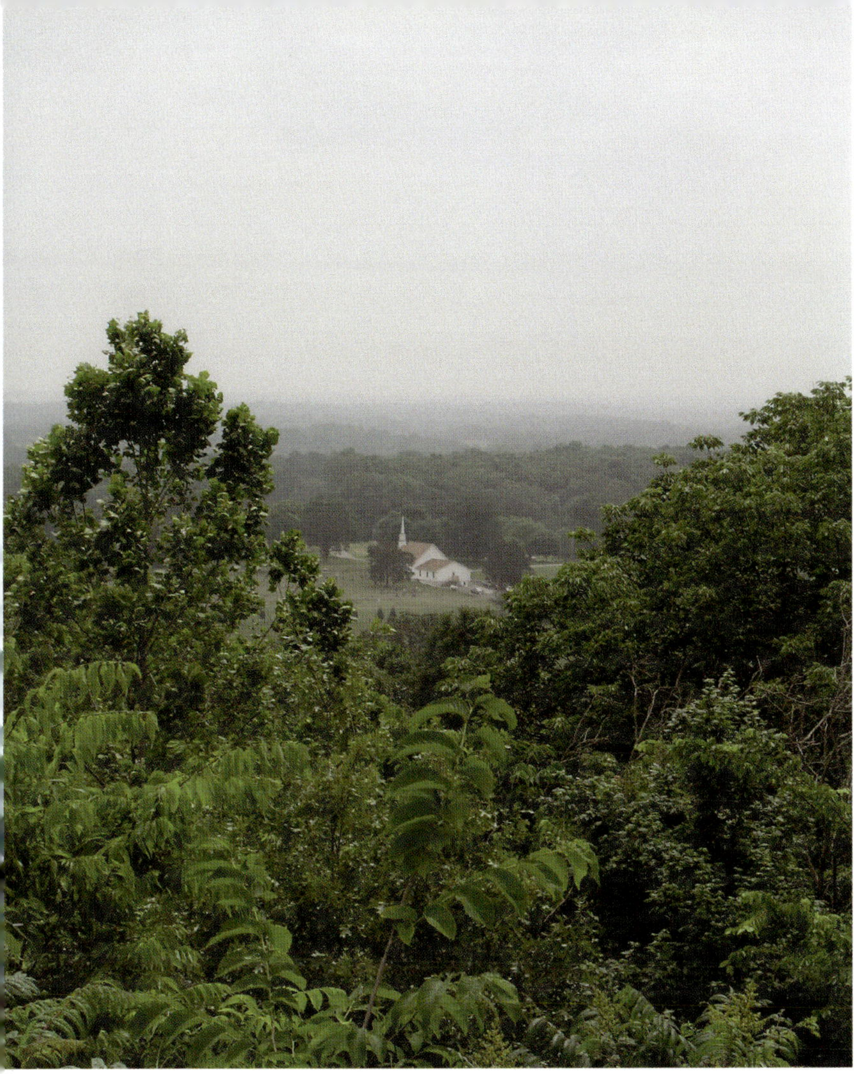

George Rogers Clark and his men passed near the site of this church on their way to attack the British at Kaskaskia in July 1778. Route 37 near Buncombe, Johnson County. Photo courtesy of Shannon Woodworth

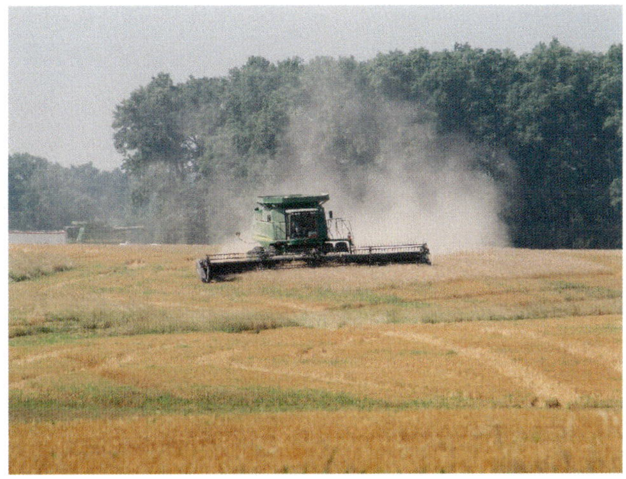

A farmer harvests wheat near the trail taken by Clark and his men. Route 4 near Oraville and Ava. Photo by Herbert K. Russell

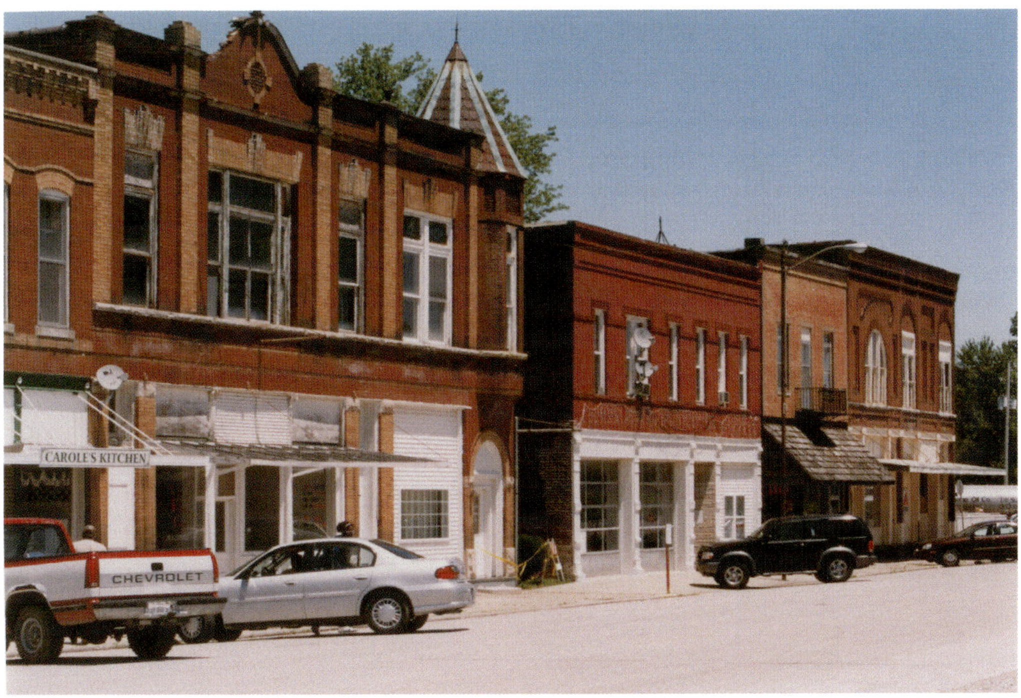

The site of Xenia was on the trail between Cahokia and Vincennes and witnessed the passage of George Rogers Clark and other important persons before assuming its modern role as a quiet farm town. Photo by Herbert K. Russell

> A comical little drummer had afforded them great diversion by floating on his drum and other tricks. Such incidents greatly encouraged them and they really began to regard themselves as superior to other men and as persons whom neither floods nor seasons could stop.
>
> —From George Rogers Clark's memoir, *The Conquest of the Illinois*

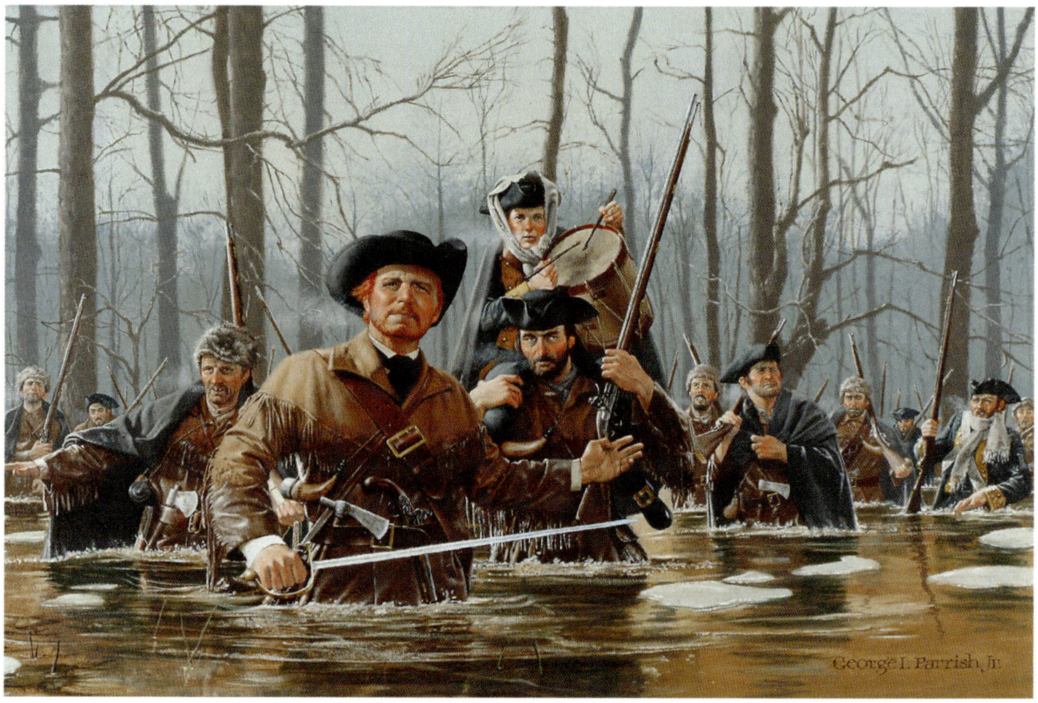

Illustrations of Clark's army crossing Southern Illinois highlight the bone-chilling journey made through the Embarras and Wabash River bottoms near Lawrenceville in February 1779. Painting by George I. Parrish Jr.; courtesy of the Illinois State Historical Society

Xenia and south of Flora to the Wabash River, which he crossed near St. Francisville. The final leg of the journey was made through flooded bottomlands clogged with brush and ice, and many days ended with soggy meals and little sleep. The campaign required three weeks but yielded what Clark had hoped for—the complete surprise of the British and their surrender of Vincennes. He had now neutralized British forts at Kaskaskia and Vincennes and brought the strategic site of Fort Massac under American sway without losing a single man.

Clark's small army later turned back a British thrust at Cahokia and remained a threat to Detroit and other British-held areas for the remainder of the Revolutionary War. The British recognized this danger, and in the treaty of 1783—following skillful negotiations by Benjamin Franklin—England turned over to the Americans all lands between Pittsburgh and the Mississippi River from Cairo to Minnesota. The new territory—called the "Northwest Territory" because it was northwest of the Ohio River—doubled the size of the United States.

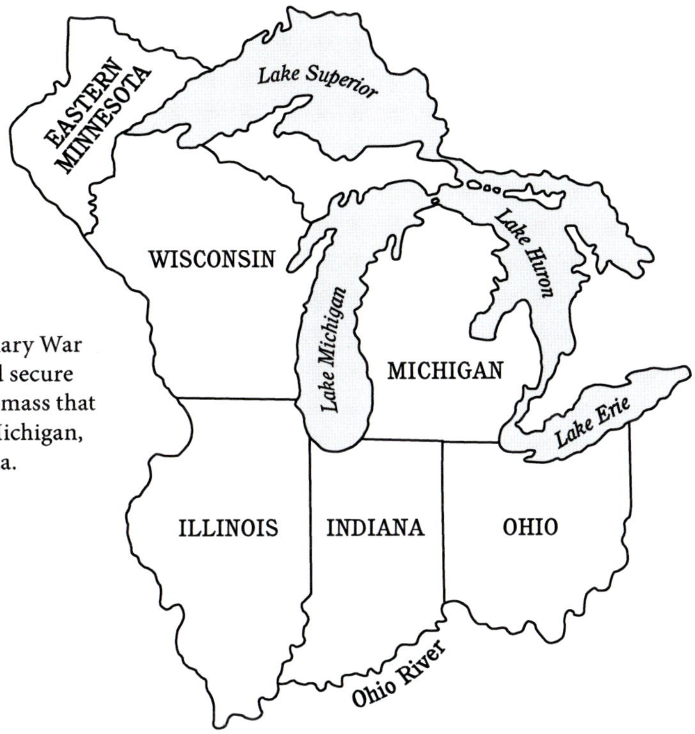

George Rogers Clark's Revolutionary War daring in Southern Illinois helped secure the Northwest Territory, the land mass that became Illinois, Indiana, Ohio, Michigan, Wisconsin, and eastern Minnesota.

One of the first military uses of the Southern Illinois lands came near the Pulaski County town of New Grand Chain in 1801 when the U.S. Army established Cantonment Wilkinson on the Ohio River upstream from Cairo. Named for its temporary nature ("cantonment") and General James Wilkinson, the site was home to 1,500 soldiers in the days when Native Americans were a threat from the south and France and Spain held interests west of the Mississippi. After Indian fears abated and the Louisiana Purchase ended immediate concerns about European nations, Cantonment Wilkinson was abandoned and eventually returned to forest.

It was now that another member of the Clark family made his way around Southern Illinois. George Rogers Clark's younger brother William was co-leader with Meriwether Lewis on the expedition that explored the Louisiana Purchase, the area west of the Mississippi River purchased from France by Thomas Jefferson in 1803. In 1803–04 they recruited some of the expedition's men from the Southern Illinois sites of Massac and Kaskaskia. In May 1804 the expedition left its winter quarters on the Wood River in Madison County, crossed the Mississippi, and began the journey up the Missouri River toward the Rocky Mountains and the Pacific Northwest. The group reached Oregon and the Pacific Ocean in 1805 and brought back information about a "new" Northwest, one that lay 2,000 miles beyond "the Old Northwest," the five-state area that includes Illinois. The expedition's winter camp at Wood River has long since been swept away by the Mississippi, but a handsome interpretive center tells their story at nearby Hartford, Illinois.

Although the Revolutionary War had driven the British out of Illinois, several eastern states held old land claims to the

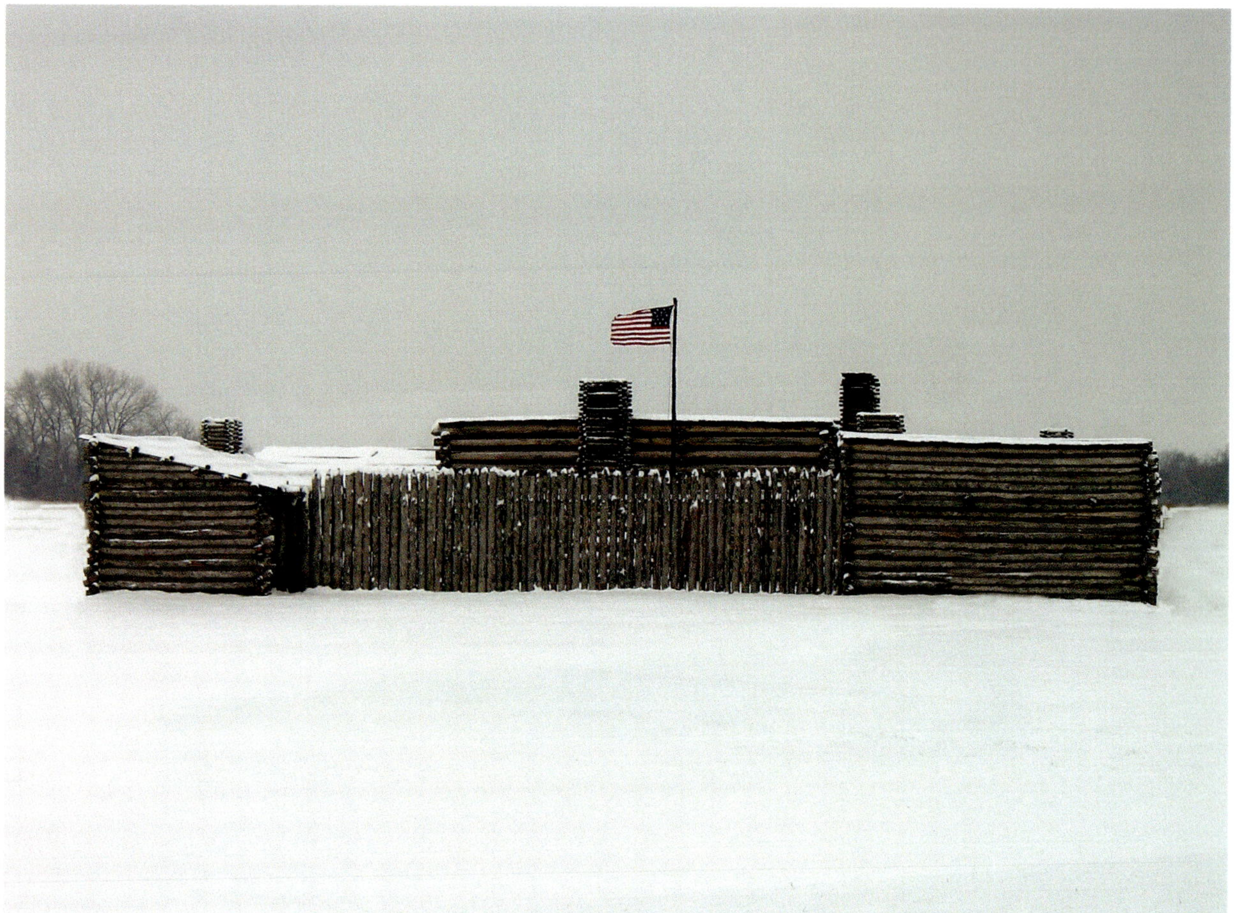

Snow swirls about Lewis and Clark's reconstructed winter quarters at Hartford in Madison County. The expedition spent the winter of 1803–04 near here before heading up the Missouri River toward the Pacific Northwest. The Mississippi has long since destroyed the original structure. Photo by Mike Stout; courtesy of Lewis and Clark State Historic Site

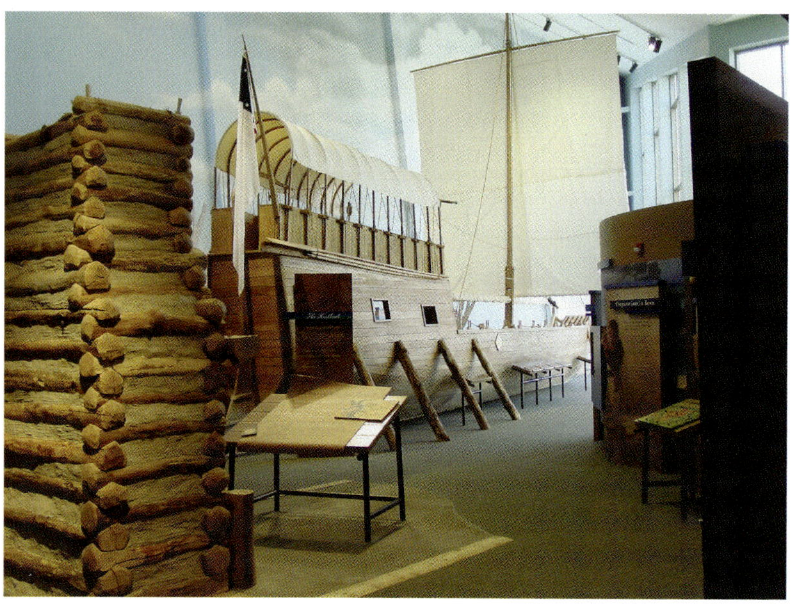

Lewis and Clark's reconstructed keelboat is a highlight of the Corps of Discovery Museum at Hartford. Photo by David Blanchette; courtesy of Lewis and Clark State Historic Site

Midwest. In a series of remarkable transfers, these states now relinquished their claims and gave the land to the federal government. Uncle Sam subsequently sold the land in small parcels to individuals and applied the proceeds to the national debt created by the Revolutionary War. The people thus came to own the land, and the U.S. government received the money it needed. Southern Illinois was still owned by the state of Virginia at the end of the war, but its land transfer came with costly conditions. The federal government could have Virginia's Illinois land, provided the Illinois inhabitants could keep their properties. This apparently reasonable request, agreed to in 1784, meant that those who owned slaves in Illinois could keep them, and so the institution of slavery was passed along once again.

It was at this point in 1784 that Thomas Jefferson tried his hand at drawing the region's boundaries. Jefferson had gone to Congress the year before and found himself chairing several committees, including one governing lands received from the British. He proposed to begin the process toward statehood by dividing the area into fourteen regions. His map of Southern Illinois included parts of southwestern Indiana and western Kentucky and had its northern border on the 39th parallel near Vandalia. He named the area "Polypotamia," a "land of many rivers."

Jefferson's plan would have appealed to many of Illinois' first settlers. Seventy-five percent of these came from the South, and no state sent more people to early Illinois than Kentucky. Southern Illinois replicated the hills, woods, and wildness of the land they had left, and that was enough. It looked like home, and they stayed. And the same could be said for many who first passed through southwestern Indiana and then into Illinois. Some took a ferry across the Wabash River at Vincennes or crossed into Illinois at Mt. Carmel, St. Francisville, or near New Haven.

Jefferson's state of Polypotamia would have been every Egyptian separatist's dream. A state that ran east-west on its long sides instead of north-south would have placed Southern Illinois among friends from the Mid-South, far from the strange ways of Chicago. Such a state would have developed at its own pace, somewhat like the southern Appalachians or Missouri Ozarks, but would have faced one call to secede: it would have come during the Civil War and would have asked whether Polypotamia should join the Confederate States of America. But this question never arose, for not even Jefferson won all his battles. When his fellow members of Congress rejected his plans for future states, Jefferson's active mind turned to a trip to France. By the time he left for Paris, Polypotamia was dead in the water. An unrelated 1805 proposal to join the southern portions of Illinois and Indiana into a single state also failed.

Of course no one could control the Midwest until the American Indian presence was addressed. Native Americans had probably been in Southern Illinois intermittently since about 9500 B.C. They were here at the time of Christ and through the first millennium, hunting, gathering, traveling, trading, and gardening, growing more sophisticated in the use of tools and weapons and oblivious to the changes that Europeans would bring. Before the Revolutionary War, the British had treated land north of the Ohio River to Canada as Native American hunting ground and as a buffer between

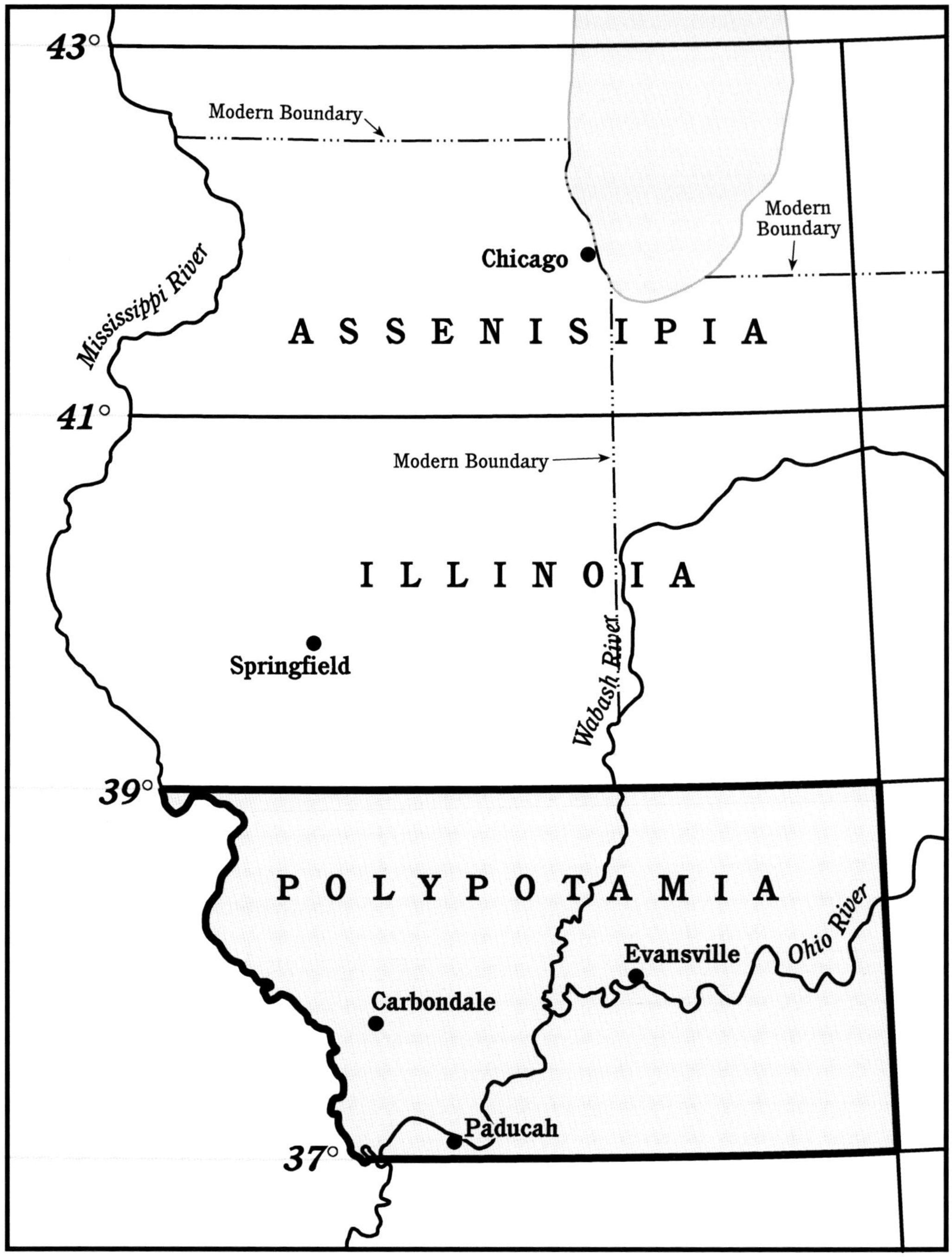

Thomas Jefferson's planning map for Southern Illinois created a hypothetical state that would have been southern in climate and culture and named "Polypotamia," the land of many rivers. Springfield would have been in the state of "Illinoia" and Chicago in "Assenisipia."

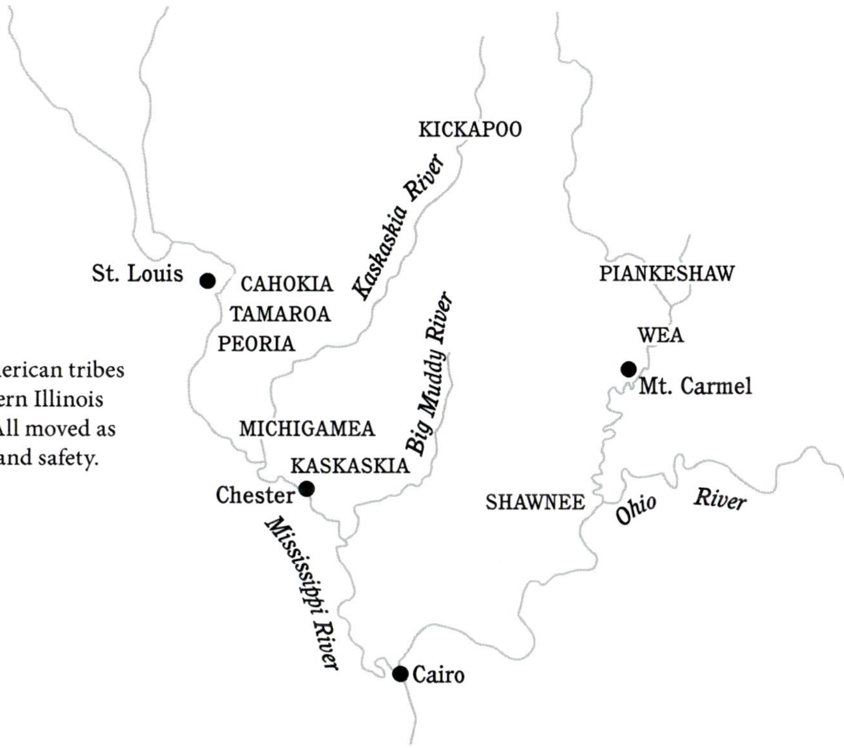

Some Native American tribes in or near Southern Illinois included these. All moved as needed for food and safety.

French and British interests. But even before the war ended in 1783, a few whites had moved north across the Ohio, and after their numbers grew in the early 1800s, the two cultures clashed.

Estimates of the number of Native Americans living in Illinois at the beginning of the nineteenth century vary widely, with 30,000 being a rough average. Certainly, the number of Indian attacks in Southern Illinois was small in contrast to other parts of the nation, but when they did occur, no news traveled faster, and revenge was nearly certain. The often-repeated story of John Moredock illustrates. When his family was killed by Native Americans in 1786 on the Mississippi shoreline at present-day Grand Tower in Jackson County, Moredock undertook a years-long revenge on all Indians, murdering so many in Illinois and Missouri that he became known as "the Indian hater," a nickname applied to several such men in various locales.

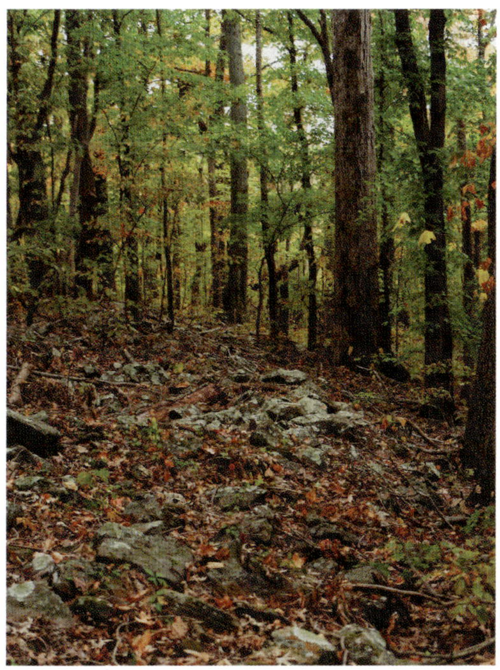

Only a few rocks remain where Native Americans constructed a large stone wall on a hill between A.D. 400 and 900 in what is now Saline County. White settlers assumed the wall was for defensive purposes and named the village of Stonefort after it. Similar walls on eleven high hills once dotted the region. Photo courtesy of Andrew Martin

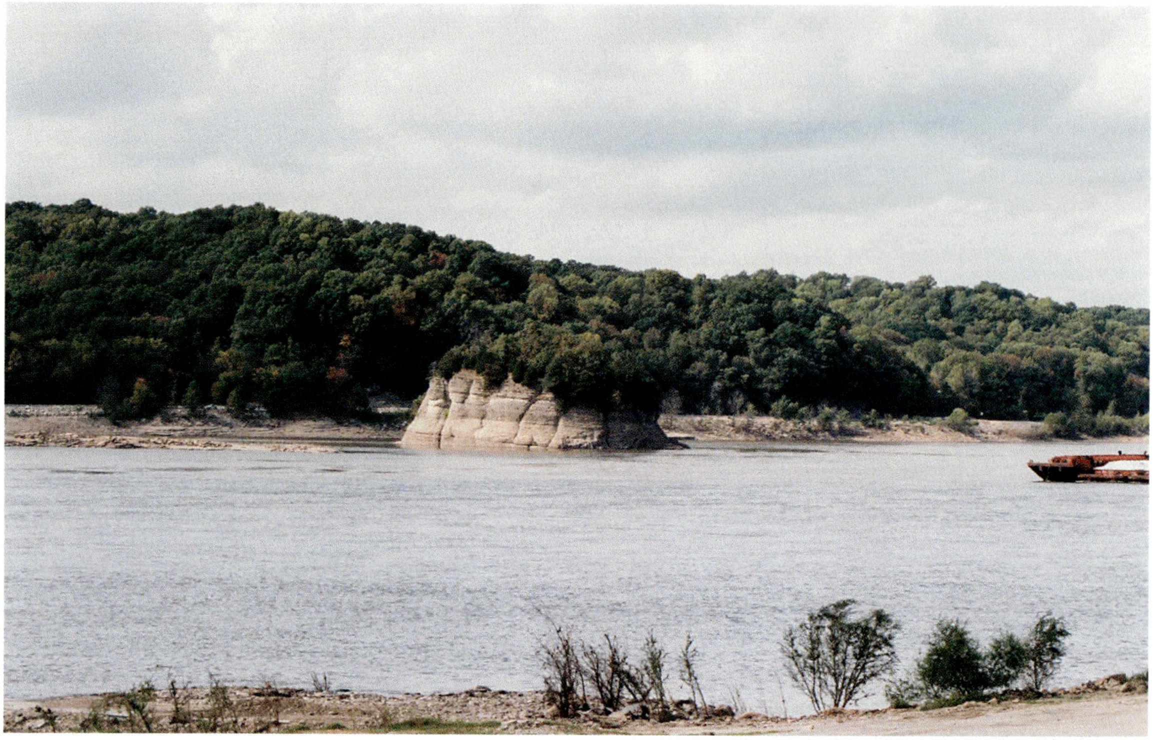

Stony sentinel to history, the "grand" tower of rock on the far shore witnessed the 1786 Moredock massacre on the beach in the foreground before lending its name to the nearby town of Grand Tower. A downstream barge enters the picture at right. Photo by Herbert K. Russell

Moredock's killings went unchallenged by local authorities, and he subsequently lived a long life and died of natural causes.

Midwestern Native Americans might have delayed white migration if they had banded together, but there was no lasting Indian confederacy, and intertribal jealousies and overwhelming numbers of whites ended the tribal presence in Illinois. The life and death of Pontiac, the Ottawa chief, illustrates. Clever and tenacious, he was an opponent to be taken seriously on any terrain and is generally given credit for organizing multitribe attacks against the British before the Revolutionary War. Later, overwhelmed by the great number of whites occupying former Indian lands, he turned to alcohol to ease his sorrow and was murdered by enemies while visiting Cahokia in 1769.

Intertribal rivalries also vanquished the normally peaceful Kaskaskia Indians. They controlled much of the land between the Mississippi and the Big Muddy River from Benton to Murphysboro before being worn down by enemies such as the Fox. The Kaskaskia presence lives on in the town of Du Quoin, named for the Kaskaskia's partly French chief, Jean Baptiste Ducoigne. In 1803 most of the remaining Kaskaskia voluntarily moved to a Native American reservation in Jackson County's Sand Ridge Township, where they were joined by remnants of other tribes. In 1833 they were moved west and merged with the Peoria tribe.

The Shawnee also were overpowered and removed. During the War of 1812 the Shawnee chief Tecumseh organized several tribes in a last effort to retain hunting grounds in

Old Chief of the Kaskaskias,
Do you know who got your name?
A town got it and nailed it down with hammers.
—From "Du Quoin" by Stanley Kimmel

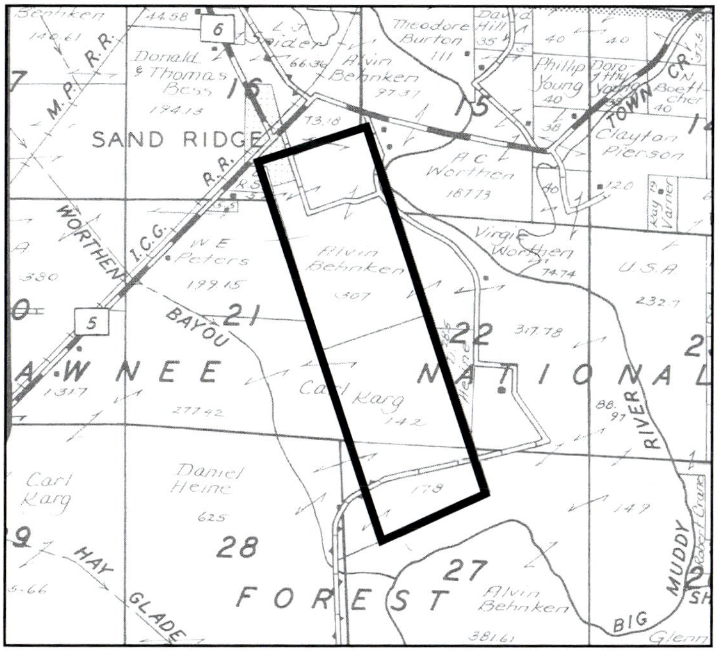

The Indian reservation at Sand Ridge in Jackson County retains its early-nineteenth-century outlines in this late-twentieth-century map. The Kaskaskia and other Native Americans occupied the reservation from 1803 until 1833, when they were moved to western lands.

Illinois, Indiana, and Ohio. The Shawnee had once lived and hunted in southeastern Illinois (hence the name *Shawneetown*), and Tecumseh reportedly passed through Bone Gap in Edwards County and Marion on his way to the South to recruit warriors. His braves made deadly attacks on several Southern Illinois families but were suppressed by Army cavalry and by federally paid local rangers, so named because they were organized to "range" across the area as needed. Articulate and intelligent, respected and feared, Tecumseh died in battle in Canada, far from the Shawnee National Forest named for his tribe.

Two decades later, Southern Illinoisans trooped north to the state's last Indian uprising, the Black Hawk War of 1832. It lasted only a few weeks, with the result that Southern Illinois largely escaped the Indian wars that racked other parts of the country—in part because the federal government reached agreements with local tribes before white settlement became common, in part because Native Americans still had adequate hunting grounds after Illinois' early settlers arrived. In the end, the only Indian drama of consequence to take place in Southern Illinois was the forced migration of a southern tribe, the Cherokee, across the tip of the state.

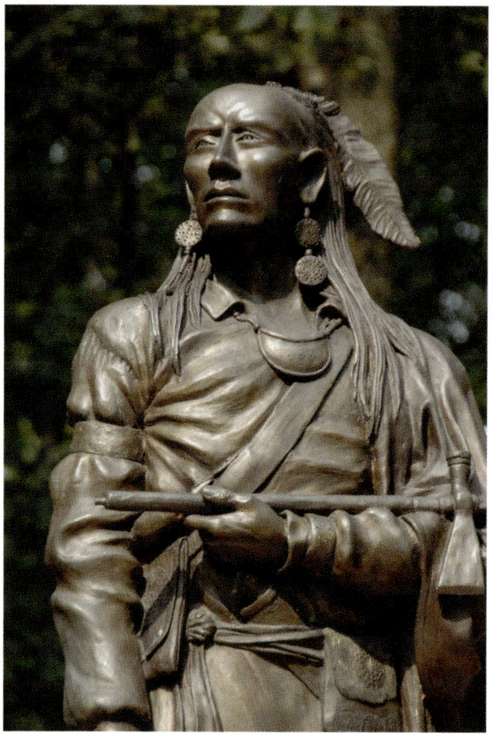

Sculptor Tom Allen's *Tecumseh* gazes into the forest the Shawnee once roamed, now a part of the Saline County Fish and Wildlife Area near Harrisburg. Photo courtesy of Shannon Woodworth

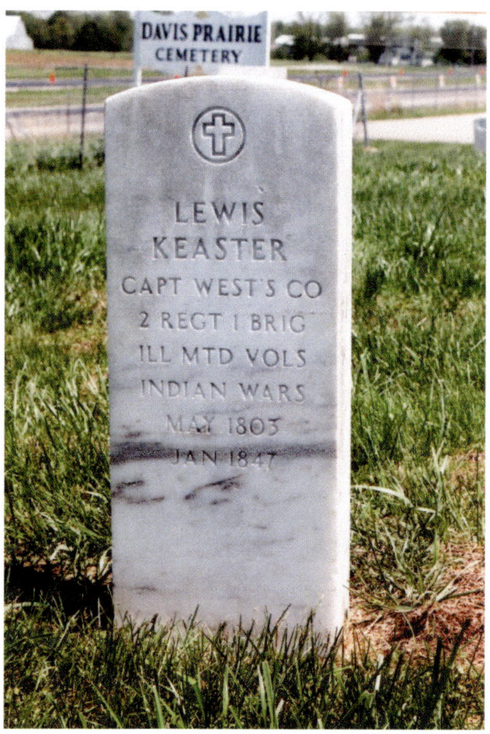

Franklin County's Lewis Keaster served as a private in the Black Hawk War as a member of the Illinois Mounted Volunteers. Davis Prairie Cemetery, Williamson County. Photo by Herbert K. Russell

Among the most sophisticated tribes, the Cherokee had a knack for prospering near white societies, and intermarriage with whites was common in the Appalachian Mountains of Tennessee, North Carolina, Georgia, and elsewhere. Several Cherokee had white wives, wore white men's clothing, lived in frame or brick houses, owned farms with black slaves, and practiced Christianity. Not surprising, perhaps, is that a good many Southern Illinois families claim a Cherokee ancestor in their past. Cherokee occasionally married free persons of color, and triracial ancestries of red, white, and black are not uncommon.

By the 1830s the Cherokee were outnumbered by whites in their southern homelands, and after some of the Cherokee negotiated with the federal government, plans were made to remove the tribe from their southern tribal lands to Indian Territory, now Oklahoma. Scholars disagree on the number of those making the journey as well as on the number of deaths and births. The Cherokee departed from their homeland at various times, some by water and some by land. Some had U.S. Army escorts and some did not. Some Cherokee went voluntarily to departure camps, but many were coerced, and some died in the camps. Others avoided capture by hiding; and some who did not live on Cherokee tribal lands remained on the Tennessee–North Carolina border.

To avoid land travel in the heat of the summer of 1838, some of the Cherokee asked for, and were granted, permission to delay departure until cooler weather prevailed, a delay that would later strand some in Southern Illinois during the winter. The Cherokee making the land journey began the 800-mile trip in several different groups traveling several days apart. Crossing the Ohio River by ferry at Golconda was time-consuming, and at one point some of the Cherokee were in Illinois, some in Kentucky, and others already in Missouri. Once in Illinois they made their way west along or near contemporary Route 146, passing through or near Dixon Springs, Vienna, and Mt. Pleasant toward Jonesboro where, as winter came on, many found their way blocked by large ice floes on the Mississippi. The miles-long column stopped.

Ancestral lore of numerous Southern Illinois families tells that some Cherokee escaped into the hills while hunting food or water and later intermarried with local families. This is possible, for some Cherokee did escape. There is also the story of "Priscilla," a slave girl purchased from the Cherokee and freed by Brazilla Silkwood, owner of the Silkwood Inn at Mulkeytown. Some of the Cherokee had to establish winter camps near Jonesboro, and many perished in the winter of 1838–39. The Cherokee would later summarize their forced migration to Oklahoma as "the trail where we cried"—the Trail of Tears.

As Native American control of Southern Illinois declined, the federal government established land offices on the Mississippi River at Kaskaskia, on the Ohio at Shawneetown, and at Edwardsville. Beginning in 1814 federal officials had the responsibility for overseeing sales of government land to settlers, many of whom came originally from the British Isles—England, Scotland, Wales, and Ireland. A good many were "Scots-Irish," a hardy breed more Scottish than Irish who had lived in England, Scotland, and occasionally Ireland and been abused and starved by the English over various centuries. They grew up hating the English (who grew up scorning them), and when both groups migrated to the American East Coast, they again found themselves in conflict. The English and others owned the flatlands on the coast, and the Scots-Irish were pressured to head south and west into the Appalachian Mountains and the Cumberland Gap—which led some, after many a winding turn, to Southern Illinois. All of this would be important years later when

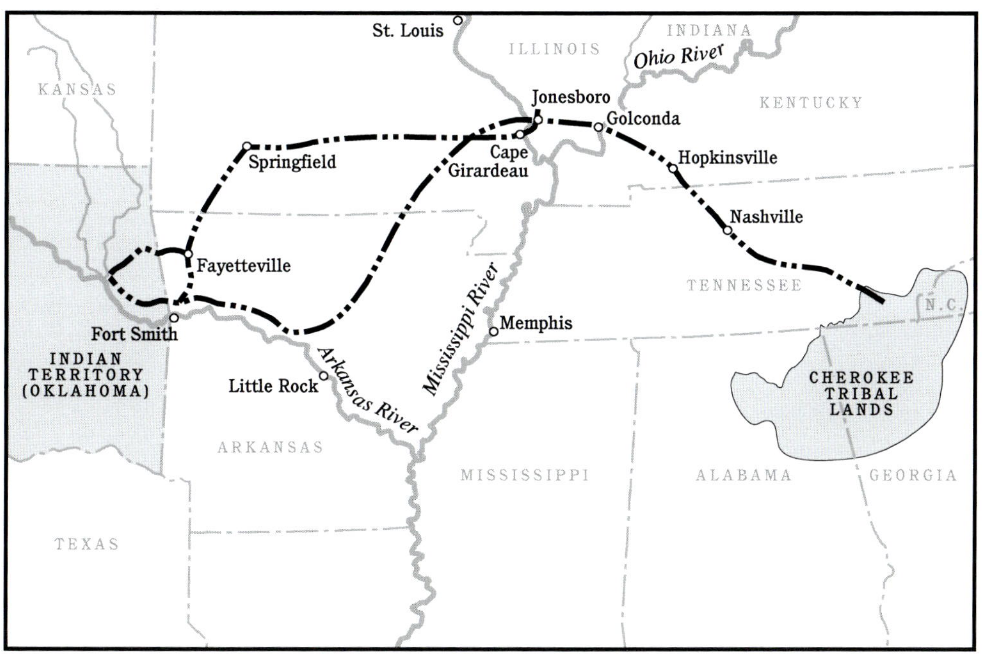

The Cherokee Trail of Tears led southern Indians through the Southern Illinois hill country to Missouri and Arkansas before delivering them to Indian Territory, now Oklahoma. The travelers came north to what is now a part of Illinois Route 146 to find an east-west road that would accommodate wagons.

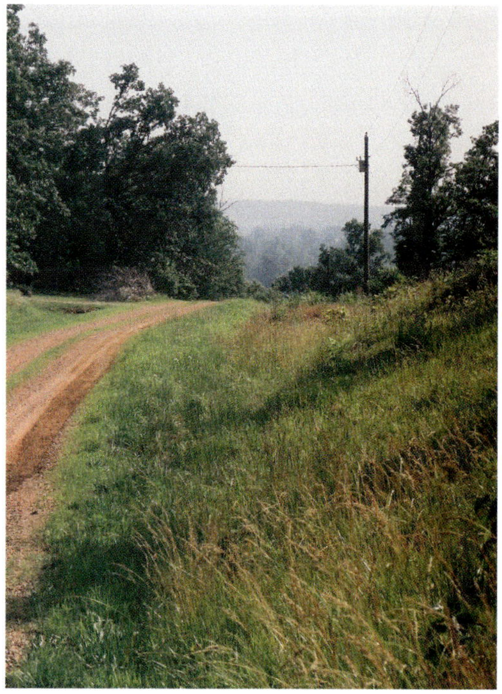

The Trail of Tears emerges from a deep valley near its Southern Illinois beginnings at Golconda in Pope County. Photo by Herbert K. Russell

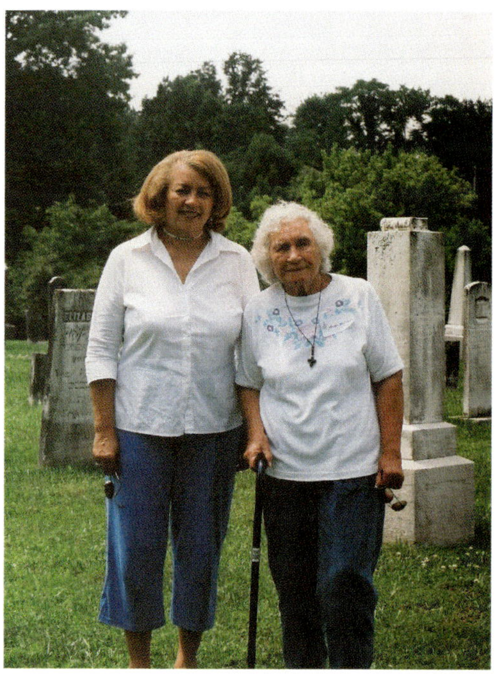

Visitors to the Trail of Tears include those with Cherokee ancestry, here at Camp Ground Church east of Anna, where several Cherokee are thought to be buried. Photo by Herbert K. Russell

parts of northern Illinois were settled by natives of New England and New York ("Yankees and Yorkers"), some of whom traced their roots to Old England and looked down their noses at the Scots-Irish of Southern Illinois, or "Egypt," as it was soon to be called.

> I have heard that there is corn in Egypt: get you down thither, and buy for us from thence; that we may live, and not die.
>
> —Genesis 42:2

Nearly all of Illinois' early settlers passed through or lived a generation or two in southern states such as Kentucky, Tennessee, Virginia, the Carolinas, and occasionally Maryland, Georgia, or Alabama. Two north-flowing rivers—the Cumberland and the Tennessee—ran out of the South toward Paducah and Southern Illinois, and at least one visitor to Kentucky mentioned the name "Egypt" in association with abundant grain in Kentucky. Arthur Singleton's *Letters from the South and West*, published in 1824, shows this in an 1818 "Letter from Kentucky": "*From the poorer states, when there is a famine in the land, they are fain to send to this Egypt [Kentucky] to buy corn.*" Borrowed from a story in the Bible and popularized in the nineteenth century, the name "Egypt" has never been exclusive to Southern Illinois but has been used in various states, including New Hampshire by 1816 and later in New Jersey to indicate areas with full granaries.

Many of these first settlers in Illinois were "upland" southerners, poor whites from the rural backcountry and hilly or mountainous areas where small farmers eked out a living.

Only a few came from the lowlands—the flatlands associated with prosperous river bottoms, the delta, and coastal areas where slaves worked on plantations. While the typical poor white of the Old South owned no slaves (many did not even own the land they farmed), the misconception remains that the majority of those who came to Southern Illinois were slave owners who brought slaves with them. This was fueled in part by N. Dwight Harris' influential 1904 study, *The History of Negro Servitude in Illinois*: "most of the settlers owned slaves."

Harris did not provide a footnote for this assertion, probably because he could not. He did not actually count slaves and settlers—he was a hundred years too late for that—nor could he rely on the first federal census of Illinois Territory made in 1810: its totals are still available, but details of individual households are lost except for a fragment. Nor would the territorial census of 1818 or federal census of 1820 be of much use: through 1820 census takers used varying criteria and sometimes estimated populations; sometimes failed to distinguish between free and slave populations; and sometimes failed to distinguish between black and white populations. After 1818 the state constitution curtailed slavery, and an 1824 effort to revive it failed. In other words, Harris' often-cited remark about settlers owning slaves is unsubstantiated. Based on the poverty of those who came to Illinois, one can conclude that the typical settler in Southern Illinois had no slaves, had no money to buy them, and as historian John Y. Simon noted, was seldom descended from slaveholders.

Many early travelers and immigrants to Southern Illinois came by land or water through Kentucky or arrived by flatboat on the Ohio River at Shawneetown. The northward-flowing Cumberland and Tennessee Rivers delivered southerners to the very doorstep of Southern Illinois.

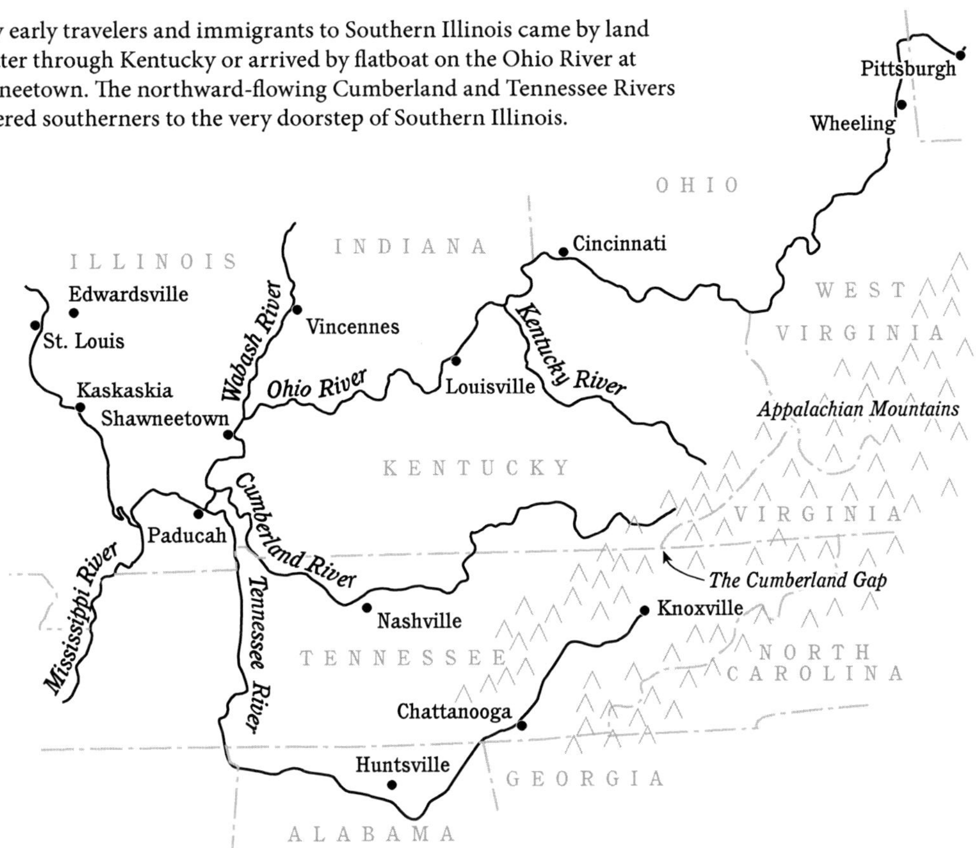

Some of Illinois' early settlers felt slavery was a moral wrong, but most were indifferent to it, and if few believed in racial equality, the majority did not want plantations or slavery in Illinois. When Englishman William Oliver visited Southern Illinois, he described one man's situation as follows: "On asking him why he had removed from the South, we got the old story, that a man who had not a number of slaves and a large estate was despised by the planters [plantation owners], and was, in fact, almost deprived of society." Some of these early Southern Illinoisans had also been deprived of their properties by fair means or foul, and it was land that brought them to Southern Illinois, "good land dog-cheap," as one immigrant put it. They lined up by the thousands at land offices to begin their lives anew. Because the federal government had wisely insisted that the land be surveyed before it was sold, buyers could be reasonably sure they would avoid the expensive land squabbles that had troubled other states.

In addition to those who came through Kentucky and Tennessee, some came down the Ohio River, perhaps on a flatboat manned by the legendary Mike Fink, the colorful boatman whose deeds and misdeeds earned him a place in American history and folklore. Related stories about Cave in Rock being headquarters for thieves, murderers, psychopaths, whores, and counterfeiters have proven to be largely folklore, and most boats drifted by the cave without incident. One of the most important Illinois settlements was Shawneetown, a boatman's layover town where crews might rest or roister before traveling on to river towns such as New Madrid, Missouri, and Natchez, Mississippi.

Travelers arriving in Shawneetown in the 1820s found a village that met many of their needs: a bank, hotel, post office, a medical doctor, a lawyer or two, various shops, and of course the land office. Shawneetown was smoky, dirty, malodorous, and subject to flooding from the Ohio, but it was easy to access by those coming down the Ohio or across from Kentucky and had a necessary supply of salt. Early trails meandered out of town over uncertain footing toward the first capital of Illinois at Kaskaskia and to present-day Equality in Gallatin County, site of the salt supply.

The ancient oceans that had covered Illinois some 300 million years earlier had not taken all the sea water with them when they receded but left part of it trapped in underground cavities to become salt springs. These were easily identified by the animals that came to lick at the salty soil, including the large Half Moon Lick near Equality. Salt was essential for home use and as a meat preservative, and the federal government acquired two strong salt springs from Native Americans near the Saline (or salty) River in Gallatin County. Because the frontier was short on manpower, and because Illinois had few slaves, those leasing the springs from the government usually leased slaves from Kentucky or Tennessee to work at the salt springs. Free African Americans and area whites also worked there, and salt making became a major industry in early-nineteenth-century Illinois.

Shawneetown soon had several trails leading from it, including a second and drier route to Kaskaskia, one that offered the comfort of the Silkwood Inn in Franklin County. Another popular trail was

Some rows up, but we floats down,
Way down the Ohio to Shawnee Town.
And it's hard on the beech oar, she moves too slow,
Way down to Shawnee Town on the Ohio. . . .

There's whisky in the jug, boys, and wheat is in the sack.
We'll trade 'em down in Shawnee Town and bring the salt back.
And it's hard on the beech oar, she moves too slow,
Way down to Shawnee Town on the Ohio.

—One of several versions of "Shawnee Town"

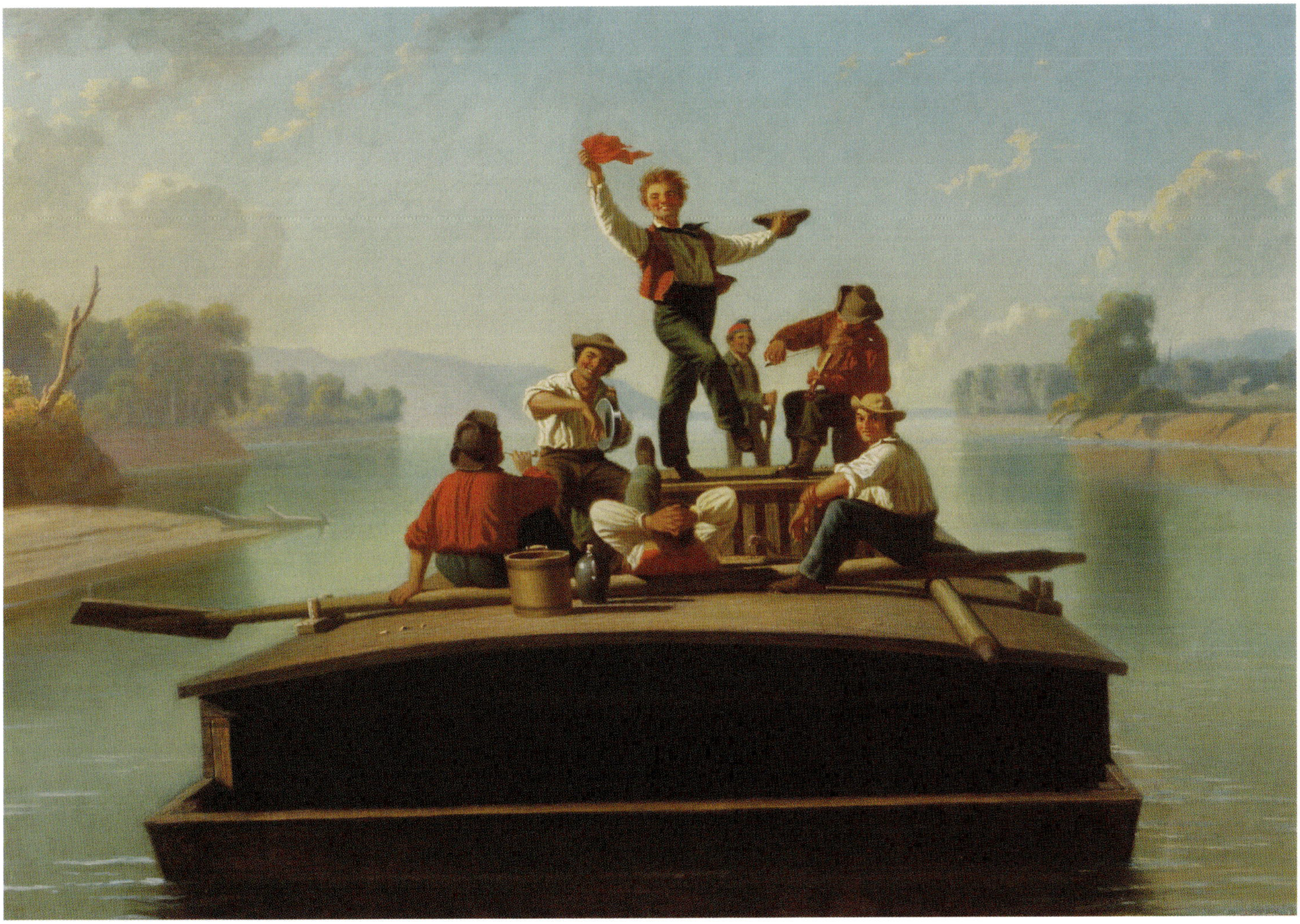

George Caleb Bingham's *Jolly Flatboatmen* shows the amusements of travel, as well as the cramped quarters on some boats. Cargoes were usually carried in barrels. Bingham, George Caleb (1811–1879); *The Jolly Flatboatmen*, 1877–78. Oil on canvas, 26 1/16 × 36 3/8 in. Daniel J. Terra Acquisition Endowment fund, 1992.15.; Terra Foundation for American Art, Chicago, IL, U.S.A. Terra Foundation for American Art, Chicago / Art Resource, NY

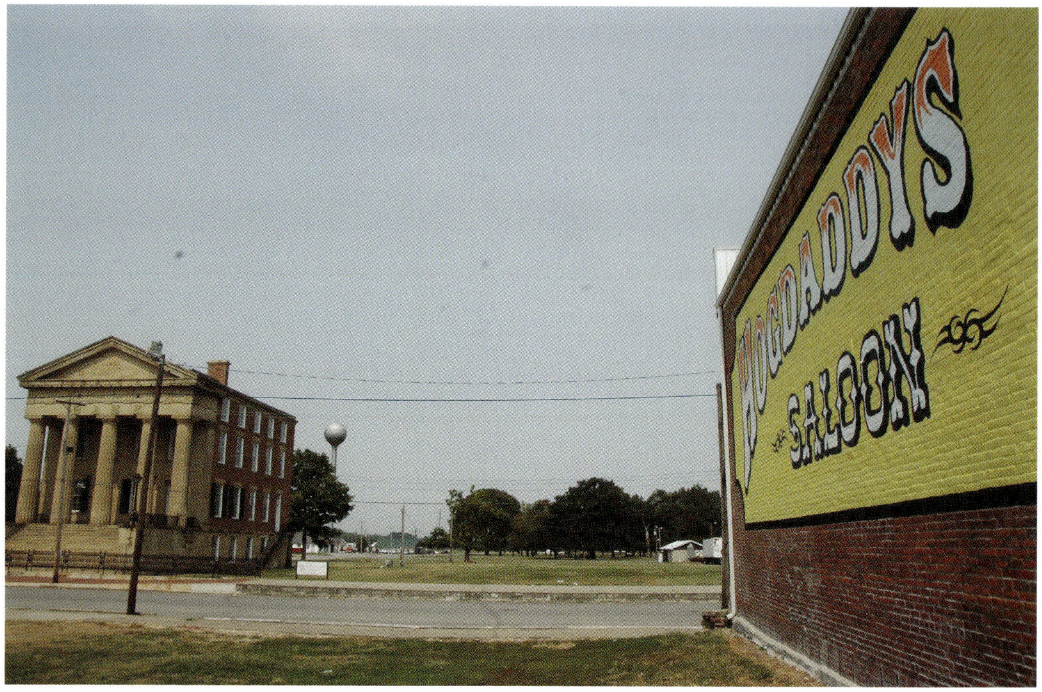

Its glory days long gone, Old Shawneetown's business district has been reduced to a few buildings. The classically designed state bank, dating to the 1830s, stands idle on the street where Lafayette, Lincoln, and John A. Logan walked. Photo courtesy of Shannon Woodworth

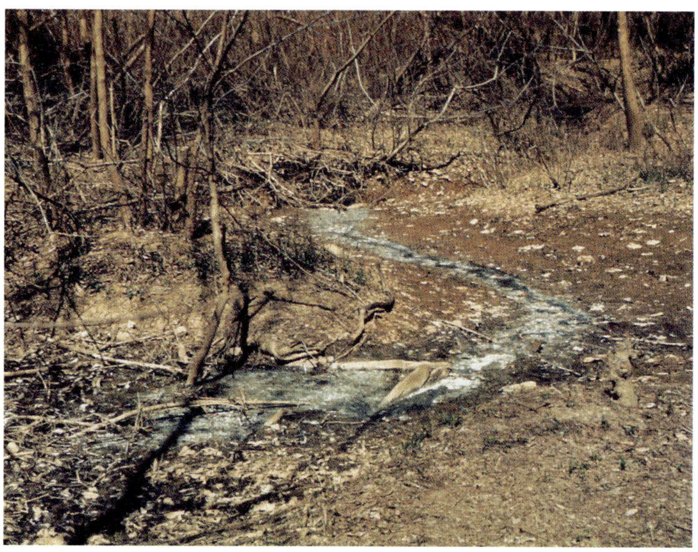

Historian John W. Allen's photo shows one of the Gallatin County salt springs in its natural state, circa 1960. Water removed from the well was boiled in kettles until only the salt remained. John W. Allen Collection, Special Collections Research Center, Morris Library, Southern Illinois University Carbondale

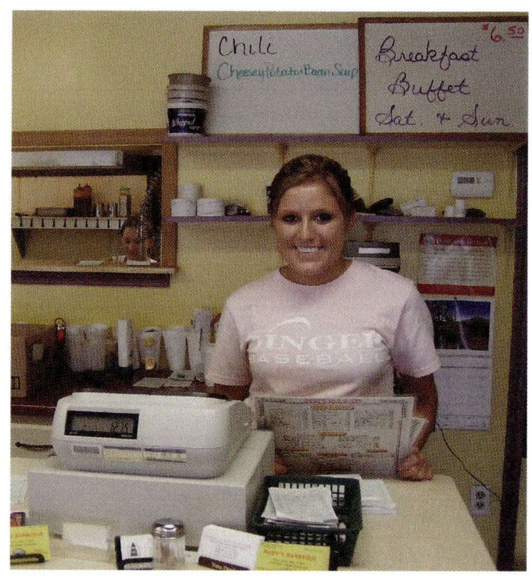

A new Shawneetown built on higher ground after the great flood of 1937 includes the county courthouse and various businesses, including Rudy's Barbeque. Photo courtesy of Shannon Woodworth

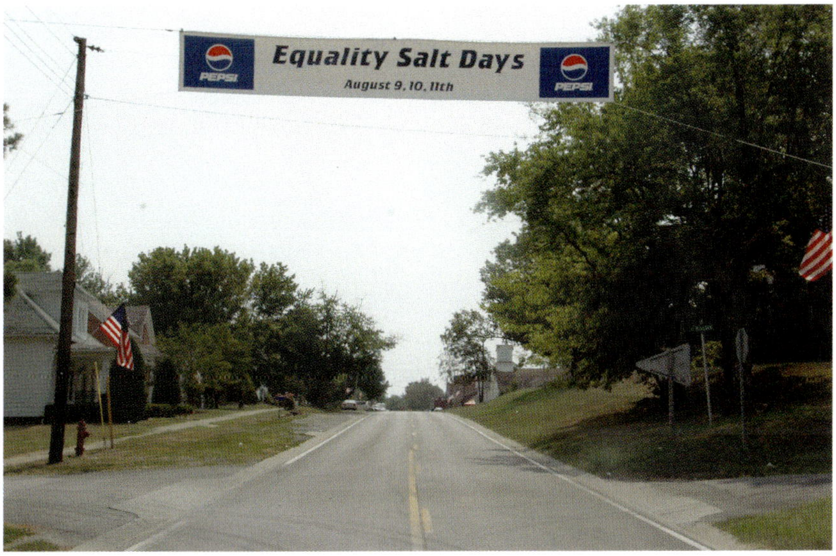

The town of Equality observes its role in helping to settle the state. Photo courtesy of Shannon Woodworth

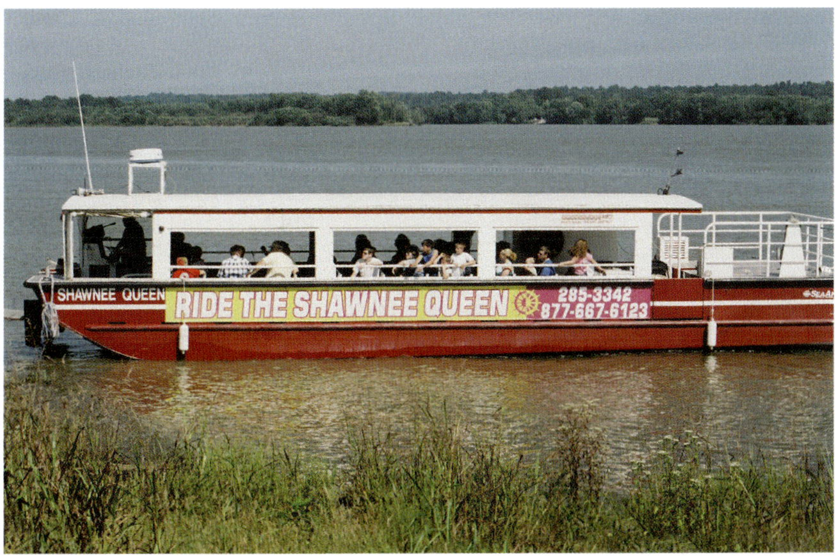

The *Shawnee Queen*, an Ohio River taxi and excursion boat, leaves Golconda for a run to Rosiclare, Elizabethtown, and other river communities. Photo by Herbert K. Russell

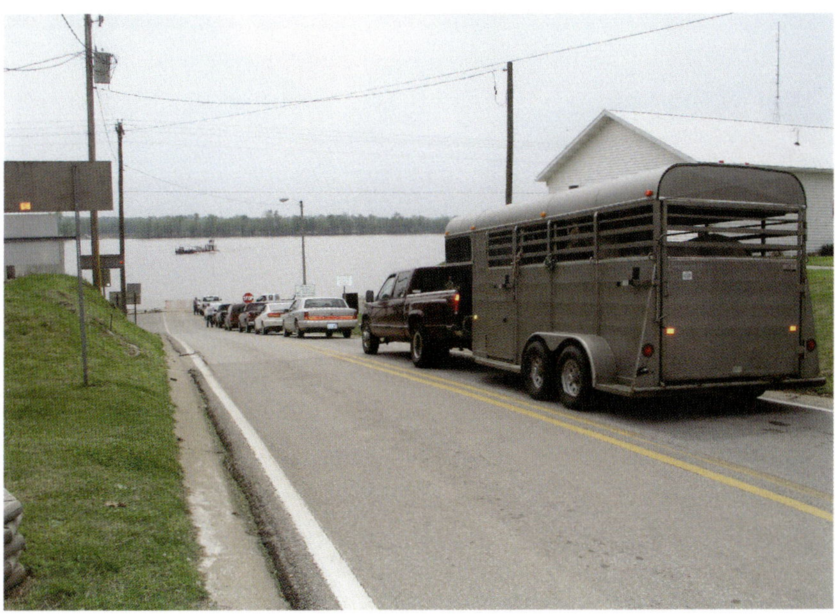

Commuters line up for the rush hour at the Cave in Rock ferry on the Ohio. Photo courtesy of Shannon Woodworth

the "Goshen Road" from Shawneetown to the Edwardsville area and nearby Alton, a jumping-off place for those moving north into the Military Tract, land in west central Illinois given free to veterans of the War of 1812. The Goshen Road passed from Shawneetown through or near Equality, Eldorado, McLeansboro, Mt. Vernon, Dix, and Walnut Hill to Carlyle, where travelers had a choice of routes: west through Cahokia and the Mississippi bottoms to St. Louis, or northwest to Glen Carbon and Edwardsville and land so rich that settlers compared it to the Bible's Land of Goshen.

A man on his way to St. Louis saw in the Bottom a hat on top of the ground. The man got off his horse to pick up the hat, and found a man under it. The man under the hat said, "I am safe, but under me is a wagon and four horses mired in the mud, and I think they are in a bad fix."

—The perils of early travel—as reported in *A History of Columbia . . . , Monroe County*

Trails were aptly named, for most were simply dim paths. Improved trails might become "traces" or "wagon roads," roads from which trees had been cut low enough for an axle to pass. The best-known road in Southern Illinois in the 1820s was the Vincennes-to-St. Louis Trace, also known as the St. Louis Trace or Vincennes Trail, depending on one's destination. It offered an east-west stagecoach route across Illinois and the hospitality of the Halfway Tavern east of Salem, founded in 1823. Some early inns and stagecoach stops still standing in the twenty-first century include the Mermaid House in Lebanon, the Ratcliff Inn in Carmi, and McFarland's Tavern in Elizabethtown, now known as the Rose Hotel.

Those who could not afford to ride might walk. It was not uncommon for a man to walk from Tennessee or North Carolina (or Pennsylvania or elsewhere) to see whether Illinois looked promising. If he liked what he saw, he would return home, after which he might walk back with his family, the oxen pulling their goods on a sled or tied to a "snake," a forked tree branch. Or perhaps a young couple scouting Illinois simply showed up, arrived in the state with one horse or a mule and took turns riding it, or perhaps neither rode as the animal carried all their goods. Or maybe the family cow pulled a two-wheeled cart, or perhaps they themselves pulled the cart, a barrel mounted on wheels. Some were like Ann Rutledge's father, who settled near Enfield in White County with his family and baby daughter in 1813 and remained a dozen years before pushing on to New Salem to start a mill on the Sangamon River. Others were like Abraham Lincoln's father, Thomas, who had lost his land in both Kentucky and Indiana. He and his family crossed Egypt's northeast corner near Lawrenceville in 1830 and kept on going.

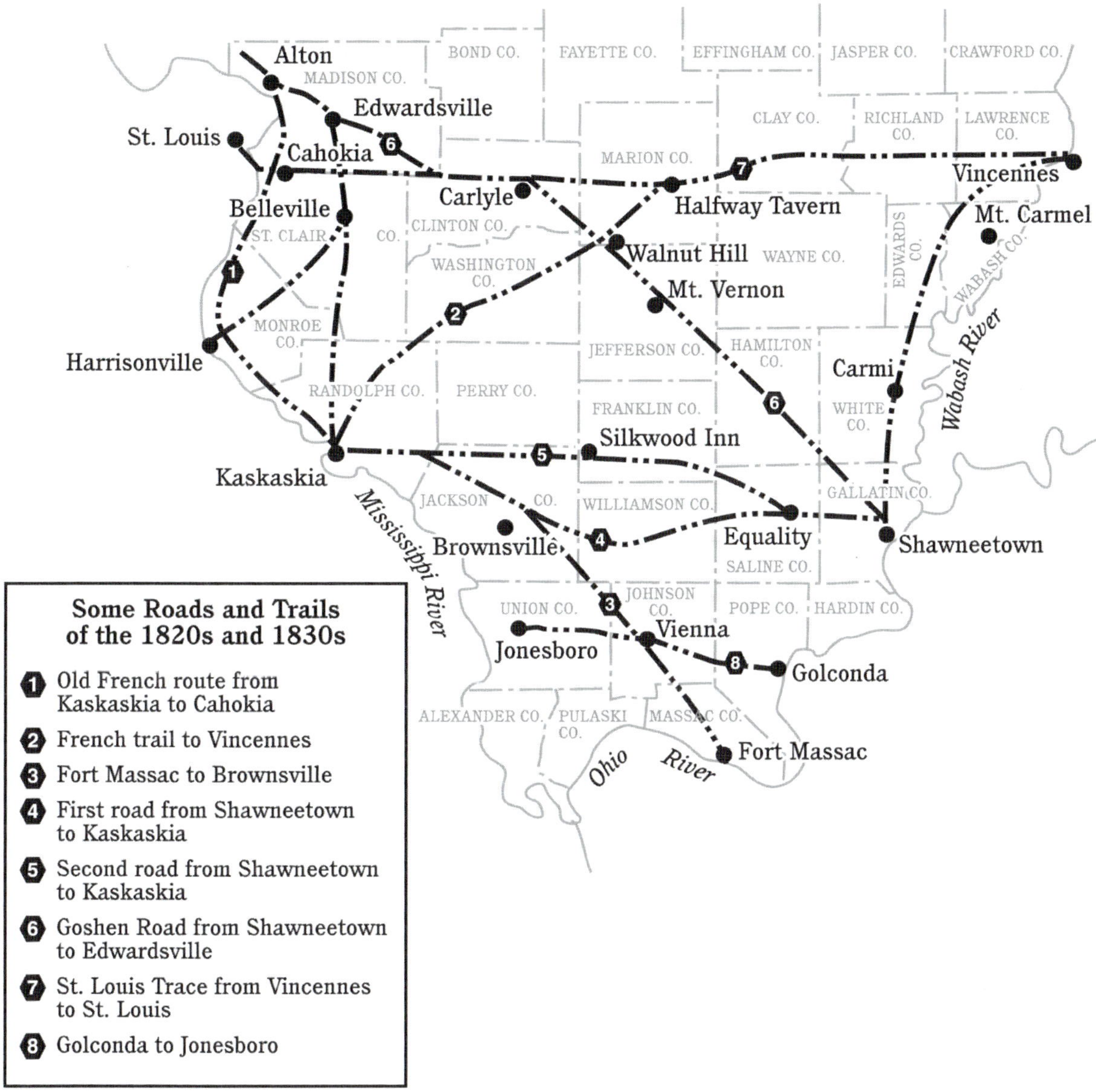

Settlers who reached their destination would spend several years killing trees and "shrubbing off." Nearly every reminiscence of the 1820s, '30s, and '40s has an account of log rolling, a community get-together at which the men would use their own brute strength and that of oxen to move the trunks of giant trees into bonfires to create open spaces for corn, a patch of garden, and later, wheat and tobacco. Poor roads prevented the marketing of crops, and the best-paying of these had to be processed into portable forms: wheat flour and corn whisky. Home-brewed whisky had a prominent place at the table—some families made it available for all meals—and it was always present at social gatherings. Farm animals could be walked to markets on the major rivers, but in

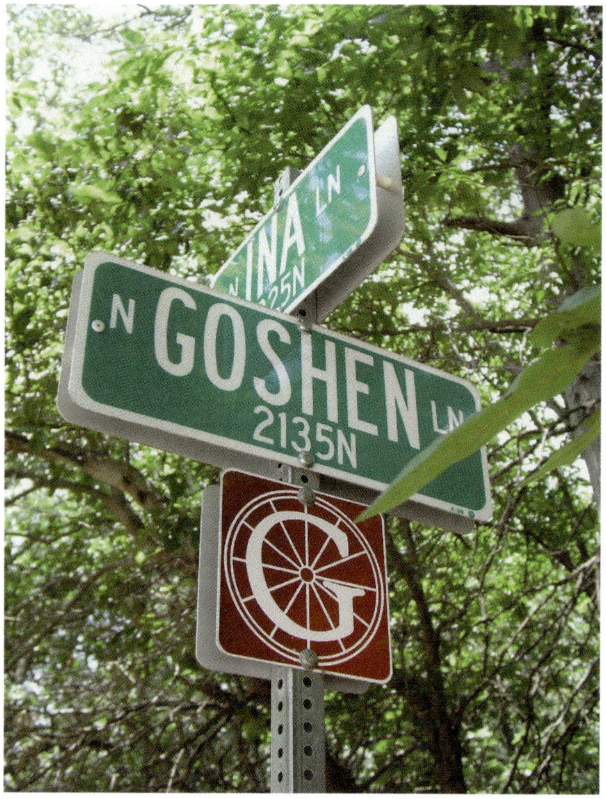

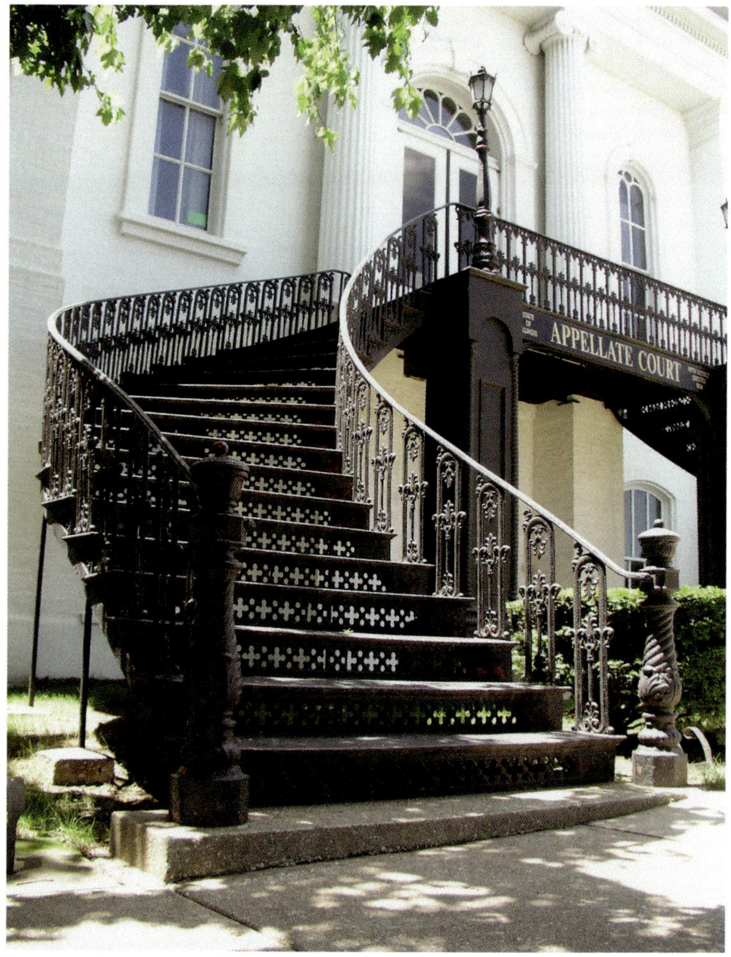

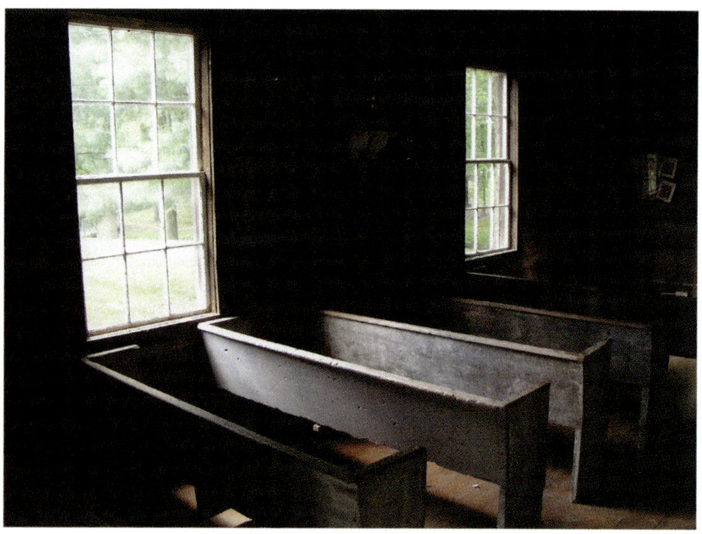

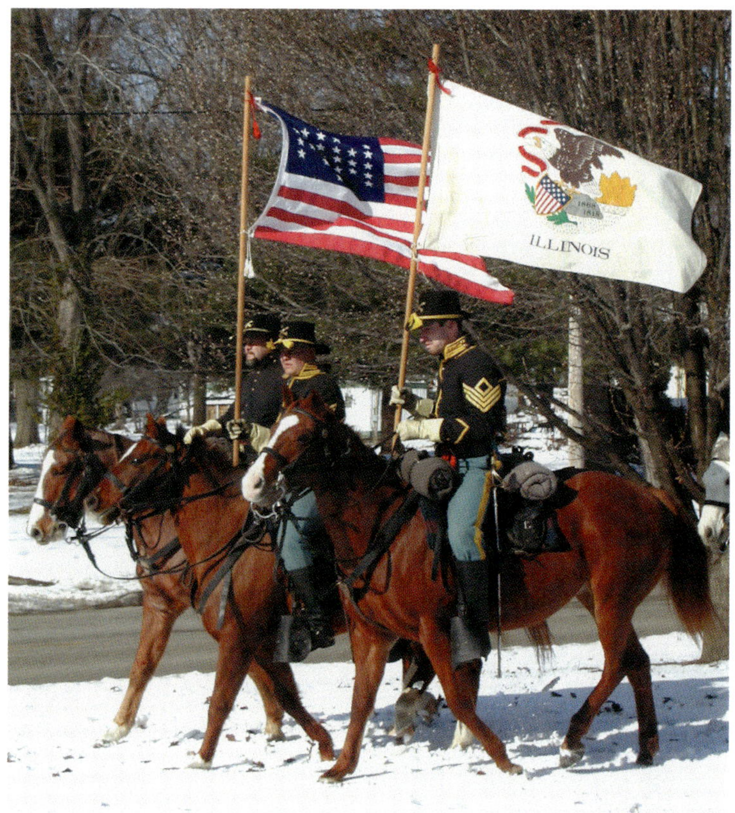

(*Top, left*) Parts of Illinois Route 142 between the towns of Equality and Mt. Vernon follow the pioneer-era Goshen Road, as indicated by the brown "G" on this sign. (*Top, right*) The Goshen Road passed near Mt. Vernon, which gained the appellate courthouse in the 1850s. (*Bottom, left*) An 1837 log church is included in the nearby Jefferson County Historical Village. (*Bottom, right*) Cavalry in the snow add an extra touch to pioneer observances in Jefferson County. Photos courtesy of Shannon Woodworth

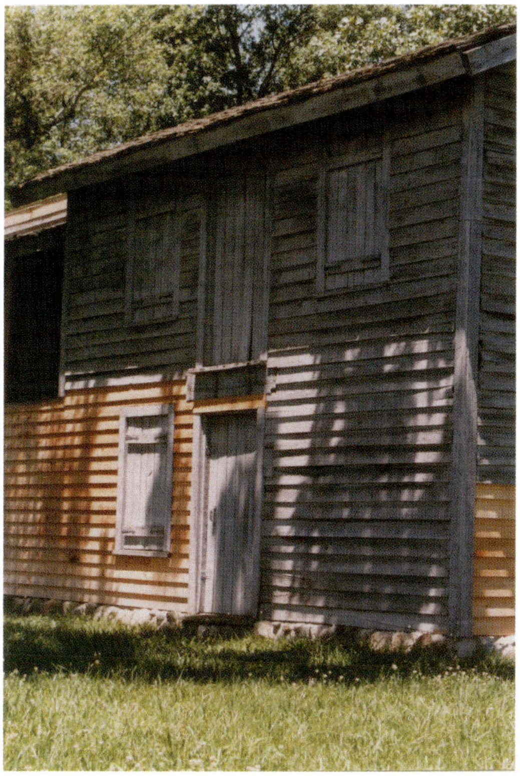

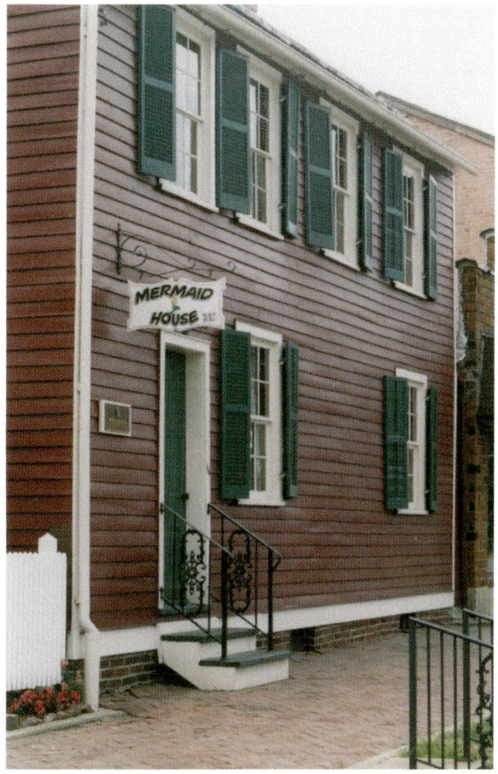

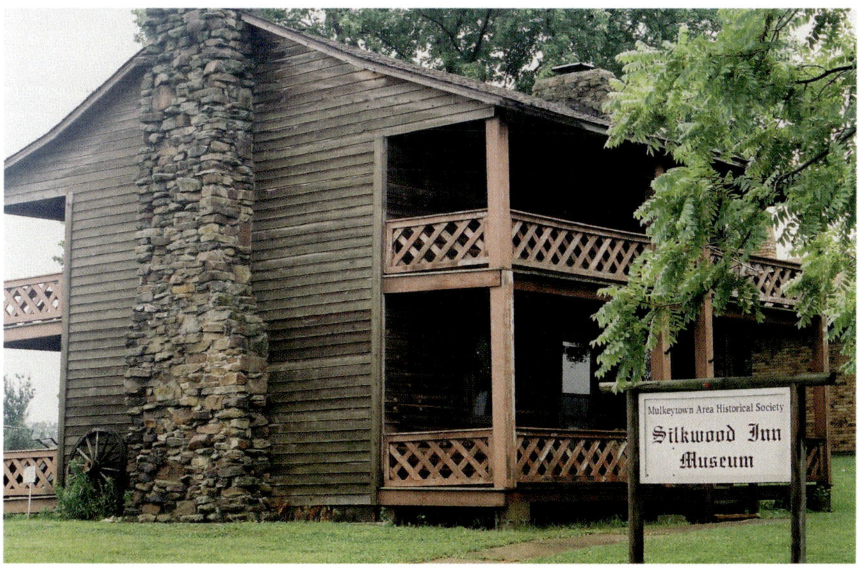

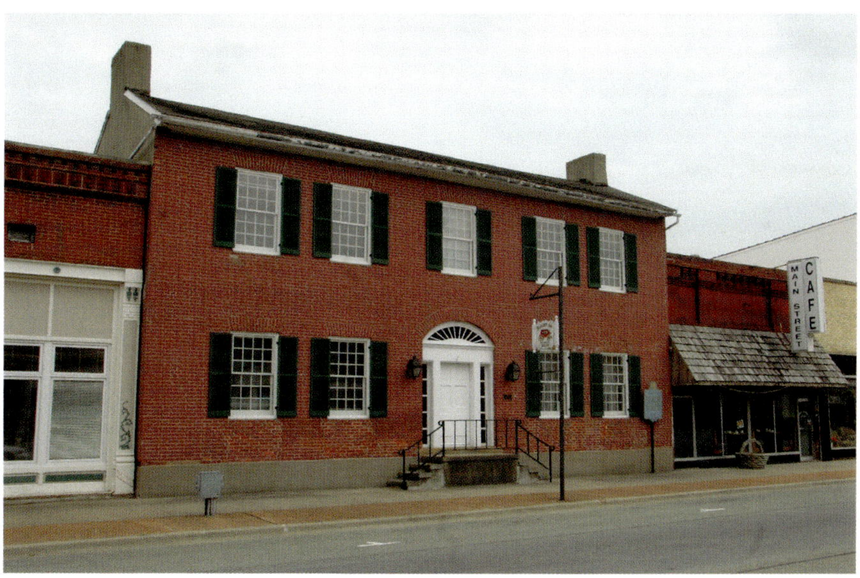

(*Top, left and right*) The sun-dappled Halfway Tavern east of Salem and the Mermaid House at Lebanon offered food and lodging to those crossing Illinois on the trail that became U.S. Route 50. (*Middle*) Travelers on the road between Shawneetown and Kaskaskia relaxed on the porches of the Silkwood Inn at Mulkeytown, west of Benton. (*Bottom*) The Ratcliff Inn at Carmi was the place to stay in White County. Photos of Halfway Tavern, Mermaid House, and Silkwood Inn by Herbert K. Russell; photo of Ratcliff Inn courtesy of Shannon Woodworth

The Weev'ly Wheat

A nineteenth century kissing and courtship song and dance

Oh I don't want none o' your
weev'ly wheat,
An' I don't want none o' your
barley,
But I want some flour in half an
hour,
To bake a cake for Charlie.

* * *

The higher up the cherry tree
The sweeter grows the cherry;
The more you hug an' kiss a gal
The more she wants t' marry!

* * *

Over the river t' feed them sheep
On buckwheat cakes an' barley;
We don't kear what the ol' folks
says—
Over the river t' Charlie.

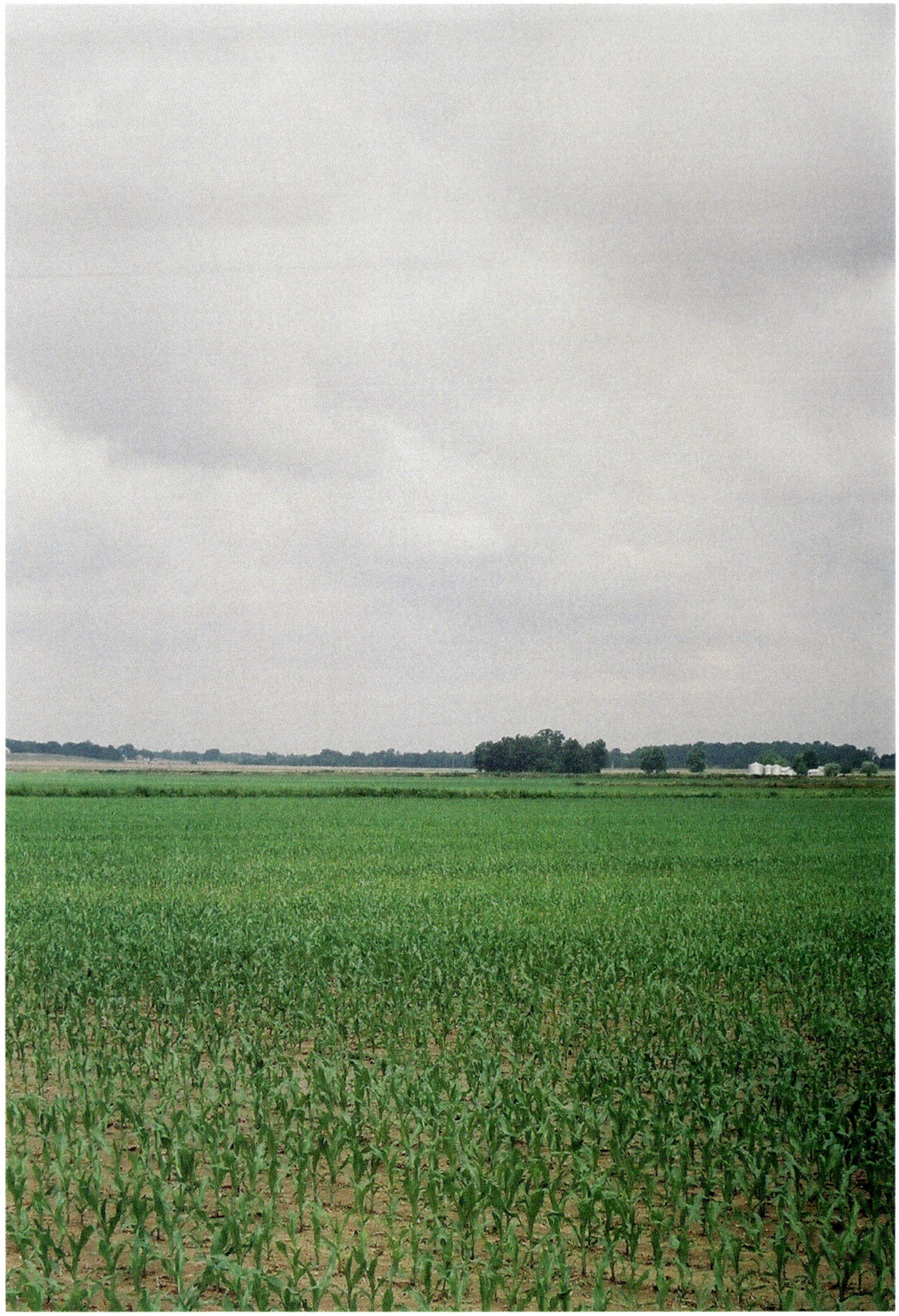

Uncertain skies cloud White County's Seven Mile Prairie, where Lincoln sweetheart Ann Rutledge spent her girlhood. The Rutledges lived southeast of Enfield from 1813 to the mid-1820s, when they moved to central Illinois. Photo by Herbert K. Russell

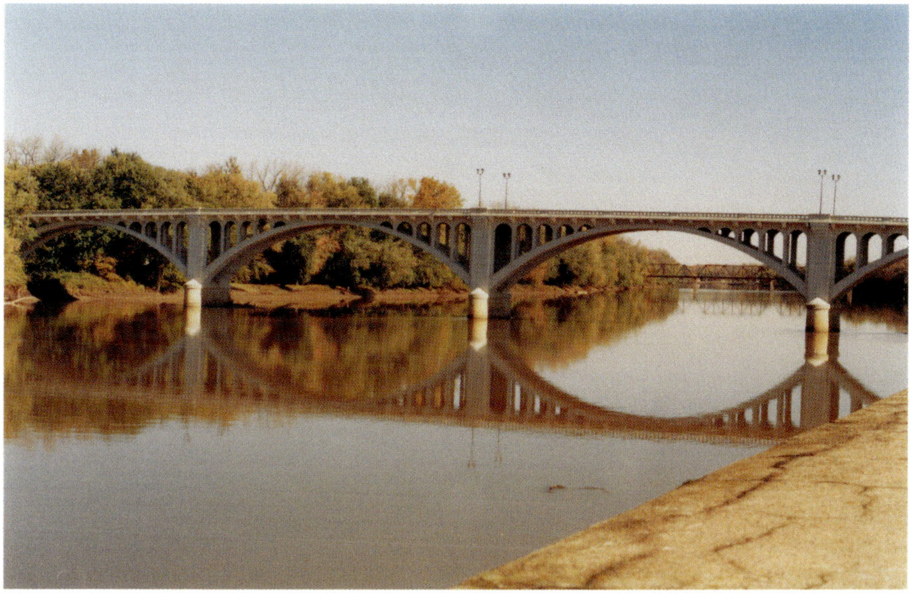

Abraham Lincoln crossed the Wabash River into Illinois in 1830 at the Lawrence County ferry landing on the far shore. Photo by Herbert K. Russell

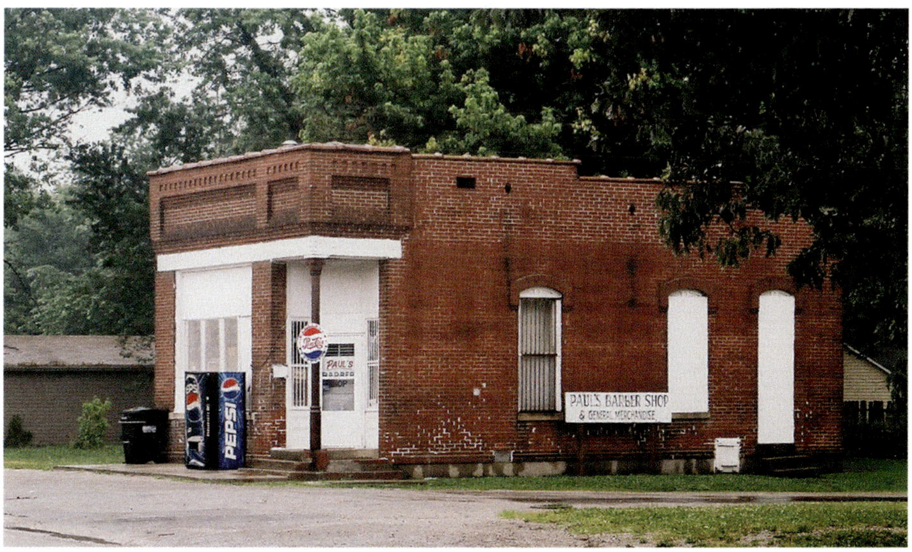

Once a lively crossroads town where the Goshen Road met the Kaskaskia-to-Vincennes Trail, Walnut Hill proceeds at a more serene pace in the twenty-first century. Jefferson County. Photo by Herbert K. Russell

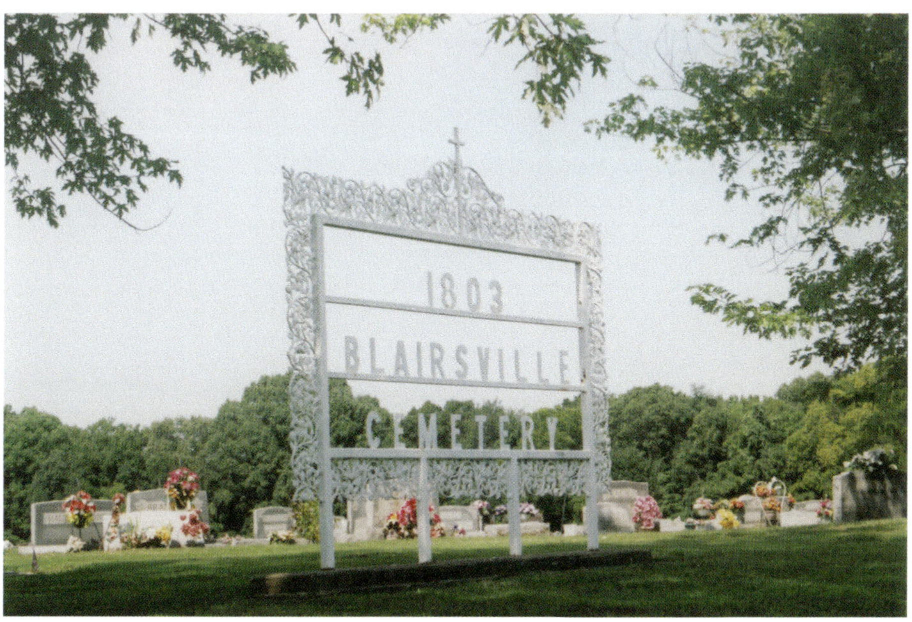

Burials alongside the state's first trails, once common, were possibly the origin of this early cemetery near a crossing of the Big Muddy River in Williamson County. Photo by Herbert K. Russell

an age when crops and gardens were fenced and much of the countryside open, animals strayed. The trip could easily take more than a week and was stressful on man and beast—all the while the beasts lost weight and the owner lost profits.

> The breed of hogs in this part of the country is very bad; they are long-nosed, thin creatures, with legs like greyhounds, and . . . think nothing of galloping a mile at a heat, or of clearing fences which a more civilized hog would never attempt.
>
> —William Oliver, *Eight Months in Illinois*, 1843

Marketing became easier after steamboats came to the Ohio River in 1811 and to the Mississippi in 1817. Early steamboats were powered by boilers heated by burning wood, and Southern Illinois landowners living along the rivers did a brisk business in firewood. This activity spawned numerous shoreline hamlets and landings and provided economic encouragement to emerging towns on a half dozen major and minor rivers. The wood-fueling station at Jenkins Landing matured into the Mississippi River town of Grand Tower, complete with iron furnaces fired by Egyptian coal and dreams of becoming an important industrial site. Upstream, Chester became a processing center for castor beans, the oil of which served as

Several mansions, such as Riverlore, remain in Cairo and other old river towns. Photo courtesy of Shannon Woodworth

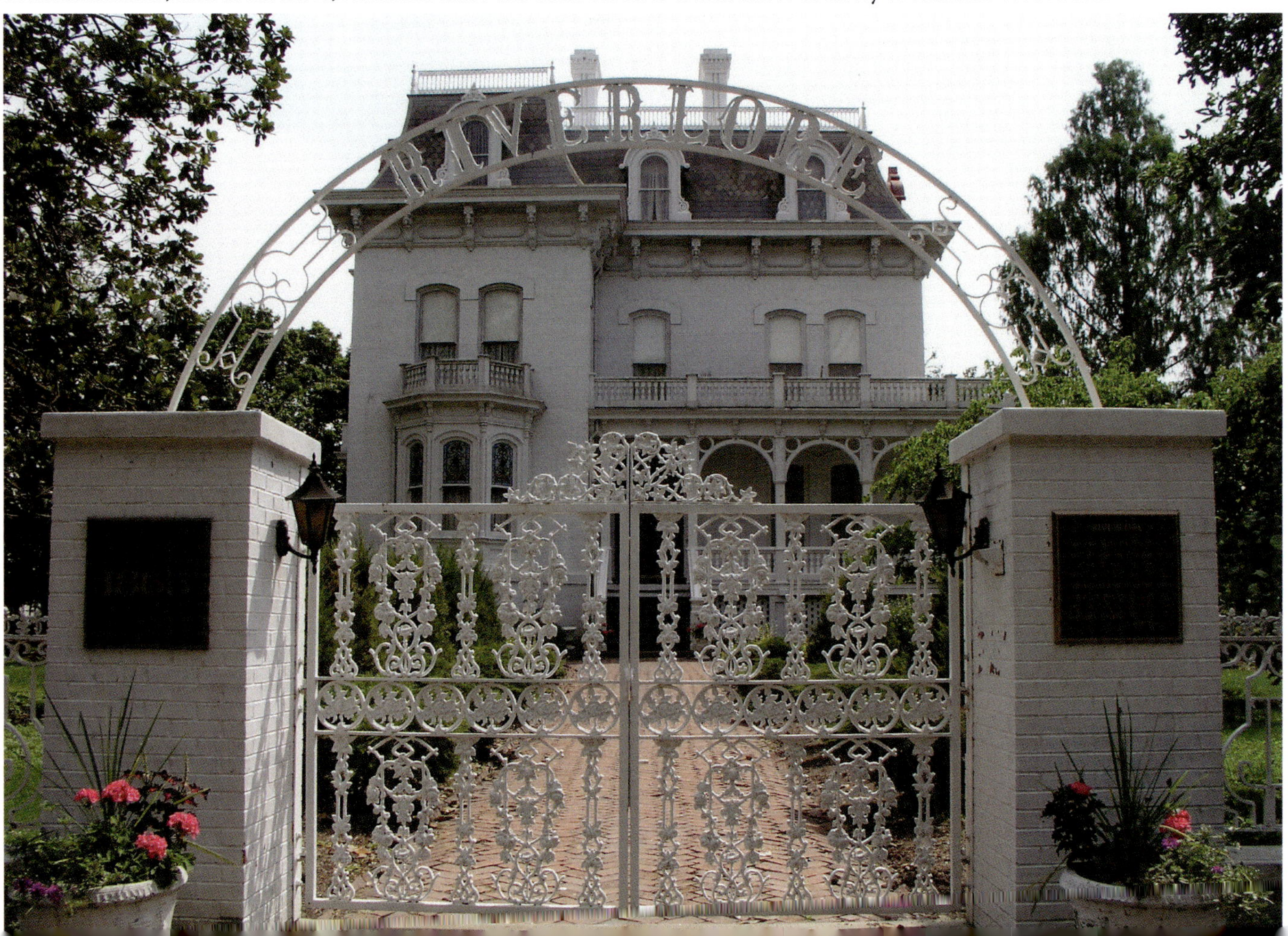

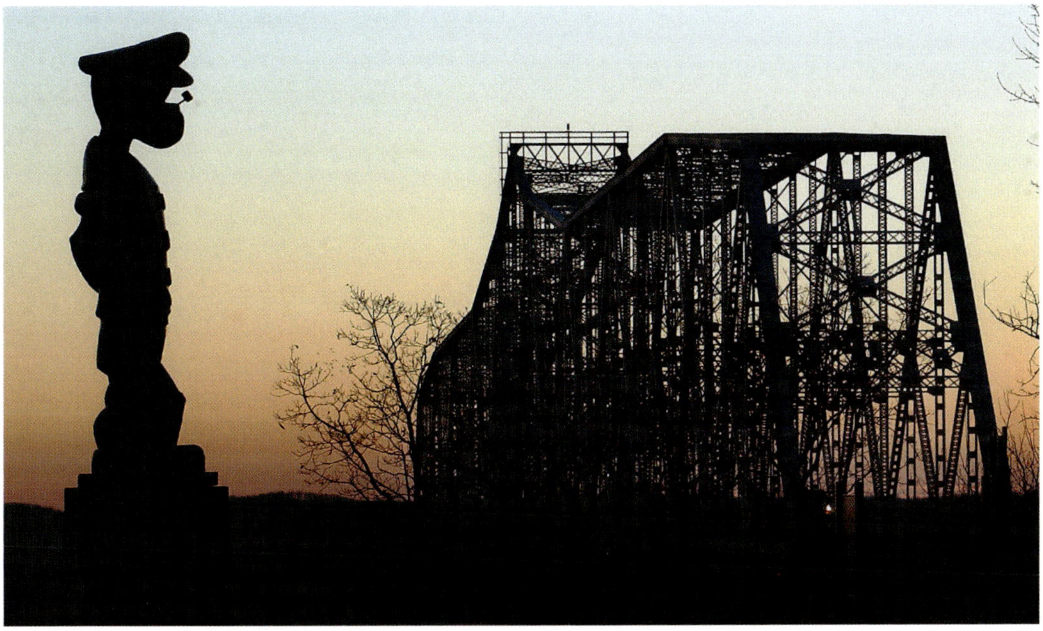

Popeye observes a rosy sunset at the Chester bridge. Photo by Steve Jahnke; courtesy of the *Southern Illinoisan*

a lubricant in the days before petroleum, and as the nineteenth century's favorite cure-all, castor oil. (Chester's ties to the castor bean achieved a sort of permanence when Chester cartoonist Elzie Segar made his way to the big city and created cartoon characters named Castor Oyl, Olive Oyl, and Popeye.)

In the end, it was Cairo that benefited most from river traffic. Some two dozen rivers carried over a third of the nation's river water toward Cairo, and some people thought it would become a port for oceangoing vessels, especially when it attracted as many ships as St. Louis. Unfortunately, Cairo was not a good site for a town. It was low lying, a target for floods on both the Ohio and the Mississippi, and had an unstable foundation of sand and river sediment. Chronic wetness necessitated pumps and pumping stations, and major floods sometimes defeated the levees. Still, Cairo and its magnolias flowered for the better part of a century. It developed a mystique as a southern city visited by boats such as the *Cotton Blossom*, the *Robt. E. Lee*, and the *Natchez*. Busy commercial streets, imposing homes, and an obliging nightlife kept Cairo in a prominent position, along with its status as a port of entry with a customs house empowered to tax river traffic.

Interviewing for a teaching position in pioneer days:

"Is the world round or flat?"

"I can teach her either way."

—Derived from *The Old Northwest Pioneer Period, 1815–1840*, II

Large families were the norm in Illinois' early days, but the young might or might not attend schools, which might or might not have textbooks. Some schools were taught by competent teachers, others by the community failure, still others by itinerant teachers and wanderers who imparted what they knew and moved on. In the absence of clocks and watches, instruction began when the teacher indicated and ended likewise. Lighting came from a "light hole" made by cutting out part of a log on one side of a building, or from an enlarged version of the hole made by removing most of one log. Greased paper or glass sometimes kept out the elements. In the half light of the schoolhouse with the smoke of an open fire going up a chimney, a hole in the roof, or several holes provided by Mother Nature, students learned what they could during the brief school year. Most pioneer schooling was offered for about three months, typically from December through February, although some of Egypt's schools closed for the month of January, and a few included fall or warm-weather instruction. The school year advanced to six months in the decades after the Civil War, but some of Egypt's log buildings remained in use as schools into the 1890s—to the wonderment of visiting city dwellers.

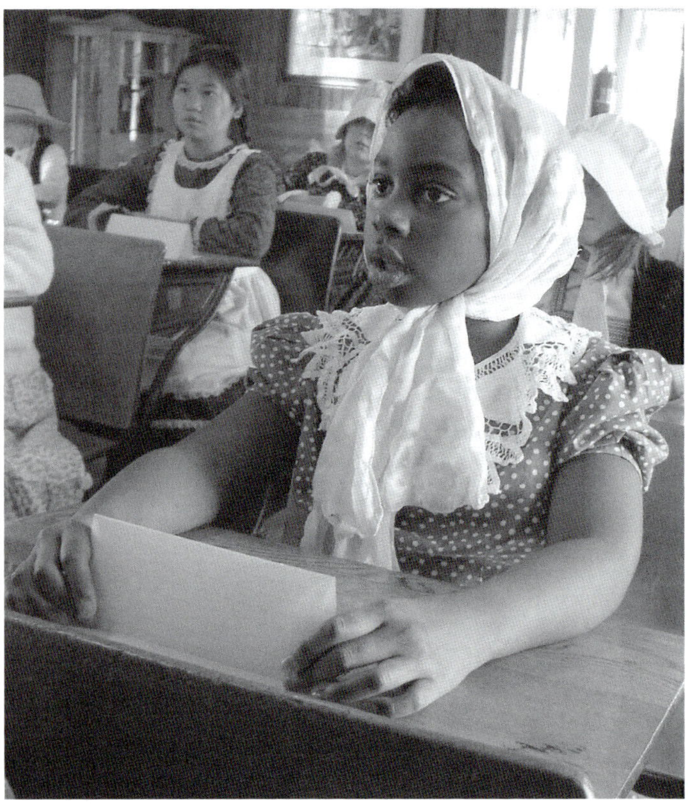

Dressed in period outfits, students enjoy a day in an 1854 schoolhouse using texts and recess games from the early 1900s. Purdy School, John A. Logan College, Carterville. Photo courtesy of Shannon Woodworth

I was your queen in calico,
You were my bashful barefoot beau,
And I wrote on your slate,
"I love you, Joe,"
When we were a couple of kids.

—"When We Were a Couple of Kids"

A defining moment in Egypt's relationship with the rest of Illinois came in 1818 when territorial leaders at Kaskaskia applied for statehood. Illinois did not have enough people to become a state, but those taking the census knew what was expected. They generously overestimated populations in some areas, counted families passing through Illinois as permanent residents, counted some people twice, and went as far north as the Wisconsin River to tally the inhabitants of an old French settlement. That too was allowed, since the northern border of Illinois had never been fixed, but it was this uncertain northern border that would become very important in the future.

Preliminary plans called for Illinois' boundary to go as far north as the southern tip of Lake Michigan. Later, the territorial legislature in Kaskaskia approved a ten-mile extension north so that Illinois could have a port on the lake, but this extension was increased by the legislature's delegate to Washington, Nathaniel Pope. Pope, deciding on his own that ten miles was too little, told Congress that Illinois wished to place its northern border more than sixty-two miles north of the southern tip of the lake. In 1818 Congress approved Pope's request along with statehood—and added all or part of fourteen future counties that would include Chicago, most of its suburbs, and major towns such as Rockford and Aurora. This extension of Illinois northward helped create a cultural divide that continues to this day and is behind the occasional calls for Egypt to secede and become the state of Southern Illinois.

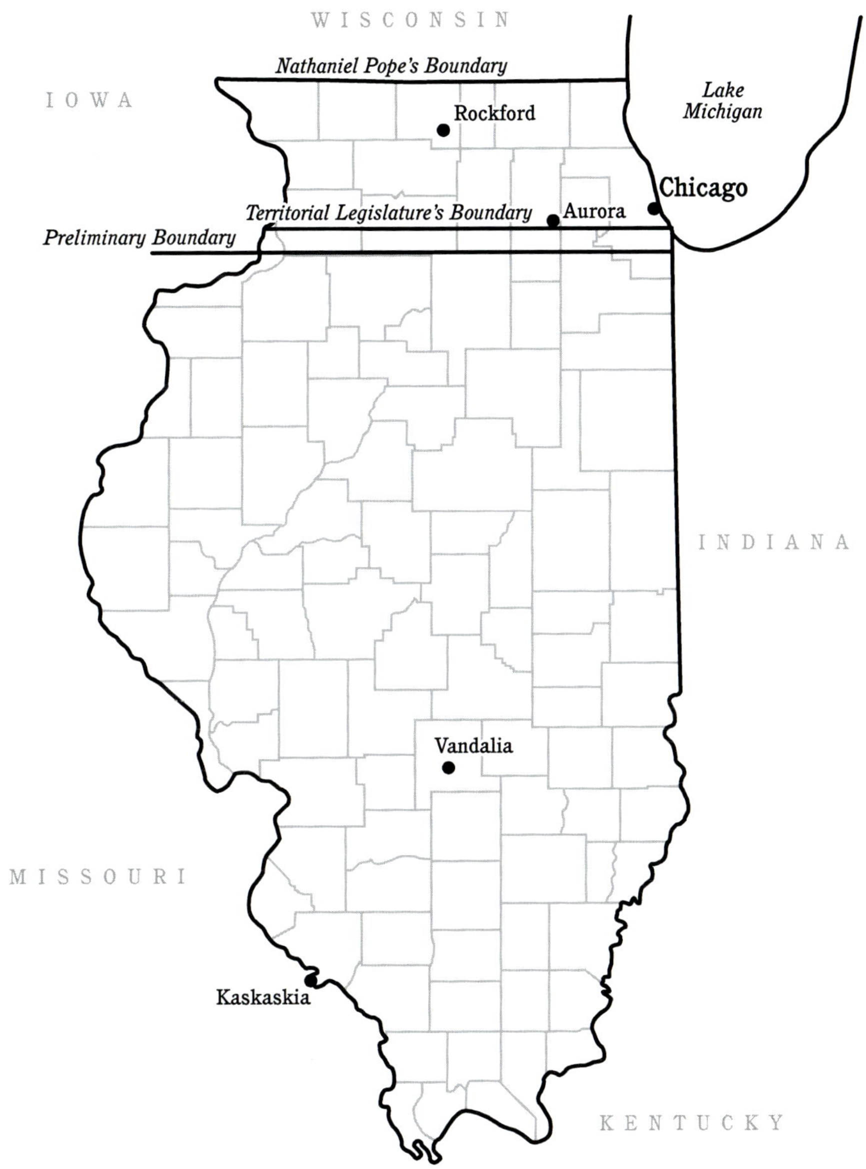

But none of this could have been forecast in 1819 when the state legislature in Kaskaskia moved the capital eighty miles up the Kaskaskia River to Vandalia. The town's

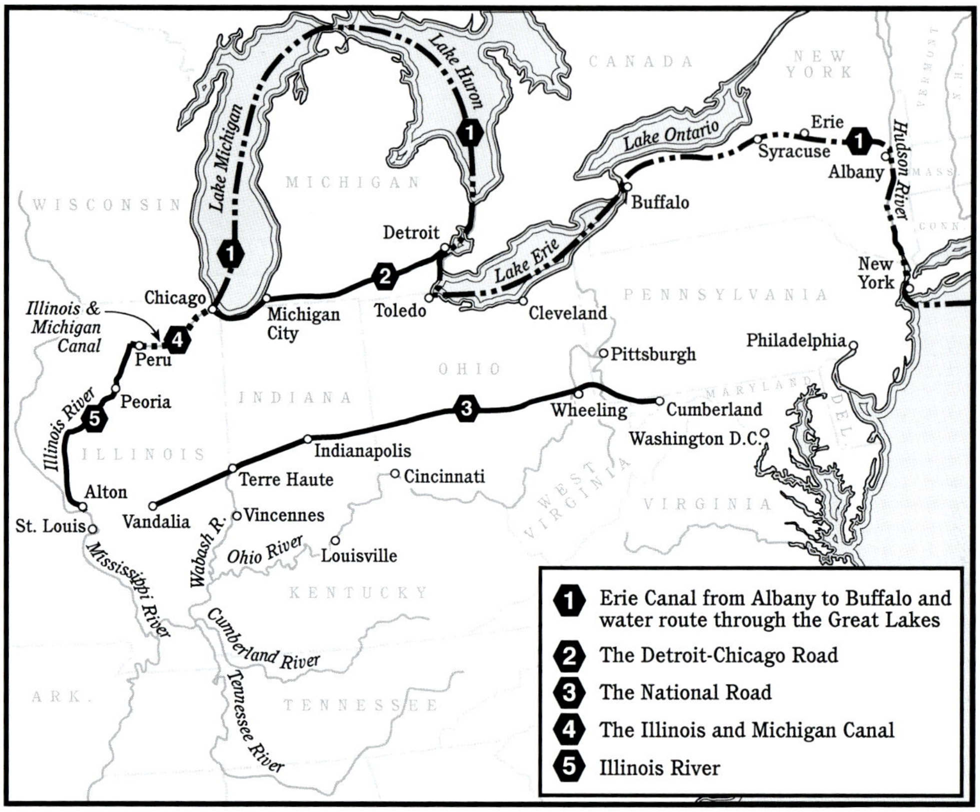

The Erie Canal (1) ran west from Albany to Buffalo and Lake Erie and connected New York City and the Hudson River with the Great Lakes. The Detroit–Chicago Road (2) offered a shortcut. The National Road (3) provided a graded highway from the East to Vandalia, while the Illinois and Michigan Canal (4) connected the Illinois River (5) with Lake Michigan.

unusual name was probably borrowed from a plan by several pre–Revolutionary War businessmen (including Benjamin Franklin) to create in 1768 a *fourteenth* British colony, this one to be located on the west side of the Appalachian Mountains in present-day West Virginia. To win the approval of King George III (the story goes), the colony would be named "Vandalia" in honor of his wife, who claimed to be descended from the Germanic tribe named "Vandals," the same who helped sack Rome. This fourteenth colony never materialized, but the name "Vandalia" lingered on, an entrepreneurial hope from the East waiting to be exploited in Illinois a half century later.

Meanwhile, changes that would affect Southern Illinois were under way elsewhere. In 1825 the Erie Canal connected New York City's Hudson River with Lake Erie and provided a northern route to Illinois (see nearby map). Eastern travelers could now journey by water all the way or get off at Detroit and take a newly made road to Chicago. Safer and less expensive than the route down the Ohio River, the Erie Canal was only forty feet wide, with barges pulled by mules on a towpath, but it helped populate northern Illinois with easterners, immigrants, and New England Yankees. By the 1840s more than three-fourths of settlers in northern Illinois had nonsouthern roots,

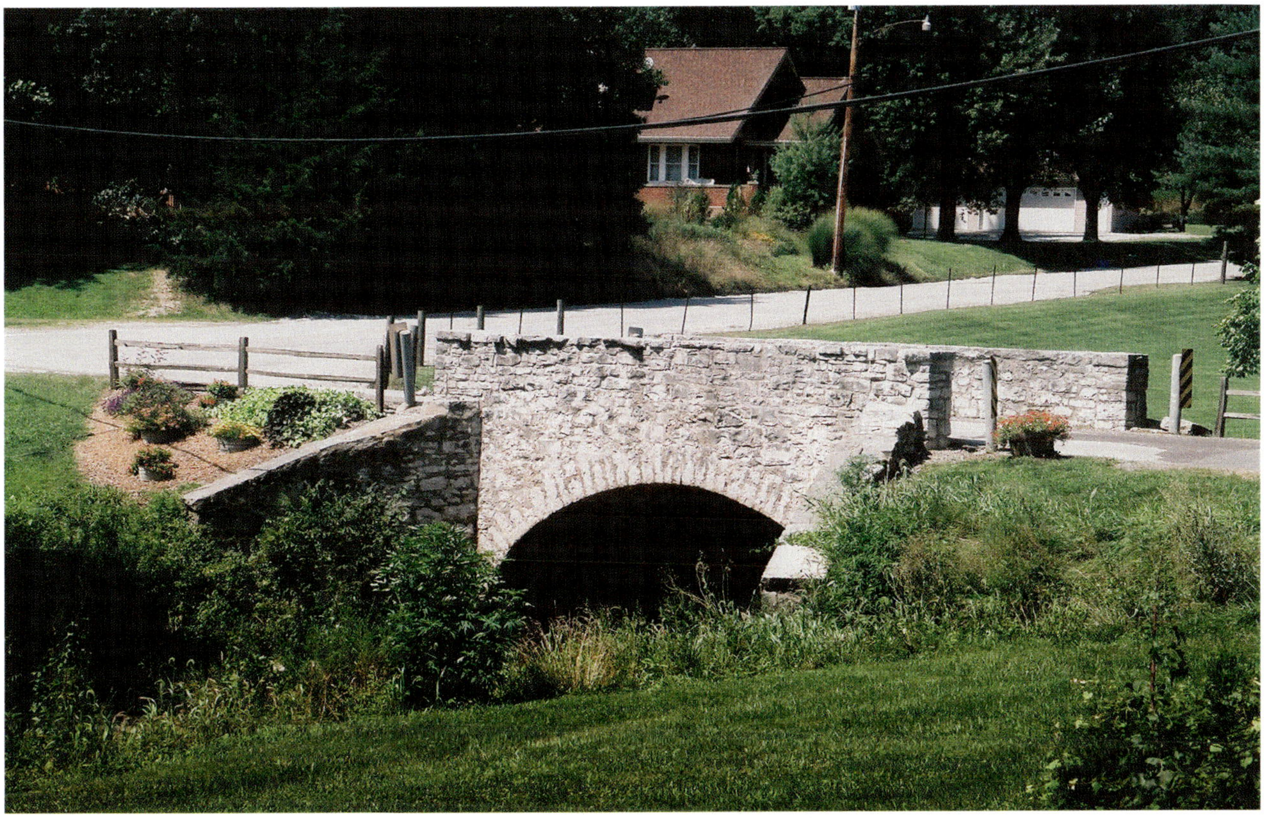

Many German immigrants settled in Monroe County, site of this arched bridge in Maeystown, a hill-and-valley community on the National Register of Historic Places. Photo by Herbert K. Russell

while the opposite was true in the southern end of the state—and so the stage was set for the future cultural clash between the regions.

At about the same time, America's first interstate highway arrived in Illinois as a dirt road. In 1806 President Jefferson had signed legislation calling for a road to run from Cumberland, Maryland, west to the Mississippi River. Known as the National Road, National Trail, Cumberland Road, and by other names, it wound through Pennsylvania and modern-day West Virginia, then through the capitals of Ohio and Indiana toward Illinois' new capital. In the 1830s the highway (which became U.S. Route 40) inched through the Illinois towns of Marshall, Greenup, Teutopolis, and Effingham before stalling at Vandalia in 1839. As Washington politicians dithered about whether the road should end at Alton or St. Louis, a steady stream of newcomers reached Vandalia. Nearly all of them turned north toward unsettled lands in the northern and western parts of the state, but many German-speaking immigrants pushed on toward St. Louis' growing German population to settle in and near Belleville, Germantown, Maeystown, Waterloo, and elsewhere. No part of the National Road penetrated Southern Illinois, and most of Egypt remained distinctly "southern."

As the National Road was approaching Effingham, plans were under way for a canal linking the Illinois River to Lake Michigan. The Illinois was navigable from its mouth

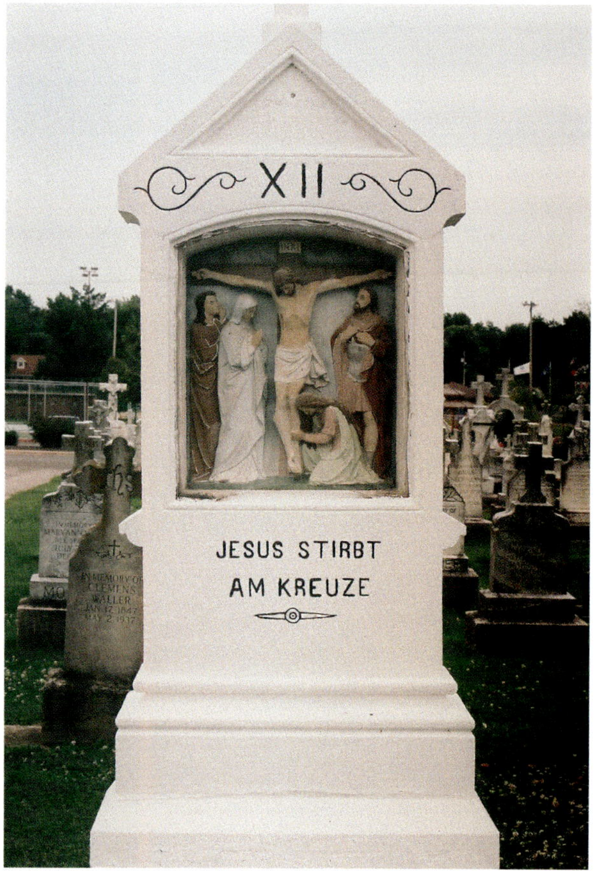

The farming community of Germantown remembers its heritage through a summer *Spassfest*—a fun festival—and religious signage in German. Clinton County. Photo by Herbert K. Russell

west of Alton upstream through Peoria to the towns of LaSalle and Peru, where rocks and low water often prevented further navigation. If a canal of some ninety miles could be dug from La Salle–Peru to Lake Michigan, the Illinois River and Lake Michigan would be joined. And so between 1836 and 1848, the Illinois and Michigan Canal came into existence. It opened a more efficient way for central and northern Illinois farmers to ship grain to large eastern markets instead of sending it south to New Orleans, around Florida's peninsula, and up the East Coast. The canal also operated in reverse, of course, providing yet another means for New England Yankees and other easterners to populate the Illinois heartland.

Completion of the Illinois and Michigan (I&M) Canal diminished the importance of what had been presumed to be Illinois' future great port, Cairo; and it enhanced the value of whatever city would rise to become the shipping center on Lake Michigan. The enterprising commissioners of the I&M Canal had already thought of that. In 1830 they laid out a village ten blocks long and six blocks wide in an area where a sluggish stream made its way through a field of wild onions into Lake Michigan. The village was called "Chicago," the French pronunciation of an Indian word for "onion" or "skunk."

History might have turned out differently if at this point Southern Illinois had become a leader in the development of a state railway system. That chance briefly existed through a popular state representative from Murphysboro, Captain Alexander Jenkins. He had trooped north to fight Chief Black Hawk in 1832 and, after getting soaked while crossing one too many rivers, concluded there was a better way to travel. Jenkins used his position as speaker of the Illinois House of Representatives to propose a railroad that would run north-south from Cairo through central Illinois to the lead mines at Galena (galena is the mineral from which lead is extracted). Galena was then the most important town in northern Illinois but could not be reached by boat when the Mississippi froze. Jonesboro's John S. Hacker sponsored the bill—which

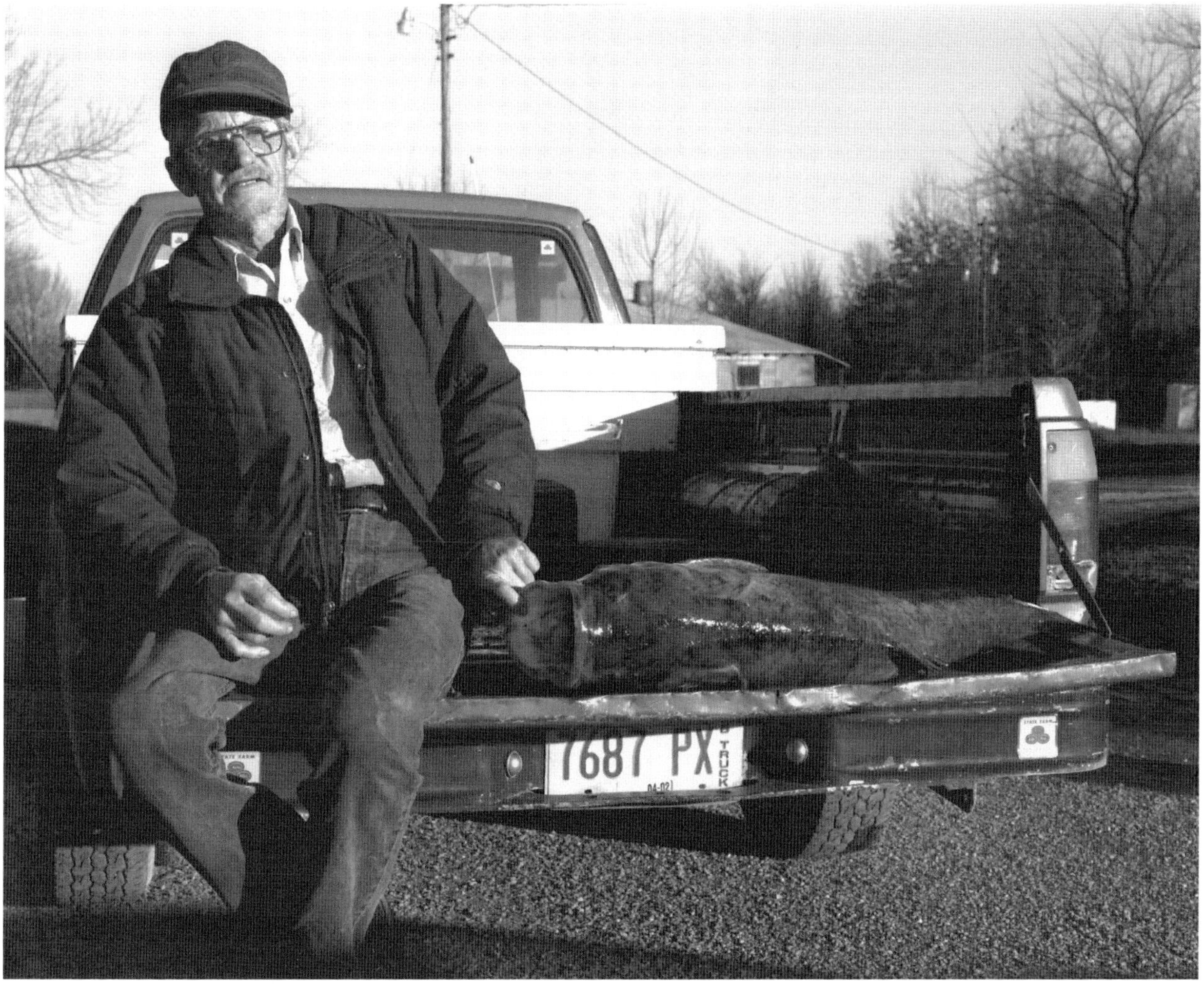

Fisherman with Mississippi River catfish. Tamms, Alexander County. Photo courtesy of Eric Robinson

passed just in time for the state to go broke in 1837. Southern Illinois did have one railroad in St. Clair County (Belleville), but it was private, powered by horses pulling coal cars over wooden rails, and had only six miles of tracks.

Thus Egypt had no public, working railroad at all when Chicago's first rail line began operations in 1848. The spikes in its ties were the same as nails in the coffin of Southern Illinois' early dreams. Within a dozen years Chicago had become the railroad hub of the nation. Its trains carried midwestern grain, pork, and beef to the hungry East and brought back unprecedented numbers of easterners and newly arrived European immigrants. The combined effects of the canals, the roads, the rise of Chicago as a rail center, and access to the Great Lakes caused the northern part of the state to prosper.

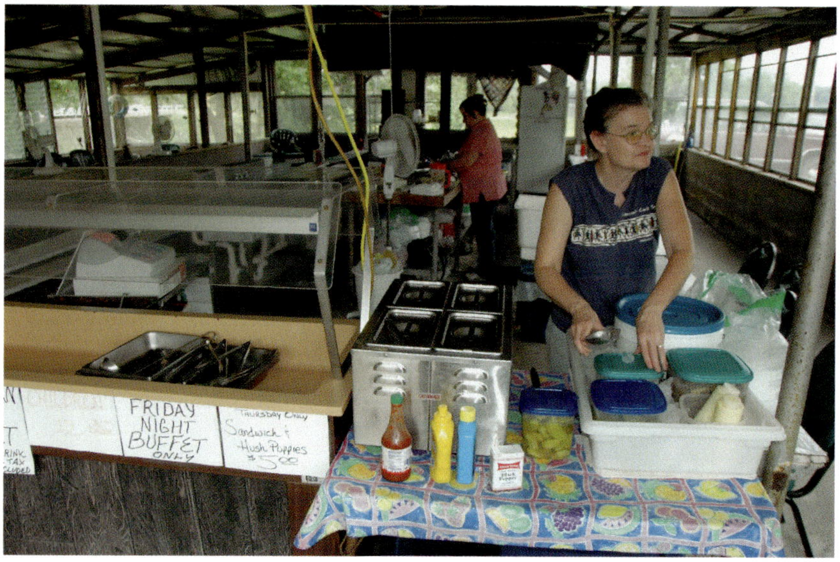

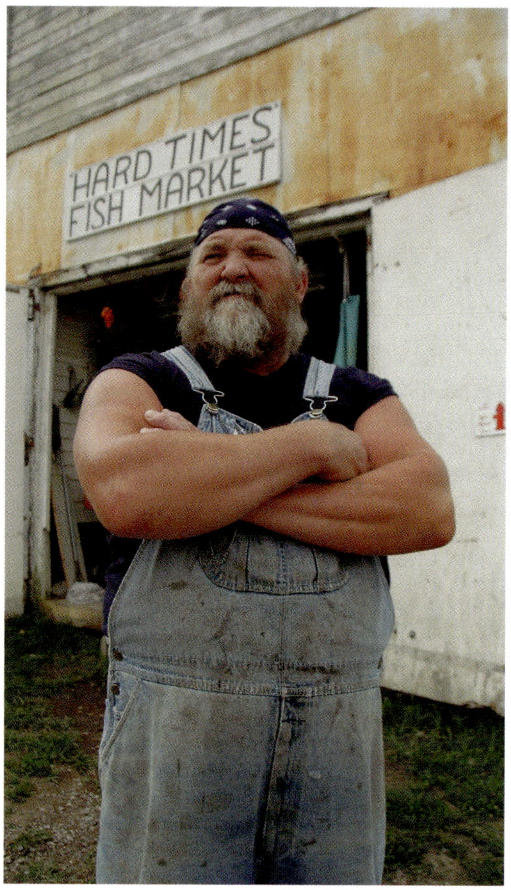

The Friday special at the Grayville Fish House restaurant (*top*) is pulled from the Wabash River and cleaned at the Hard Times Fish Market (*bottom*). Photos courtesy of Shannon Woodworth

This prosperity and the arrival of eastern and European immigrants heightened differences between Southern Illinois and the rest of the state. The nation itself was developing a divisiveness in which the East, with some justification, regarded the Midwest as crude and unsophisticated. Meanwhile, large portions of the North developed a disdain for the agricultural South and its slaves. Newly arrived Yankees in northern Illinois and their city cousins in the East often held all southern cultures in contempt regardless of whether they were in the Deep South, Mid-South, or Southern Illinois. Northeastern publications fueled these negative images by portraying poor white southerners in unflattering ways: the men were lazy, the women uneducated, the children dirty, their teachers and ministers primitive, and all of them ragged and hopeless. The popular East Coast humorist Thomas Haliburton depicted Illinois' southern settlers as tobacco-chewing whisky drinkers who took life easy amid corn, hogs, and mud. They "don't care shucks for law, gospel, or the devil," he told his readers. The *New England Farmer and Gardener's Journal* went a step further in its issue of July 1838. "A Northern State is better than a Southern State, and the north end of a Northern State better than the south end of the same State." (Cultural historian Thomas Beer would later note such biased writings and remark on "the odd blending of smugness and hypocrisy with which Northern editors treat all Southern affairs.") When this condescension migrated with the people from New England and New York to northern Illinois, the melting pot of Chicago looked at Egypt's pioneer kettle and called it black.

> I sleep fine nights.
> I sleep pretty good mornings.
> But in the afternoons I gets kinda restless.
>
> —Legendary hillbilly saying

When Yankee attitudes collided with Southern Illinois' unhurried Egyptians, the mistrust and misunderstandings were immediate, mutual, and lasting. Southern Illinoisans were regarded as inhabitants of a "coon and catfish" society that wanted to be left alone, a stereotype that had some truth to it. Yankees were regarded with suspicion if they built frame houses instead of log cabins or if they shunned whisky—the more so after northern peddlers found they could unload cheaply made northern goods on less sophisticated folk. (Humorist Haliburton also validated this phenomenon, by creating a smooth-talking Yankee peddler named "Sam Slick.") An Egyptian housewife who paid too much for a cheap New England clock was said to have been "Yankeed." Northerners were assumed to be money-grubbing opportunists, a stereotype that also had some truth to it, and Illinois' early nickname of "the Sucker State" was given a new meaning as wandering Yankee peddlers unloaded shoddy goods on the "suckers."

Visitors to Egypt sometimes remarked that its inhabitants seemed shiftless and listless, and this was often true, not only because a significant percentage of the population suffered from malaria, the effects of which include chronic tiredness, but also because some of the first Southern Illinoisans were riffraff fleeing a posse. But on the matter of lifestyle, Yankees and Egyptians could never agree: what a Southern Illinois farmer regarded as an agreeable and self-sufficient life, his northern Illinois acquaintances invariably viewed as subsistence-level living that needed "improving"—which always meant that Egyptians should stop acting as themselves and begin behaving as Yankees.

Isolated by the rivers and by the times, by the aristocratic plantation society they had fled, and by the Yankee invasion to the north, Egypt's inhabitants were in many ways cut off. Their political isolation began in 1819 when the capital was moved from Kaskaskia to Vandalia and increased in 1839 when it was moved north to Springfield. Meanwhile, states to the east filled up, and Missouri became a slave state. Unable to return to the South, unwilling to move north, many Southern Illinoisans stayed put. Perhaps it was then that the capital *S* often seen on *Southern Illinois* began to gain legitimacy. Southern Illinoisans increasingly felt they were living in a separate state, and in a moment of rare accord, the rest of the state agreed.

> There shall be neither slavery nor involuntary servitude in the said territory.
>
> —Northwest Ordinance of 1787, Article 6

Slavery was bound to be an issue in Southern Illinois, not only because of its proximity to Dixie but also because of a Pennsylvania army officer named Arthur St. Clair. Appointed to govern the Midwest after the Revolutionary War, St. Clair's responsibility was to oversee the area until new territories

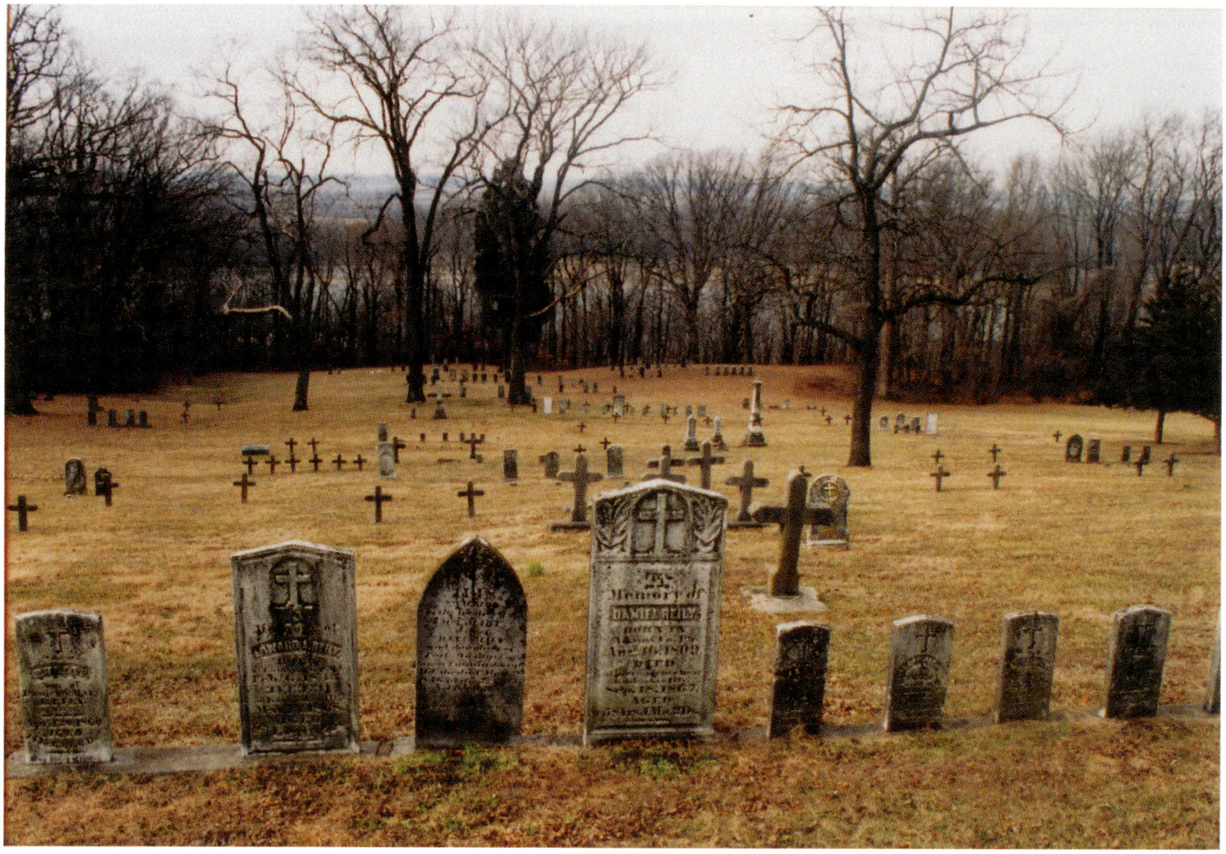

Remains of Kaskaskia's early settlers were moved to this hill overlooking the Mississippi River after floods destroyed the town, Illinois' first capital. Randolph County. Photo by Herbert K. Russell

and states began to take shape. Article 6 of the federal Northwest Ordinance of 1787 had banned slavery in what became the Midwest, but every law is subject to interpretation, and it was St. Clair who interpreted this one. In 1790 he left his territorial offices in Ohio to visit Illinois where he ruled that Article 6 meant only that no *new* slaves could be introduced. Those already enslaved would remain so. Thus the so-called French slaves in Illinois would remain slaves along with others who were slaves before the federal ordinance was passed. St. Clair's decision was consistent with eighteenth-century thought in many parts of the world: slaves of all skin colors were regarded as property, and freeing them outright would have deprived their owners of that property. (The word *slave* is itself derived from *Slav*, a reminder that white Slavs and other Caucasians have also served as slaves.) With St. Clair's decision as precedent, the way was smoothed for the use of black slaves at the federally owned salt springs near Shawneetown, at the federally owned lead mines at Galena in northern Illinois, and elsewhere. St. Clair's actions underscore a recurrent pattern in Southern Illinois: it is "southern" in many ways but

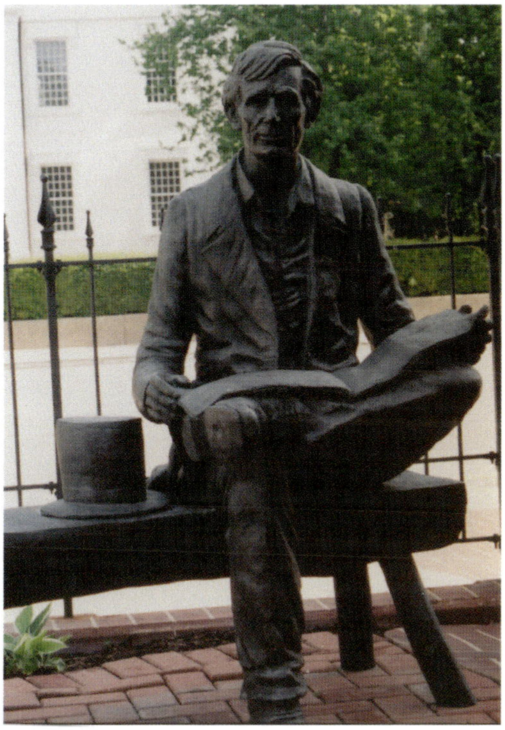

Young Abraham Lincoln waits in the shadows across the street from Illinois' second capitol, the Old State House at Vandalia. Sculptor John McClarey's work is titled "Sitting with Lincoln." Photo by Herbert K. Russell

has often been shaped by people and events associated with the East and the North.

Illinois did not require a war to ban the slavery prolonged by St. Clair. Rather, the state's behavior resembled that of several of the older, eastern states. New England farmers and merchants in Maine, Massachusetts, Vermont, New Hampshire, and Connecticut had owned both black and Indian slaves. The Rhode Island cities of Newport and Providence were major ports for African slaves brought to the Northeast, but slavery was seldom profitable on small farms dominated by long New England winters, and many of these slaves ended up in New York City's slave markets (forgotten slave graveyards were still being discovered in the 1990s near Manhattan's old slave market). Slave ships and slave sales bought comfortable houses for northeasterners and helped found New England Ivy League colleges such as Yale and Brown. As slavery fell out of favor after the Revolutionary War, many easterners registered their slaves as "indentured servants," an indenture being an agreement that binds one person to work for another for a period. People of many sorts served indentures (to pay for their ship passage to America, for example, or to learn a trade, as Benjamin Franklin did), but indentures were subject to abuse if the period of indenture was made for many years, as happened, for example, with a New Jersey slave whose indenture was for ninety-nine years.

By the 1820s and '30s, many easterners disapproved of slavery but did not think it could be abolished overnight without economic turmoil. Unskilled laborers in cities feared immediate abolition for the same reason they feared cheap immigrant labor and cheap convict labor: wages would plummet if large numbers of free blacks suddenly came north to enter the workforce. Nor were well-off Connecticut carriage makers eager for southern slavery to end after they noticed how many carriages and other pricey goods they could sell to southern plantation owners. The same could be said for Massachusetts linen mills dependent on southern cotton and thousands of businesses in New York City. There exists a general impression that the North approved of the antislavery

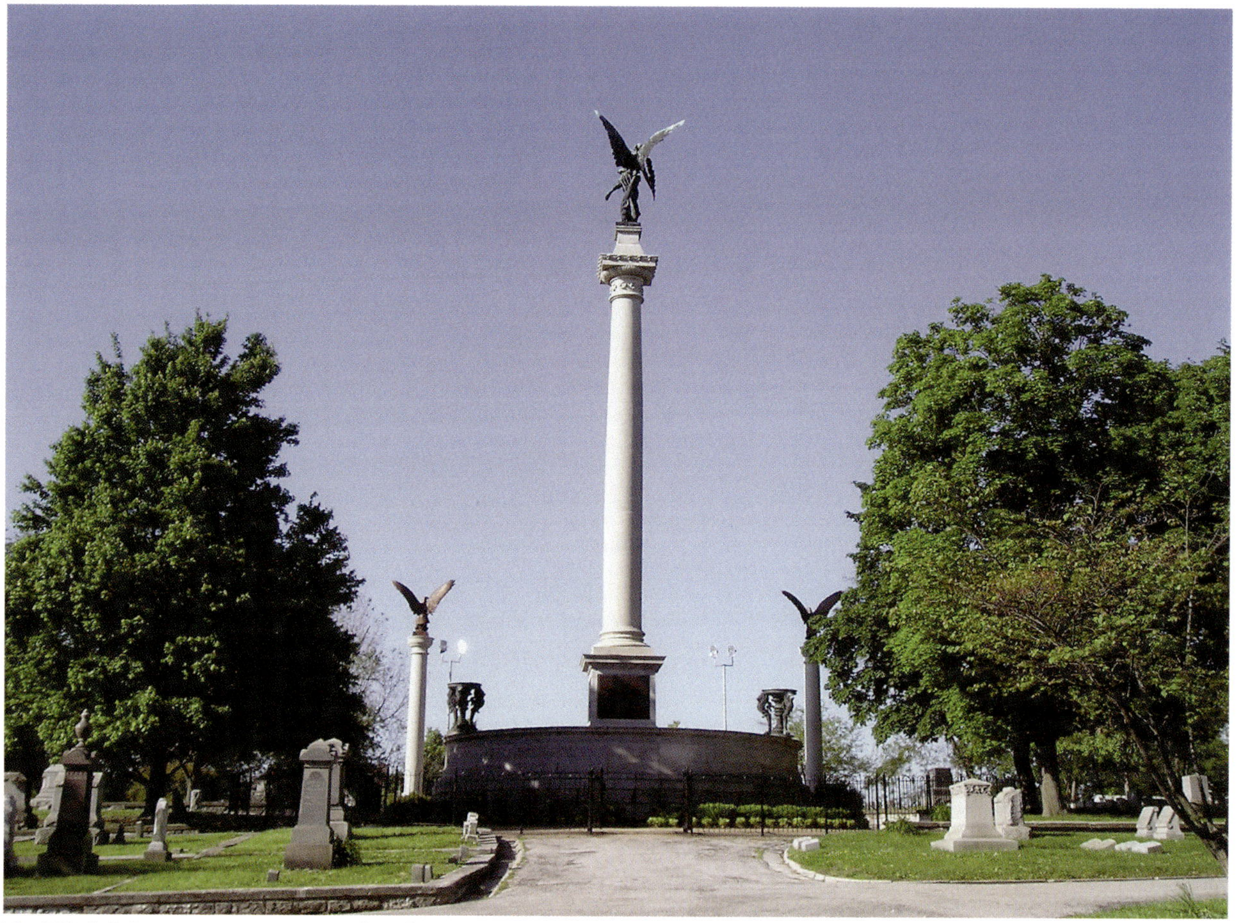

The Elijah P. Lovejoy Monument in the Alton cemetery honors the Midwest's best-known abolitionist. Photo courtesy of David Schwan

writings of William Lloyd Garrison—but Bostonians nearly killed him, and residents of other places drove abolitionists out of town (one thinks of the poet John Greenleaf Whittier in Concord, New Hampshire). Throughout the North, abolitionists were often attacked or regarded as fanatics standing in the way of moderate reforms and the orderly eradication of slavery. Maine and New Hampshire witnessed *proslavery* demonstrations, and mobs *opposed* to the abolition of slavery rioted in New York City in 1834, made threats in Philadelphia, and twice destroyed an abolitionist press in Cincinnati in 1836, events that were northern rehearsals for what happened to the Rev. Elijah Lovejoy in St. Louis.

A Presbyterian from Maine, Lovejoy was intolerant of the religions of others. He was appalled at how Baptists kept the Sabbath (too much merriment) but hated Catholics with a special fervor and in 1833 moved to St. Louis, where he wrote newspaper articles denouncing that city's large Catholic population. He briefly rented a slave named "William" (William Wells Brown, a future reformer) but eventually turned to articles denouncing slavery and urged its abolition.

Missouri was in the process of doubling its slave population in the 1830s (it had 58,000 by 1840, 114,000 by 1860), and no county in Missouri had more slaves than St. Louis County. After mobs repeatedly stole or destroyed his printing equipment, Lovejoy moved his family across the Mississippi River to Alton, Illinois, in 1836.

Here he began another newspaper, telling financial backers that he would use it principally for religious discussions, but he immediately printed articles on slavery and helped bring a meeting of the Illinois Antislavery Congress to Upper Alton. This gathering was advertised as open to all who wished to speak, but Lovejoy's abolitionist friend Edward Beecher tried to prevent the proslavery men from speaking. This apparent inequity created ill will, since Lovejoy, the champion of free speech, now seemed to be denying it to others. He printed an article claiming that "more than half" of those who criticized abolitionists had had sexual relations with slave women, a remark that libeled much of the nation. And he continued with his anti-Catholic articles, a religious bigot denouncing racial bigotry. He fueled the anger building against him by taunting his detractors: "You may hang me. . . . You may burn me." Not long afterward, he was shot dead while trading gunfire with a group bent on getting rid of him or his press. He remains the outstanding example of New England's long bout with "white guilt" over black slavery, one who attempted to atone for the sins of his forefathers by his own death.

The pity of Lovejoy's death is that it need not have occurred. It was unwise of him to print a lie about his enemies' sexual behavior and then taunt them, the more so as he had a press at his disposal, while most of them did not. Moreover, Illinois had already voted down by 57 percent to 43 percent an attempt to make it a slave state, and the Illinois Constitution had banned the use of slaves at the salt springs after 1825 and set emancipation ages for children born of slaves. Illinois circuit and state courts were dismantling the indenture system, and circuit courts were issuing freedom papers to runaway slaves whose owners had not reclaimed them at the end of one year, as required by law.

In the end, Lovejoy's courage in the face of mob action advanced the causes of abolition and freedom of the press, but it did not hurry history: after becoming a state in 1818, Illinois required thirty more years to bring slavery under control, about the same as some slave-owning eastern states. Nearly three decades after the Revolutionary War, for example, the states of New York, Pennsylvania, and New Jersey still held over 17,000 black people as slaves or indentured servants. Connecticut did not formally abolish slavery until 1848, and New Jersey waited until 1860. In other words, geographic location was not an accurate predictor of how people felt about the abolition of slavery: in northern Illinois a citizens group in Peoria tried with considerable success in the 1840s to stifle all discussions of abolition.

Illinois had borrowed the idea of indentured servants from Indiana and counted 331 slaves and indentured servants in the federal census of 1840. Some of the long-term indentures were essentially life sentences in slavery, but lawmakers were slow to make reforms and were adamantly against immediate abolition. In the pre–Civil War era, nearly all Southern Illinoisans were Democrats. The Whig Party was perceived as too aristocratic, and the Republican Party did not come into being until the 1850s. Democrats had for years maintained party loyalty by reminding voters that freed slaves would work for lower wages and take jobs from poor whites. Party leaders might also raise the fear of "race amalgamation," marriage between blacks and whites, or assert that Negroes, like the Indians, would become dependent on public aid. This is not to say that such views were restricted to one party: many in the emerging Republican Party would hold these same views. A belief in white supremacy and black inferiority threaded its way through many assumptions, as did the belief that the abolition of slavery would cause the northern states to be overrun with African Americans.

Several eastern states had faced these same concerns after the Revolutionary War. Massachusetts decided flogging would discourage black newcomers from remaining more than two months, and New Jersey barred free blacks from settling in the state, thus establishing some of the nation's first "Jim Crow" laws preventing the physical and social mobility of African Americans. None of the eastern states offered slaves immediate freedom after the Revolutionary War unless they had served as soldiers, and only gradually ended the indenture system. In the end, most Illinois slaves and indentured servants slowly became free in the same ways that their eastern counterparts did: they were voluntarily freed by their owners, often through the owner's will or after the owner recouped his investment in a slave; gained freedom upon reaching a certain age or after indentures expired; were freed by the courts after indentures were declared invalid; or purchased their freedom with monies earned when they were permitted to work for themselves, perhaps on Sundays, at specified hours of other days, or when tasks were completed.

Illinois officially ended slavery in 1848 but confounded matters in 1853 when the legislature followed the northern examples of Iowa (1851) and Indiana (1852) and passed a law aimed at stopping black migration into Illinois. Southern Illinois Democrat John A. Logan guided the bill to passage and earned the nickname "Dirty Work" Logan by defending the return of runaway slaves to the South. Some said the law forbidding black migration was not consistently enforced, but it reflected a viewpoint common in the Midwest: the East had profited from black slavery; the South had flourished because of it; and it was these areas and not the Midwest that should deal with what newspapers called the "Negro problem."

But this is only a small part of the black experience in Egypt. On the eve of the Civil War the 1860 federal census showed 3,202 *free* African Americans residing in Illinois' twenty-eight southernmost counties. (The figure does not include Madison County on Egypt's northern border, an area with a transient population of runaway slaves from St. Louis and Missouri.) Mainstream historians have virtually ignored the stories of Southern Illinois' free African Americans, and this is unfortunate, for it was they who knew the most about black life in Egypt before and during the war.

Numerous free people of color lived in the East and South when they were slave societies, and these people were attracted to Illinois because the Northwest Ordinance of 1787 had curtailed slavery and because an 1824 attempt to make Illinois a slave state had failed. Many of Southern Illinois' free African Americans lived as their white neighbors did, by farming land they often owned, sometimes on individual farms and sometimes in small communities. A few of these African Americans are mentioned in county histories published in the nineteenth century, but far more appear in census, genealogy, and courthouse records as free farmers, carpenters, laborers, preachers, teachers, businessmen, settlement founders, and so on. We know that many black people were abused in nineteenth-century Illinois, but such reportage usually paints them as passive victims instead of self-sufficient participants in their own communities. What follows may help balance their pre–Civil War history in Southern Illinois.

About 5,000 free and slave African Americans served in the American Army during the Revolutionary War (1776–83). Slaves who served as soldiers were given their freedom. A few free blacks were in Southern Illinois during the French period (1673–1763) and during Illinois' early days as a territory (1809–18), but more arrived after 1815 when the Indian threat had ended. Many of these free black settlers came from Virginia and North and South Carolina. Children of mixed race were common in these states but were not always the result of white masters having their way with submissive female slaves, as is usually reported. Genealogist Paul Heinegg has shown in his *Free African Americans of North Carolina, Virginia, and South Carolina*, a genealogy of 488 black families, that sexual relations between white females and black men both free and slave produced a good many mixed-race children. (Both African American and Caucasian researchers pointed this out in the 1950s and '60s but were largely ignored.) Common-law and formal marriages between blacks and whites took place before and after the Revolutionary War, and considerable racial mingling is reflected in Virginia and North Carolina deeds, court cases, land transfers, marriage and tax records, baptismal records, registries of free Negroes, references to mulatto children, and so on.

Race relations deteriorated as the slavery issue gained political prominence in the early 1800s. The 1831 slave rebellion led by Nat Turner in Virginia worried many slave owners, and life in the South became more difficult for free African Americans when states such as North Carolina prohibited free blacks from voting or carrying a gun without a license. The migration of free African Americans to Southern Illinois (and Indiana, Ohio, and elsewhere) followed as southern laws against their freedoms became more stringent. The prospect of cheap land and a fresh start were major incentives, and free blacks often came to Southern Illinois for the same reason their white neighbors did: they hoped life would be better in Egypt than the place they had left. Some southern slave owners felt the same way, a well-known example being that of the Virginian Edward Coles. He freed his slaves, saw that each family received 160 acres of land near Edwardsville, Illinois, and was later elected Illinois governor.

Many free African Americans enjoyed satisfactory relations with their white neighbors before the Civil War, a point borne out in several instances in which free blacks were kidnapped to the South but rescued by their Southern Illinois neighbors and returned to their Egyptian homes. White citizens in Pope County raised a reward to find four mixed-race children kidnapped from their homes; they were located in Mississippi and rescued. Conscientious lawmen from Pope and other counties found themselves on the trail of kidnappers of free blacks in slave states such as Kentucky, Missouri, and Arkansas and were sometimes able to achieve a rescue. The prominent newsman-attorney Henry Eddy, of Shawneetown, successfully interceded with Illinois' Governor Ford on behalf of three African American men wrongfully imprisoned at the Alton state prison, and the future Union Army general Michael Lawler fought self-appointed "regulators" who were making life miserable for African Americans near the Ohio River. A runaway slave named "Harry" (afterward Harry Dougherty) went from being property to being a property owner in the years after Union County attorney John Dougherty bought Harry in Vienna and freed him on Christmas day 1835. And a Franklin County man traveled to Missouri to buy slaves he had known previously and resettled them as free people near his own home.

The "Emancipation Baptists" (more formally, the Baptized Churches of Christ, Friends to Humanity) also had friendly relations with African Americans. They organized their first church in 1809, the year in which Illinois became a territory. Their antislavery "missionaries" encouraged the growth of Emancipation Baptist congregations across Southern Illinois, including Shawneetown's Colored Emancipation Baptist Church, which listed fifteen African Americans as members.

Of interest too is an event in Hamilton County (McLeansboro) about 1819. The setting is a prayer meeting conducted in a private dwelling by white settlers in need of both a church and minister:

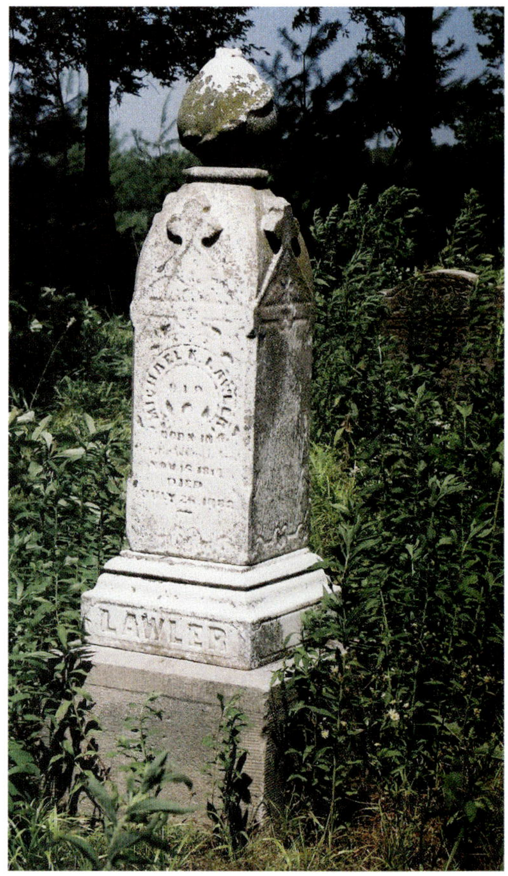

Among those friendly to free African Americans in pre–Civil War days was Michael K. Lawler, who is buried in a rural cemetery near Equality. Lawler tried to protect black people from bands of thugs in the Ohio River county of Gallatin and became a Union Army general during the Civil War. Photo by Herbert K. Russell

An old colored man, an entire stranger, made his appearance and announced himself as a preacher. Of course no excuse would be taken and the old man had to preach! He did so and preached the first sermon ever preached in Hamilton County. This sermon of the old colored man pleased the people so well that they determined that he should teach them at a school. . . . In a very short time, the colored preacher was engaged in training or teaching the first school ever taught in the county.

The preacher-teacher may have been Pros Robinson, who was teaching several miles south of McLeansboro near present-day Omaha, Illinois, about 1820.

Although Illinois law forbade marriage between Caucasians and people of color, those in Union County (Jonesboro) sometimes married anyway, as historian Darrel Dexter has shown in his *Free and American: A Study of Eleven Families of Color.* The bride was usually white and the groom black or mulatto, but the opposite also occurred. Free blacks also carried cases to court and won in the counties of Union and Jackson (Murphysboro), both in deep Southern Illinois. Dexter's revisionist study, based on courthouse records and genealogy searches, suggests that free blacks in Union County were found innocent as often as guilty when charged with crimes or misdemeanors. "Black laws" passed by the Illinois legislature are often accepted as defining the quality of life

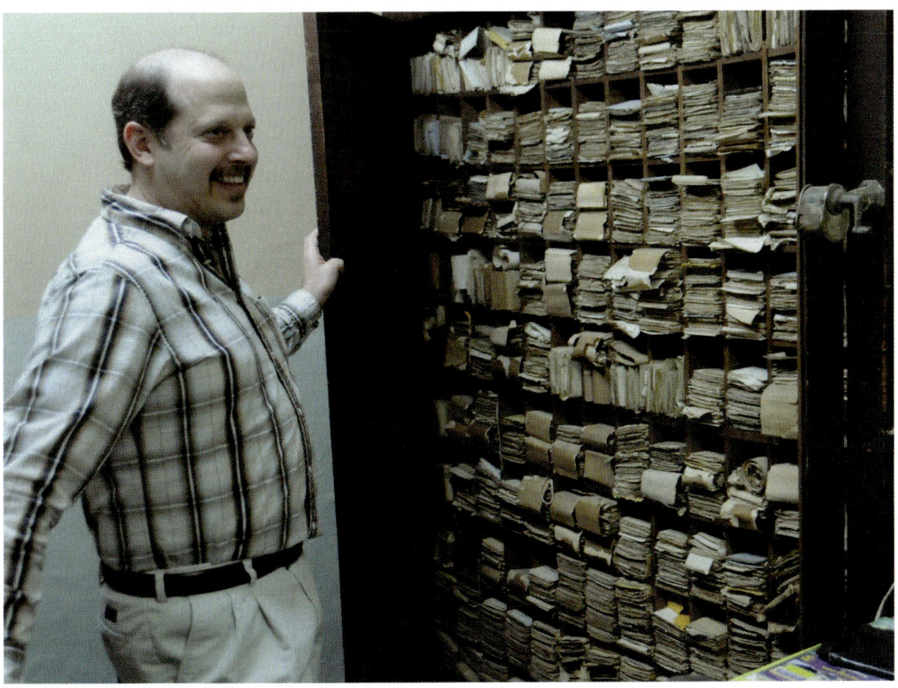

Historian Darrel Dexter examines legal documents from the 1830s and '40s stored in the janitor's room of the Union County Courthouse at Jonesboro. Dexter's *Free and American: A Study of Eleven Families of Color* revises several commonly held views of black-white relations in early Southern Illinois. The study is accessible via Internet. Photo courtesy of Shannon Woodworth

for African Americans, but the courthouse records of individual counties must be consulted in conjunction with census data and newspapers to determine whether these state laws were enforced locally. A review of several free black settlements provides more information about the pre–Civil War African American experience in Egypt.

In 1812 free African Americans and white settlers "forted up" together at Russellville in Lawrence County when Tecumseh's braves threatened; after hostilities ended, some black families created a settlement in the Pinkstaff-Lackey area, later moving south into Lawrence Township. The Saline County hamlet of Nigger Hill (renamed Grayson) was established on the Goshen Road southeast of Eldorado when a free black man named Neal or Cornelius Elliott opened an inn in the 1820s; Grayson later attracted a post office and railroad and ended its existence as a small coal mining town in the 1920s. In nearby Gallatin County, an area known as Nigger Spring (or Springs) was settled southeast of Equality by former slaves who had worked at the salt springs and bought their freedom.

The free black settlement of South America (named for missionary activities of the Emancipation Baptists) was sited among friendly whites near the Saline-Williamson county line and had a post office by 1853. A nearby black community southeast of Carrier Mills was named both Pond and Lakeview and was settled by free African Americans from North Carolina after 1815. Two inhabitants, Mr. and Mrs. Joseph Cole, were fondly remembered by Southern Illinois author W. S. Blackman in *The Boy of Battle Ford and*

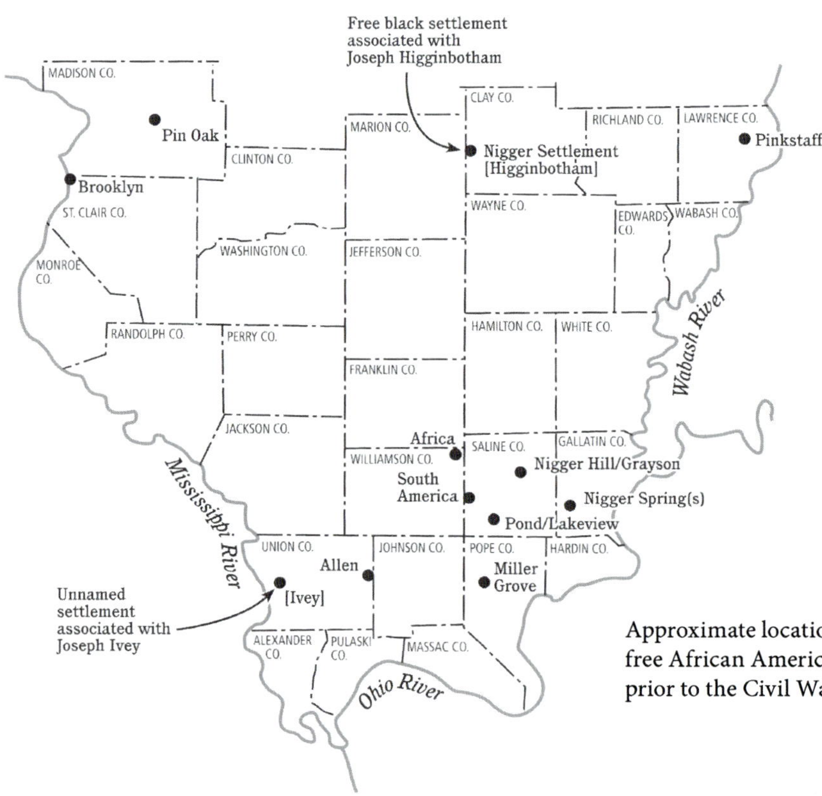

Approximate locations of several free African American settlements prior to the Civil War.

the Man: Ann Cole brought young Blackman a gift of wheat biscuits when he was ill; Joseph Cole shared his seed wheat with white neighbors after the drought of 1854. Blackman also tells of an integrated baptism in a local creek. Not far away, the black settlement of Miller Grove was sited in Pope County north of Glendale in the 1840s by emancipated families from Tennessee. They had peaceful relations with white antislavery neighbors before the Civil War, and after the war were joined by white neighbors for annual barbecues, baptisms, and revivals. Like many other settlements, Miller Grove's most enduring benchmark would be its cemetery, now a part of the Shawnee National Forest.

> The pioneers were so few and scattered that it was not until 1824 that a school could be established and maintained. . . . The first teacher's name that we are able to record in this part of the county was a colored man by the name of Sweat.
>
> —Education comes to north Edwards County, *Combined History [of] Edwards, Lawrence, and Wabash Counties*, 1883

One of Egypt's best-known black settlements was Africa and its post office of Locust Grove near the Franklin and Williamson County line. Founded by indentured servants whose indentures had expired and by former slaves who had been freed, the settlement nearly came to an end shortly before the Civil War when Southern sympathizers told its inhabitants to leave. The African Americans had packed their goods and were departing in three wagons on the Sabbath when they passed the Liberty Methodist Church three miles southeast of Thompsonville. White churchgoers urged them to stay, and they did, opening a schoolhouse with white teachers. Africa subsequently remained an African American community for much of the twentieth century before losing its black population to time and migration.

Twenty miles northeast of Salem, a former slave named Joseph Higginbotham settled in Clay County's Oskaloosa Township in the 1830s or '40s and bought land in the Skillet Fork area. Other free African Americans added to the community, and it came to be known locally as "Nigger Settlement." The community existed at least through the time of the Civil War, when it reportedly sent a son to the Union Army in whose service, it was said, he lost an arm. Nigger Settlement ("Higginbotham" would be a better name) has long since passed from existence, but some of its former inhabitants are buried in Higginbotham Cemetery in Oskaloosa Township.

Near Jonesboro, Joseph Ivey had purchased property in the Union County bottoms west of Ware by 1830 when he and several "free persons of color" were counted in the federal census. Ivey had a good head for business and soon bought 400 acres and was hired by the Union County commissioners in Jonesboro to build a bridge over the waterway known as Running Lake. State laws notwithstanding, Ivey did not register his free status with the county clerk. (The county kept a record of such registrations in "Negro Book A.") The bridge may have helped steer customers to Ivey's grist mill, and by 1835 thirty-five free African Americans

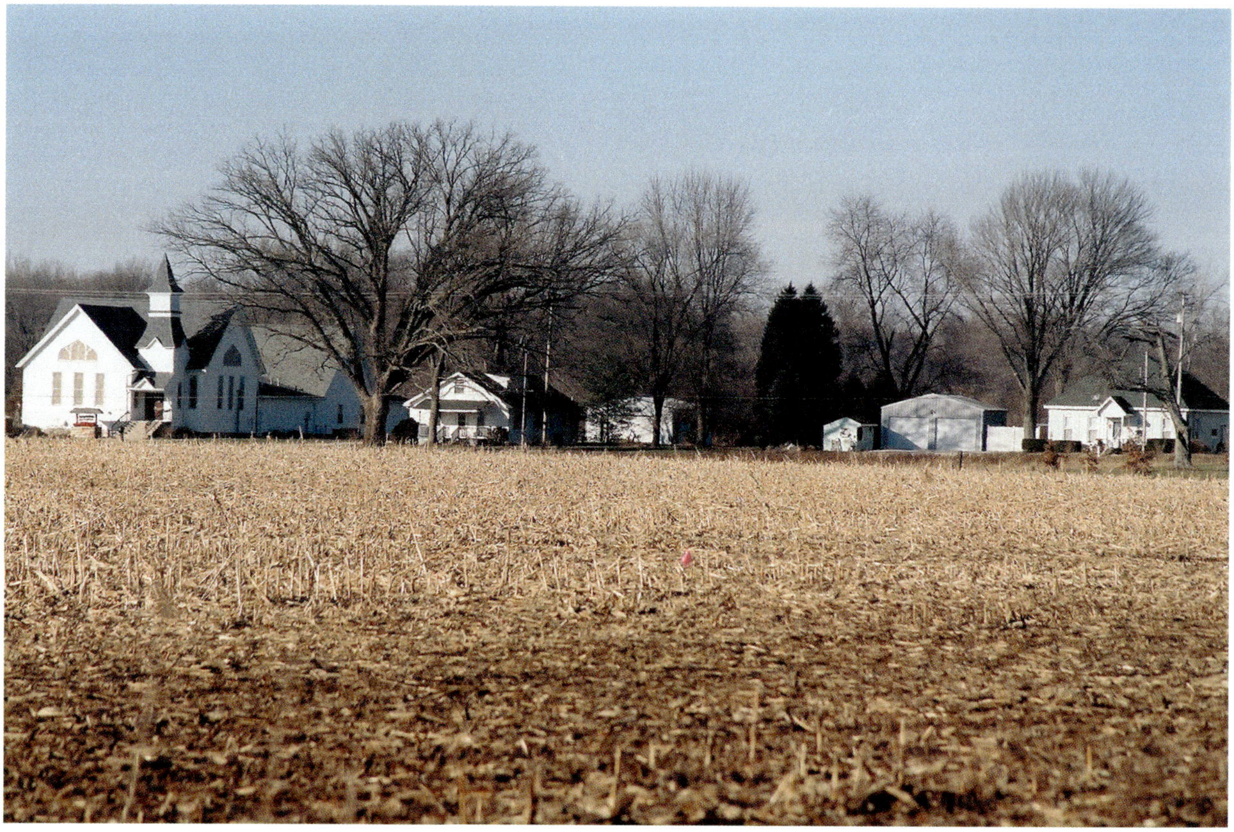

One of the earliest free black settlements in Southern Illinois, Pinkstaff is now a country village flanked by cornfields. Lawrence County. Photo by Herbert K. Russell

and a number of white friends were living nearby. The settlement of "Ivey" (call it that) came to an end after two of its members were indicted for a plan to murder a nearby racist politician. The charges were dropped, but Ivey and his friends had moved on by the 1840 census.

On the eastern side of Union County, the African American settlement of Allen was more enduring. It began in 1828 when Arthur and Patience Allen moved from North Carolina to a plot of land northeast of the village of Mt. Pleasant where the 1830 census identified them as farmers. Like the Iveys, the Allens never registered their free status at the Jonesboro courthouse as required by Illinois law, a situation suggesting that both families were judged by their behavior rather than their skin color. A half century later, the Allens had purchased more land, and the Union County history of 1883 describes the Allen community as "the only regular negro settlement in the county." The Allens got along with white neighbors, including peaceful Quakers in nearby Johnson County, the 1925 history of which shows the Allens "proved themselves substantial citizens."

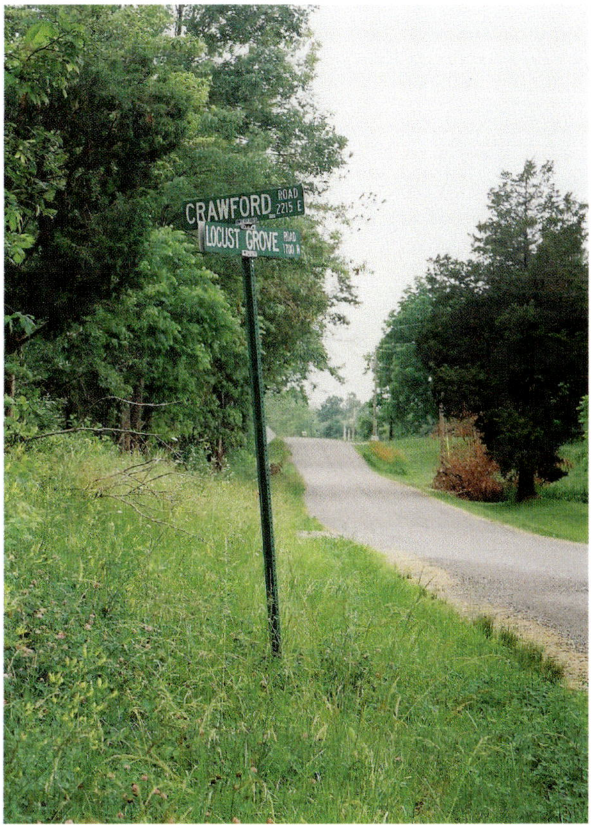

Little is left of the all-black community of Africa except country roads, signposts, and a cemetery. Northeast Williamson County. Photo by Herbert K. Russell

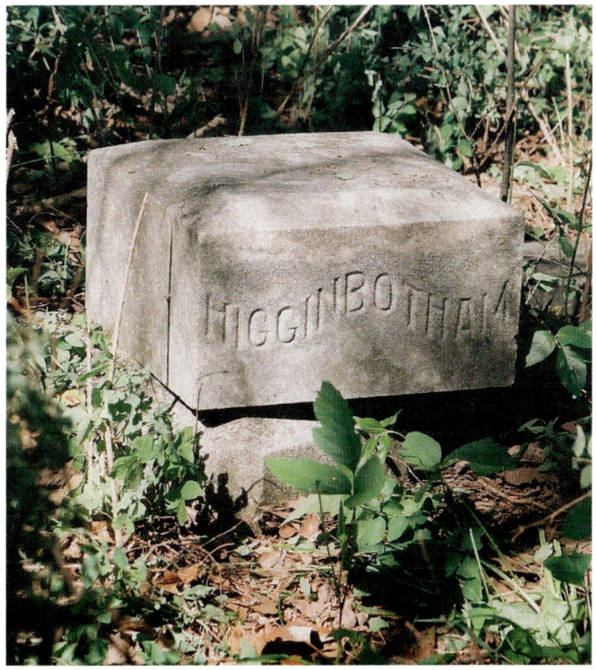

The Higginbotham Cemetery is a reminder that a free black settlement was sited northeast of Salem in Clay County's Oskaloosa Township circa 1840–60. Photo by Herbert K. Russell

Several miles north, in St. Clair County, runaway slaves and free blacks settled tiny Brooklyn in 1829–30. Northeast of Brooklyn was Pin Oak, where the slaves freed by governor Coles sought a new beginning. Pin Oak was also where former runaway slave Harry Dougherty, freed on Christmas day 1835, lived out his life as a landowner, and where his heirs continued to own land into the twenty-first century.

A few miles south near Collinsville, the Emancipation Baptists' Bethel Church is sometimes described as a station on the Underground Railroad (UGRR). In northeastern Randolph County, antislavery Reformed Presbyterians known as "Covenanters" had established a church at Eden by 1819 and were probably the guiding force behind that area's reputed station on the UGRR. Indeed, we have court records of a Covenanter-farmer in the Eden-Sparta area aiding a black mother in her flight north with her children in 1842. Like many runaways, she was eventually apprehended, but runaway slaves apparently continued to make their way to the Eden area. Legend and community lore agree that

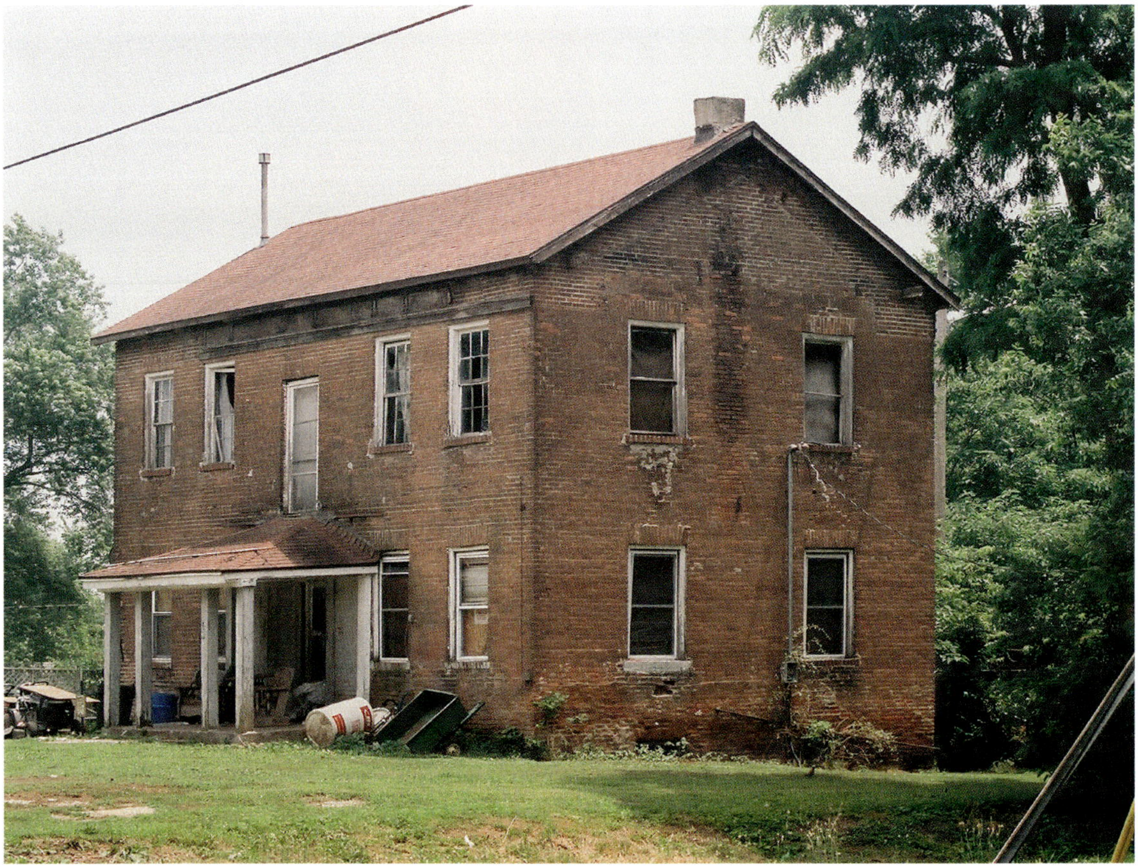

The Burlingame House in Eden was reportedly on the Underground Railroad. Randolph County. Photo by Herbert K. Russell

a residence near the Washington County village of Oakdale was also on the UGRR.

Southern Illinois has several stories of the Underground Railroad and hiding places for runaway slaves. Some of these have credible paperwork, such as the above-mentioned court records; others lack supportive paperwork and must be regarded as folklore—stories that have been repeated through the years but are difficult to prove or disprove. The latter usually lack evidence beyond the alleged hiding place itself—a stairway closet discovered during remodeling, an empty cistern with an old story, a trap door leading to an underground storage area, a potato bin filled (it turns out) with family lore.

A related question is how much help runaway slaves received from Southern Illinois' free African Americans. We know from the court case *Rodney v. Illinois Central Railroad* that an unnamed free black woman from Cairo assisted one runaway slave in the purchase of a ticket to ride north on the Illinois Central during the 1850s. And we have a transcription of a letter from 1896 in which African American railroad porter George J. L. Burroughs indicates that he hid one runaway slave girl on a freight train at "St.

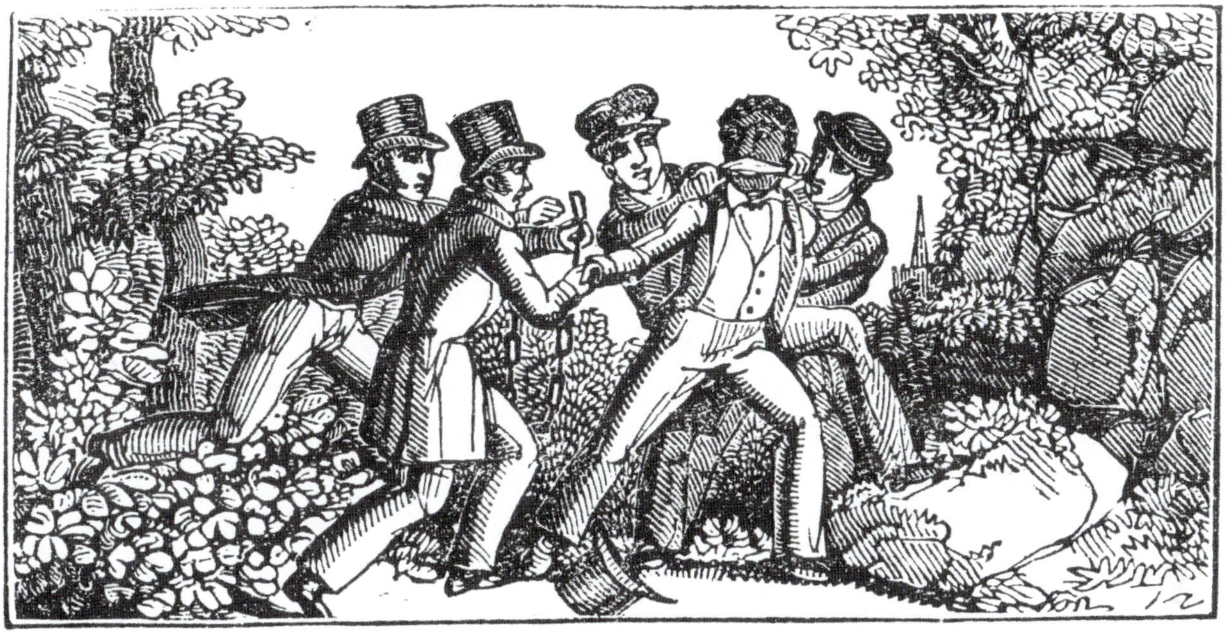

Kidnapping of free African Americans and selling them into slavery was a problem in northern states, including New York, above. In Southern Illinois, "Negro catchers" and "slave catchers" targeted free African Americans and escaped slaves near East St. Louis, Shawneetown, and Cairo, river communities offering easy access to nearby slave states.

Louis Junction" (near Centralia) during the 1850s. We know too that in 1850 a southern runaway named "Patrick" sought a free black man in the settlement of South America west of Harrisburg. But whether such occurrences were common or unusual we do not know.

In any event, Southern Illinois' free black settlements and interactions between free people of color and area whites illustrate an important part of the region's pre–Civil War history: the two races often got along as individuals and families, as rural neighbors and farmers, as townspeople and churchgoers, as teachers and students, and occasionally as partners in marriage in spite of prejudices of the day and inhumane laws from the Illinois legislature. In the not-too-distant future, some would also be soldiers in the same army.

A strong oral tradition alleges that Gallatin County businessman John Hart Crenshaw kidnapped free blacks and runaways and sold them into slavery and that some of his misdeeds took place at Hickory Hill, the mansion and grounds where he lived with his family east of Equality. One of the local stories is that Crenshaw kept slaves and runaways on the third floor, where they were imprisoned and used for breeding in small, barred closets with shelves for bunks. Crenshaw died in 1871, and several families lived at Hickory Hill before one owner, A. J. Sisk, began charging admission to tour the mansion during the Great Depression of the 1930s. It was during this commercialization of the house that the family names of *Hickory Hill* and *Crenshaw Mansion* were replaced by the name *Old Slave House*.

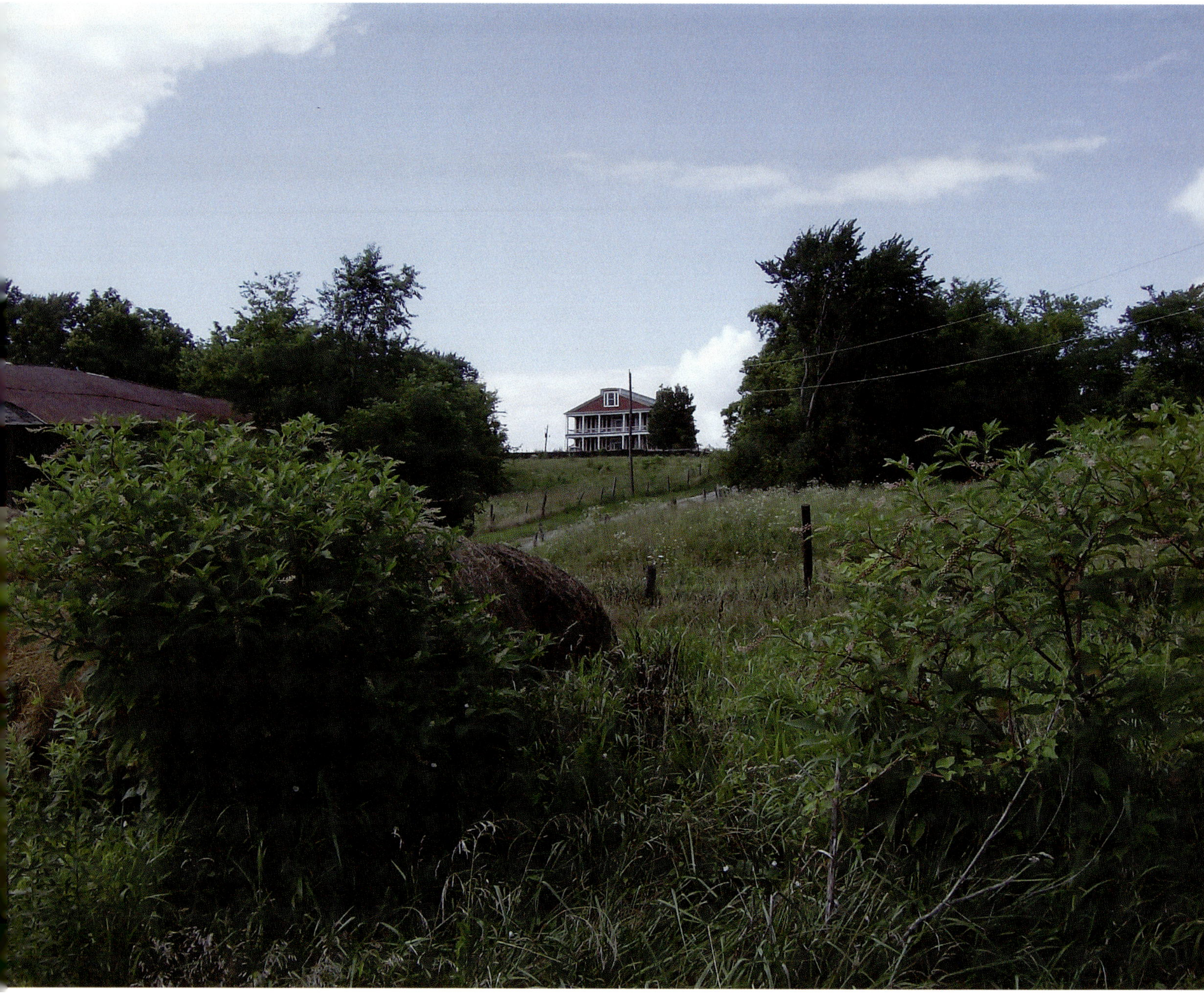

Hickory Hill, the "Old Slave House" of Gallatin County. Beginning in 1828, house owner John Hart Crenshaw leased the state salt springs near Equality, built a mansion with a mysterious third floor—and created the most restless ghosts in Egypt. Photo courtesy of Brian DeNeal

In 1947 a 111-year-old former slave named Robert "Uncle Bob" Wilson told a social worker in Elgin, Illinois, that he had been kept as a "stud slave" on the house's third floor and that he had fathered some of his hundreds of children there. There seems to be no credible evidence that Wilson was ever in the house, but Sisk used Wilson's claims as advertising to attract tourists. Sisk decided that Wilson had fathered 300 children while at the house and provided visitors with this information. Sisk also identified as torture devices two wooden frames on the third floor and displayed ball-and-chain sets reportedly found at the site.

During the second half of the twentieth century, additional ball-and-chain sets were displayed, and the house acquired a reputation for being haunted. Various individuals tested their courage by volunteering to spend a night on the house's creaky third floor, but most frightened themselves into hysterical anxiety and fled before dawn. Several historians have inspected the house, but no one has shown how the purported torture devices work, and they are sometimes referred to as "whipping posts." A competing oral tradition says that the mansion at Hickory Hill was a station on the Underground Railroad. A third opinion is that none of the above is true. John Crenshaw completed his house in the 1840s, and it is now owned by the Illinois Historic Preservation Agency.

John Crenshaw's attorney, Henry Eddy of Shawneetown, once began a legal document for one "John Granger" before lining out "Granger" and writing "Crenshaw," a moment that underscores problems of research on Crenshaw. He followed a Virginia and South Carolina family tradition of pronouncing his last name as *Granger* and was known to many, including fellow Methodists, by his nickname, *John Granger.* Those who followed Crenshaw also confused matters. House promoter A. J. Sisk attracted tourists by advertising the house's legends, but his sensational approach was that of a sideshow barker ("See the breeding room"), and what he and others could not explain (the two wooden frames) became props in a house of horrors. Jon Musgrave's *Slaves, Salt, Sex, and Mr. Crenshaw* enjoys a provocative title and contains useful research but is confusingly written. A 2002 report for the Illinois Historic Preservation Agency suggests that some stories about Crenshaw may be true but does not particularize. Various people have shown a willingness to accept wishful suppositions about the mansion (e.g., that Abraham Lincoln slept there); others accept none of the stories unless they are accompanied by documentary (paper) evidence from Crenshaw's era. Some combine research with the legends and believe the evidence remains strong that Crenshaw/Granger kidnapped free African Americans and hid them until he or his friends could move them south and sell them as slaves.

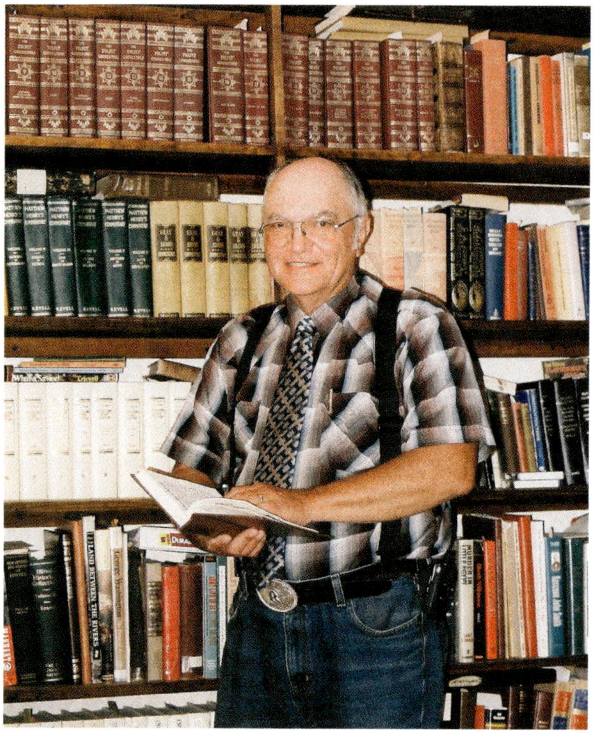

Historian Ronald L. Nelson has conducted extensive research on John Crenshaw's house, grounds, and business dealings. Nelson's research suggests that Crenshaw may have kidnapped free blacks and kept some on the third floor of his house before selling them into slavery. Photo by Herbert K. Russell

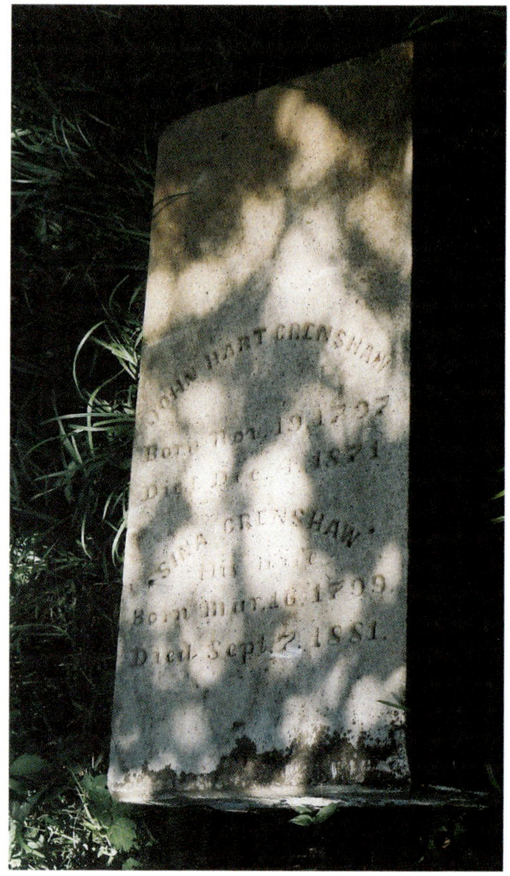

Shadows of leaves play on the toppled tombstone of John Hart Crenshaw in a hilltop cemetery near his home. His name is misspelled as "Crinshaw." Photo by Herbert K. Russell

By 1858 it was impossible for Southern Illinoisans to be unaware of the possibility of a civil war, especially after the darling of the Democratic Party, Stephen A. Douglas, debated the rising star of the Republicans, Abraham Lincoln, at Jonesboro in a race for the U.S. Senate. "Trot him down to lower Egypt" and see what he says, Douglas had remarked of Lincoln's antislavery words, and so the two had come to a grove of trees on the north edge of Jonesboro. The audience was swollen by visitors from Cairo, then an important city, and from Centralia, site of that year's Illinois State Fair. Many arrived in cars of the recently completed Illinois Central Railroad, which Douglas had helped bring into existence earlier in his political career. The Illinois Central ("the IC") was Douglas' great achievement and helped ensure his popularity.

Douglas argued that future American states should enter the Union as either slave states or free, according to the inhabitants' wishes. Lincoln remarked on Douglas' New England upbringing in Vermont, a politically astute move aimed at Egypt's distrust of Yankees. "I know this people better than he does," Lincoln said. "I was raised just a

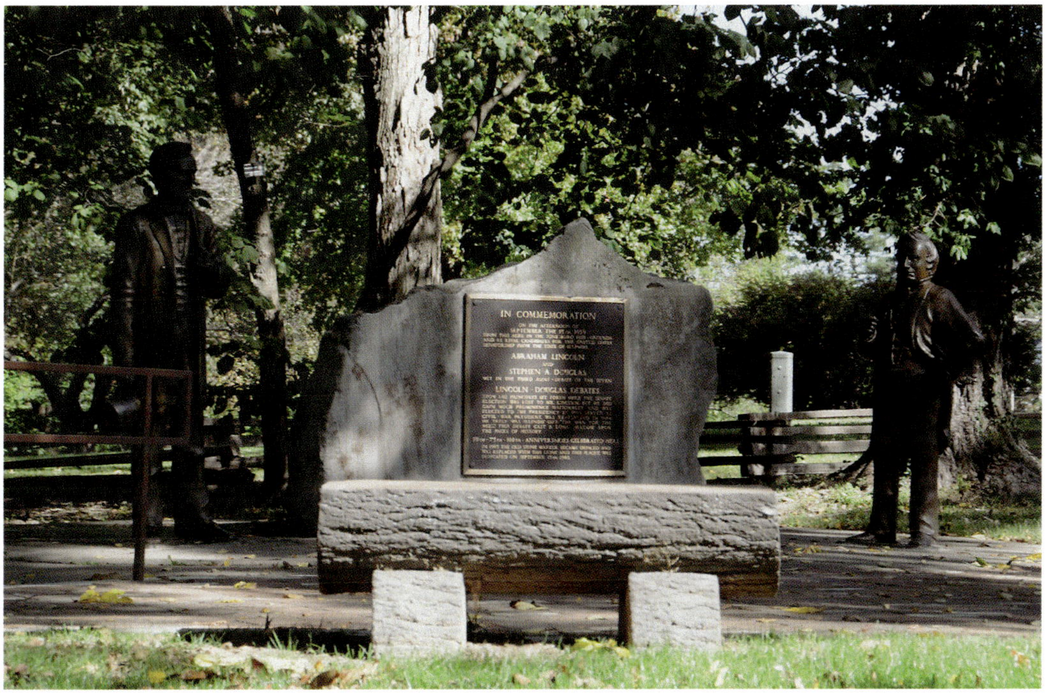

One of the best-known debates in American history took place at Jonesboro when Abraham Lincoln and Stephen A. Douglas met here on September 15, 1858. The statues were sculpted by Tom Allen. Photo courtesy of Shannon Woodworth

little east of here. I am a part of this people." And this was true: Lincoln had been born in the southern uplands in the hills of Kentucky; had been raised "a little east of here" in southwestern Indiana; and came from a family similar to those of his listeners—dirt poor, southern, and backward. His audience nibbled fried chicken, spat tobacco juice, and looked unconvinced. They favored Douglas, in part because he had name recognition, in part because nearly all Southern Illinoisans were Democrats. Douglas would go on to win the senate race in 1858, but Lincoln would win the more important race for the White House two years later, just as Southern states began to secede and the Civil War broke out in April 1861.

Most Egyptians found themselves in one of three groups soon after the war began. "Peace Democrats" wished the war to end quickly through Northern recognition of the Confederate States of America as a separate country. "War Democrats" sided with Lincoln and preservation of the Union. Those in between did not like Lincoln or Yankees, but they did not necessarily want war. Newspapers fed the dispute. Scholars who view Egypt as an extension of Dixie often quote the *Cairo City Gazette* for December 6, 1860: "The sympathies of our people are mainly with the South"—but this statement should not necessarily be taken as a desire to secede. In 1861, as war drew near, the same newspaper (now named the *Cairo City Weekly Gazette*) printed articles in favor of saving the Union; after war broke out, the paper urged reconciliation. Southern Illinoisans studied their choices through the summer of 1861

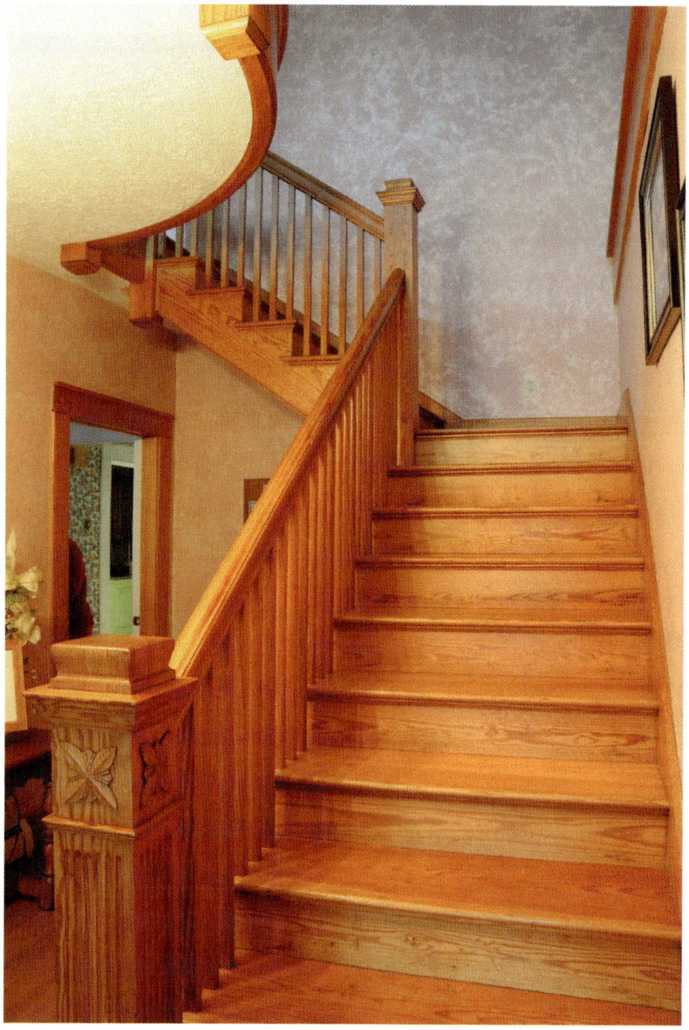

Lincoln ascended these stairs to his bedroom in the Anna home of David L. Phillips on the nights before and after his debate with Douglas. Photo courtesy of Shannon Woodworth

and then overwhelmingly chose the region that had been better for them. This turnabout from secessionist talk to loyalty received an important boost when Stephen A. Douglas realized he could not accept the breakup of the United States and began openly supporting the North.

A native of the Northeast, Douglas had moved to Illinois as a young man and remained to become an important political figure. After the war began, Douglas urged preservation of the Union in speeches in Springfield and Chicago. He said he could not support Southern secession and urged fellow Democrats to support the North—and then Douglas suddenly died, leaving his followers in need of a leader. The role of many Southern Illinois Democrats was not defined until several weeks later, on August 19, 1861, when the popular Democratic congressman John A. Logan addressed a large crowd on the Marion square.

Before the war Logan had made remarks supporting both the North and the South, but a good many voters assumed he was a southerner at heart. When the war began in April, Logan failed to inform his constituents as to which side he supported, and drifted politically during the war's early weeks. Now, four months after the war began, he finally told Southern Illinoisans where he stood. He borrowed ideas Stephen A. Douglas had used successfully at Springfield and Chicago ("every man must be for the United States or against it") and implored fellow Democrats to do as he had done, turn their backs on Southern allegiances and follow him in support of the North. They did so in overwhelming numbers, and it was he (and the ghost of Douglas) who led much of Egypt into the Union Army.

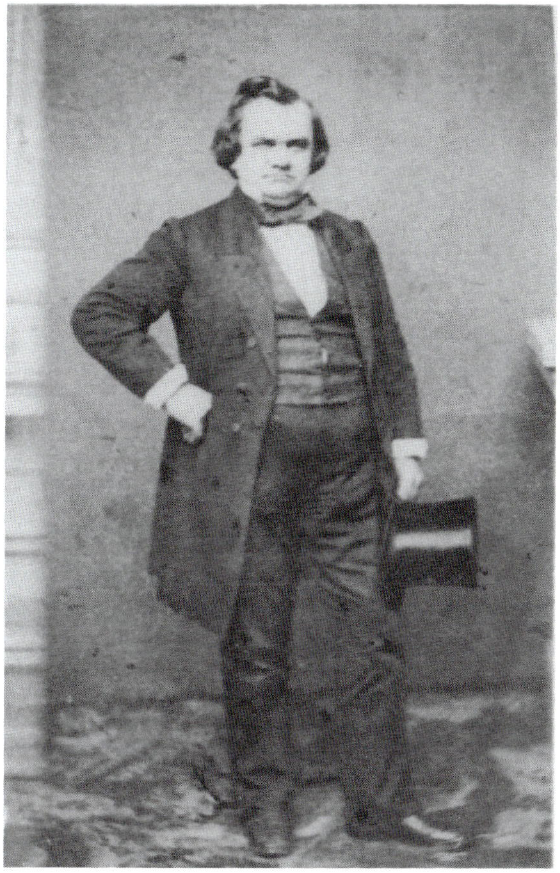

Stephen A. Douglas' antisecession speeches helped bring Illinois Democrats into the Union camp at the start of the Civil War. Douglas had earlier championed the building of the Illinois Central Railroad from Cairo through Centralia to northern Illinois and tied Egypt's economic future to the North. Photo courtesy of Abraham Lincoln Presidential Library and Museum (ALPLM)

Egypt's new immigrants also supported the North. Chief among them were Germans, numerous Irish (who helped build the IC), some Scots, Welsh, Dutch, a few Swiss, and many Scots-Irish. A progressive English settlement had also taken root. The English had come to Illinois in search of a better life and inexpensive land and found both on the prairies of Edwards County in 1817. They established the county seat of Albion (an old name for England), opened the state's first public library, and, coincidentally, demonstrated that Illinois' flat, wet prairies could be encouraged to grow crops through the expedient of ditching. Many of the English actively opposed slavery.

Many Southern Illinois churches also turned against slavery, including the first to do so, the Emancipation Baptists. Their church philosophy was nurtured in Kentucky by the slavery-hating Baptist minister Josiah Dodge, who carried his message to New Design near Waterloo, Illinois, where he baptized James Lemen, a former Virginian, in 1794. Lemen made opposition to slavery a part of his religious beliefs by 1796, when religious services were held in his home, and helped establish churches near New Design and Collinsville by 1809. "Being opposed to slavery" became a central part of Emancipation Baptist doctrine, and church membership and communion were denied those who felt otherwise: *"We believe it to be our duty to extend our friendship (that is, justice and mercy) to human nature, let it appear in whatever dress or complexion God may see fit to order, whether white, red, yellow, or black, and not when it appears in white only."*

Lemen and his five antislavery sons, four of whom were ministers, were active politically, and one of them, James Jr., was elected to the Illinois territorial legislature and later to the state legislature. He became part of the coalition organized by Governor Edward Coles to prevent Illinois from becoming a slave state, and is remembered for arguing that slaves "could not be property" because they were "part of the human family." From the pulpit and through circulars the Emancipation Baptists influenced like-minded individuals in 1824 and helped Illinoisans vote down a constitutional convention that could have legalized slavery. They evangelized successfully from the Shawnee Hills to Salem, as far north as Springfield, Illinois (a slave-holding town), and crossed into Missouri. By the 1840s they counted 2,400 members and sixty-four churches, including the appropriately named Liberty Baptist Church near Harrisburg and three black churches in St. Clair and Madison Counties. Black and white ministers occasionally exchanged pulpits, and they practiced what they preached.

Methodists also would be prominent in the antislavery fray, and those in Franklin County established their own Liberty Church. (It was they who had halted the Sunday morning exodus of free African Americans from the nearby settlement of Africa and encouraged them to remain in their homes.) Individual Protestant churches often wavered or split over the slavery issue, but the trend among state and regional associations and church leaders was to condemn it. Led by an eastern-born Baptist named John Mason Peck and a fire-eating Methodist from Kentucky, Peter Cartwright, Illinois' two largest religious bodies supported the North, as did German Lutherans, Presbyterians, the region's few Congregationalists, and other Protestant churches. Many Catholic soldiers would also serve in Mr. Lincoln's army.

> What a wonderful and stupid nonsense the newspapers give us. They are a nuisance, destroying important facts . . . and confusing the record of the times.
>
> —War Diary of William Camm, 14th Illinois Infantry, 1862

In Illinois' sixteen southernmost counties where Democrats ruled and Confederate sympathies were once assumed to be the strongest—areas south of Chester, Benton, and Carmi—about 40 percent of the men between the ages of eighteen and forty-five had enlisted in the Union Army by August 23, 1862. The enlistment rate for the rest of Illinois for this same period was only about 28 percent. These figures from the *Adjutant General's Report* might have ended questions about Southern Illinois' loyalty but did not, in part because of instances such as the following.

Three days after the Civil War began, several Williamson County men, including Southern sympathizers Thorndike Brooks, John M. Cunningham, and Henry C. "Harry" Hopper, met in a Marion saloon and planned a resolution calling for Southern Illinois to secede and join the Confederate States of America. The wording of their four-part resolution is reported in slightly different ways by different newspapers and historians, but the most important part means the same in all versions: "The interest of the citizens of Southern Illinois imperatively demands at their hands a division of the State. We hereby pledge ourselves to use all means in our power to effect the same, and attach ourselves to the Southern Confederacy." This gathering is sometimes referred to as a "mass meeting," and perhaps it was, but Williamson County historian Milo Erwin wrote in 1876 that only "ten or fifteen men got together in a saloon in Marion." Two later historians could count only twelve men at this gathering and agree that only eleven supported the resolution.

This Marion saloon resolution had no legal significance beyond calling attention to the eleven men who supported it, and a larger group met in Marion the day after its adoption and voted to repeal it. But such was the inflammatory spirit of the times (and the willingness of humanity to pass along a good story at any time) that other instances of Egyptian disloyalty seemed to follow naturally. In the summer of 1861 the Northern press led by the very Republican *Chicago Tribune* scanned Egypt's newspapers and reported (and sometimes distorted) suspicious acts in Democrat-controlled Southern Illinois until Civil War disloyalty became the perceived norm and was still being repeated as fact when the twenty-first century dawned. Interestingly, future general Ulysses S. Grant wrote from Anna in May 1861 to say that stories of Egypt's disloyalty were untrue.

Meanwhile, the secessionists noisily announced plans to destroy the Illinois Central Railroad's large, wooden bridge over the Big Muddy River four miles north of Carbondale—an excellent military target. The Illinois Central was laid out as an enormous Y: Galena and its lead mines were at the upper left, Chicago at the upper right, and Cairo at the bottom. Repair shops were in Centralia, a company town created by, and named for, the Illinois Central. In 1860 Illinois had over 2,800 miles of railroad tracks, but only 118 miles lay south of Centralia: the Illinois Central had a 112-mile stretch of single tracks from Centralia to Cairo, and the Ohio River town of Mound City enjoyed a six-mile short line connecting it to the IC's main line at Mounds. If travel on the Centralia–to-Cairo tracks could be disrupted, it would seriously impede the Northern war effort.

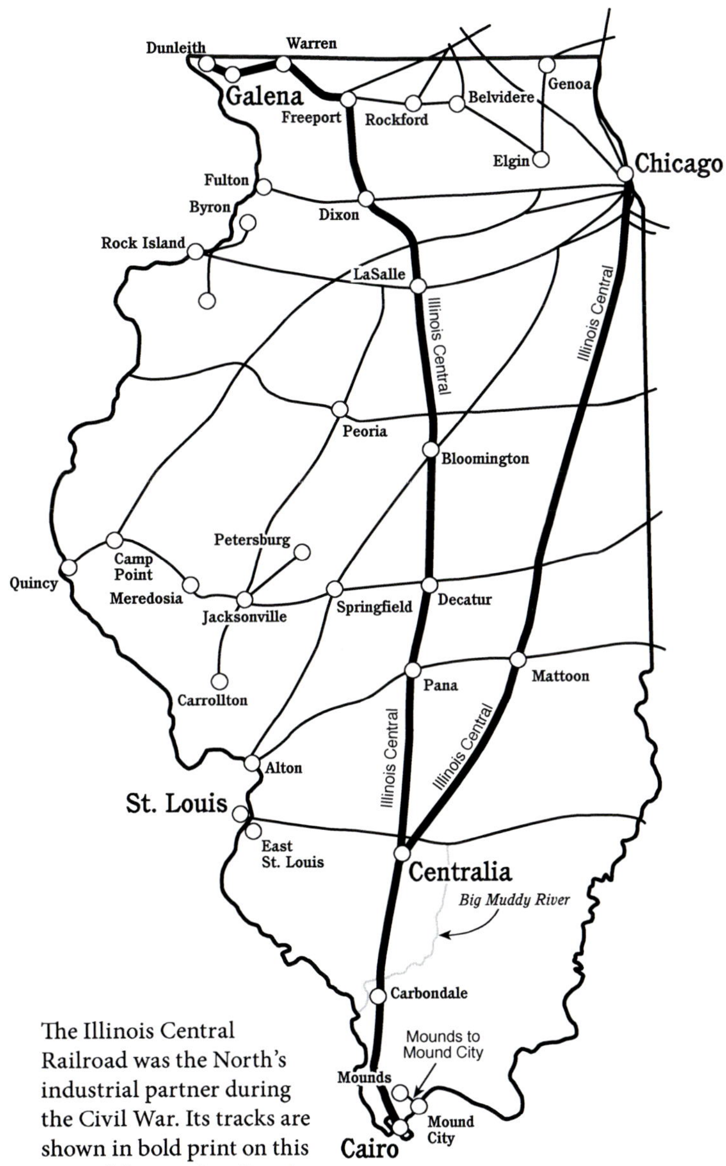

The Illinois Central Railroad was the North's industrial partner during the Civil War. Its tracks are shown in bold print on this map of the state's railroad system at the start of the war.

Word of the planned attack on the Big Muddy railroad bridge reached Carbondale's cofounder, Daniel Brush. A Yankee from Vermont, Brush had helped develop the town on the Illinois Central Railroad and had started several businesses, including a bank, a portion of which served as the area's telegraph office. When Marion's Thorndike Brooks and other secessionists showed up to urge destruction of the railroad bridge and enlistment in the Confederate Army, Brush sealed the public entrance to the telegraph office and shielded the operator from secessionists wishing to know what messages were being sent and received.

On April 22, 1861, Union troops passed through Carbondale on their way to Cairo, and on the following day, Daniel Brush made a well-received speech in support of the Union on Carbondale's town square. He made another speech two days later, in the course of which he climbed to the top of his building on the southwest corner of Main and Illinois (now Routes 13 and 51), waved the American flag, and stood there daring anyone to tear it down. His two speeches helped put a damper on secession—and created an interesting tension in Southern Illinois history: Daniel Brush the Yankee was doing in April what John A. Logan of Egypt failed to do until August, rally the home folks and keep them loyal.

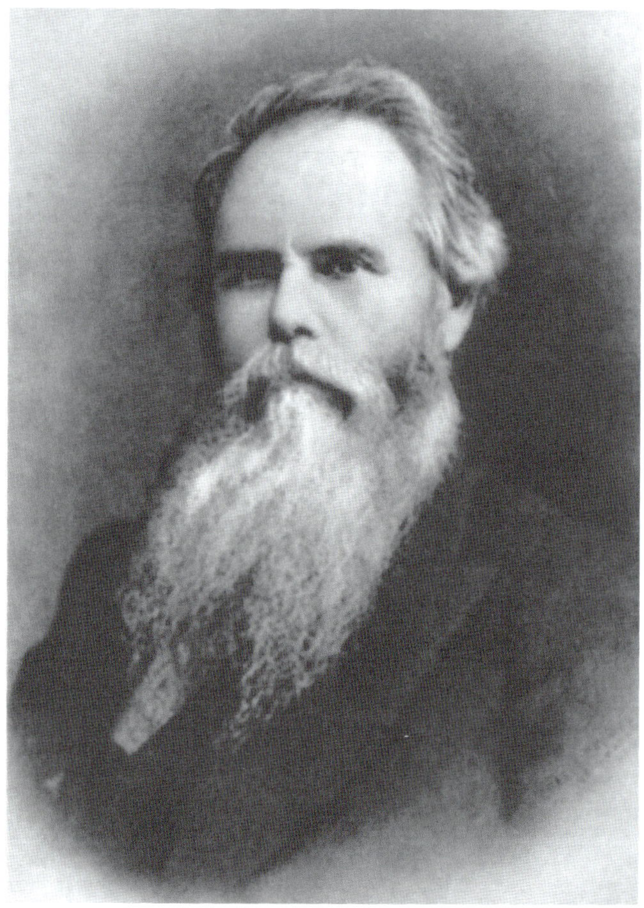

During the opening days of the Civil War, Carbondale businessman Daniel Brush made effective public speeches supporting the Union and later wrote an important memoir. Photo courtesy of Gordon Pruett

But Brush is also important as a historian. He noted in his memoir (first published in 1944) that "the rampant rebels of this region to the number of 25 or 30 . . . held a meeting [in Carbondale], as they had been doing in other southern Illinois towns, for the purpose of inducing that portion of the State lying south of the Ohio and Mississippi Railroad [Salem] to secede. . . . Secessionists generally went in a body from town to town in this section [of Illinois], assembled where they were allowed a room, and with astonishing unanimity passed the resolutions to transfer this end of the State to rebeldom. They came here without publicity and passed their resolves . . . , and it was proclaimed that the people of Carbondale were strong for the South."

In other words, the "*25 or 30*" ringleaders did not depend on Carbondale's 1,100 citizens to approve the resolutions but brought their own men ("*went in a body*") and successfully created the impression that Carbondale and "*other southern Illinois towns*" supported secession. The choreographed nature of the meeting was confirmed in 1992 when John Y. Simon's introductory essay written for the Crossfire Press edition of Brush's memoirs identified by name twenty-four men at the Carbondale meeting, among whom were the familiar trio of Brooks, Cunningham, and Hopper of Marion, their friend William Joshua Allen of Marion, well-known Southern sympathizers Israel Blanchard and Anderson Corder, and others of the same persuasion. Unfortunately, some newspapers reported that citizens of an entire county had met to secede when only a few men had done so. An example is the untitled telegraph story from "Cortos" in Cairo printed on the front page of the *Chicago Tribune* for April 26, 1861: "Williamson County passed resolutions on Wednesday, declaring preferences for the Southern Confederacy, and deprecating the [Illinois] Governor's call for troops." That only eleven men had supported the resolutions was somehow forgotten.

In the end, it was a thing—the Illinois Central Railroad—that did as much as any person to still the threat of secessionists. On April 21, 1861, nine days after the firing on Fort Sumter, the U.S. Army sent 595 soldiers south from Chicago on the IC. The train dropped off Union troops and artillery to guard the railroad bridge over the Big Muddy River and went on to Cairo. For the rest of the war the Illinois Central carried Union soldiers, guns, ammunition, horses, food, and other supplies south to Cairo. When the war disrupted the North's supply of cotton, IC railroad officials encouraged Southern Illinois farmers to increase their own cotton acreage. The railroad sought out the best cotton varieties and sold these to Egypt's farmers, who profited from inflated war prices. And so it was that Southern Illinois cotton (and tobacco and sorghum) went north on the Illinois Central toward Chicago, along with Confederate prisoners of war and Union dead being returned to their homes.

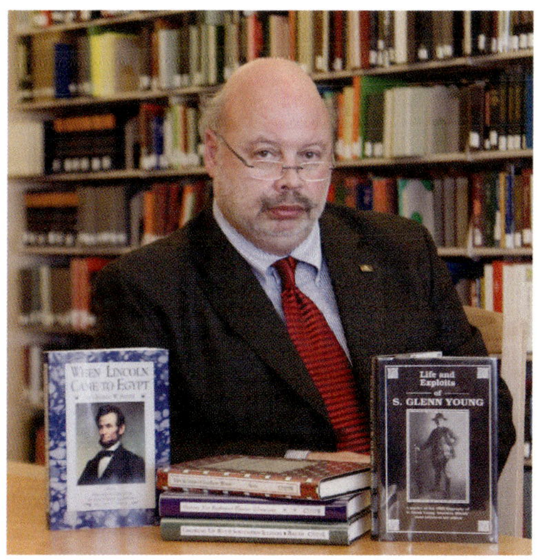

Gordon Pruett's 1992 Crossfire Press edition of Daniel Brush's *Growing Up with Southern Illinois* includes details suppressed in the 1944 edition and identifies some of the secessionists who traveled "from town to town" and created the impression that Southern Illinois wished to secede. Pruett is pictured with reprints from his Crossfire Press. Photo courtesy of Gregory Wendt

The war turned Cairo and the shipyards of nearby Mound City into camps of soldiers, sailors, gamblers, peddlers, and spies as well as a variety of nurses. Wounded soldiers at Cairo's hospitals were comforted by that city's Mary Jane Safford, "the Angel of Cairo," and by Galesburg's "Mother" Bickerdyke, volunteers whose nicknames came from the soldiers they served. Catholic nuns from Indiana managed the large hospital at Mound City and the U.S. Navy's hospital ship *Red Rover.* Recently freed African American women served as nurses on the hospital ship and elsewhere. Wounded Confederate soldiers and freed African Americans were also treated at these hospitals.

Cairo and Mound City had for years enjoyed their days and nights as rowdy river towns for crews from flatboats and steamboats, and the arrival of the IC Railroad, followed by units of the Northern Army and Navy, made them the most important military staging points in the Midwest. The U.S. Marine Ways at Mound City helped construct the heavily armed and heavily armored gunboats *Mound City, Cairo,* and

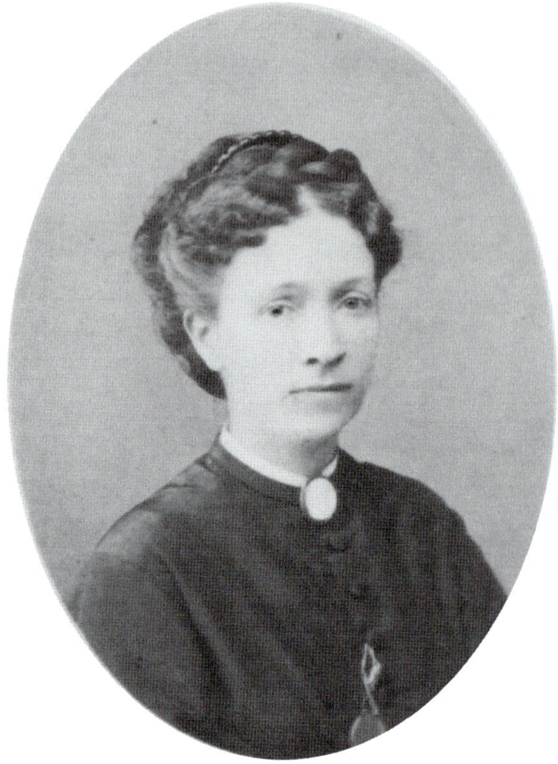

"The Angel of Cairo," Mary Jane Safford acquired her nickname by helping wounded soldiers at Cairo's military hospitals before traveling south to care for casualties from the battles of Belmont, Donelson, and Shiloh. A native of New England, she later became a physician in Boston. Photo courtesy of Abraham Lincoln Presidential Library and Museum (ALPLM)

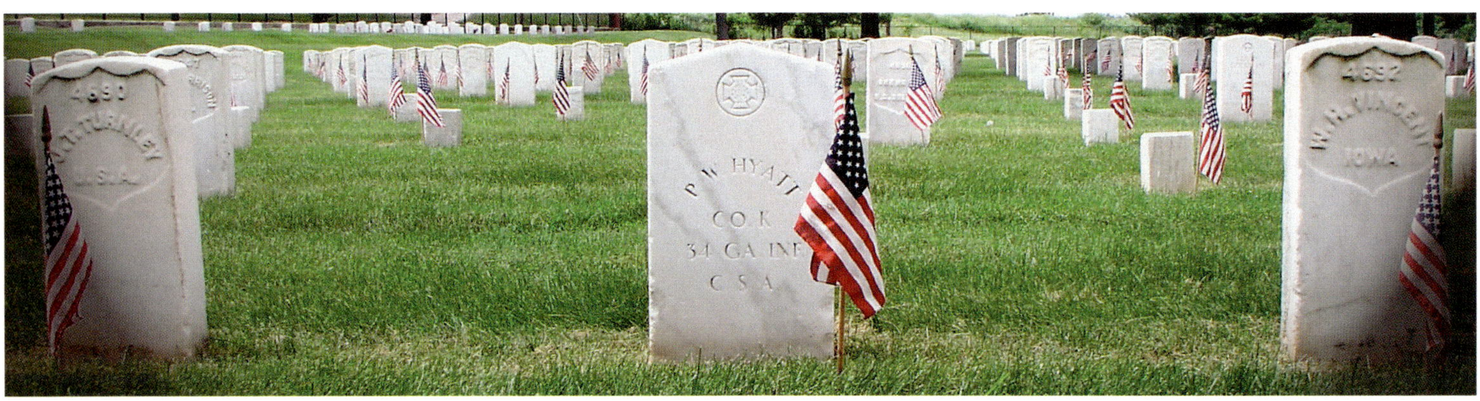

A rebel far from home, P. W. Hyatt of the 34th Georgia Infantry found his grave between two Union soldiers in the Mound City National Cemetery in Pulaski County. The pointed top of his stone and initials *CSA* at the bottom show Hyatt was a soldier in the Confederate States Army. He probably died in one of the nearby Union hospitals or on a prisoner-of-war train to the north. Photo courtesy of Shannon Woodworth

others; and it was from Cairo that General Ulysses Grant launched campaigns against Southern troops near the Cumberland, Tennessee, and Mississippi Rivers. Union victories drove Southern troops out of Tennessee, while the Union victory at Perryville, Kentucky, encouraged that state's citizens to support the North.

> Come tighten your girth and slacken
> your rein;
> Come buckle your blanket and
> holster again;
> Try the click of your trigger and
> balance your blade,
> For he must ride sure that goes riding
> a raid.
>
> —From "Riding a Raid," a
> Confederate raiding song

The Civil War years were tense along the lower Wabash River and in Ohio River towns, especially after 1862 when Confederate colonel Adam "Stovepipe" Johnson crossed the Ohio and raided a town near Evansville, Indiana. Operating under Confederate commander John Hunt Morgan, Adam Johnson and his men returned two years later, on August 13–15, 1864, this time to threaten Shawneetown, skirmish with its civilian home guards, and plunder Ohio River steamboats of cattle, clothing, corn, and oats. The *New York Times* reported that "Rebel Commander Johnston" (Johnson) and his men were "stealing and bushwhacking" in a line twelve miles wide and heading south along the Kentucky side of the Ohio. The *Louisville Journal* subsequently reported that "ten guerillas" crossed into Illinois "ten miles above Smithland," Kentucky, on August 19 and raided the McCormick Store "at Bayfield" (one mile north of present-day Bay City). Some of the raiders said "they belonged to Adam Johnson's command [and] proceeded to rob the store. They took near $3,000 worth of goods, including boots, shoes, hats, [and] broadcloths." The raiders followed the Confederate directive that a receipt be left for civilian goods seized for military purposes, and one of them, "Henry Johnson," signed the receipt. The Louisville paper said that the store owner would be compensated in full.

The McCormick family kept the receipt, hoping for restitution that never came (for the South lost the war), and the receipt spent the next eighty years in a trunk before being framed by the family historian. The signer of the document, Henry Johnson, is listed in Stephen Lynn's *Confederate Soldiers of Kentucky* (2002) as a member of the 3rd Kentucky Cavalry, Company A. The Bayfield raid would be one of the last actions initiated by his superior, Colonel Adam Johnson: two days later he was blinded in a raid on Union forces forty miles east of the McCormick Store.

Fear of raids from Missouri heightened tensions in Egypt, as did the Knights of the Golden Circle, a secret society of Southern supporters in Ohio, Indiana, and Illinois. The Knights did what they could to stir up discontent with the war and Lincoln, and hoped to free Confederate prisoners of war in northern Illinois prisons at Chicago and Rock Island and in Indianapolis. Tall talk and supposition magnified their deeds and numbers. The Knights were said to threaten and bushwhack Union soldiers home on leave, murder pro-North civilians, burn the

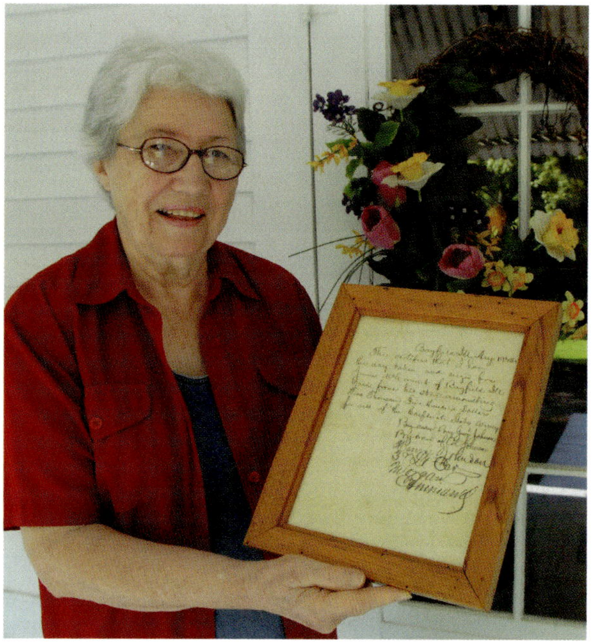

Pope County historian Mildred McCormick holds the 1864 receipt left by Southern raiders at the McCormick Store in Bayfield. The receipt was subsequently donated to the Abraham Lincoln Presidential Library and Museum, Springfield. Photo courtesy of Shannon Woodworth; used with permission of Mildred B. McCormick

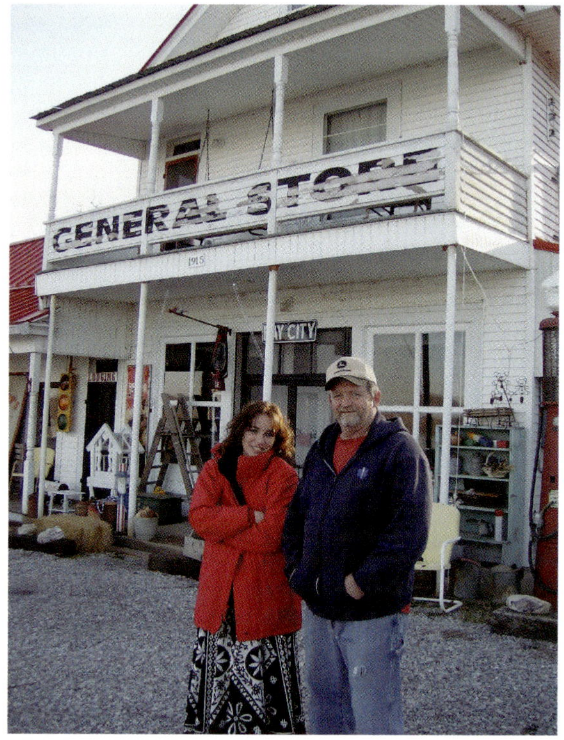

The present-day Bay City General Store stands a mile south of the McCormick Store of the 1860s. Photo courtesy of Brian DeNeal

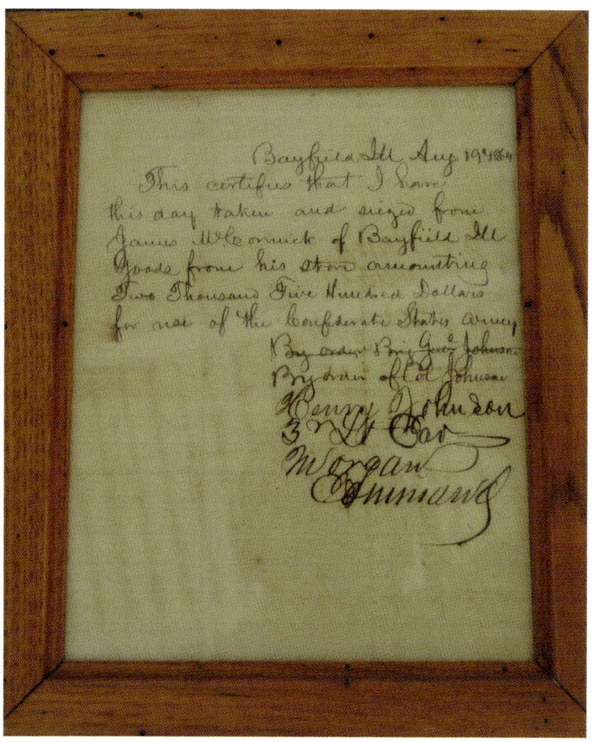

Bayfield Ill Aug 19 1864

This certifies that I have
this day taken and seized from
James McCormick of Bayfield Ill
goods from his store amounting
Two Thousand Five Hundred Dollars
for use of the Confederate States Army

By order Brig Genl Johnson
[lined out]
By order of Col Johnson
Henry Johnson
3rD Cav
Morgan
Command

Confederate receipt. Colonel Adam Johnson was recommended for promotion to brigadier general, but his promotion was denied by the Confederate Congress. This may explain why "By order Brig Genl Johnson" is lined out and replaced with "By order of Col Johnson." Photo courtesy of Shannon Woodworth; used with permission of Mildred B. McCormick

barns of Northern supporters, and harbor deserters. (A pro-North group known as the Union League was accused of similar crimes against Southern supporters.) Illinois' deadliest clash between Northern and Southern supporters did not come in Egypt but in the central Illinois town of Charleston, a pro-South stronghold, where nine soldiers and civilians died in an 1864 shootout at the Coles County courthouse.

The Knights of the Golden Circle and other Southern sympathizers were often referred to as "Copperheads," a reference to the snake that supposedly strikes without warning. During the war's opening weeks, thirty-four men from the counties of Williamson and Jackson left to enlist in the Confederate Army. It is this group that is sometimes referred to as a "company" of soldiers, an inaccurate description of a Civil War company, which usually consisted of about 100 enlisted men plus officers instead of the 200–250 common to later times. The thirty-four men were placed in Company G of the 15th Tennessee and saw action at various locales. When their history was published as *Illinois Rebels* in 1996, it was discovered that only one of the thirty-four had been born in Southern Illinois and that he soon returned home. John A. Logan's brother-in-law, Hibert Cunningham, was among those who served in the 15th Tennessee. Born in Virginia, Cunningham dutifully left Marion with other Southerners and survived several battles before becoming disillusioned and deserting to the North where he one day showed up at his brother-in-law's tent. Logan made him an aide, and he served the Union for the rest of the war.

The soldiers Logan recruited on the Marion square were assigned to his 31st Volunteer Infantry Regiment, nearly all of whom were from Southern Illinois. They were a rough bunch who settled disputes with fists, and Logan was the perfect leader for them. Some officers liked to remain out of the profile of battle and observe it through binoculars. Logan often led his men, usually from atop one of the big horses he preferred. He addressed the soldiers as his "boys" and "Thirty-Onesters." "Remember the blood of your mammas," he advised them at the Battle for Atlanta, an allusion to the slaughter that would follow if rebel armies invaded Southern Illinois.

Of course slaughter had been present all along—first at Belmont, Missouri, south of Cairo in 1861 where the 31st fought against the 15th Tennessee and Logan's brother-in-law—and later at Fort Donelson and Vicksburg and in three dozen other battles and skirmishes. Disease and capture also took their toll, and none of Illinois' 150 infantry regiments suffered greater losses than did Logan's 31st Illinois Volunteers. With his

There are bonds of all sorts in this world of ours,
Fetters of friendships, and ties of flowers. . . .
The boy and the girl are bound by a kiss,
But there's never a bond, old friend, like this,
We have drunk from the same canteen.

—Miles O'Reilly, "We've Drunk from the Same Canteen"

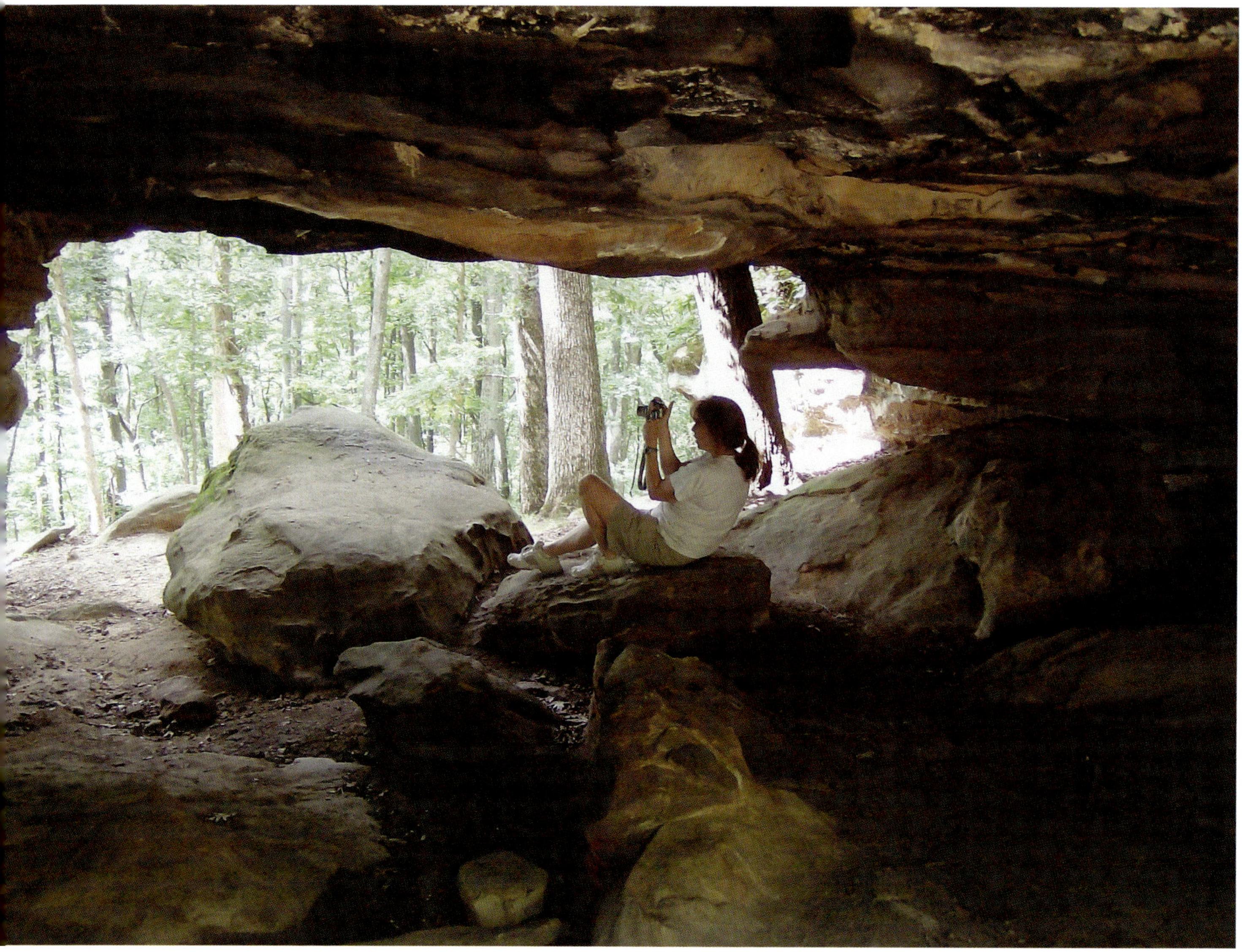

Folklore says this entrance to a “stone corral” was used as a Civil War hideout by the Knights of the Golden Circle, a pro-South organization active in Ohio, Indiana, Illinois, and elsewhere. Garden of the Gods, Saline County. Photo courtesy of Brian DeNeal

large black eyes, long black hair, and drooping black moustache, Logan was both handsome and savage, an easy figure to see on the coal-black stallion he called "Slasher." The enemy spotted him easily also and gave him several wounds. He usually ignored such things until he had to notice them and was promoted to two-star general.

Lincoln's 1863 Emancipation Proclamation freeing slaves in rebel-held states, as well as his use of the military draft, offered his political opponents an opportunity to defeat him in the 1864 presidential election. It was bad enough that rich men who were drafted could buy an exemption for $300 or purchase a substitute. Far worse was that Lincoln had earlier said the war was not about ending slavery but about maintaining the Union. Now he had broken his word, in response to which some Democratic politicians and newspapers advanced the most successful propaganda of the Civil War: white men would be drafted, they said, to liberate Negro slaves —who would come north and take their jobs, intermarry with whites, and so on. New York City's predominantly Irish (and desperately poor) lower class accepted the propaganda outright. White mobs destroyed draft offices, looted homes of the wealthy, burned the Colored Orphan Asylum, and hanged, drowned, or beat to death twenty-three free African Americans. Another seventy were missing. Police and soldiers also died, and "the worst riot in American history," as James McPherson called it, spread throughout the North from Vermont to Minnesota. Desertion rates soared in the Northern Army. In Southern Illinois, the Democratic Party in Jonesboro called for the immediate cessation of the war and discharge of soldiers.

After emancipation, some freed slaves remained where they were, some followed the Union Army or found work with it, some scattered to the four winds, and some made their way to Southern Illinois. Some ex-slaves were sent north on trains and boats to Cairo. When an officer with Egypt's desertion-racked 109th Infantry saw large numbers of African Americans heading northward, he wrote to the *Jonesboro Gazette* that it confirmed earlier predictions: emancipation would cause the North to be overrun with free black people and result in lower wages for everyone. In 1862, after Cairo became overcrowded with war refugees, some freed slaves were placed in cars of the Illinois Central Railroad and moved north to other towns, but not all towns would accept ex-slaves: Chicago refused both employment and support, and some people in Quincy and Olney threatened violence to the blacks and their employers if ex-slaves were sent there. Some freed slaves are said to have arrived by train in Carbondale, where about thirty are believed to have died of smallpox in 1864. Like many others with this contagious disease, they may have been quarantined in a separate building, provided meals in a bucket on the end of a pole, and left on their own to survive or die.

> The iron gate of our prison stands half open. One gallant rush from the North will fling it wide open.
>
> —Frederick Douglass, "Men of Color, to Arms!"

The Emancipation Proclamation offered black men and women a chance to defeat the Confederacy that had once enslaved them. The American Navy had always enlisted African Americans, and some were serving in the Union Army even before the Emancipation Proclamation took effect on January 1, 1863. They now enlisted or were drafted from Illinois and elsewhere until they comprised approximately one-tenth of the Union Army. Official records show 1,811 African Americans from Illinois served in the infantry, artillery, and cavalry in over two dozen Northern units from various states, including the 54th Massachusetts Colored Infantry, memorialized a century and a quarter later in the movie *Glory*. African Americans also worked in military commissary units as cooks and bakers, served as nurses and teamsters driving wagons, and functioned in other capacities. Illinois had only one all-black military unit, the 29th U.S. Colored Infantry sworn in at Washington, D.C., in April 1864.

Composed of former southern slaves and free African Americans from Southern Illinois and elsewhere, the 29th figured in several battles, including the 1864 Battle of the Crater, a fight for a railroad junction vital to the Confederate capital at Richmond, Virginia. Black and white soldiers and both armies occasionally killed prisoners of war, and such killings took place at the Crater when several African Americans with the 29th were murdered in what appears to be the war's worst massacre of prisoners. The 29th U.S. Colored Infantry Regiment was last stationed on the Texas border and was discharged in Springfield in 1865.

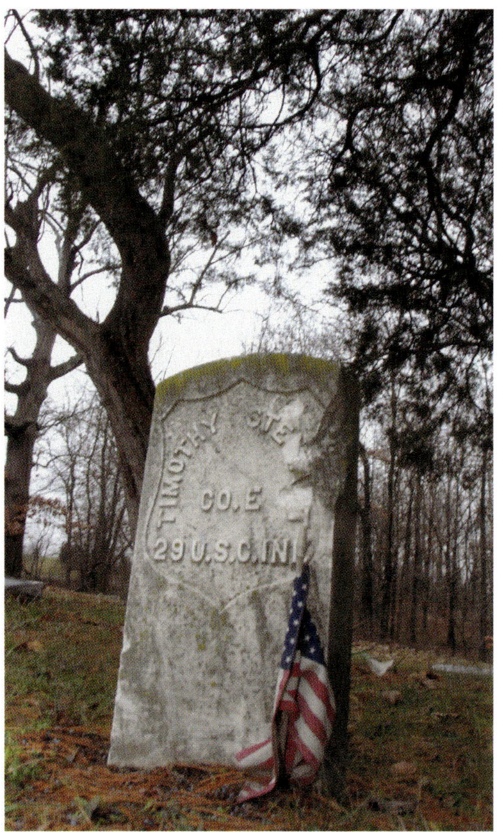

The grave of Union Army soldier Timothy Stewart of the 29th U.S. Colored (U.S.C.) Infantry, Illinois' only African American unit in the Civil War. His grave is in the cemetery of Africa in Williamson County. Photo courtesy of Shannon Woodworth

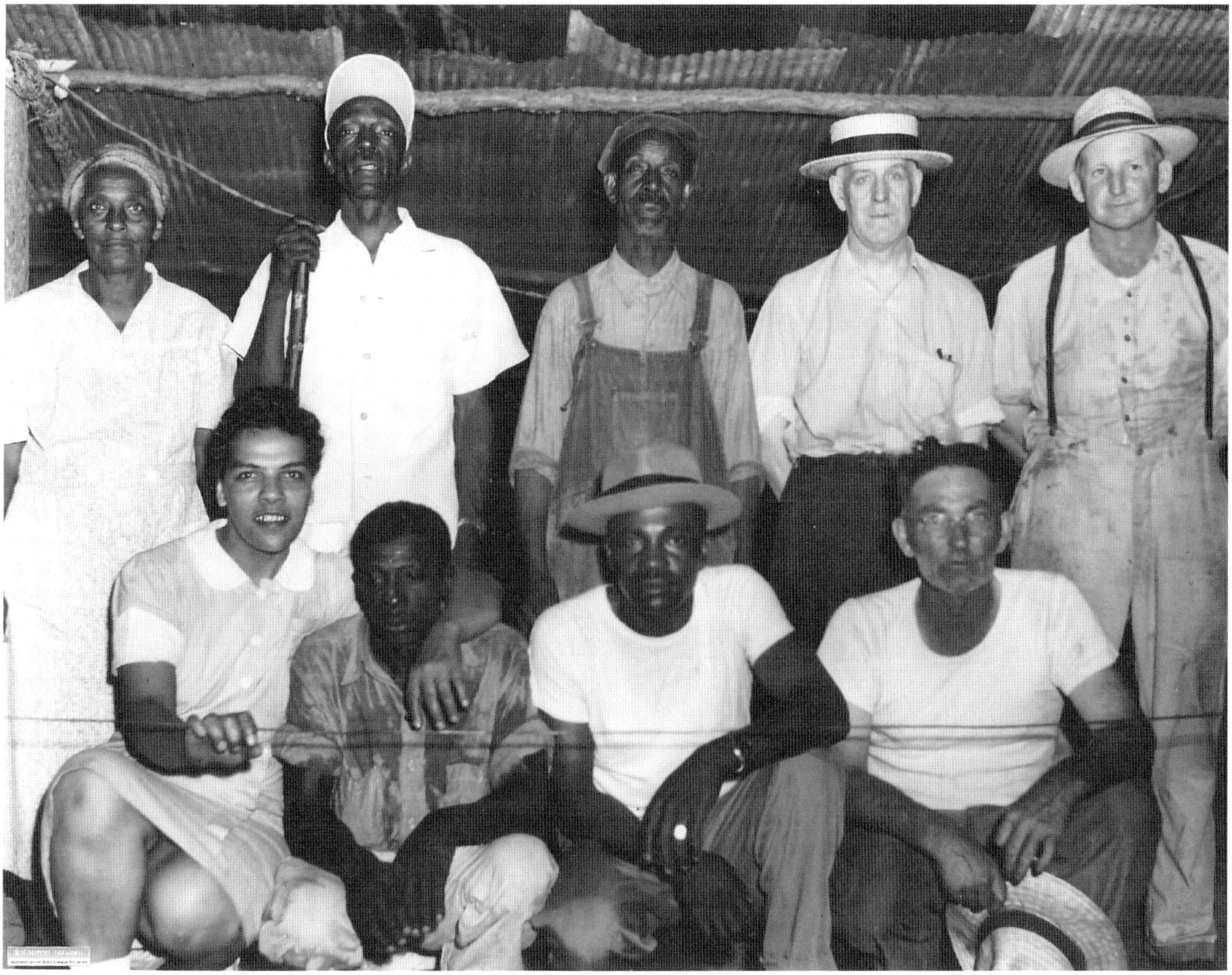

Beginning in the 1880s, Emancipation Day, conceived to celebrate the abolition of slavery, was observed annually in several Southern Illinois communities, here at a barbecue in Elizabethtown in 1940. Emancipation Day was also observed in Brookport, Metropolis, and Carbondale. Photo by Harry L. Porter; courtesy of the *Hardin County Independent*

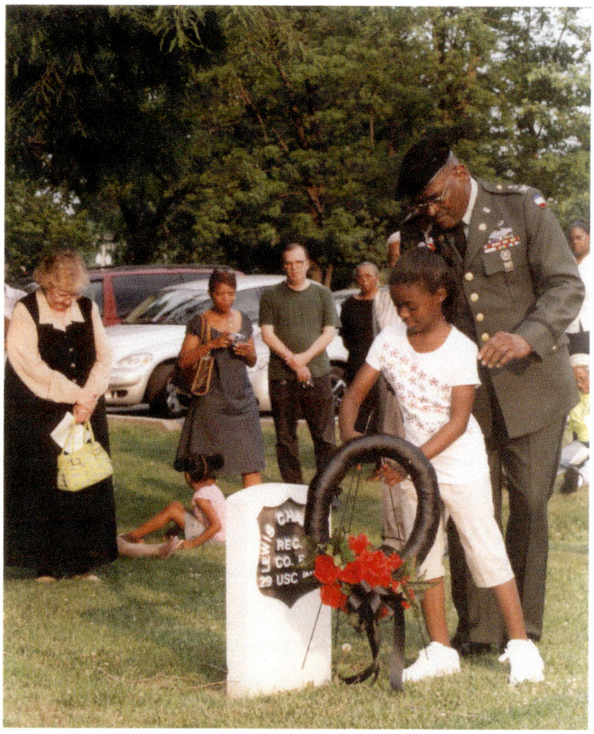

"Juneteenth" ceremonies are named for a day in June 1865 when southern slaves in remote areas learned they were free. (*Left*) Participants in Carbondale's Juneteenth observance at Woodlawn Cemetery place a wreath at the grave of African American soldier Lewis Chambers of the Union Army's 29th U.S. Colored Infantry Regiment. (*Below*) A nearby tombstone tells the unhappy ending of several freed slaves. Photos by Herbert K. Russell

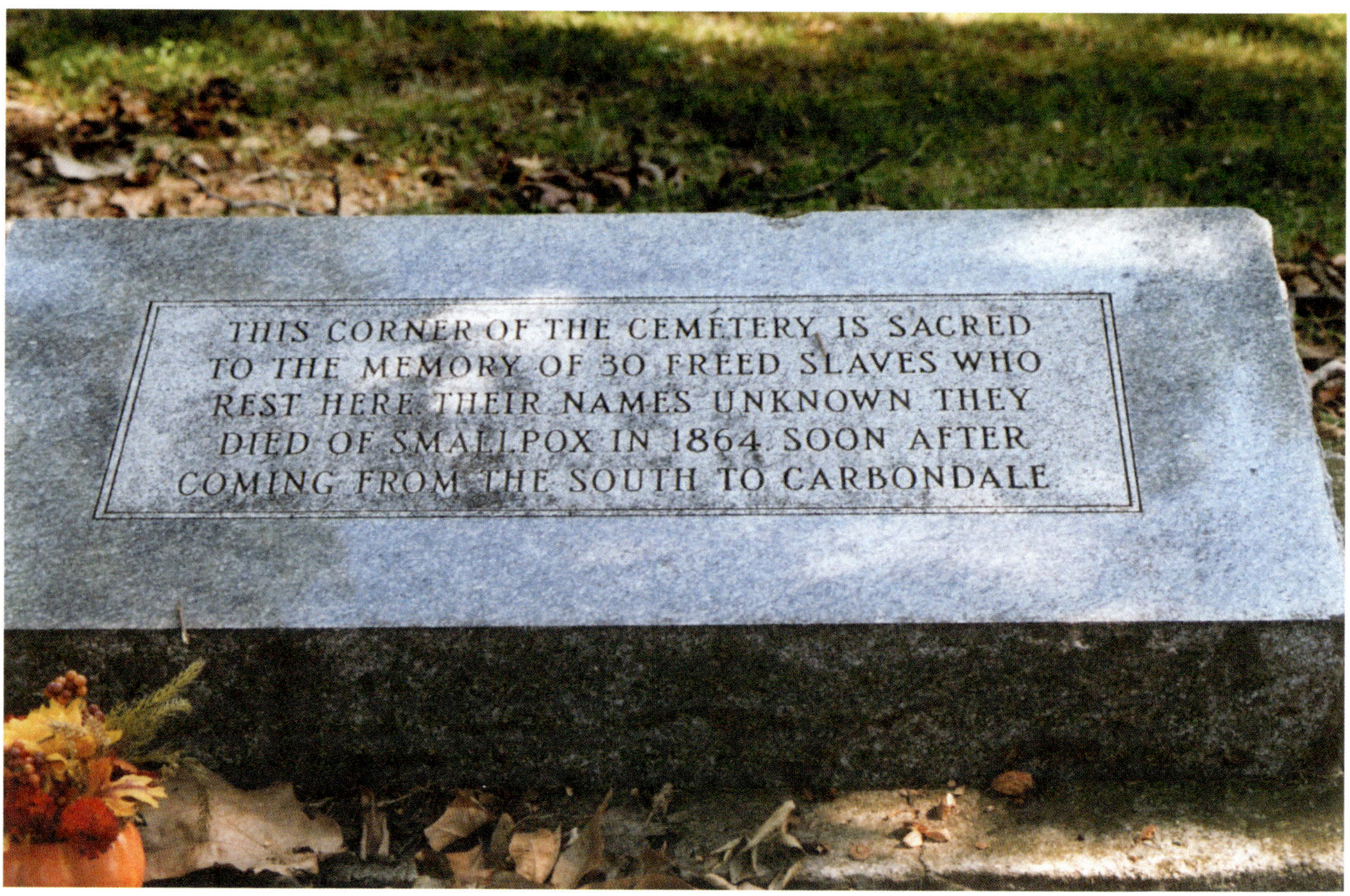

John A. Logan emerged from the war larger than life. As a U.S. senator, he would sponsor civil rights and education legislation and run unsuccessfully as the Republicans' candidate for vice president in 1884. He is the subject of numerous statues, including two at the Carterville college that bears his name. Chicago held a Logan Day a decade after his death in 1886, and his hometown of Murphysboro has both a statue and a museum devoted to him and his family's memory. He was the natural choice to lead the Grand Army of the Republic, a civilian organization designed to assist Union Army veterans and their families, and it was this group that helped him organize a national Memorial Day.

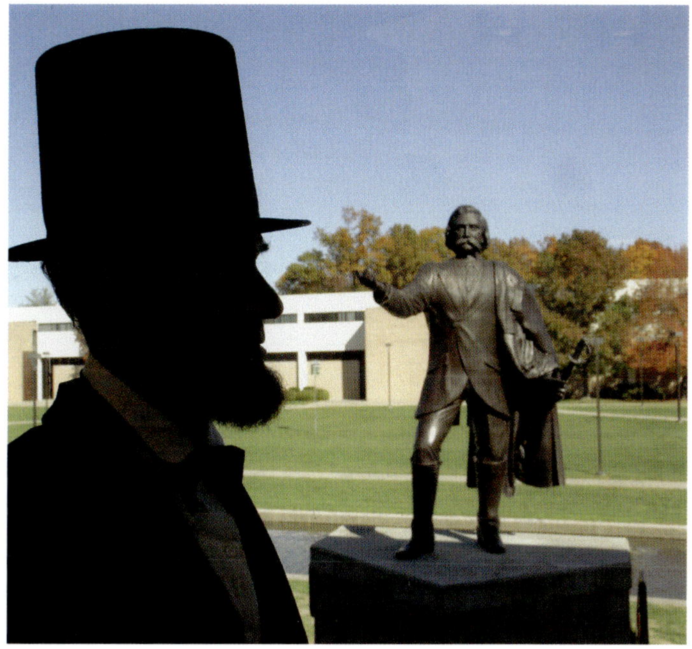

Overshadowed by Lincoln but important in his own right, John A. Logan sets aside his sword and Army coat and returns to civilian life in Marshall Hyde's statue at John A. Logan College, Carterville. Photo courtesy of Shannon Woodworth

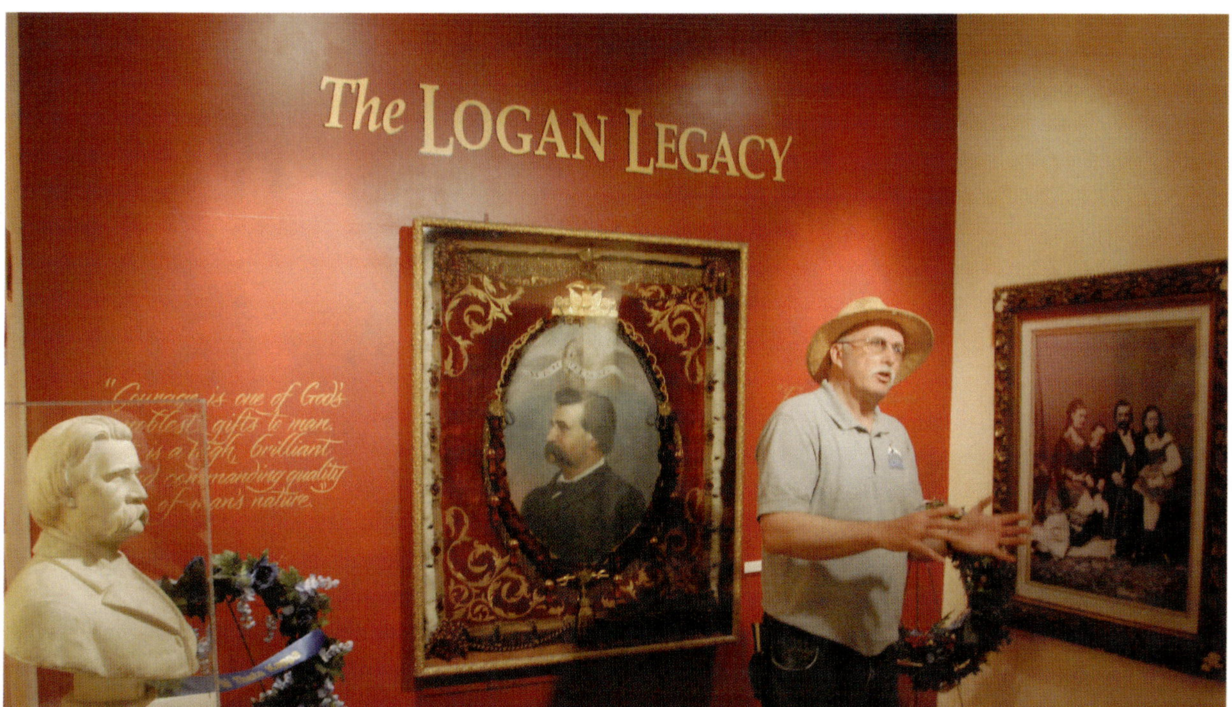

Curator P. Michael Jones is shown in the General John A. Logan Museum in Murphysboro. Photo courtesy of Shannon Woodworth

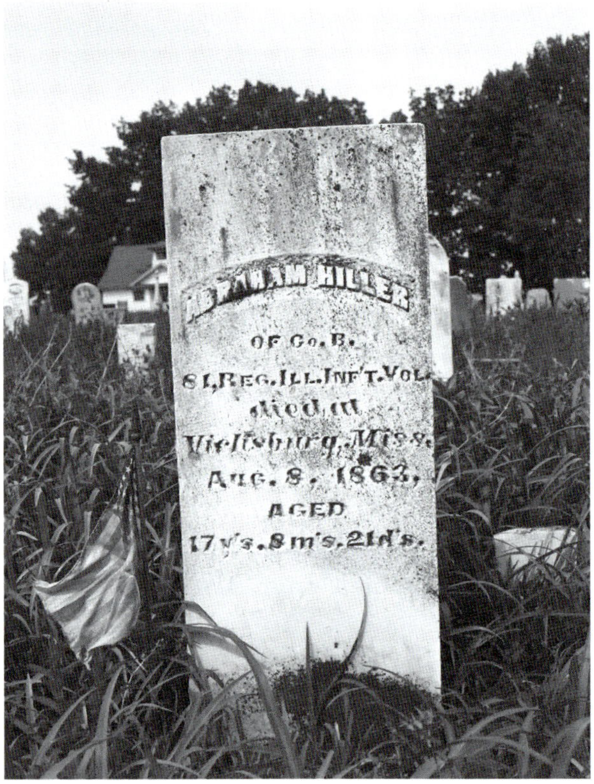

Southern Illinois' impulse for Memorial Day began on April 15, 1866, at Hiller Cemetery and adjacent Crab Orchard Christian Church with the decorating of graves, including that of Abraham Hiller, dead at Vicksburg at the age of seventeen years, eight months, and twenty-one days. West Pleasant Hill Road near Carbondale. John W. Allen Collection, Special Collections Research Center, Morris Library, Southern Illinois University Carbondale

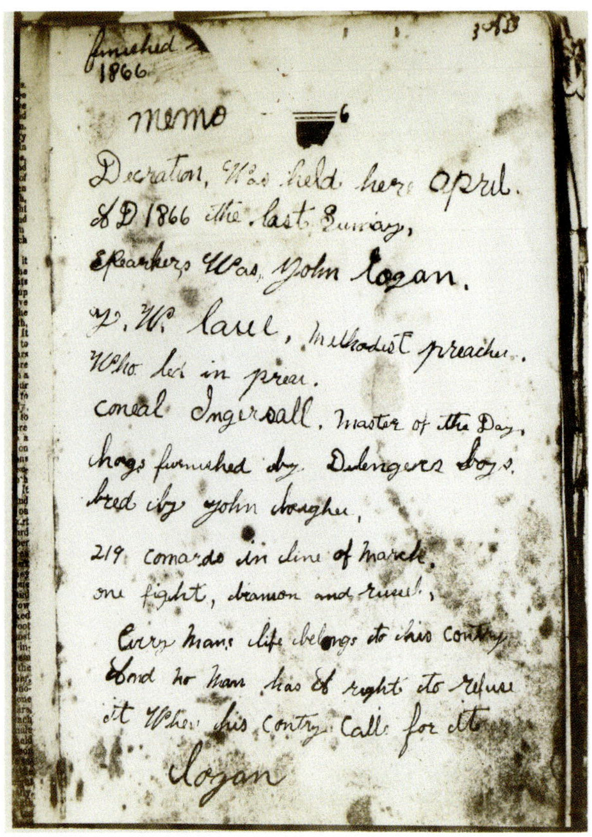

Memo
Decration, Was held here April.
A D 1866 the last Sunday,
Speaker,s Was John logan,
J. W. lane, Methodist preacher,
Who led in prear.
coneal Ingersall, Master of the Day,
hog,s furnished by Dilengers boys,
bred by John borgher,
219 comards in line of March,
one fight, branson and russel,
Every Man,s life belongs to his contry
And no Man has A right to refuse
it When his contry Calls for it
logan

Handwritten and transcribed note from 1866 Decoration Day. John W. Allen Collection, Special Collections Research Center, Morris Library, Southern Illinois University Carbondale

An early version of Memorial Day was held in Carbondale's Woodlawn Cemetery on April 29, 1866, in the course of which cemetery caretaker John Green used a blank leaf in a book to take notes, here shown at left with a transcription. The Rev. Lane offered a prayer, Colonel E. J. Ingersoll was master of ceremonies, and the Dillinger family provided hogs for a barbecue. Town baker John Borger furnished the bread, and John A. Logan reminded listeners that "every man's life belongs to his country." Line two's "Decration" shows the early name of the future national holiday, Decoration Day.

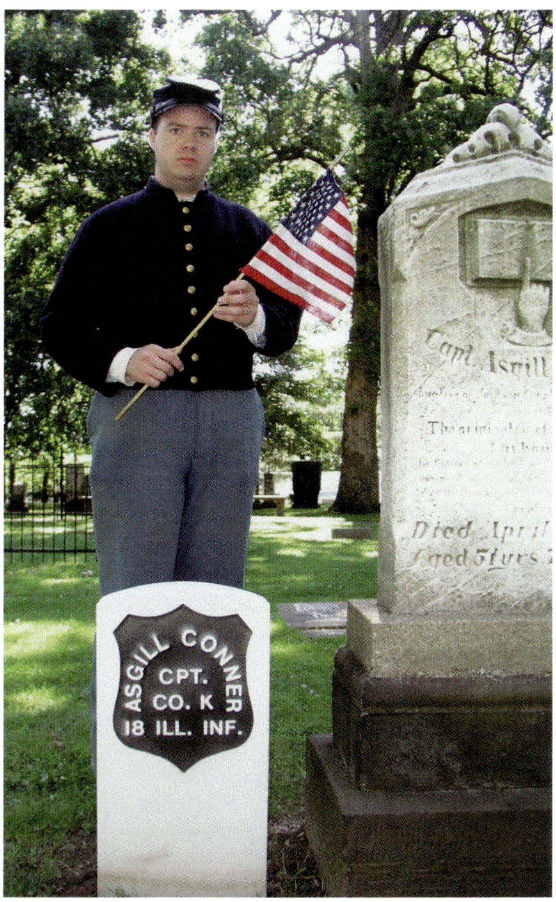

A reenactor stands by a Union soldier's grave in Carbondale's Woodlawn Cemetery, site of the first nationally organized Memorial Day. Photo courtesy of Shannon Woodworth

During the half century between the end of the Civil War in 1865 and the end of World War I in 1918, the railroads would lead Illinois into the future—and accentuate differences between Egypt and the rest of the state. Chicago's transportation, manufacturing, and banking capabilities made it a major city by 1880, and its boosters promoted it with nicknames such as "Boss City of the Universe," an example of the windy boasting that helped give Chicago its permanent nickname, "The Windy City." The new metropolis had an endless supply of jobs, promptly filled by immigrants, easterners, and midwestern villagers who wanted to see for themselves this miracle called "Chicago." The world's first skyscraper of ten stories appeared in Chicago, along with Millionaires' Row on Prairie Avenue, mansions on Lake Shore Drive, and that inevitable sign of wealth, local philanthropists importing foreign art. Prestigious suburbs such as Lake Forest, Hyde Park, and Kenilworth came into being while Oak Park and other

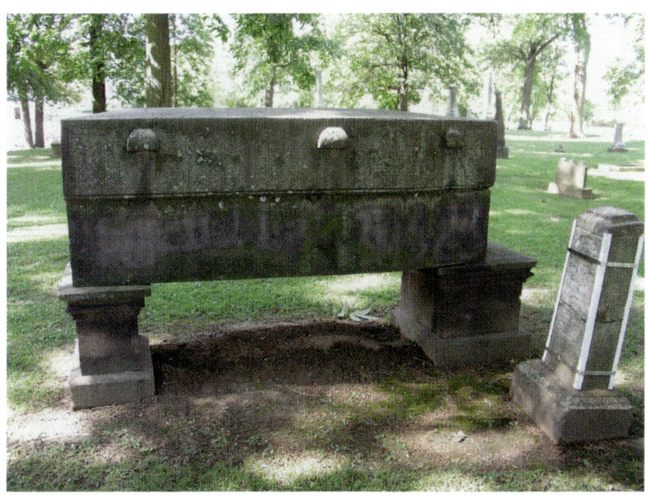

Above it all, a stone coffin thought to contain the remains of southern-born Mrs. J. W. Landrum reflects her wish not to be buried in northern soil. Woodlawn Cemetery, Carbondale. Photo courtesy of Shannon Woodworth

upscale suburbs served the slightly less affluent. Excursion steamers provided working families with a day on Lake Michigan and carried the middle and upper classes to summer homes in Michigan and Wisconsin. All of this happened in a very few years and produced enormous wealth that downstate Illinois would contribute to and share in.

The Illinois Central Railroad between Effingham and Chicago passed through the prairie of east central Illinois and towns such as Mattoon, Tuscola, Champaign, and Rantoul. These flatlands were the last of Illinois to be settled because of poor drainage, mosquitoes, biting flies, and a dark black soil so tangled with centuries of grass roots that it defeated all plows. In 1837 an eastern transplant named John Deere perfected a self-scouring steel plow that turned over the sod, but it was low technology gleaned from the prairies in Edwards County—the humble ditch—that made the prairies profitable: they had to be drained. When this was done in the decades following the Civil War, the central Illinois prairie became productive. Farmers grew mile after mile of wheat, oats, and corn; the corn was fed to cattle and hogs; and the livestock were shipped by train to Chicago where the great packing houses of Philip Armour, Gustavus Swift, and others processed the meat. Railroads then carried the beef and pork, now in cans, to the East and everywhere else. Chicago became the grain pricing center of the world and the nation's marketplace for livestock.

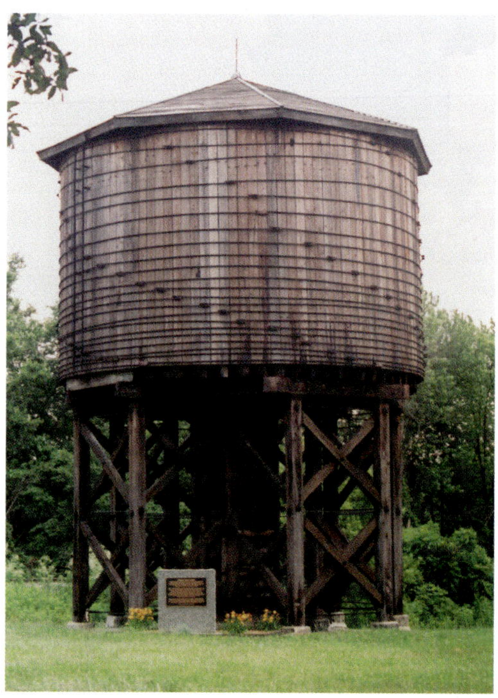

The power behind coal-fired locomotives was water—vast quantities of water heated to steam and released under pressure to turn the drive wheels. Trains made frequent stops to take on water from tanks such as this hundred-thousand-gallon tower that served the Illinois Central Railroad. Route 37 near Kinmundy. Photo by Herbert K. Russell

In Southern Illinois railroads opened up Egypt's interior in the 1870s, '80s, and later and created dozens of towns that still exist. Major railroads added spurs and branches, independent short lines came into existence, and plans for never-to-be built lines (such as the Golconda to Effingham route) emerged from roll-top desks. In 1889 the Illinois Central achieved a major engineering feat by bridging the Ohio River. Prior to this, trains bound for New Orleans had to stop at Cairo and be ferried across the Ohio a few cars at a time on "transfer steamers." By the 1900s railroads wound across much of Egypt like grapevines through a forest.

Towns that were bypassed by railroads usually lost population, and some communities moved their town and town name to the railroad, as did Du Quoin, Mulkeytown, Marissa, Bone Gap, and Stonefort. People who stayed behind soon discovered that their place of habitation had acquired a different name—*Old* Du Quoin, *Old* Mulkeytown, *Old* Marissa, *Old* Bone Gap, *Old* Stonefort. Oblivion followed many of these towns, its signature written in the broken bricks and out-of-place daffodils where houses and stores once stood.

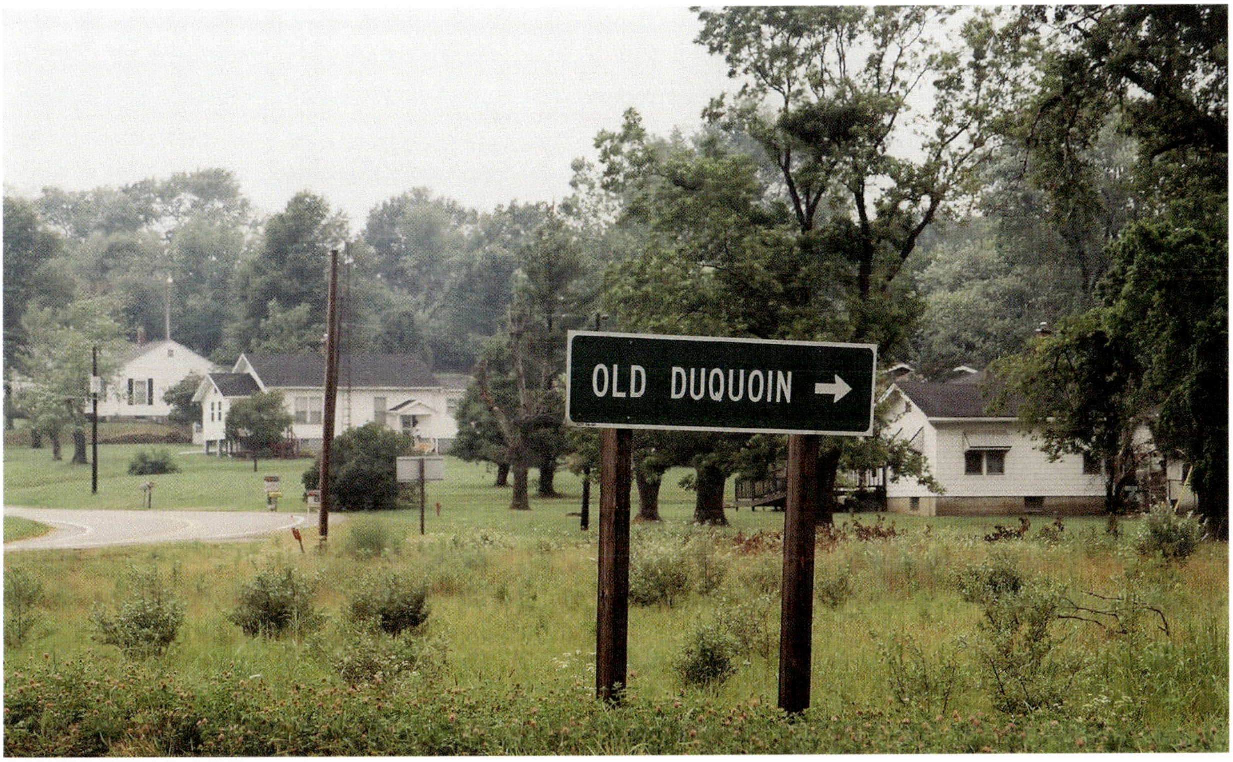

Many towns died when bypassed by railroads, but some residents of Old Du Quoin stayed where they were, and the town remains. Photo by Herbert K. Russell

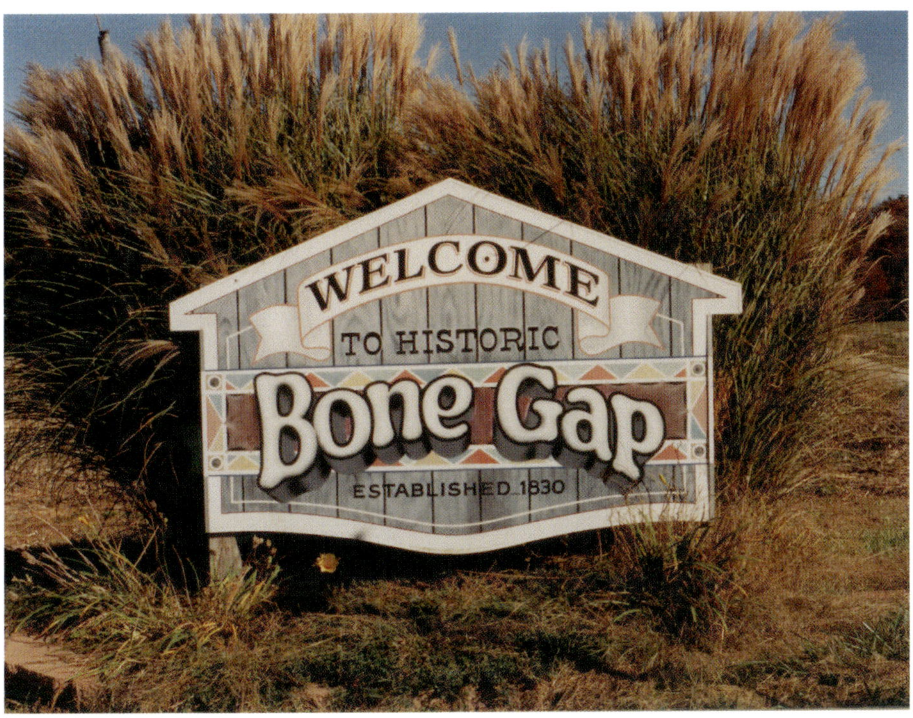

The flatlands near Bone Gap were among the first Illinois prairies to be farmed and helped bring a railroad to the town. Edwards County. Photo by Herbert K. Russell

East-west railroads strove to be the first to connect an Ohio River city with a town on the Mississippi, an ambition reflected in the name of the first rail line to do so, the Ohio and Mississippi. Better known by its successor name, the Baltimore and Ohio, the B&O came out of Vincennes in 1854 through or near Lawrenceville, Olney, Flora, Salem, and Carlyle and created railroad junction towns such as Sandoval and Odin. In the 1880s the Louisville, Evansville, and St. Louis (LE&SL) provided rail service through Mt. Vernon, which attracted a maker of railroad cars and wheels. At its peak in the 1920s the plant employed 2,300 workers and was said to be the nation's largest builder of railroad freight cars. For several years many Southern Illinois railroads were funneled into Cairo, which had at least seven railroads in the heyday of coal-fired locomotives. But it was Centralia that became known as Egypt's dominant railroad town. By 1925 thirty passenger trains per day and endless freights rumbled through Centralia's immense switching yards and created hundreds of jobs. Carbondale enjoyed a similar rail-related prosperity in its busy yards, as did Mounds for several years.

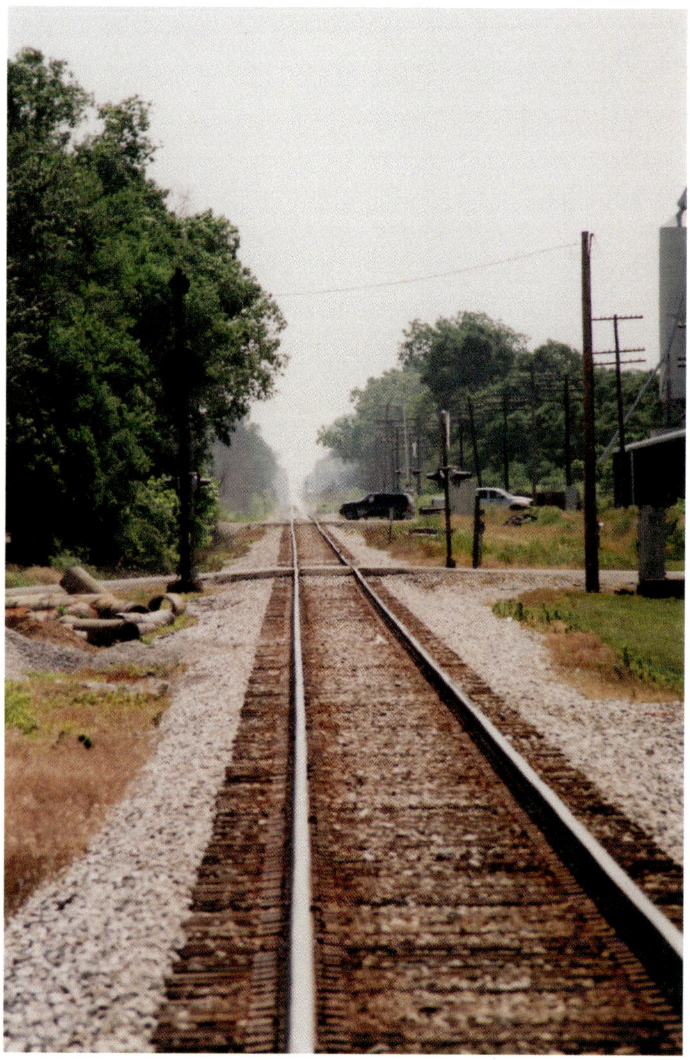

During the 1850s Southern Illinois' busiest railroad junction was at Sandoval near Salem where the east-west tracks of the Ohio and Mississippi, above, crossed the north-south tracks of the Illinois Central. During Civil War times, the O&M tracks marked an informal boundary between Egypt and the rest of Illinois. Photo by Herbert K. Russell

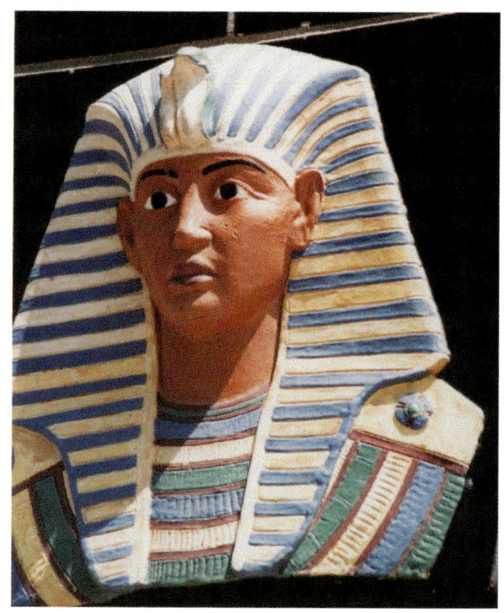

An unblinking pharaoh on the Centralia Sentinel building watches over the railroad town that called itself "The Gateway to Egypt." Photo by Herbert K. Russell

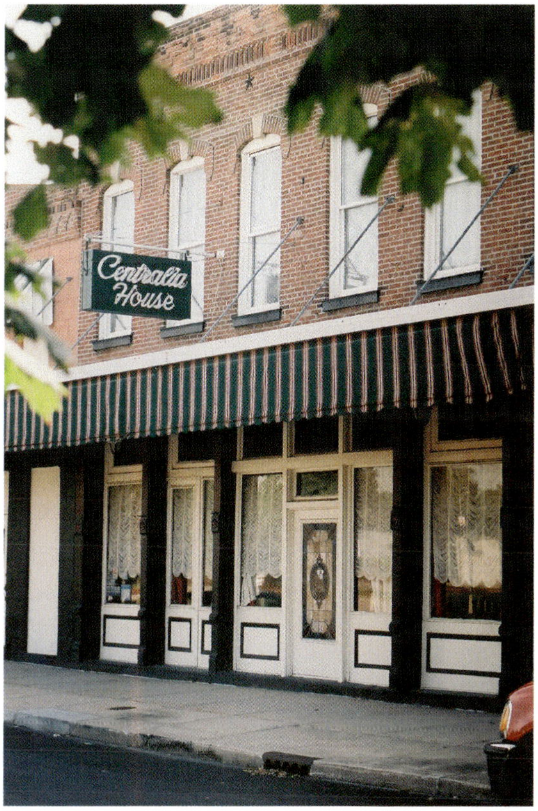

The Centralia House is a popular place to dine in the town created by the Illinois Central Railroad. Photo by Herbert K. Russell

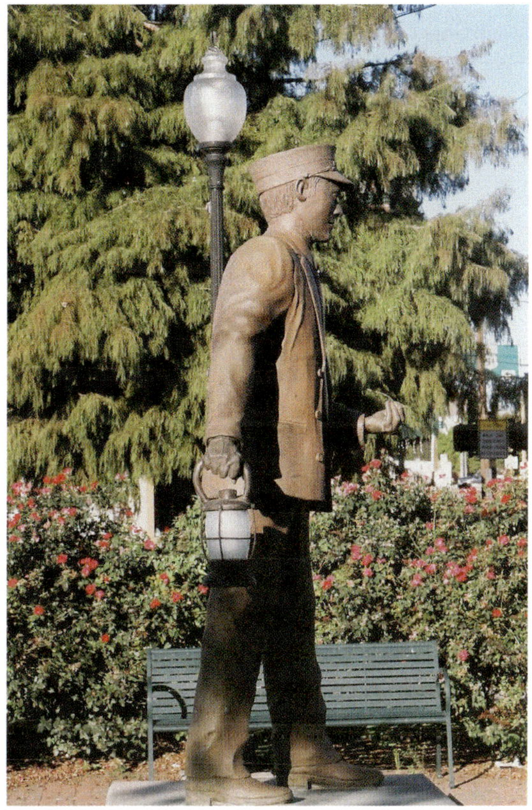

Carbondale's memorial to railroaders shows a conductor near the nerve center of the town's once-extensive rail operations. Photo by Herbert K. Russell

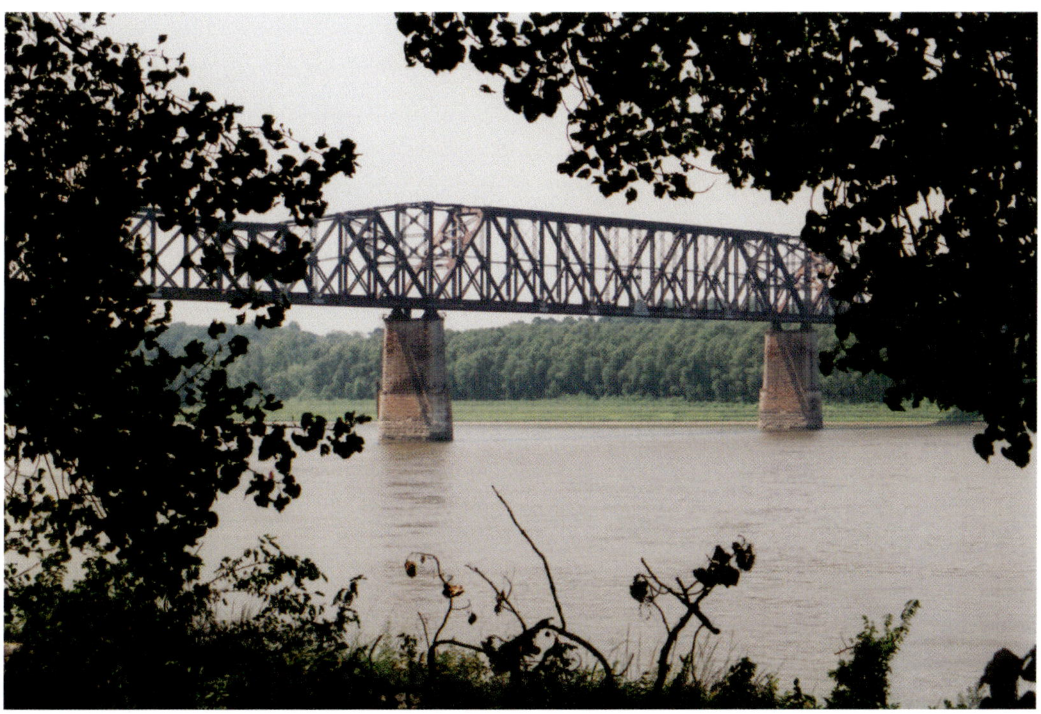

This 1904 railroad bridge over the Mississippi at Thebes increased Egypt's rail connections while decreasing its dependency on steamboats—which hastened the decline of river towns such as Cairo, Grand Tower, Chester, and Thebes itself. Alexander County. Photo by Herbert K. Russell

As rail lines expanded, a few farmers continued to raise cotton, usually marketed at Carbondale on the mainline of the IC, but most raised the turn-of-the-century favorites: corn, oats, grass, hay, and wheat—in that order of importance. (The versatile soybean was introduced between 1910 and '20 but would not become popular until the '40s.) Clover was used to "sweeten" Egypt's "sour," acidic soils, as was ground limestone, introduced in the 1920s and '30s when it was broadcast with shovels from wagons. Southern Illinoisans grew a good deal of tobacco, much of it marketed at Galatia and Raleigh, with smaller amounts in Marion. Herefords, Angus, and Shorthorns were the best beef animals, Guernseys, Jerseys, and Holsteins the favored dairy breeds. Egypt relied more on mules than did the rest of Illinois—they were the animal of choice for logging, coal mines, and some orchards—and popular mule markets came into existence at Anna, Enfield, East St. Louis, and elsewhere. Some families raised cane sorghum for sweet-tasting molasses, along with "goobers" or peanuts, and many women raised poultry, the fast food of its day.

The railroads and towns created a new type of Southern Illinois community, the sawmill settlement that turned trees into lumber. Railways always needed wooden ties and strong bridge timbers of oak and hickory. The development of underground coal mining created a need for roof supports, and numerous "prop and tie" mills came into being. Chicago relied on cypress for wooden pilings to pull itself out of the mud of the ancient lake on which it was built, and after the Great Chicago Fire of 1871, the city needed all types of lumber. During the next fifty years, sawmill settlements sprang up all over Egypt, and while a few remained viable communities into the 1950s and beyond, most died out when the trees were gone. The name of *Stumptown* near Karnak suggests both its chief activity and the reason for its disappearance.

The sawmill settlements of Delta in Alexander County (Cairo) and Aden in Hamilton County (McLeansboro) may have been typical. Delta was said to have had sawmills making railroad ties, pilings, and other lumber as well as a box factory. Aden reportedly had two sawmills fed by a lumber camp in the creek bottoms. A sawmill town might also make picket fences, shingles, spokes for wheels, tool handles, veneer, lath (vital for plastering), or furniture in addition to enjoying a store or two and a post office. Metropolis made a variety of wood products, including boats, while Chester, Grayville, and many other towns made barrel staves, always popular since a barrel usually required only one person to roll it to its appointed place.

Railroads also boosted Egypt's rock and quarry industries. Heavy limestone was used to surround culverts and to stabilize railroad beds and bridge approaches, and rock was occasionally passed through grinders and used to surface streets in towns. Some Southern Illinois stone took the train out of Egypt and became building foundations and facades elsewhere, but much was used locally. Sandstone from the Jackson County hamlet of Boskydell probably provided stone for SIU's first Old Main building.

Southern Illinois also enjoyed clays suitable for making pottery, including kaolin, a white clay valued by potters for its glazing properties. Union County's Mountain Glen and the vanished village of Kaolin prospered for several decades as the clay was

Older than the United States, this massive tree on the Stokes farm near Lick Creek survived the age of sawmill settlements to become the largest bur oak in Illinois. Union County. Photo by Steve Jahnke; courtesy of the *Southern Illinoisan*

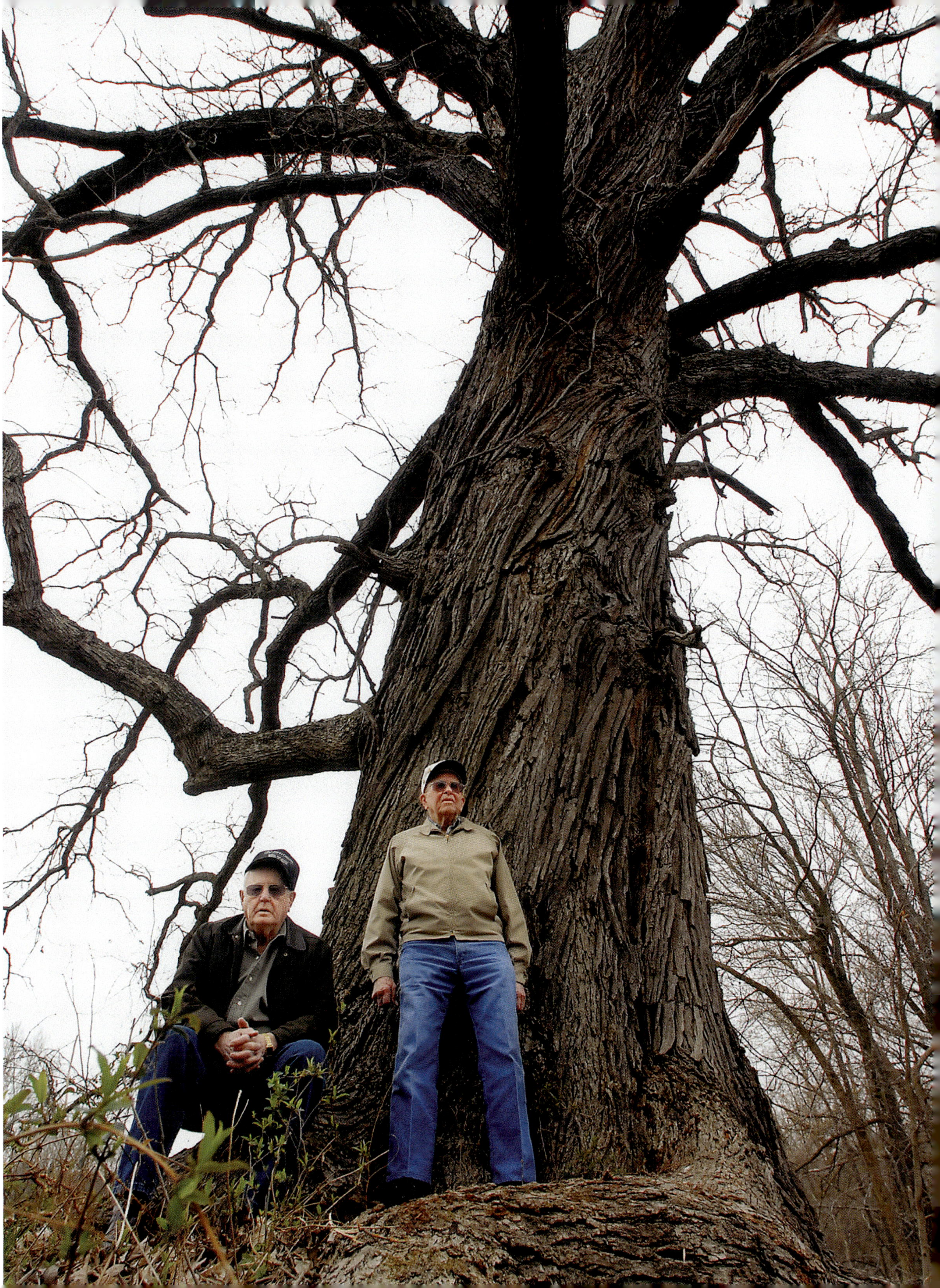

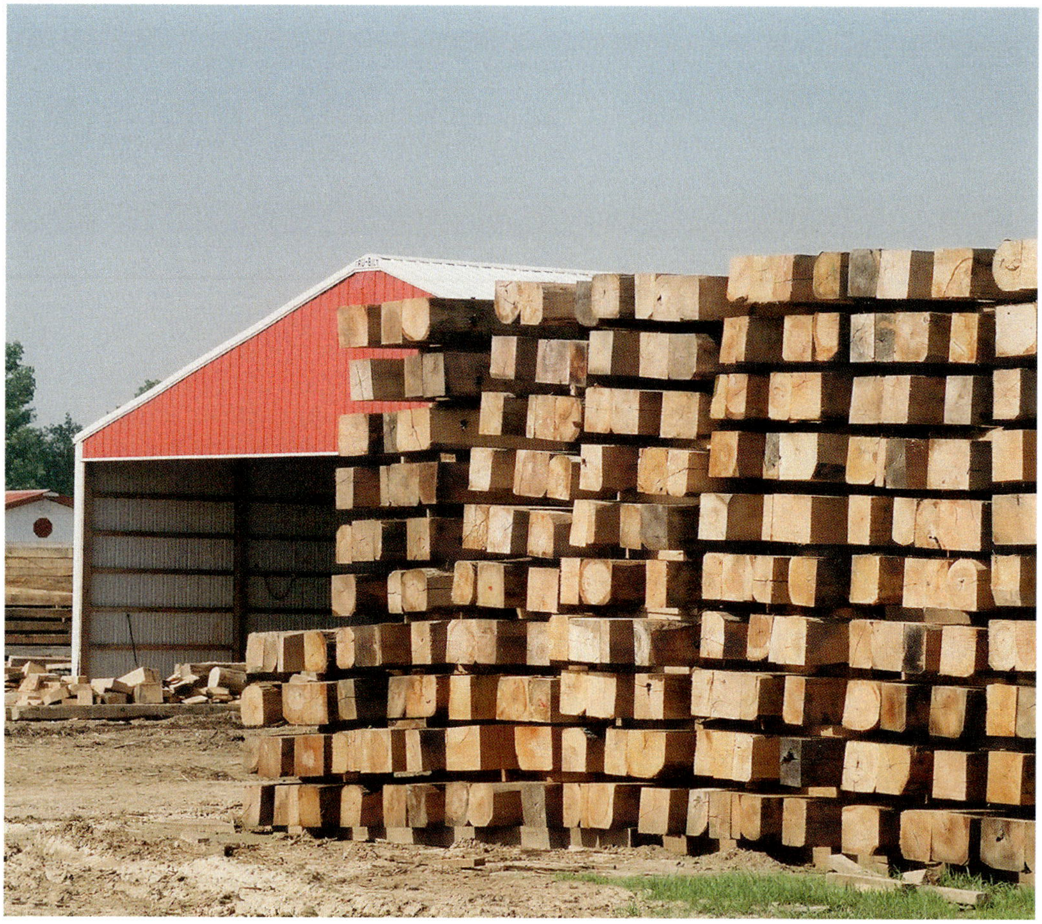

Squared away, construction timbers await shipment to job sites. Route 4 near Oraville and Ava. Photo by Herbert K. Russell

dug, processed, and shipped. The Kirkpatrick brothers' Anna Pottery relied on kaolin and achieved a niche in the folk arts with attractive, humorous, and popular creations whisked out of town to local and distant buyers on the Illinois Central.

Railroads were especially compatible with Chicago's need for fresh fruits and vegetables and Southern Illinois' early and extended growing season. Cobden's Parker Earle, a native of Vermont, experimented with fruit trees and developed a shipping mechanism that benefited everyone, the refrigerated railroad car. The city soon developed an immense appetite for Egypt's apples, peaches, and pears and could never get enough fresh strawberries from Massac and Pulaski Counties—or blackberries, blueberries, raspberries, and muskmelons from truck patches in Anna, Balcom, and Alto Pass. Cobden was known for shipping tomatoes, New Burnside for early apples, and fruit belts grew up along the tracks near Centralia and Mt. Vernon. In Makanda produce-filled wagons pulled by horses lined up by the dozens as their loads were placed on trains and sent north. Rhubarb, asparagus, and watermelons were among the crops that could be picked in Cairo or Mounds one day and arrive in

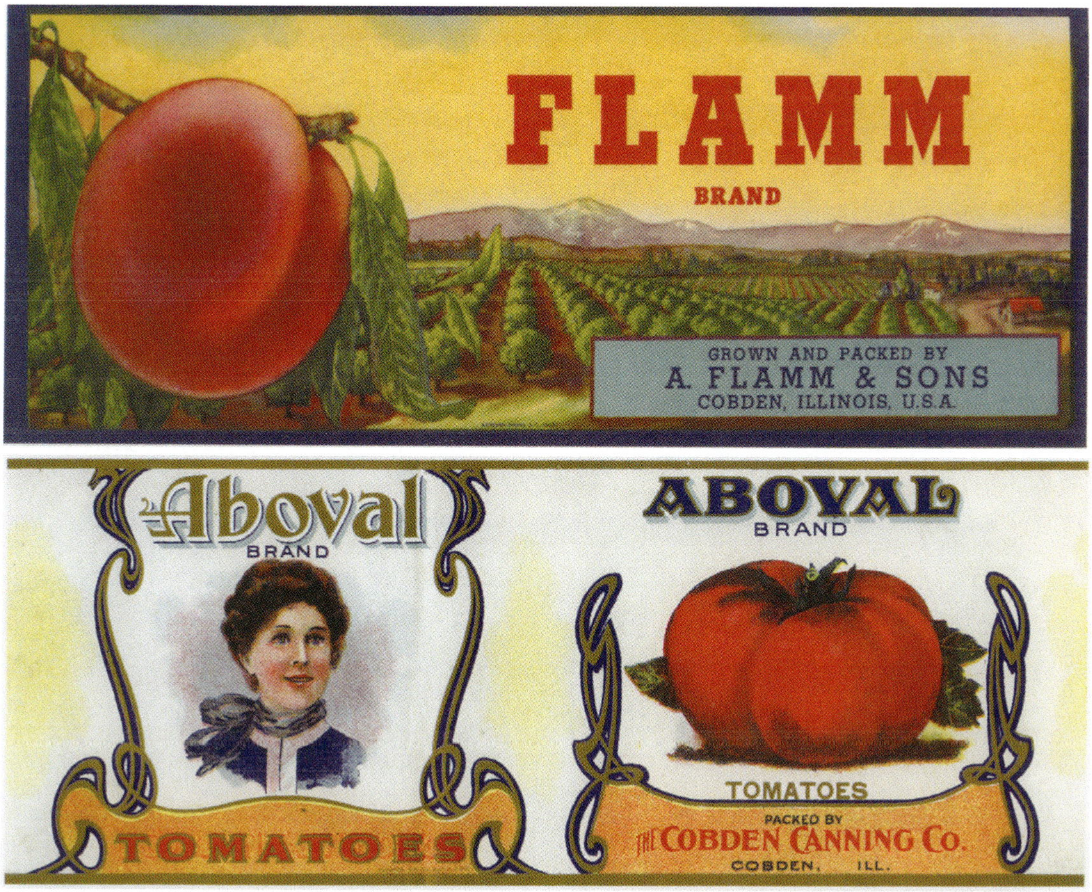

The artist for Flamm's early shipping labels placed the orchard in a California-like valley and capped the Shawnee Hills with summer snow. The Aboval name left no doubt where it stood among competitors. Courtesy of the Union County Historical and Genealogy Society

good condition in Chicago, Indianapolis, or Cleveland hours or days later. Railway refrigeration made it possible.

Changing seasons slowed down but did not stop this exodus. Potatoes could be sold or stored until the price was right, and tardy fall frosts sometimes allowed for late gardens. In winter, market hunters fanned out in Egyptian fields and bottoms, and frozen rabbits and birds also made their way north, as did dried pelts of raccoons, muskrats, foxes, and an occasional mink. Sawmill settlements and box-and-basket mills supplied the shipping containers: white oak made the best barrel staves, hickory the hoops to hold the staves together; willow was good for crates, and ash and tulip tree for boxes. Other trees were adapted as needed.

Any town on a railroad might open a fruit or vegetable canning factory, as did Alma and Sandoval near Salem, or any other kind of processing and manufacturing plant relying on local produce. Some products left on "milk trains," legendary for their slowness, the result of stopping at every one-horse hamlet to pick up cans of milk for urban "creameries." These local industries provided jobs for producers, laborers, haulers, and freight handlers, and all of Southern Illinois benefited from the railroads (the city would

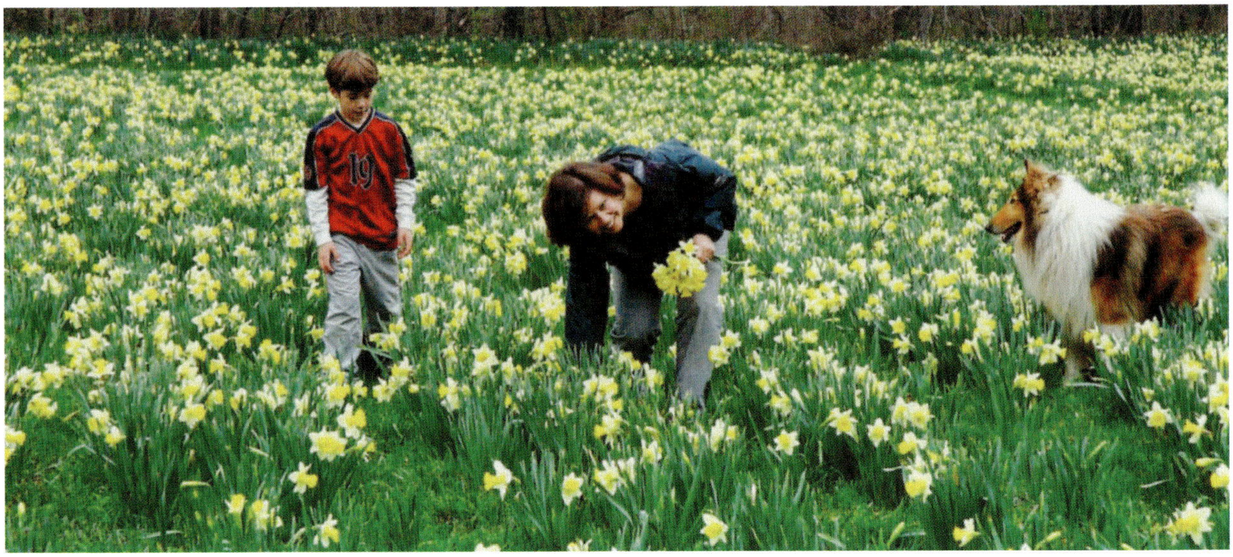

Acres and acres of daffodils renew themselves each year on this former flower farm in Union County. Photo by Chuck Novara; courtesy of the *Southern Illinoisan*

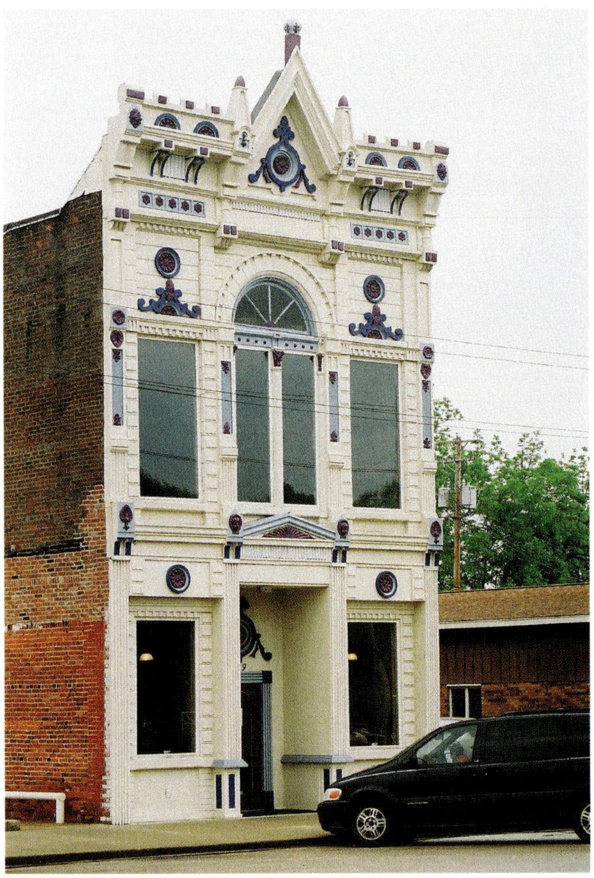

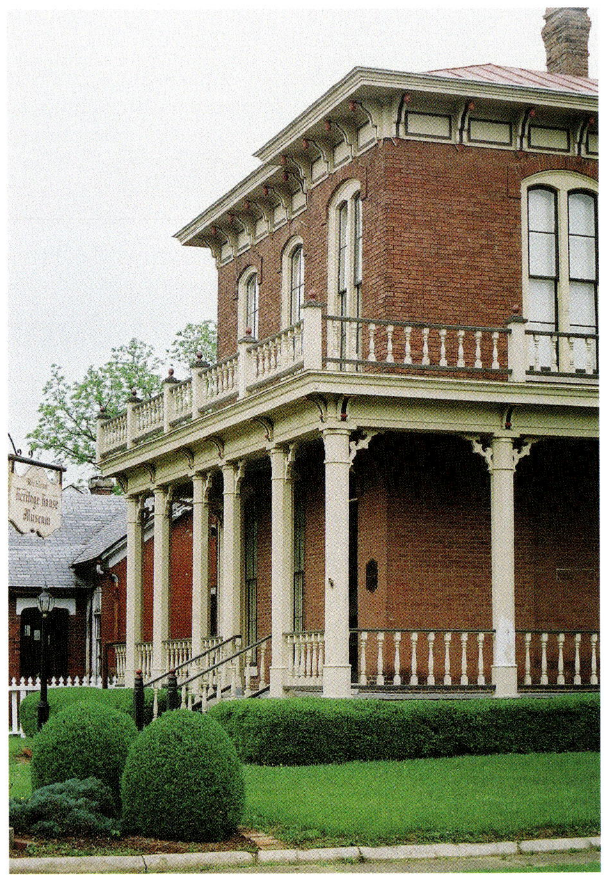

Railroads made Southern Illinois' buildings more attractive by bringing in metal facades similar to this blue and white storefront in Olney (*left*), as well as "gingerbread"—showy trim appearing as railings and column and roof supports on the nearby Heritage House Museum (*right*). Photos by Herbert K. Russell

even buy feathers and flowers), and Egypt's little towns flourished.

It was during the heyday of railroads that the Illinois towns across the river from St. Louis became more industrialized and metropolitan, anticipating their later designation as "the Metro East Area." Belleville, Edwardsville, Granite City, Wood River, and other towns provided employment in industries ranging from iron and steel to glass making, meat packing, and brewing. Because building bridges over the Mississippi was a slow task, and because St. Louis' downtown was already crowded against the river, the railroads—two dozen of them—converged on East St. Louis, which became the grimy, prosperous, industrial hub of the area. Southern Illinois' meat, milk, eggs, and produce helped feed the people; Southern Illinois coal addressed their energy needs.

Improved transportation also facilitated learning, and several towns on the Illinois Central Railroad opened educational institutions. A few miles south of Centralia, the state's first agricultural school, the Illinois Agricultural College, was chartered at Irvington in 1861; it survived through 1879. The more enduring Du Quoin Female Seminary opened for young ladies in 1855, and Carbondale made a false start with a college in 1861. The 1854 arrival of the Ohio and the Mississippi helped win a charter for the Southern Illinois Female College in Salem and made recruitment easier at McKendree College, founded in Lebanon in 1828. The LE&SL delivered students to the Southern Collegiate Institute in Albion, and several railroads augmented attendance at Shurtleff College in Alton. Some of the many other institutions benefiting from nearby railways included Ewing College, the Marissa

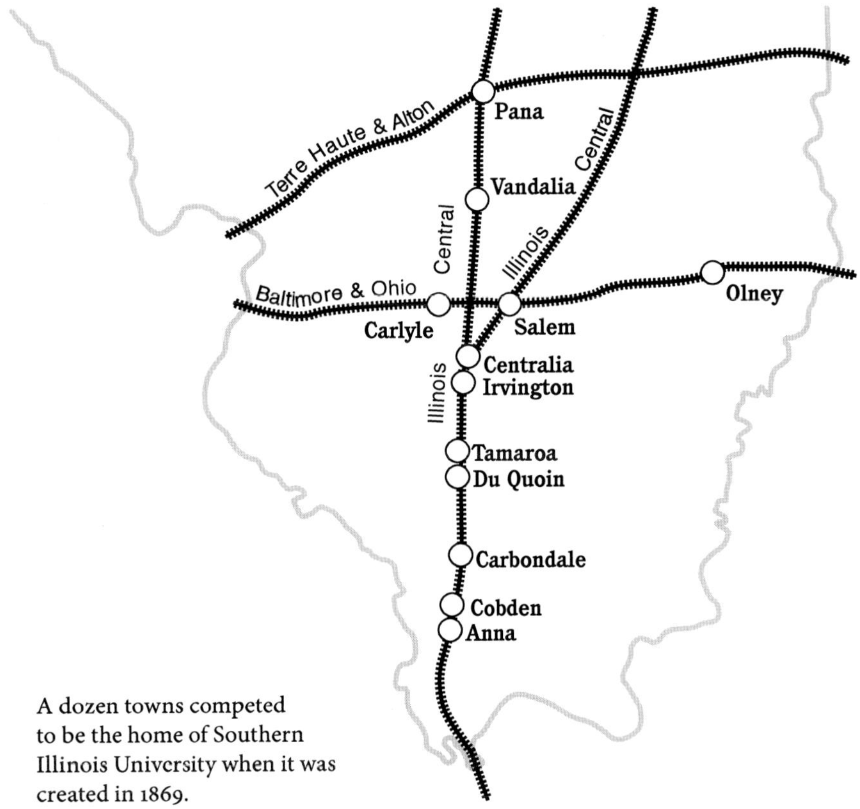

A dozen towns competed to be the home of Southern Illinois University when it was created in 1869.

Academy, and Creal Springs Seminary, all named for local towns, Hamilton College in McLeansboro, Orchard City College at Flora, Hayward College in Fairfield, and Union Academy at Jonesboro. The development of tax-supported high schools put most of the academies, seminaries, and colleges out of business, and only McKendree survived to become a university.

But no school reaped greater benefits from the railroads than did SIU, first called Southern Illinois Normal University. (It was titled a "university" even when it was only a small teachers college, or "normal," imparting educational "norms" and standards.) Planners believed the new school should be on a railroad, and in 1869 a dozen towns competed to be its home. Pana was too far north, but other towns were more acceptable. Carlyle,

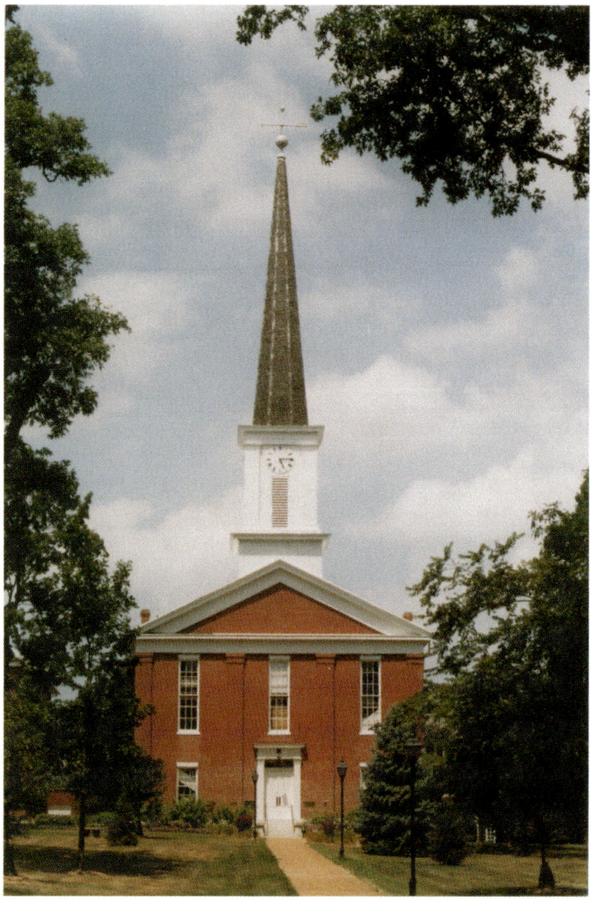

Bothwell Chapel at McKendree University in Lebanon. Founded by Methodists in 1828, the school was sited near the state's busiest east-west trail, now U.S. Route 50. Photo by Herbert K. Russell

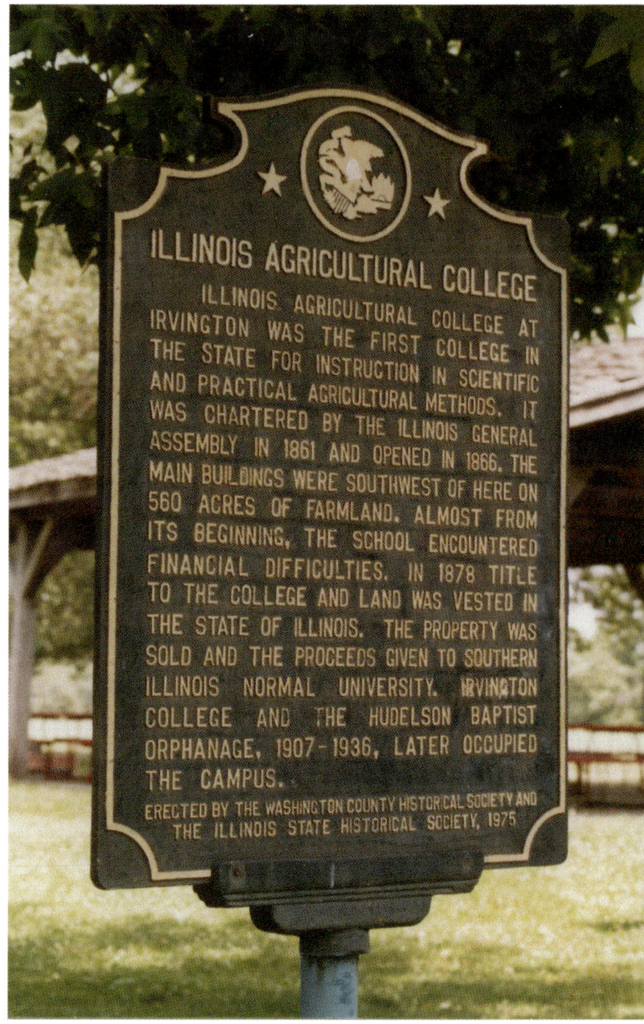

Only a sign remains of Illinois' first agricultural college at Irvington in Washington County. Photo by Herbert K. Russell

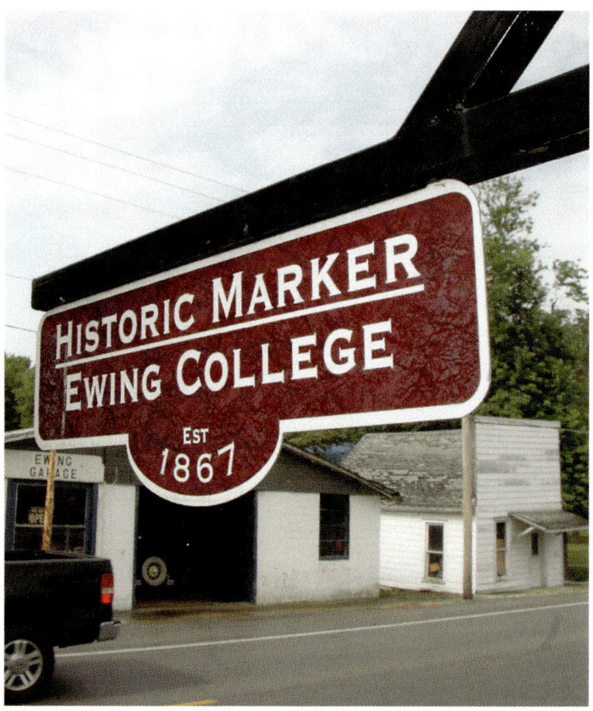

Ewing College in Franklin County was founded by Baptists and is marked by signage and other memorials. Photo courtesy of Shannon Woodworth

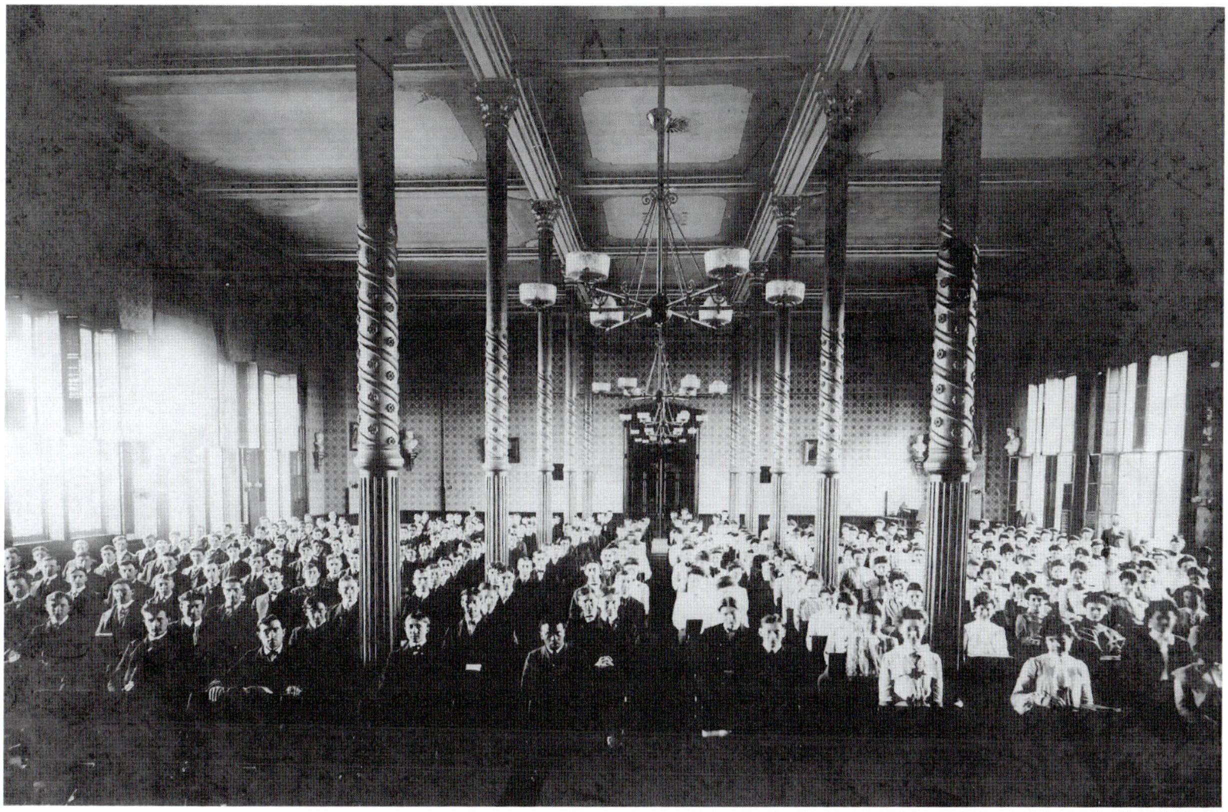

Through the second decade of the twentieth century, Southern Illinois University could seat most of its students in the assembly hall of its Old Main building. Photo courtesy of the University Museum, Southern Illinois University Carbondale

Salem, and Olney were on the B&O, and the IC passed through Vandalia, Centralia, Irvington, Tamaroa, Du Quoin, Carbondale, Cobden, and Anna. After Carbondale was selected, university trustees purchased Mrs. Sanders' twenty-acre farm one-half mile south of the depot, and the building known as the first Old Main was built on the hillock where her strawberry patch had been. By 1874 SINU was in business.

The railroads also helped shape downstate Illinois' leisure hours. A favorite recreation of those who did not live near the tracks was to visit a railroad town, watch the big engine chuff in, wave at the engineer and fireman, and hitch a dangerous ride on the cars when the train slowed for a curve. In some cemeteries it is still possible to read the last line on the tombstone of a long-gone, adventurous boy "killed by the cars." Depots became social centers, a place for a spit-and-whittle club of elderly men and town idlers to congregate and talk.

The resulting new commerce and ease of transportation helped many Southern Illinoisans enjoy recreations beyond their home counties for the first time. A favorite outing in the 1890s was to take the family on an excursion train to Jackson County's

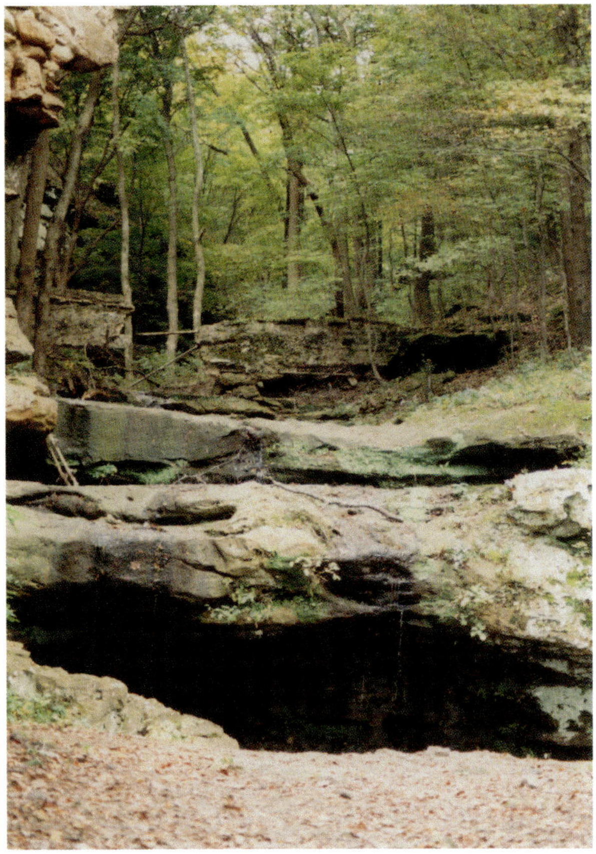

The craggy beauty of Fountain Bluff attracted excursion trains in the 1890s. Jackson County near Gorham. Photo by Herbert K. Russell

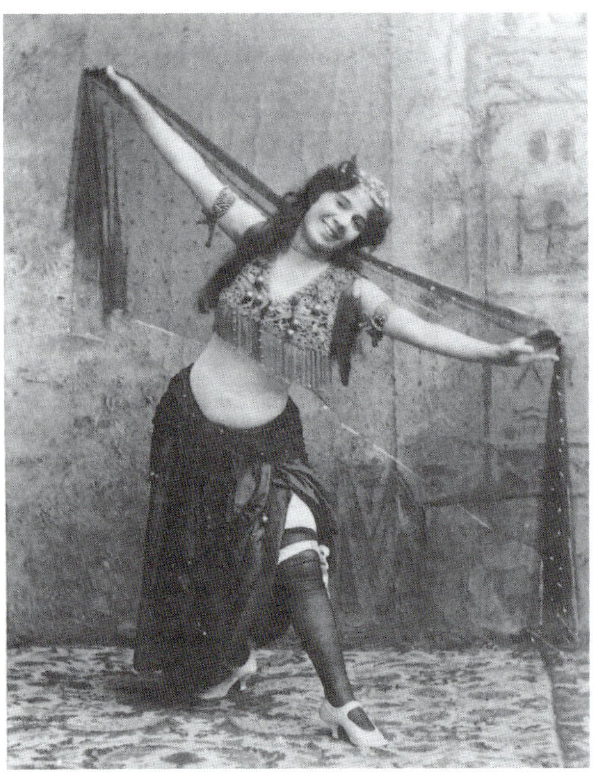

The name "Little Egypt" was popularized after dancer Ashea Wabe performed under that name for a New York City "gentleman's club" in 1896. Contrary to popular myth, no dancer performed under the name "Little Egypt" at the 1893 Chicago World's Fair.

beautiful Fountain Bluff near the Mississippi. Baskets of fried chicken would appease the appetite, the dreamy haze of Buttermilk Hill and the river would tease the eye, and the train would take everyone home, all in a day. Other excursion trains went to mineral springs and spas at Creal Springs, Dixon Springs, and Okawville, whose healthful waters when bathed in or ingested were thought to alleviate ailments such as arthritis and rheumatism. In 1893 all the trains headed north to the Chicago World's Fair to commemorate the discovery of America four centuries earlier. It was here too, folklore says, that a belly dancer named "*Little* Egypt" performed so sensationally as to dance her way into Southern Illinois geography—and confuse Egypt's first nickname for the next hundred years and counting.

This story does not, however, happen to be true. The real Little Egypt—her name was Ashea Wabe—did not dance in Chicago but was performing for a New York "gentleman's club" in 1896 when the newspapers got wind of an indecent dance, sensationalized her story, and made the name "Little Egypt" famous from coast to coast. Many years later, after Ashea Wabe had died, a woman in her sixties claimed at Chicago's centennial world's fair in 1933 that she had been known as Little Egypt at the 1893 fair. This woman, Fahreda Mahzar (one of several spellings), had indeed danced at the 1893 fair but had done so under the stage name of "Fatima." Nevertheless, Mahzar's claim and her appearance at Chicago's 1933 fair caused enough confusion to mislead newspaper and magazine editors, who repeated her story as truth. In fact, no woman danced under the name "Little Egypt" at the 1893 fair, as the fair's midway director himself said.

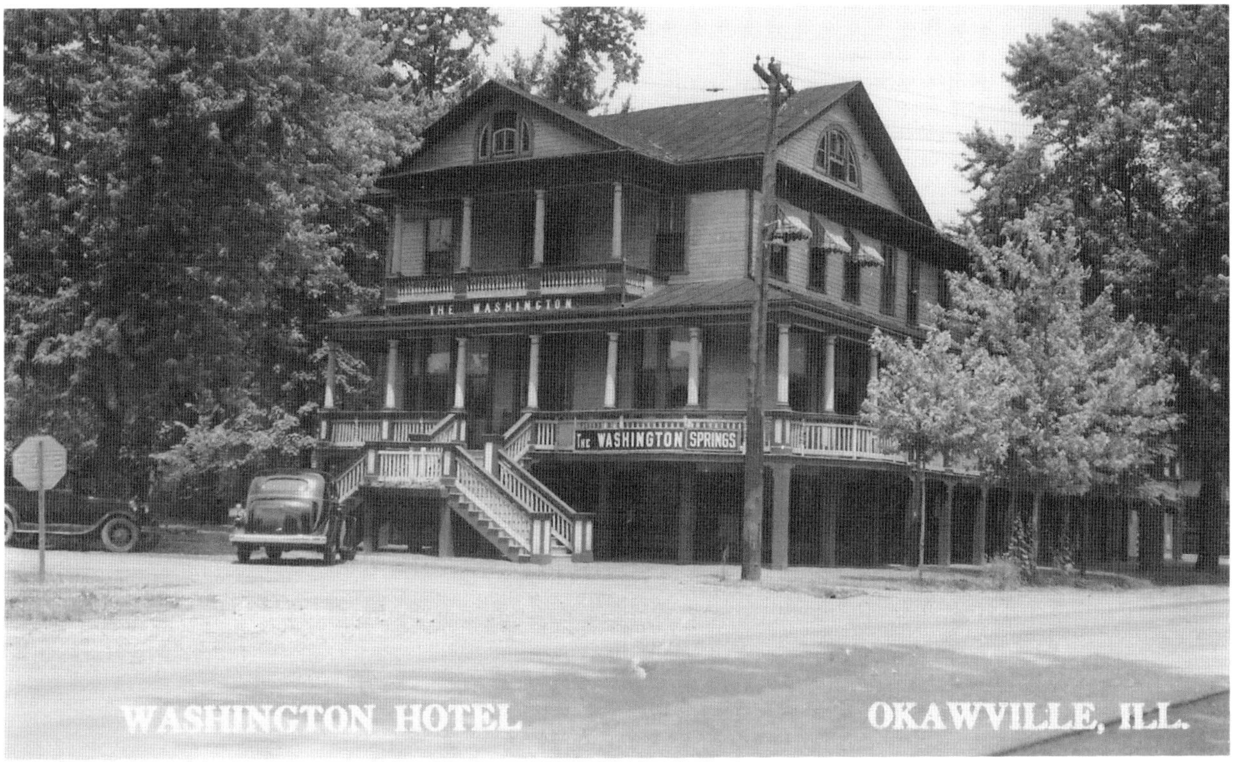

Favorite destinations of excursion trains included spas and health resorts where "grand" hotels and mineral-laden spring waters awaited travelers, here at Okawville in the 1930s. Washington County. John W. Allen Collection, Special Collections Research Center, Morris Library, Southern Illinois University Carbondale

In addition to city-made kitchen ware, stained glass windows, and faster mail service, railroads also brought city ways and words to the country. In plain-spoken Old Shawneetown (where several railroad dreams began and ended), the cemetery known for years as Joe Street's Burying Ground was rechristened *Westwood*. Other Egyptian names and places also came under urban scrutiny. Northern Illinoisans down for the summer on the train ("Is it always this hot here?") wondered why Egyptians did not give their little towns suburban-sounding names. Some said they would never live in a place named *Muddy*, *Clank*, or *Frogtown*. Of course urban values and lifestyles mattered not at all to most Southern Illinoisans, who liked the region's rural ways and small towns just as they were—an attitude that prevails to the present day.

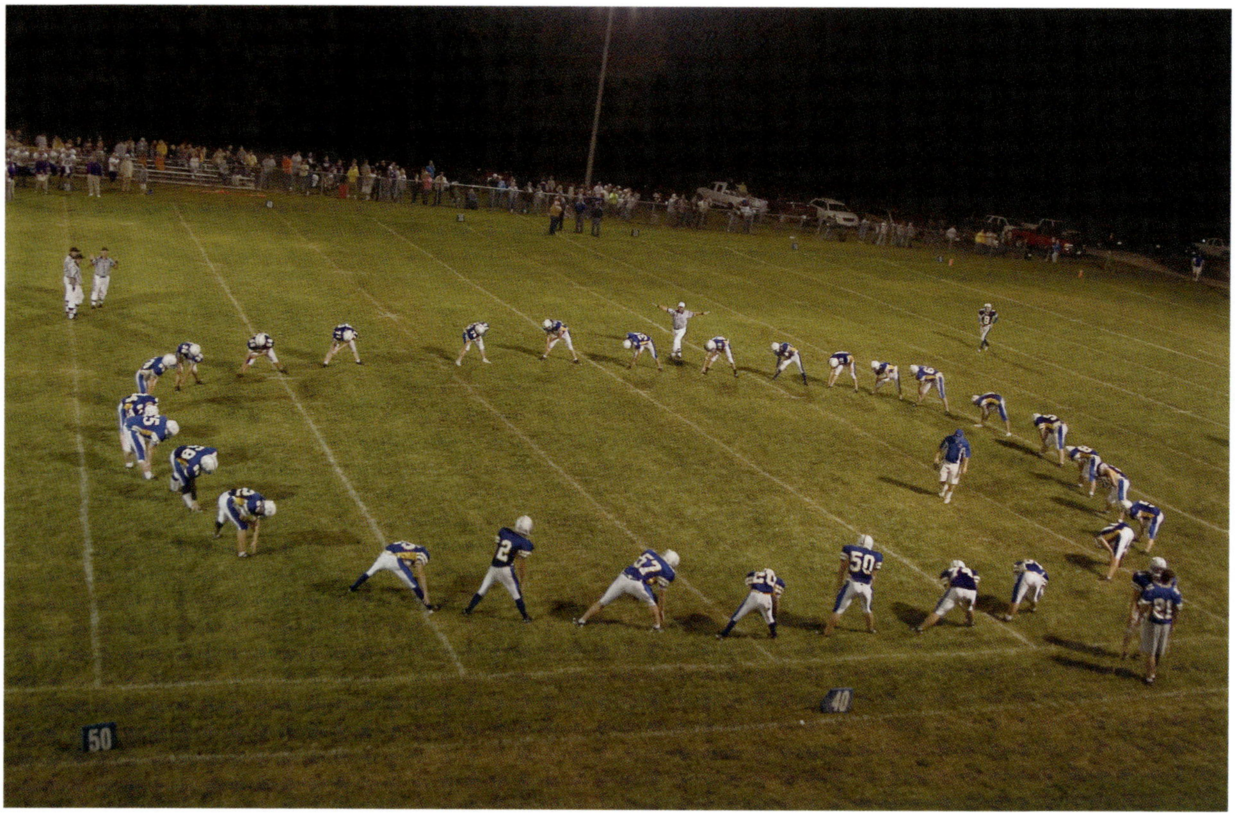

The football Falcons of Elverado. Tiny Elkville, Vergennes, and Dowell consolidated their village names and resources to create Elverado High School—and maintain a small-school atmosphere. Photo courtesy of Andrew Crook

During the 1850s officials with the Illinois Central Railroad observed that forests might someday be depleted and began experimenting with Du Quoin area coal as fuel for its steam locomotives. This experiment conducted in Centralia was successful, and within a few years railroads themselves became the largest consumers of coal. Southern Illinois' soft (or bituminous) coal also became a favorite for home heating, and after the first train nosed into coal-rich Franklin County in 1879, it made mining the dominant image of Egypt for most of the next century.

What set Southern Illinois coal apart was numbers—the number of mines and miners, the record tonnage they "hoisted," the number of railroads that hauled coal (principally to St. Louis and Chicago), the number of small towns that depended on coal for their livelihood, and the heat generated by this high-energy fuel. Moreover, Southern Illinois coal was relatively close to the surface, much of it in veins so tall and flat that a man could stand upright, a luxury to those who had worked in Kentucky's thirty-two-inch coal or in Pennsylvania's tilted seams. And Egypt's coal was incredibly abundant. Illinois enjoys the largest bituminous coal reserves in the nation, and Southern Illinois is especially rich: parts of the Herrin Seam are fourteen feet thick, although a more average thickness ranges from six to ten feet. Pleasantly surprised, coal companies hired experienced mine superintendents from Britain, recruited laborers from as far away as Europe, and settled in for some big-time mining.

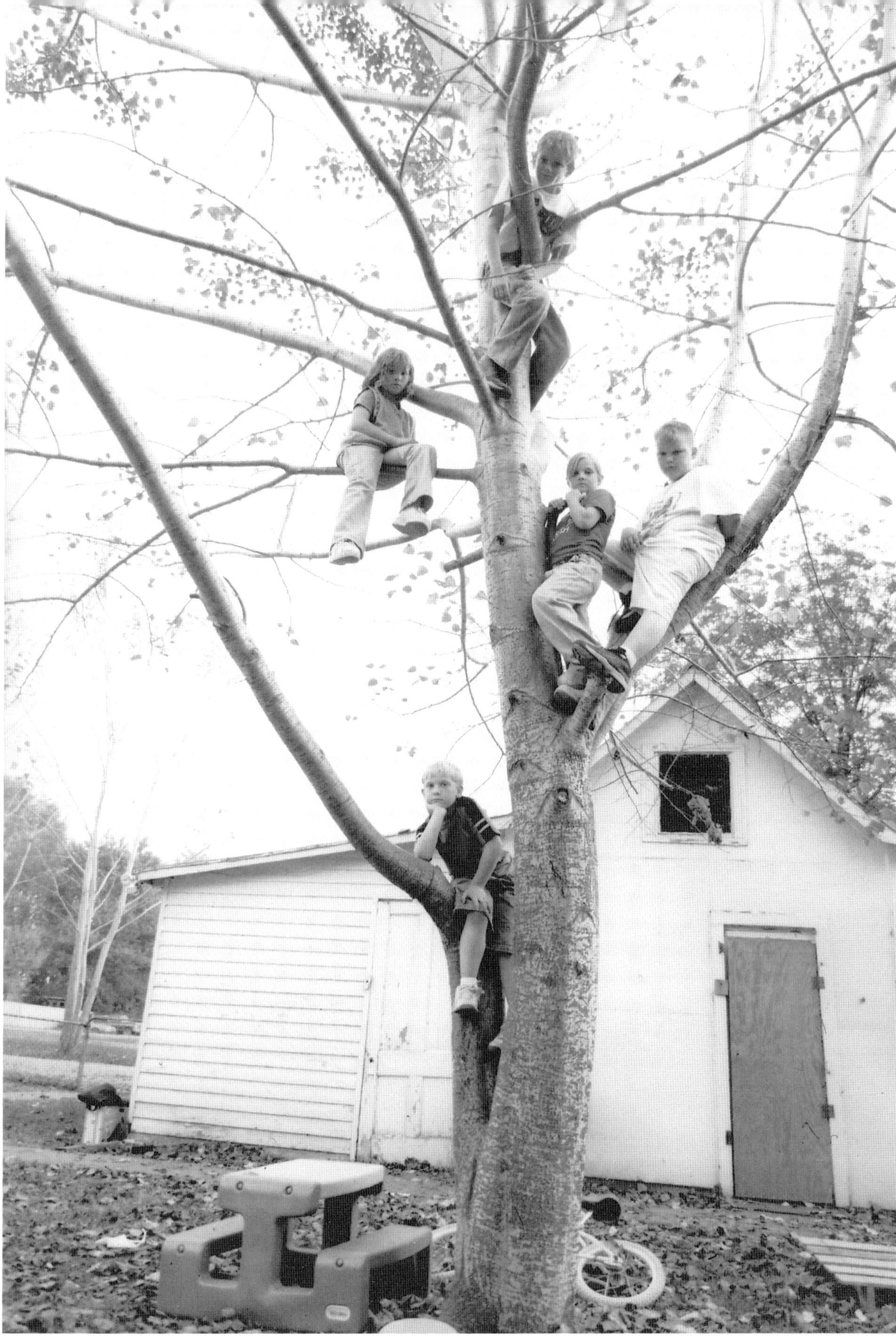

Tree-climbing youngsters in Ware, Route 146 near Jonesboro. Photo courtesy of Adam May

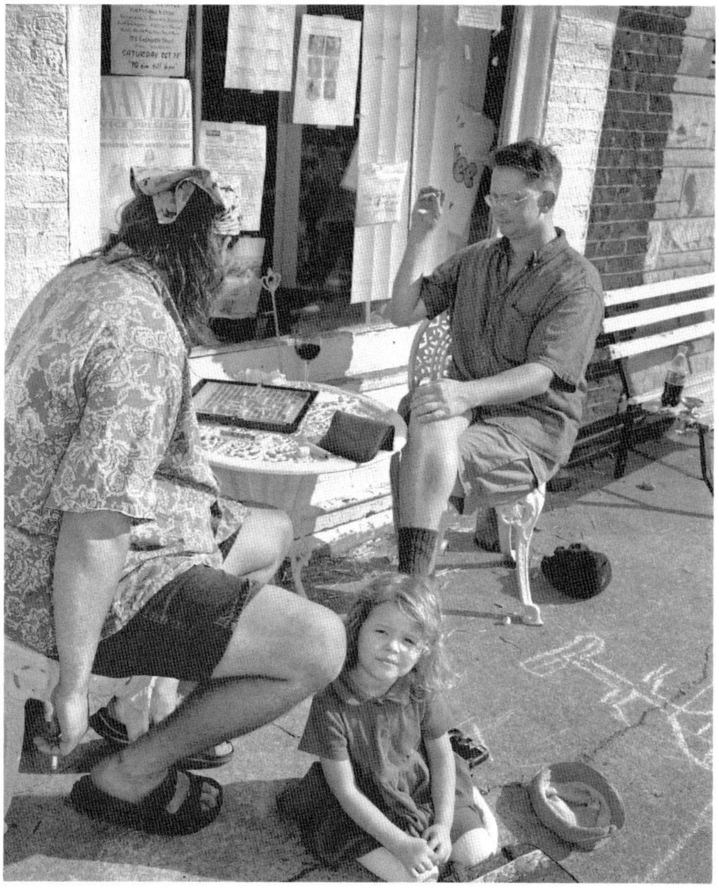

An afternoon with dad on Cobden's main street. Photo courtesy of Mike LaScola

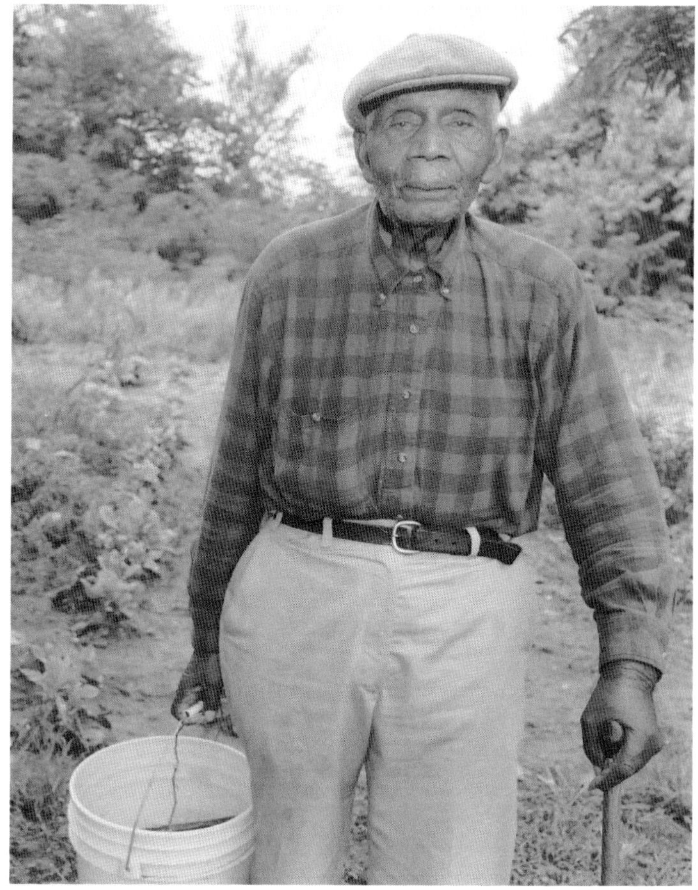

Gardening in Sandusky, Alexander County. Photo courtesy of Eric Robinson

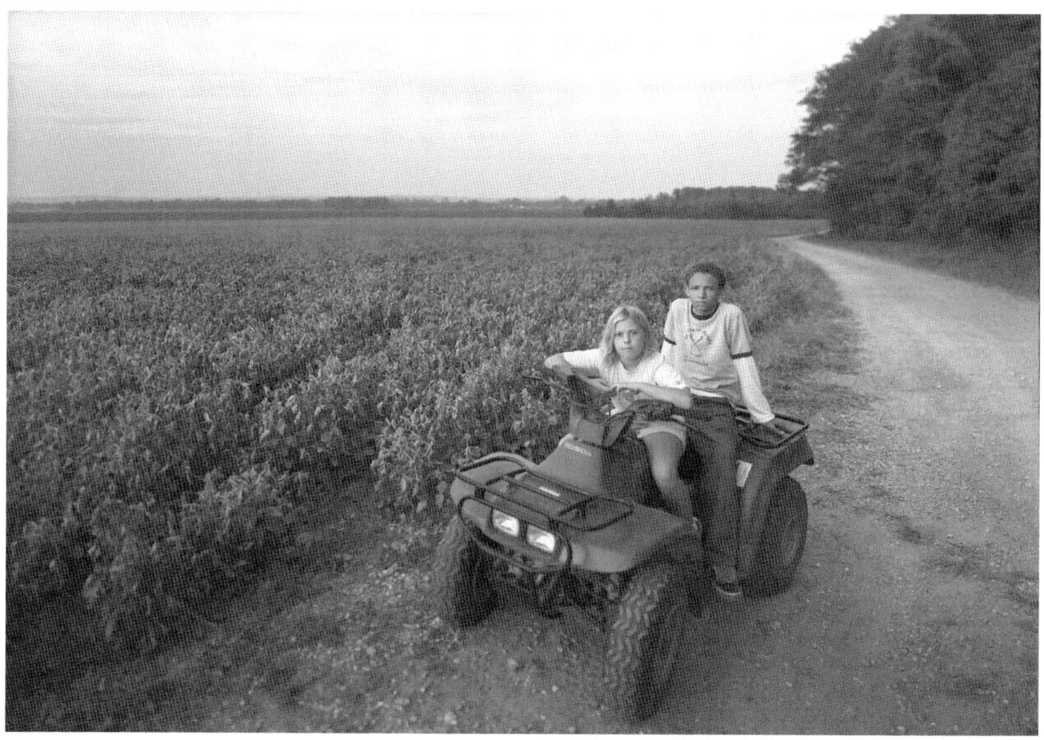

Cousins weekend near Gorham, Jackson County. Photo courtesy of Chris Walker

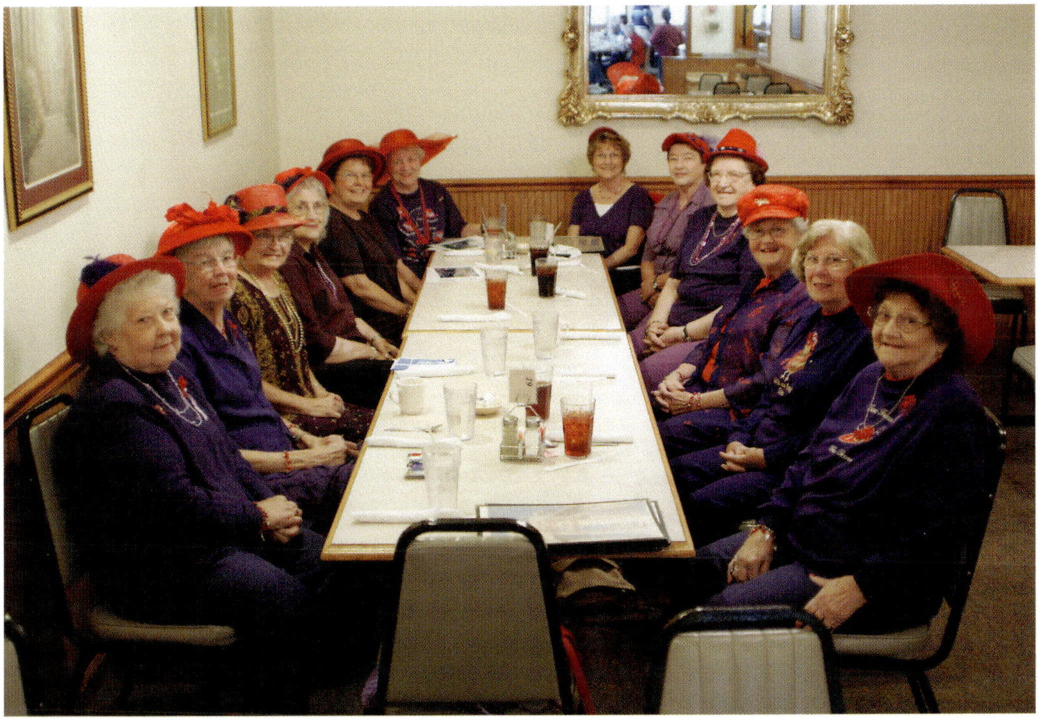

Red Hat Society, Percy. Photo courtesy of Melanie Miller

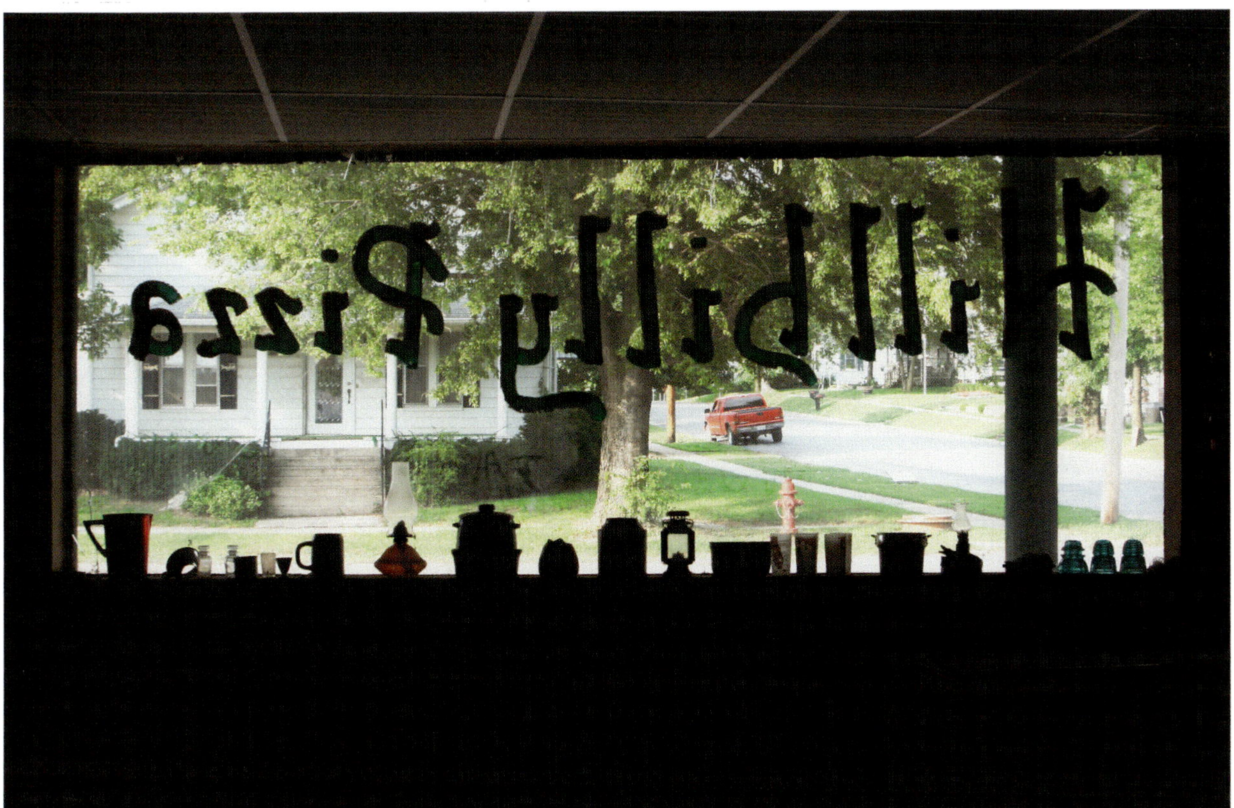

The view from Hillbilly Pizza, Campbell Hill. Photo courtesy of Amanda Voegel

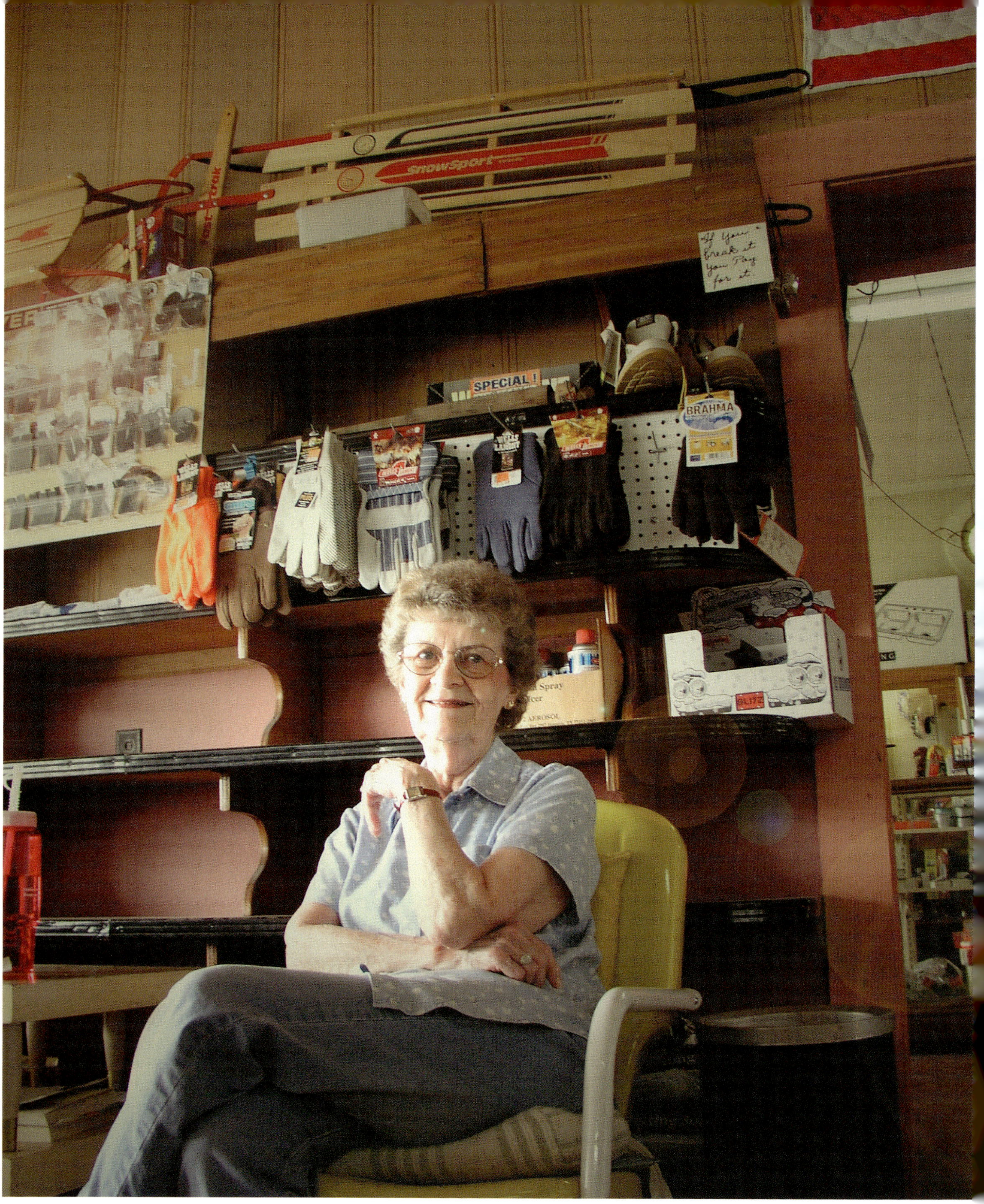

General store at New Grand Chain, Pulaski County. Photo courtesy of Shannon Woodworth

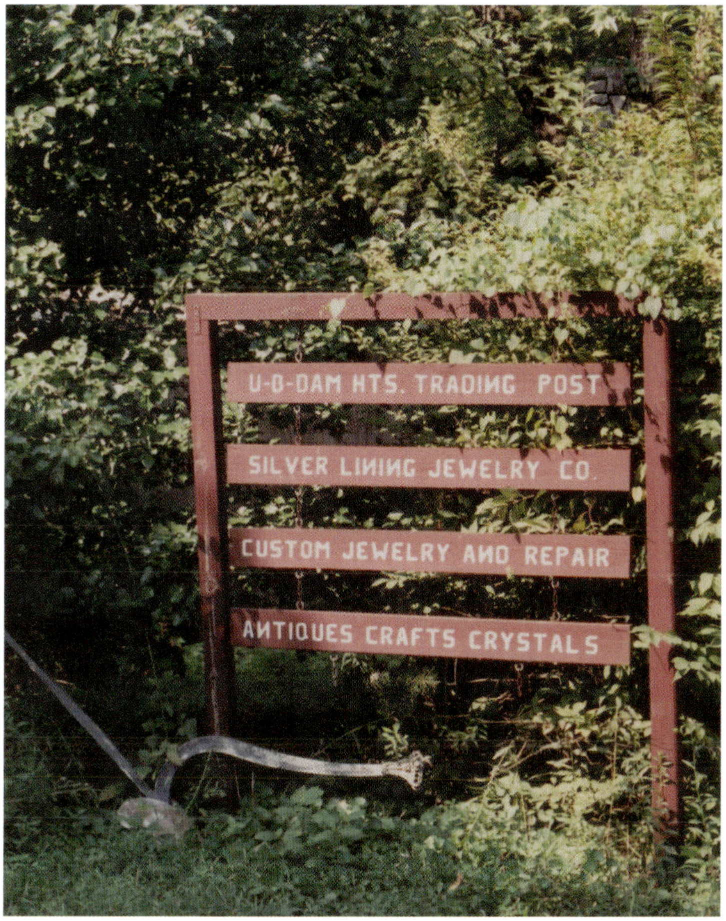

Commercial signage at You Be Damn Hollow, Old Cape Road, Union County. Photo by Herbert K. Russell

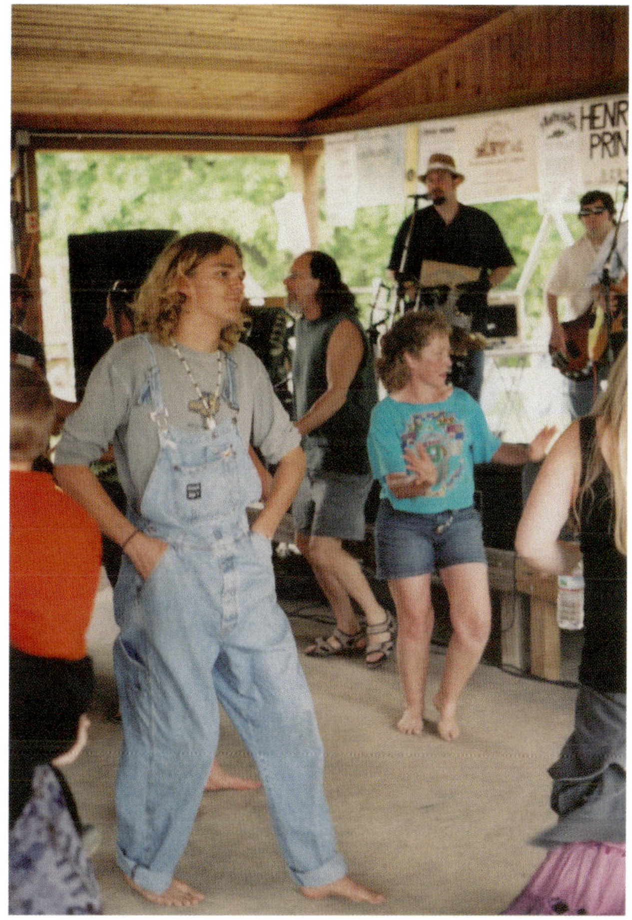

Dancers enjoying the sounds of the Woodbox Gang at the Makanda Fest, Jackson County. Photo by Herbert K. Russell

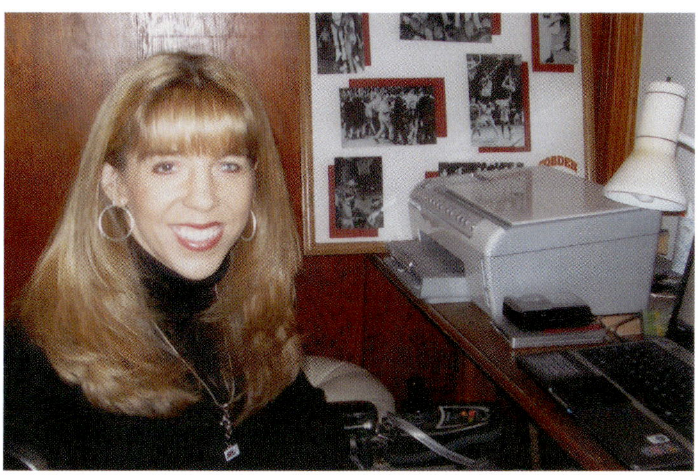

Historian of small-town heroes. Teri Campbell works on a book about the 1964 "Appleknockers," Cobden's basketball team that played for the state championship. Photo courtesy of Toni Campbell

None of this was lost on officials of the Chicago and Eastern Illinois Railroad (the C&EI). It was ready to haul coal by 1895, and by the early 1900s the counties of Franklin, Williamson, and Saline were dominated by underground, or "deep," coal mining. Johnston City enjoyed at least eight mines within walking distance of town, and Herrin was a boomtown with laborers and merchants from a dozen and a half foreign countries, notably Italy. By 1923 Franklin County alone had 16,000 underground miners. The Illinois Central soon opened its Edgewood Cutoff, a line running from Fulton, Kentucky, across the Ohio to Metropolis and north through the Coal Belt counties of Saline, Williamson, Franklin, and Jefferson to Edgewood (near Effingham), where the cutoff joined the main line to Chicago. Trains on the cutoff avoided slowdowns on the bridge at Cairo and rail yard congestion at Carbondale and Centralia and had their own maintenance center near Bluford. The development of strip, or surface, mining expanded the Coal Belt in a half dozen counties, as well as adding miles of tracks and good railroad jobs paying union wages.

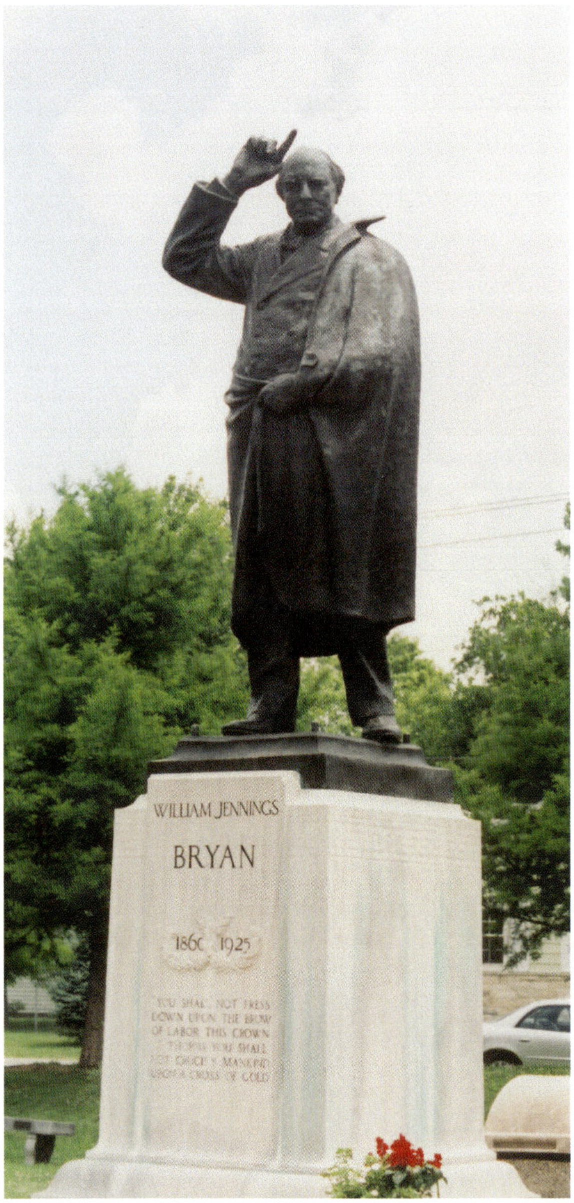

William Jennings Bryan stands up for labor in Bryan Memorial Park in Salem. Photo by Herbert K. Russell

In contrast, coal mining did not pay well at first, and an abundance of newly arrived immigrants tended to keep wages low. Some miners had experienced the benefits of unions and wanted to organize, but some stubborn mine owners disagreed. Conflict erupted in violence, beginning in 1898 at Virden (near Springfield), where a feud between miners and management cost nineteen lives before tensions moved south. The Southern Illinois Coal Belt was kept in turmoil with deadly shootouts at Cambria and Carterville in 1899 and at Zeigler in 1904.

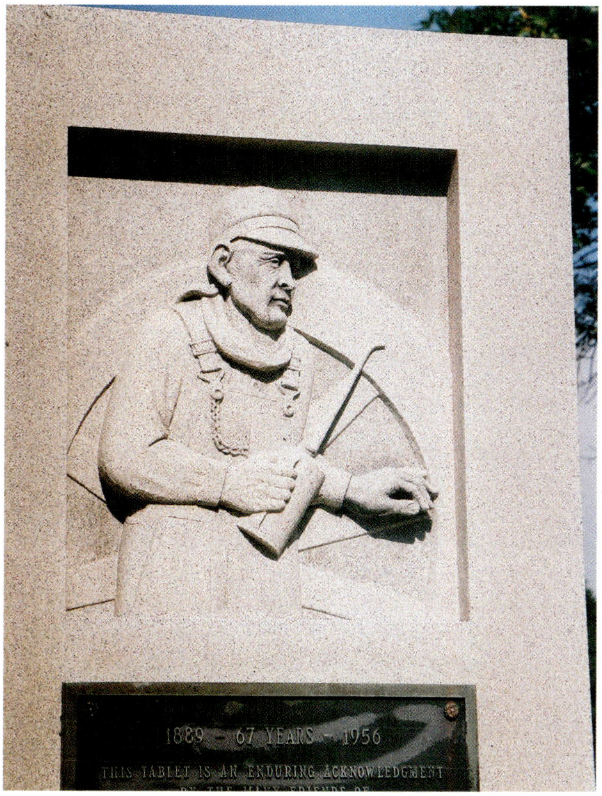

Illinois Central engineer Robert "Polecat" McMillan entered the Railway Hall of Fame after sixty-seven years on the rails. Fairview Park, Centralia. Photo by Herbert K. Russell

The nation's political leaders, including Salem native William Jennings Bryan, sometimes addressed this gap separating labor and management. Bryan led the Democratic ticket for President three times, making his famous "Cross of Gold Speech" at the 1896 national convention in Chicago. Speaking of those who controlled the country's money supply and abused the rights of workers, Bryan uttered these words of warning: "You shall not press down upon the brow of labor this crown of thorns. You shall not crucify mankind upon a cross of gold." All who listened felt it was big business that was "crucifying" blue collar workers with long hours, low wages, a hostility to unions, and a money system that relied on gold instead of a more plentiful mix of gold and silver. Bryan's words would long be remembered in Southern Illinois, which has several monuments to miners, laborers, and those who supported them, including Bryan himself. His heroic-sized statue in Salem was fashioned by Gutzon Borglum, the same who sculpted the presidential heads on Mt. Rushmore.

Powerful railroad engines, haulage cars, and cabooses also receive attention in Egypt's labor memorials and memories, along with those who lived their lives on the rails. Conductor Billy Bryan (no relation to William Jennings Bryan) never forgot that the conductor, not its engineer, manages a train (and not the Chicago bigwigs of the Illinois Central Railroad, who seemed to think they owned Billy's train). When Billy Bryan conducted *his* train between Carbondale and the Mississippi bottoms near Cape Girardeau and Ware, it stopped for every "little man" needing a ride regardless of whether the man had money or a ticket.

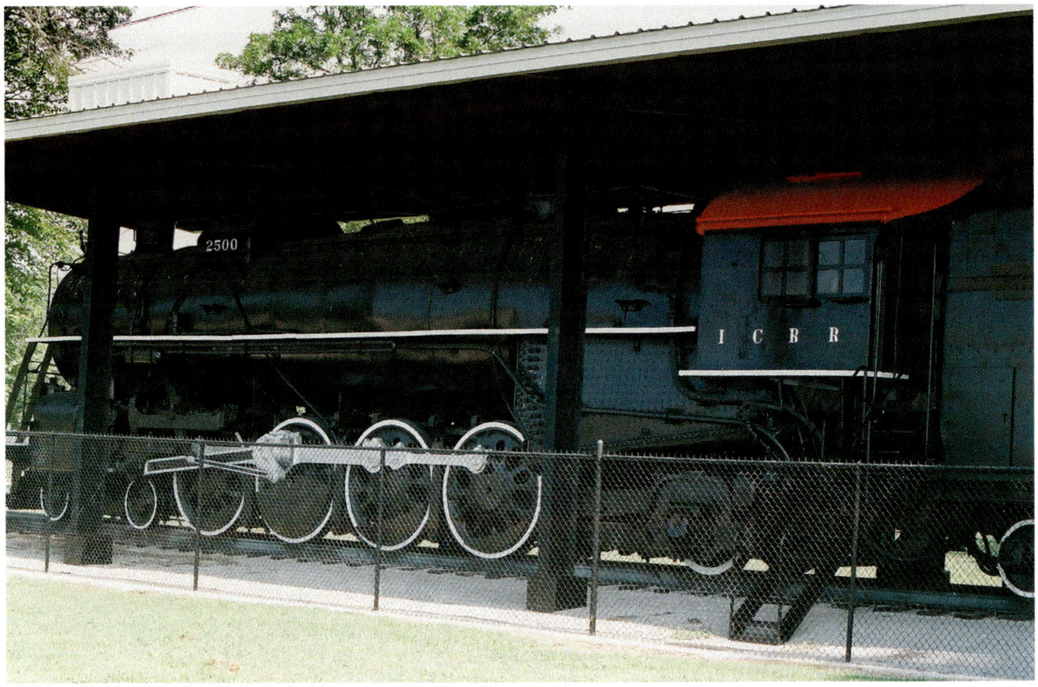

A protective roof covers the immense steam-driven locomotive in Fairview Park, Centralia. Photo by Herbert K. Russell

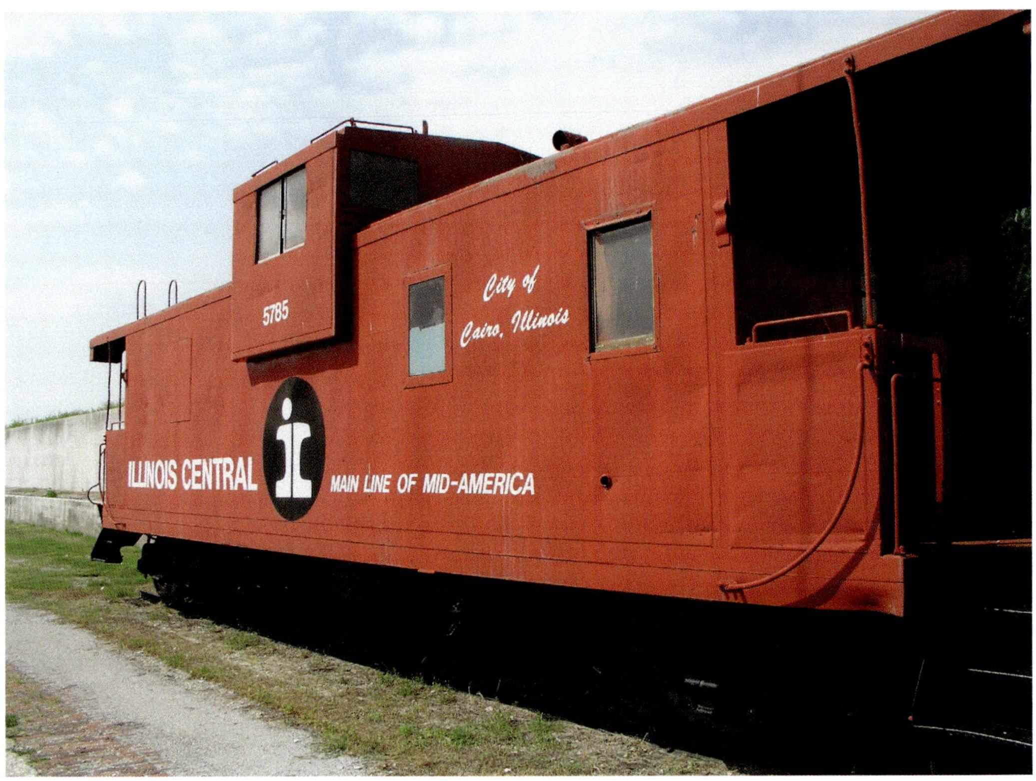

Cairo's red caboose anchors the town's prominent place in Illinois rail history. Photo courtesy of Shannon Woodworth

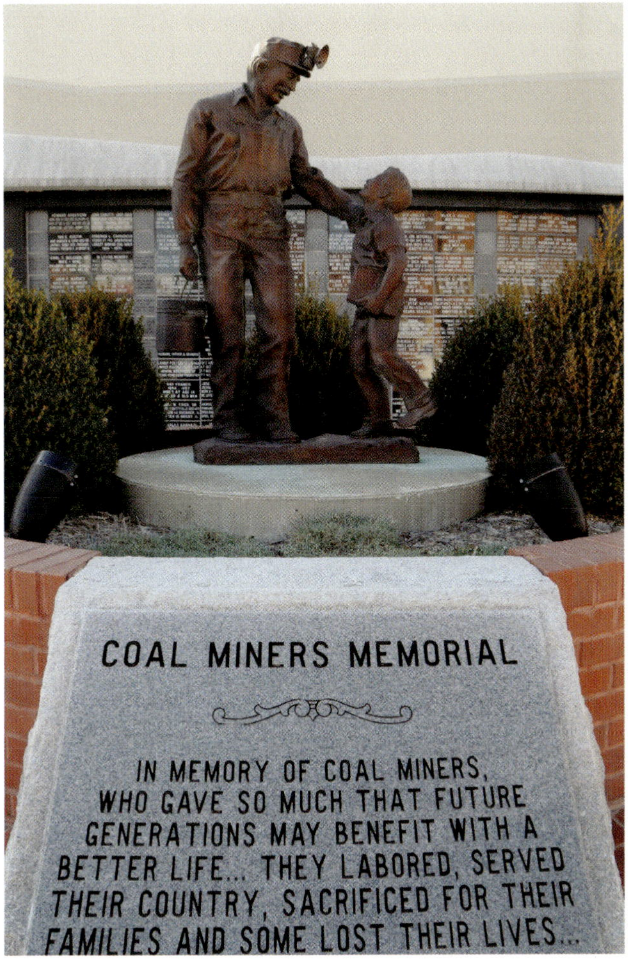

This Herrin memorial reflects the tendency of sons to follow their fathers into the mines. Photo courtesy of Shannon Woodworth

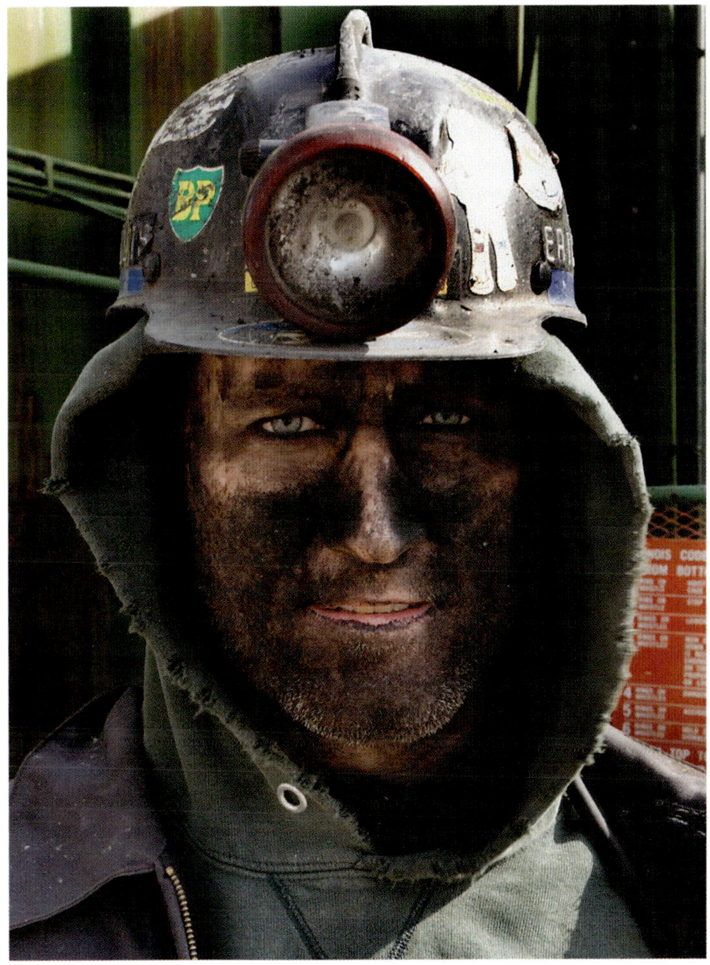

An underground miner—a longwall shear operator—comes off shift near Galatia. Photo courtesy of Andrew Martin

Coal made the railroads necessary, and the railroads made the use of coal possible.
—Albro Martin, *Railroads Triumphant*

They pulled out of Memphis nearly two hours late;
Soon they were speeding at a terrible rate.
And the people knew by the whistle's moan
That the man at the throttle was Casey Jones.
—One of several versions of "The Ballad of Casey Jones"

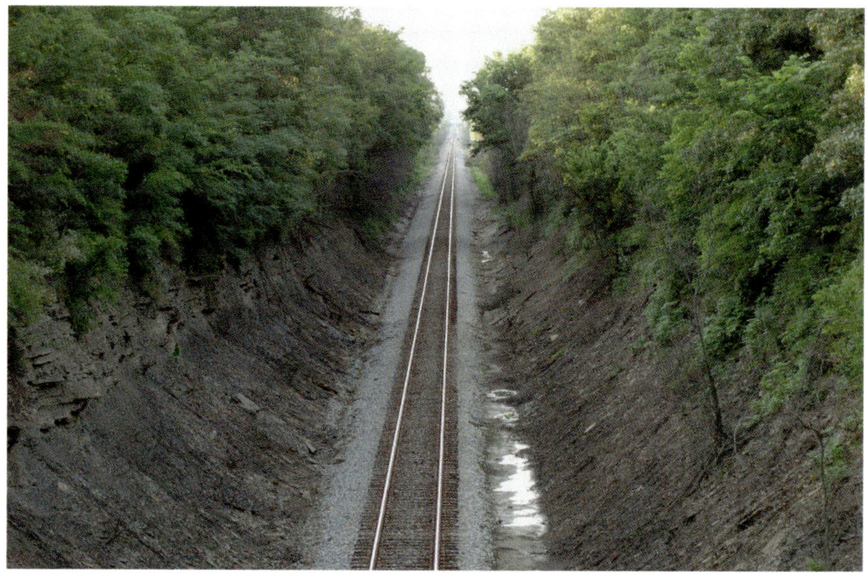

Gleaming rails of the Edgewood Cutoff slice through Franklin County coal fields on their way to Chicago. Photo courtesy of Shannon Woodworth

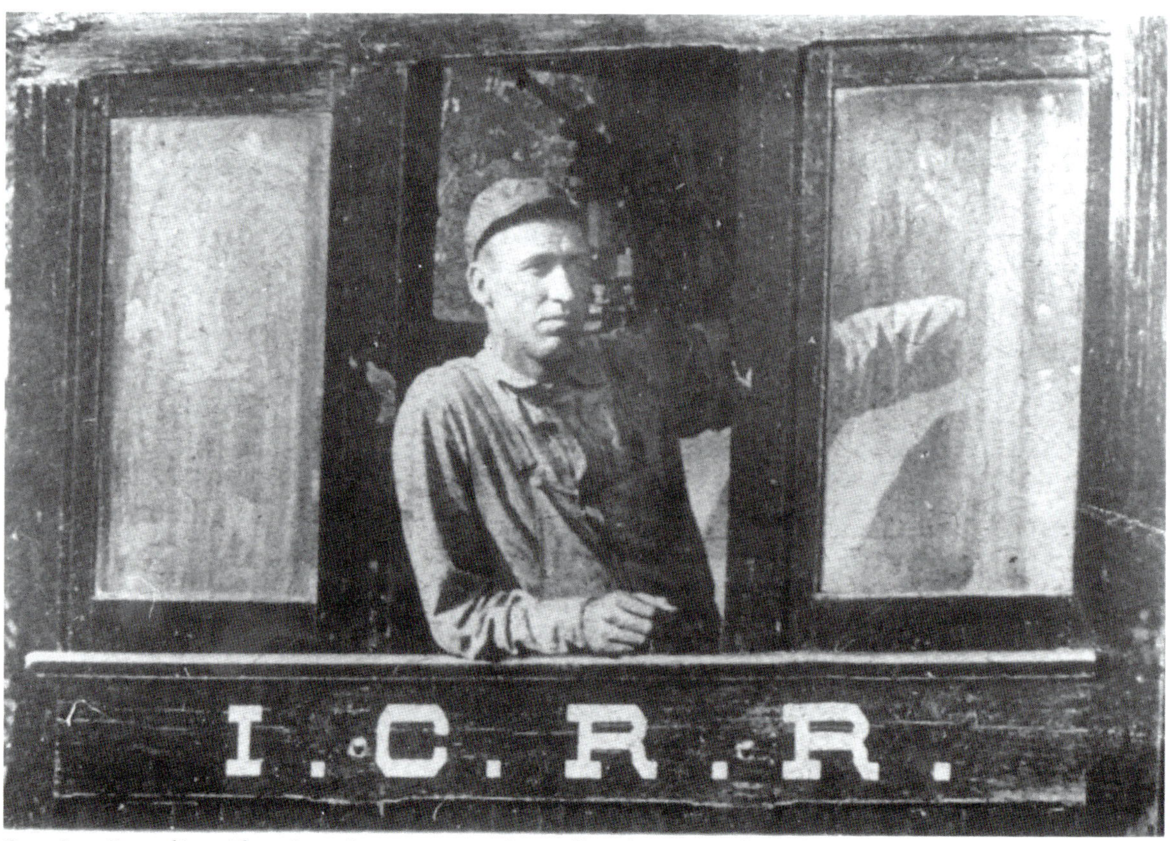

One-time Centralia resident Casey Jones seems ready to roll in this picture from the 1890s. Bruce Gurner Collection, Water Valley Casey Jones Railroad Museum

The best-known railroad personality to pass through Egypt was John Luther "Casey" Jones, an engineer with the IC who was famous for his "fast freights" even before he learned to tease a distinctive moan out of the whistle. He was adept at making up time, and one night in 1900 he made up too much, plowed into another train, and was killed. In Centralia, where Casey Jones lived in the early 1890s, an immense steam locomotive stands in Fairview Park, a permanent reminder of Centralia's considerable role in railroad history. And Cairo, which helped inspire Illinois' first public railroad, maintains a retired red caboose near the banks of the Ohio. Elsewhere, haulage cars once used for coal or fluorspar weather in the elements, their work completed.

In 1922 coal's roughneck image took a turn for the worse. A strike by 500 United Mine Workers in Williamson County led to a gun battle, in the aftermath of which unionized miners murdered nineteen unarmed strikebreakers who had surrendered and been promised safe passage out of the county. Local law enforcement officers knew what was happening but did nothing, perhaps because they feared for their own well-being, perhaps because most or all of the strikebreakers were from Chicago. Various Southern Illinois counties had long been associated with vigilante actions involving family vendettas, self-appointed regulators of justice, and visits from the Ku Klux Klan (who usually ignored Egypt's African Americans but warned, whipped, or killed whites with whom they disagreed). But this new matter was worse. The "Herrin Massacre" was immediately condemned in newspapers from coast to coast and in the capitals of Europe and was denounced by the president of the United States. Two trials were held, and while the district attorney and honest witnesses sought convictions, others were not so concerned. There is anecdotal and circumstantial evidence that some of the jurors were bribed by the miners union, and in the end, the accused were found not guilty by their friends and the fearful. "Bloody Williamson" County became a magnet to others operating outside the law.

Among the first to appear was the Ku Klux Klan, which targeted Catholic immigrants, a good many of whom had recently arrived from Europe to work in the coal fields. In 1923 a group of Protestant ministers in Marion brought in a hired gun named S. Glenn Young. His job was to enforce the nation's new Prohibition amendment regulating alcohol, a difficult task made impossible by Young's abrasive personality and highhanded methods. Homemade wine and beer were dietary staples for numerous Coal Belt immigrants, and many families of southern origin had a recipe for making "white mule," moonshine whisky named for its "kick" and its color. Both groups became victims of raids and arrests by the Klan and by S. Glenn Young. Kangaroo courts, jail time, beatings, theft, and destruction of property were common.

Local turmoil, lax law enforcement, and untaxed liquor and beer attracted organized crime, which arrived in the form of a dapper East St. Louis gangster named Charlie Birger. The Birger gang of a dozen and a half armed men and their admirers established bootlegging headquarters at Harrisburg and at a nearby pop and sandwich stand named, appropriately, Shady Rest. A few miles north, Wayne County and its county seat of

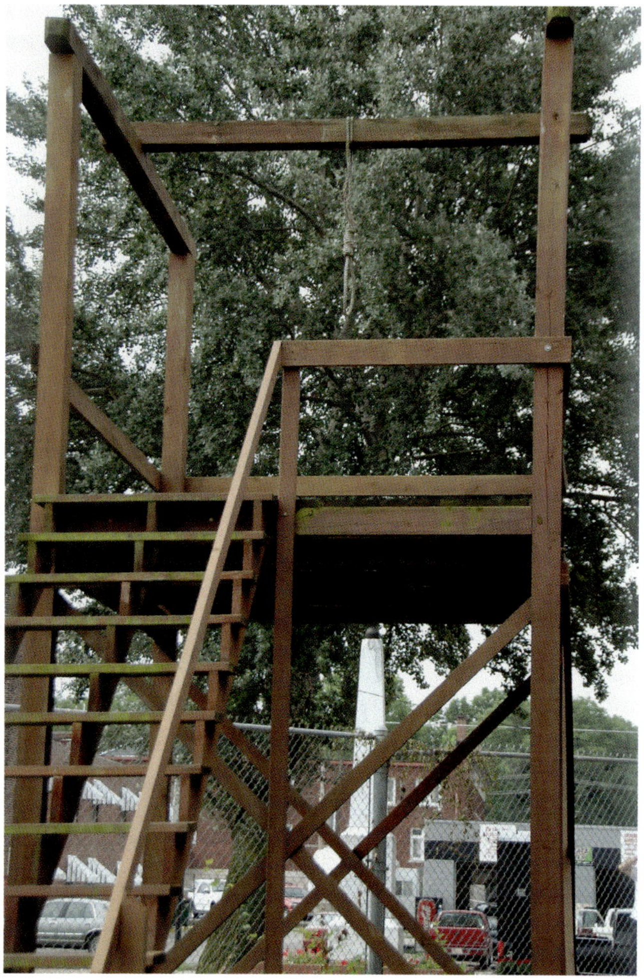

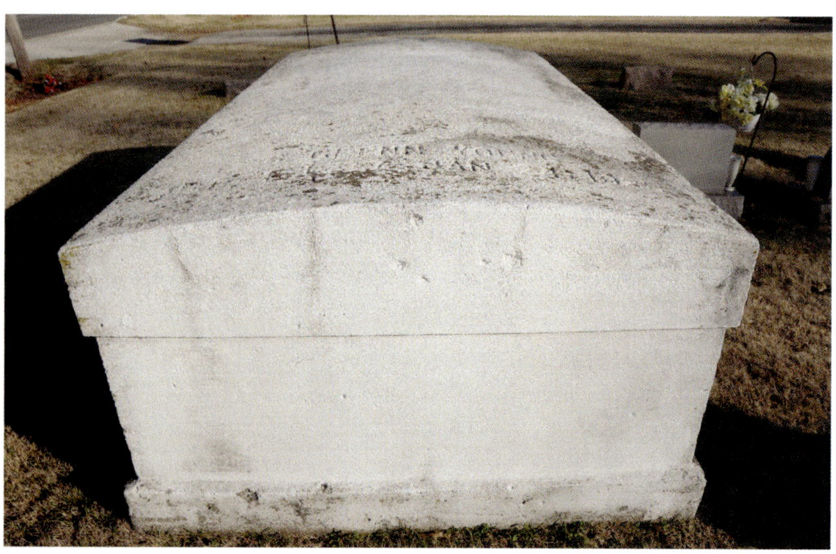

The hangman's noose (*top*) in Benton and the bullet-pocked tomb of renegade lawman S. Glenn Young (*bottom*) in Herrin are reminders of the region's gangster era. Photos courtesy of Shannon Woodworth

Fairfield grew their own thugs, the Shelton Brothers. For much of the 1920s and '30s gang members intimidated Egypt as they wished when it came to bootlegging, murder, fire bombings, prostitution, gambling, and shoot-outs with each other and police. One such incident sent Prohibition enforcer Young to his tomb, a bullet-scarred mausoleum in the Herrin City Cemetery. Some gang members lived into the 1960s and later, violent old men from the past occasionally making headlines by killing, going to jail, or dying peacefully in bed.

Little of the region's turmoil helped Southern Illinois or its blue collar workers. Miners had always faced layoffs in the summer when the nation burned less coal, but from the mid-1920s on the number of jobs declined as machines speeded coal's mining, loading, and hauling. Frequent strikes made Southern Illinois coal an undependable source of fuel, and some city markets turned to nonunion but more reliable outlets and to natural gas and oil. Some buyers are said to have boycotted Southern Illinois coal to protest the Herrin Massacre. By 1926 many of Egypt's miners found themselves unemployed while one of the most prosperous decades in American history unfolded elsewhere.

Unfortunately, a decrease in the number of miners did not guarantee a corresponding decrease in deaths. Roof falls, asphyxiation, runaway coal cars, crushing, and electrocution followed as certainly as the seasons. Men still tumbled into mine shafts, and explosions were still triggered by sparks, gas, blasting powder, and coal dust. The deaths of 230 miners in fiery holocausts at Centralia and West Frankfort in 1947 and 1951 were unusually terrible. Everyone knew Centralia's No. 5 Mine was dusty and dangerous, but little was done to prevent the disaster that followed when miners used the wrong materials to set off a charge to loosen coal. New Orient Mine No. 2 at West Frankfort had miles of tunnels and was a world record holder in production, but it also had large pockets of methane gas, a natural product of the decomposing vegetation that makes up coal. When two miners lit up forbidden cigarettes in a gassy area, the mine exploded. Disasters were invariably followed by finger pointing from state politicians eager to avoid blame and by thundering oratory from union leaders.

For much of forty years, mining's best-known labor leader was John L. Lewis, an Iowa native who had risen through the ranks in central Illinois to become head of the United Mine Workers of America, the UMWA. During the years 1932–38, competition from a powerful central Illinois union, the Progressive Mine Workers, brought on six years of tit-for-tat murders and feuding known as "the mine wars": Franklin County's Battle of Mulkeytown; a gunfight on the streets of Royalton; the explosion of a bomb at a Valier mine; and so on elsewhere—beatings administered by those loyal to Lewis, a fist in the face administered by Lewis himself. It was John L. Lewis who sealed the fate of the victims of the Herrin Massacre. Asked how the local union should treat the strikebreakers, Lewis replied by telegram: "Representatives of our organization are justified in treating this crowd as an outlaw organization and in viewing its members in the same light as they do any other common strike-breakers." The strikebreakers were beaten, stomped, shot, knifed, and hanged. Southern Illinois unions had grown aggressive.

In the 1940s and '50s labor tensions and union-imposed production levels led to the sale and eventual closing of Mt. Vernon's large railroad car manufacturing plant. Strikes were common in Cairo for decades, and nearby Joppa experienced strikes, wildcat walkouts, and labor racketeering during the 1950s construction of a power plant on the Ohio. In East St. Louis tensions were acute as early as World War I.

When East St. Louis meatpacking companies, metal works, and railroads hired recently arrived southern blacks in 1917, it sparked a story that whites were being laid off and African Americans hired in their place. An alternate story is that a labor shortage existed. In any event, after union leaders denounced the blacks as scabs and strikebreakers, a race riot broke out in which at least forty-eight people died and much of East St. Louis was burned. This 1917 incident

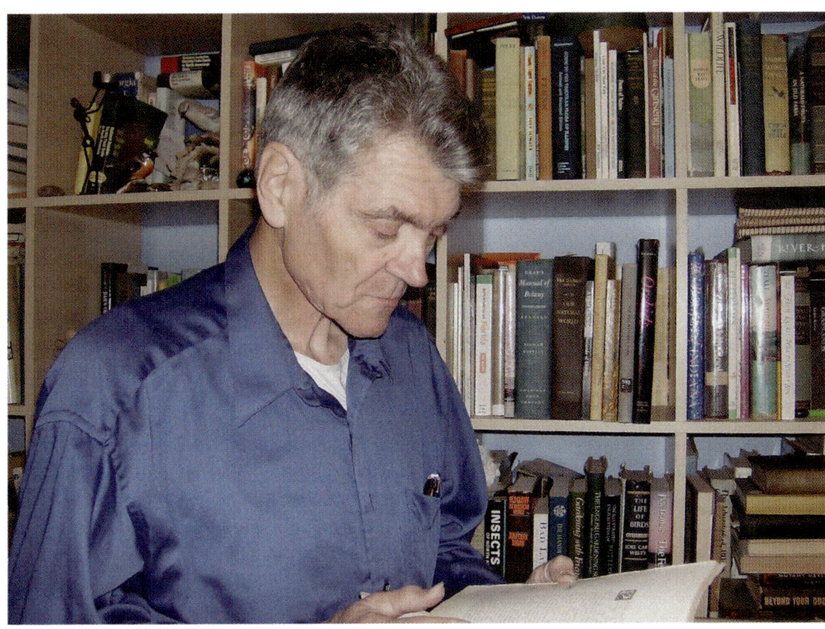

The biographer of gangster Charlie Birger, Gary DeNeal is also the editor of *Springhouse*, a magazine devoted to Southern Illinois history and culture. Photo courtesy of Brian DeNeal

was for a time the deadliest race riot of the century, and because many unions refused to let African Americans become members, labor and racial tensions festered for decades. Strong local unions kept the costs of labor high, and in the 1940s and '50s major employers such as Swift, Armour, and Alcoa began to leave, along with the National Stockyards, once the marketplace for much Southern Illinois livestock.

As the strike wore on, violence escalated,
from the ubiquitous jackrocks* to ball bats,
gunshots in the night, sabotage to equipment.
I worked uneasily on as the company replaced
224 tires in one month. Cars were trashed,
Jeff Beatty's house was spray-painted,
the family dog drowned in his daughter's
wading pool, and who knew what was next.

*Pieces of metal designed to puncture tires.

—From "Temporary Work Stoppage" by David Bond

To the extent that militant unionism was common in the North and virtually unknown in the South, it represents a major northern influence on Southern Illinois. At the same time some factory workers in Egypt might have benefited from an enlightened unionism. During much of the twentieth century, many Southern Illinois factories were sweatshops of the type one associates with the South—garment, hosiery, shoe, and glove factories paying low wages to women workers. Both images—low-paying sweatshops and militant unions—helped shape Southern Illinois' overall image.

The media invariably found Egypt's violence newsworthy. Through the 1950s few big-city reporters felt their stories were complete until they had reviewed the region's history: moonshiners, Hatfield and McCoy–like feuds, the Herrin Massacre, the Klan, coal mine explosions and mine wars, gangsters, murdered mayors and policemen, a dead wife or two, and the hangings. An obscure White County farmer named Phil Hanna performed so many court-mandated hangings in Southern Illinois and elsewhere that he became a "traveling hangman." It was he who sent gangster Birger and sixty others to their deaths, perfectly, painlessly, and without monetary compensation. National magazines such as *Life* ("Gunfire Lays Low One More Shelton"), *Esquire*, and the *Saturday Evening Post* focused on this violence when writing of Egypt. Book-length analyses covered similar ground, most famously Paul Angle's 1952 *Bloody Williamson: A Chapter in American Lawlessness.*

Cairo in particular fascinated reporters and university scholars, who traveled to it in numbers to study a town where North met South—or to experience an old-time river town with some equally old-time vices. Cairo was always open for business ("wide open," they said) when it came to illegal amusements, but it suffered from civic inertia when it needed civic betterment. Perhaps this was because a portion of the city's annual budget was spent fighting Old Man River; perhaps it was because parts of Cairo were segregated; or maybe a southern stereotype was true: things really did happen slowly in the South. Some blamed FDR. President Roosevelt's 1930s social programs offered Cairo "relief" (welfare payments) but created a chronic dependency as the city looked to

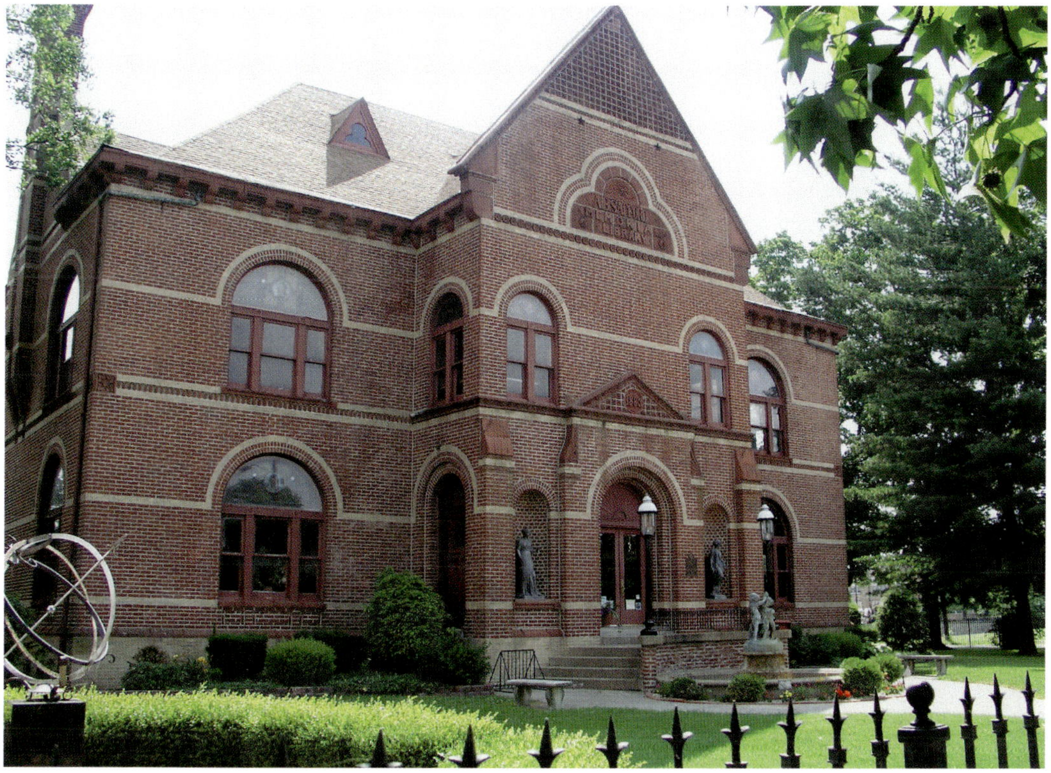

Cairo's Safford Library (*top*) is a rich repository of the city's past, but morning finds its commercial avenues deserted (*below*). Photos courtesy of Shannon Woodworth

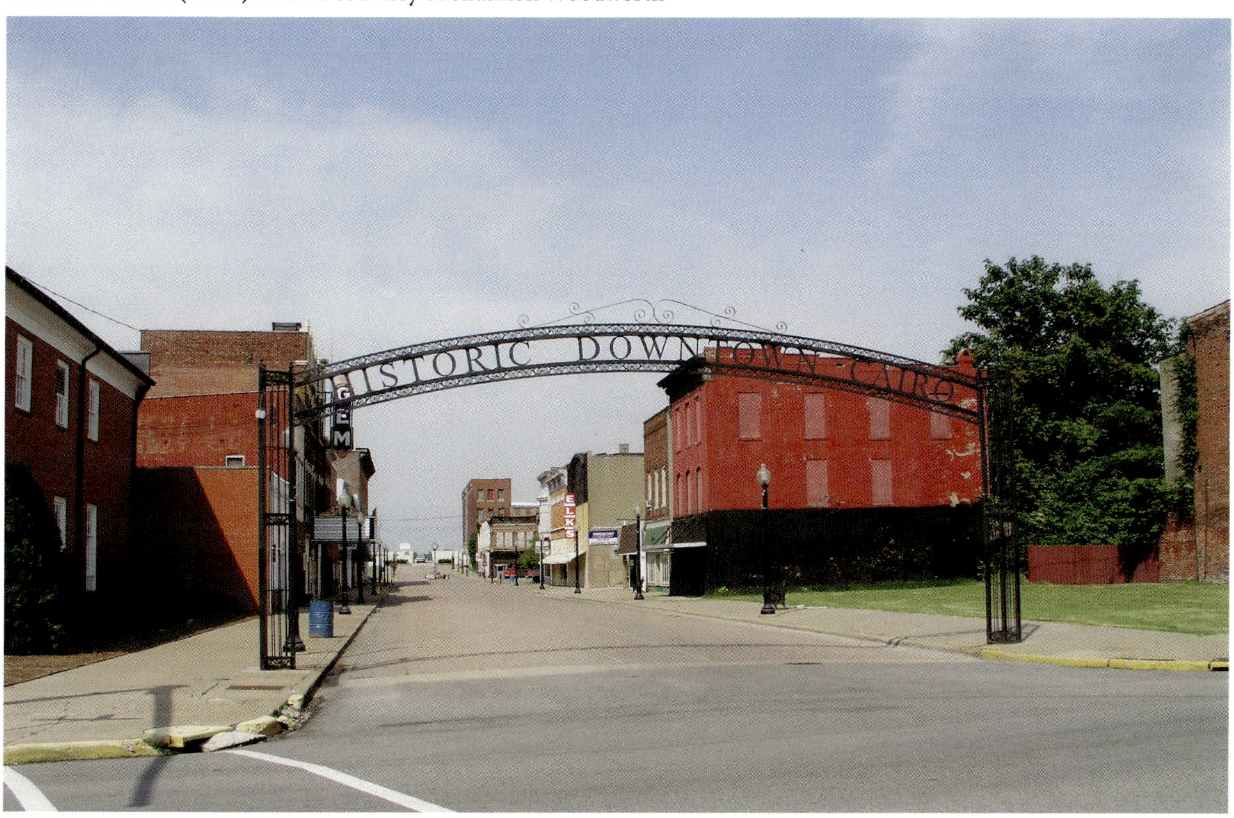

outsiders to help it into the future. Others blamed violence. Cairo was famous for a perverse instance of racial equality in 1909 when it lynched a black man and a white man on the same day. The Prohibition days of the Roaring '20s and early '30s increased local lawbreaking, and in 1937 Cairo and its surrounding county officially recorded Illinois' highest murder rate, eclipsing even Chicago and Cook County. But Chicago also had other things in common with Cairo.

In addition to suffering from one-party political rule (which stymied reform), Chicago was one of the most perfectly segregated cities in the nation. Zoning laws often excluded housing that African Americans could afford, and most blacks were crammed into "Black Belts" on the south and west sides.

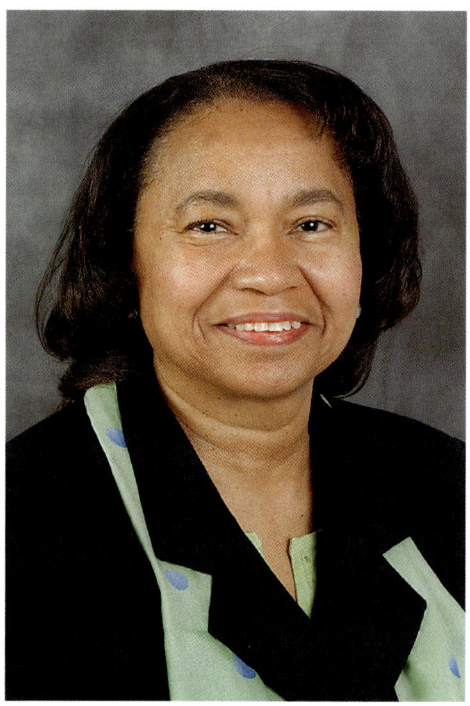

A professor emeritus of history at SIU Edwardsville, Shirley Motley Portwood recounts growing up in the segregated town of Mounds in her family history *Tell Us a Story: An African American Family in the Heartland.* Photo courtesy of Denise MacDonald

Financially successful blacks who could afford better housing were often met with violence. Through the 1940s, '50s, and early '60s, white collar Oak Park, blue collar Cicero, and numerous other Chicago suburbs used arson, bombs, or mob action to keep African Americans out. As the twentieth century closed, Chicago remained one of America's most segregated cities—but the Chicago press usually played down or ignored that city's racial problems. What was seldom or never reported thus became important in shaping how people viewed Illinois' various regions. In any event, the northern media usually looked southward for their stories on racism, and some places in "southern" Illinois fulfilled their expectations.

Through the 1950s and mid-1960s, some Illinois towns were "sundown towns," areas in which African Americans were expected to be out of town, out of the county, or in the town's "colored" section by nightfall. When the civil rights movement arrived in the late 1960s, some segregated towns experienced shooting wars. In Cairo the war began at night and continued intermittently for years as black and white antagonists exchanged weapons fire. Cars were peppered with gunfire and burned along with buildings. African American girls watched as Cairo filled its swimming pool with concrete in order to prevent integration, and an African American soldier died by suicide or lynching in the Cairo city jail. Young black men, weary of second-class citizenship, began a 1969 boycott of white businesses. The boycott lasted for years and forced many white-owned stores to close—but few businesses replaced those that closed, and out-of-towners were reluctant to locate in Cairo lest they too become the target of boycotts, bullets, or arson. Problems associated with fatherless households added to the city's unstable mix of race, poverty, and the past. Without steady jobs and a healthy tax base, Cairo went into an economic decline that continued into the twenty-first century. Forty miles north, Carbondale successfully addressed tensions associated with the death of Dr. Martin Luther King Jr. and a 1970 shootout with African American militants known as Black Panthers, but East St. Louis, with its own racial and financial problems, virtually destroyed itself. One of Illinois' most prosperous cities in the early twentieth century, East St. Louis had become so violent by 1969 that it introduced a new type of "sundown town," one in which it was dangerous for anyone, white or black, to be on its streets after dark.

All of these factors—much publicized racial tensions, unpredictable violence, and aggressive unions—caused some businesses to steer clear of Southern Illinois. That a once-violent town such as Herrin finally achieved a balance of strong unions and stable employers for years on end was seldom noted outside the area. Investors put their money across the big rivers and state lines in Evansville, Paducah, and, most often, St. Louis—at which point history repeated itself. Two hundred years earlier, social and economic upheavals and violence between the British and the Indians caused many French to abandon Illinois for Missouri, where a far-sighted businessman named Pierre Laclede had established a trading post and village he called St. Louis.

For many years, life on Southern Illinois rivers seemed tied to the past, most visibly through the wooden paddlewheel steamboats that plied the Mississippi, Ohio, and lower portions of the Wabash. Many of these were "packet boats" that carried both freight and passengers (cattle and people, for example), but in the early part of the twentieth century they began to specialize. Some of the old packets were converted to towboats pushing barges, while others became gambling boats permanently moored to city wharves, forerunners of the river casinos of later times. Still others were turned into excursion steamers offering day trips and moonlight rides, diversions that were popular through the 1920s, '30s, and early '40s. Unfortunately, boats with wooden hulls had poor safety records when it came to collisions with bridges, islands, and "hull inspectors" (river humor for snags), and a good many went to watery graves.

O the moonlight's fair tonight along
the Wabash,
From the fields there comes the
breath of new-mown hay;
Thru the sycamores the candle lights
are gleaming,
On the banks of the Wabash far
away.

—"On the Banks of the Wabash
Far Away" by Paul Dresser

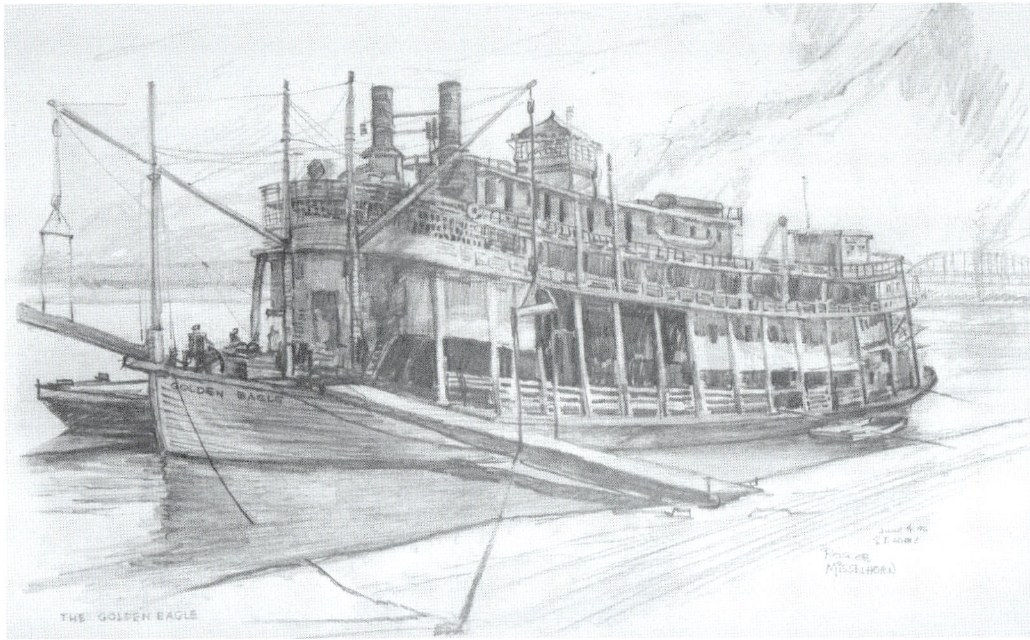

The years have destroyed nearly all of the wooden-hulled steamboats such as the *Golden Eagle*, here depicted by Sparta artist Roscoe Misselhorn in 1946. Safer steel-bottomed hulls became standard after World War II. Used by permission of the Misselhorn Art Foundation

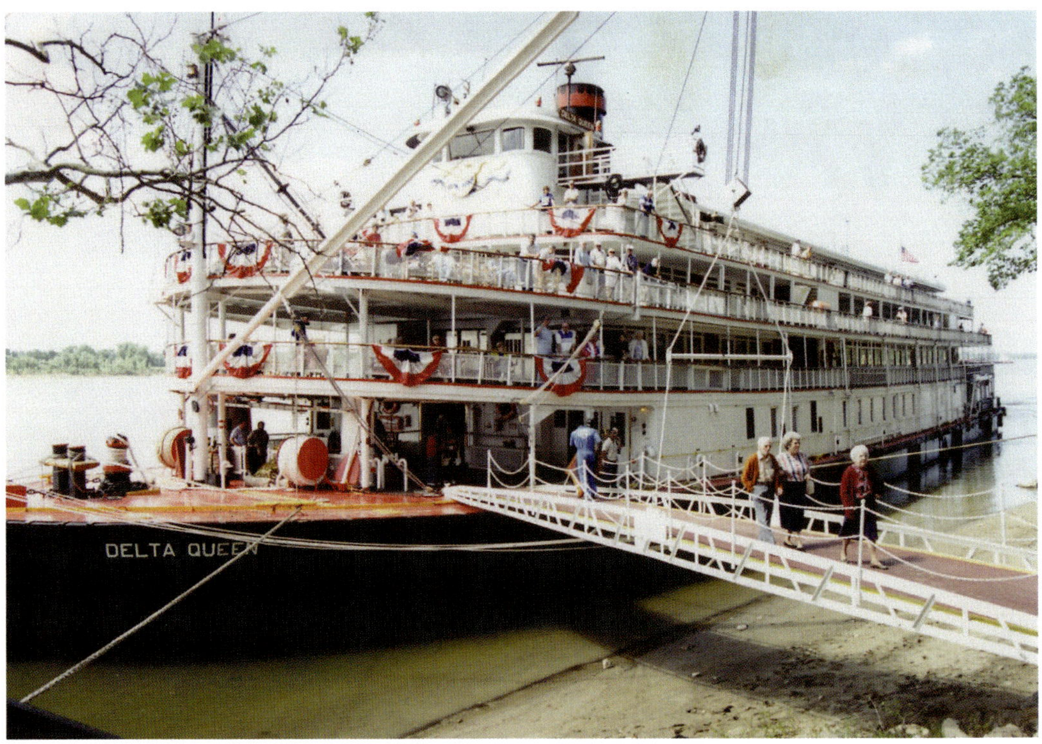

The *Delta Queen* docks at Cave in Rock. Photo by Julie Rash

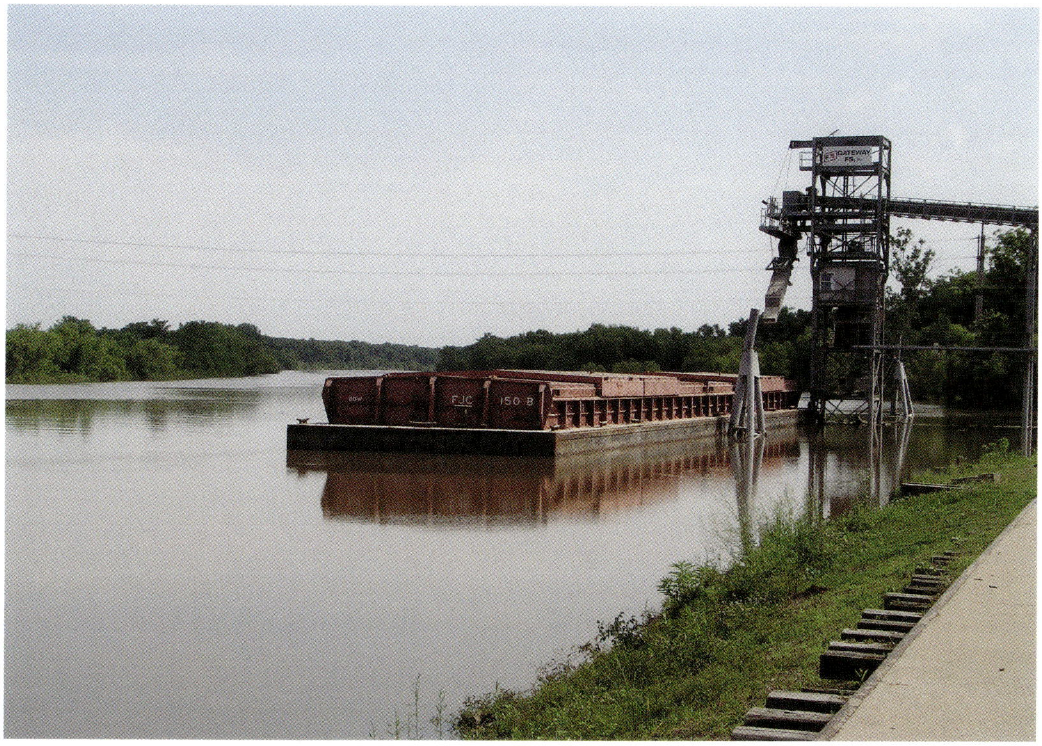

Quiet day on the Kaskaskia at Evansville, Route 3. Photo courtesy of Shannon Woodworth

The late 1940s were transitional years for steamboats serving Southern Illinois. In 1947 *The Golden Eagle*, a wooden-hulled cotton carrier built in 1903 but remodeled for passengers, plowed into the Mississippi's Grand Tower Island and never sailed again; in 1948 the steel-hulled *Delta Queen* began offering Ohio River cruises for passengers wanting to experience river travel in safer and more luxurious settings. This experiment was successful, and the *Queen* and her sister ships were still tying up at Southern Illinois ports in the twenty-first century.

The decline of steamboats hurt Southern Illinois' river towns, especially those on the Ohio. Cave in Rock, Elizabethtown, Golconda, Rosiclare, and various inland villages had always relied on the river to compensate for a scarcity of good roads and railroads in the Shawnee Hills. The hill country economy was seldom robust, and in 1930 a group of citizens met in Harrisburg and made plans for a federally funded national forest. Congress had earlier changed the name of such projects "from forest reserves to National Forests to indicate the forests are not locked up but are for use and are grown and harvested as a crop." With this in mind, planners hoped to replace eroded hillside farms providing subsistence-level living with conservation-friendly woodlands that would first bring in tourism dollars and later yield profits from logging. In 1933 Uncle Sam began buying land for the Shawnee National Forest, and young men in the Civilian Conservation Corps earned a dollar a day reclaiming gullied hillsides, planting trees, and building roads and bridges. The CCC performed similar work at state parks such as Giant City. The resulting forests, someone said, were "pretty as Eden on the morning of creation."

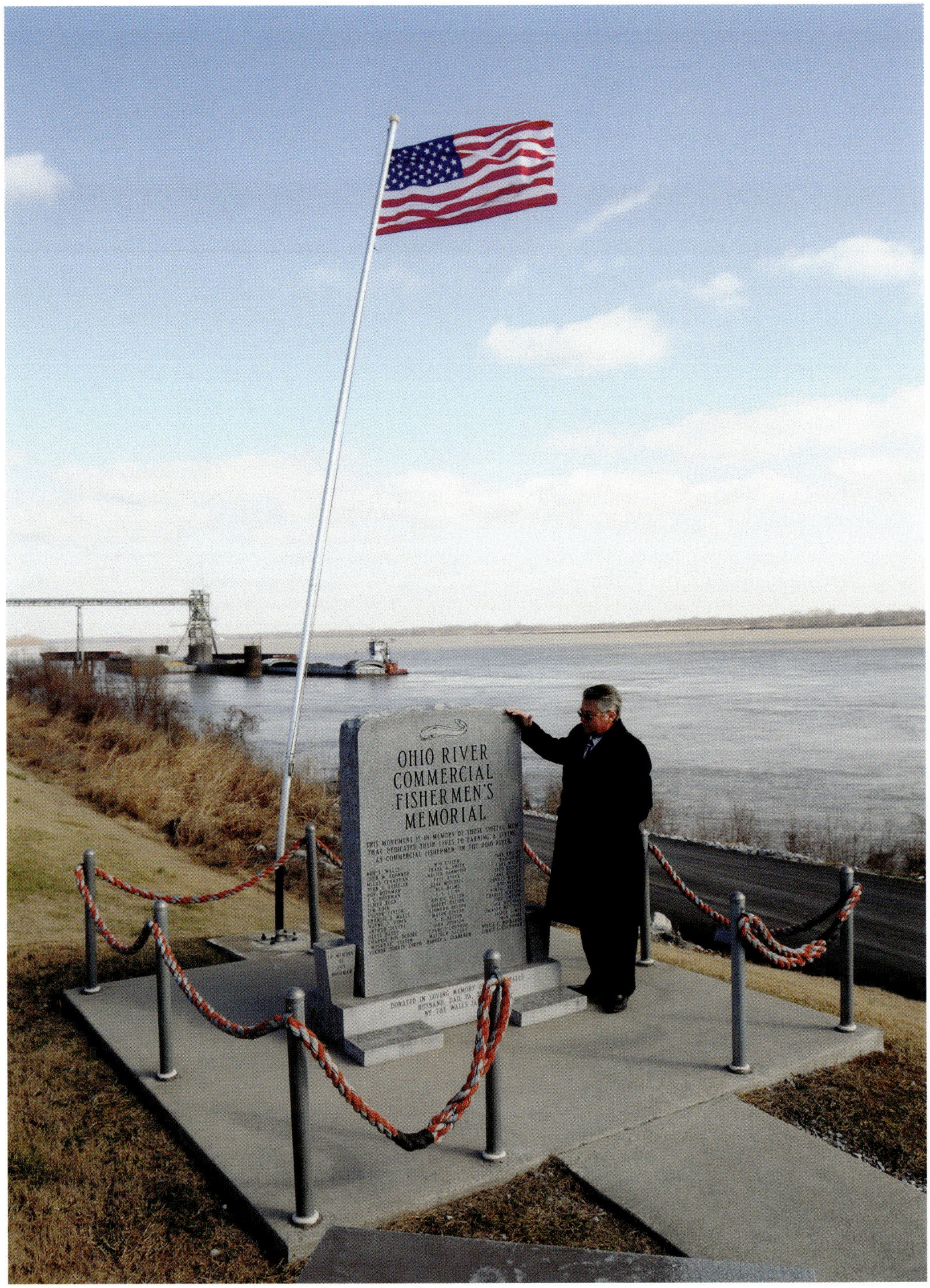

The son of an Ohio River fisherman, Buddy Walls and others erected this memorial to the area's commercial fishermen. Local rivers also supported a mussel industry yielding an occasional pearl, as well as mother-of-pearl (the shell's interior), which was shaped into buttons and sold commercially. Mound City. Photo courtesy of Shannon Woodworth

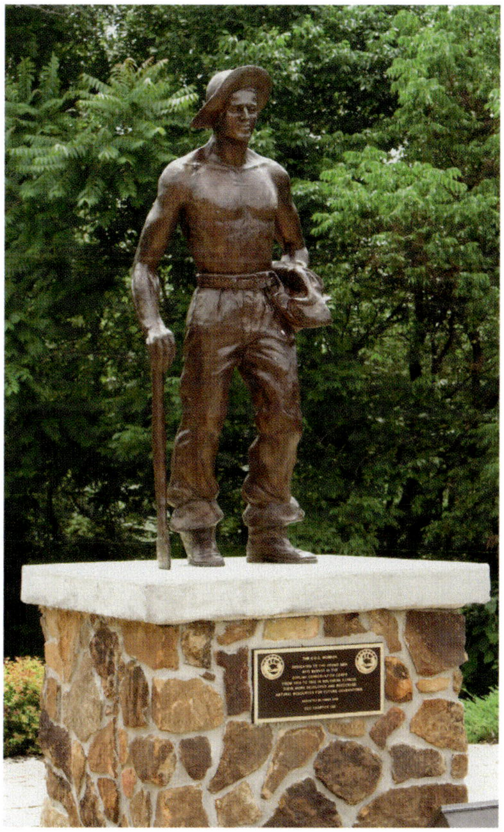

This statue memorializing the Civilian Conservation Corps stands in the plaza flanking the lodge at Giant City State Park, Makanda. The lodge and park were built by the CCC during the 1930s. Photo courtesy of David Hammond

The roads are impassable,
Hardly jackassable.
I think those that travel 'em
Should get out and gravel 'em.
—Oft-repeated poem
about dirt roads

By the end of the 1920s some Southern Illinois highways were paved with concrete, although many were only ten-feet wide and required a driver to drop two wheels off the pavement when meeting another vehicle. These first highways did little to alleviate the farmers' ongoing problems with low grain prices, but town merchants appreciated the improvements and advertised that they were now "On the Hard Road." Owners of automobiles especially liked the all-weather roads, and even during the Great Depression, cars were much in evidence in some counties.

In contrast, the new gasoline-powered farm tractors made in northern Illinois were slower to arrive. Designed for traction (hence the name), the steel-wheeled tractors from John Deere, Case, Fordson, and International Harvester were equipped with a small side wheel as well as a power take-off that revolutionized farm work. The side wheel powered a leather belt that could run a threshing machine, a saw to cut firewood, a feed mill to hammer corn into cattle feed, or anything else propelled by a belt. The power take-off "took off," or transferred, part of the engine's power to another piece of equipment, such as a mower, a corn picker, or a combine—to "combine" the processes of cutting and threshing grain. Some of Egypt's small farmers accepted the new technology; others continued farming with horses through the 1940s and into the '50s.

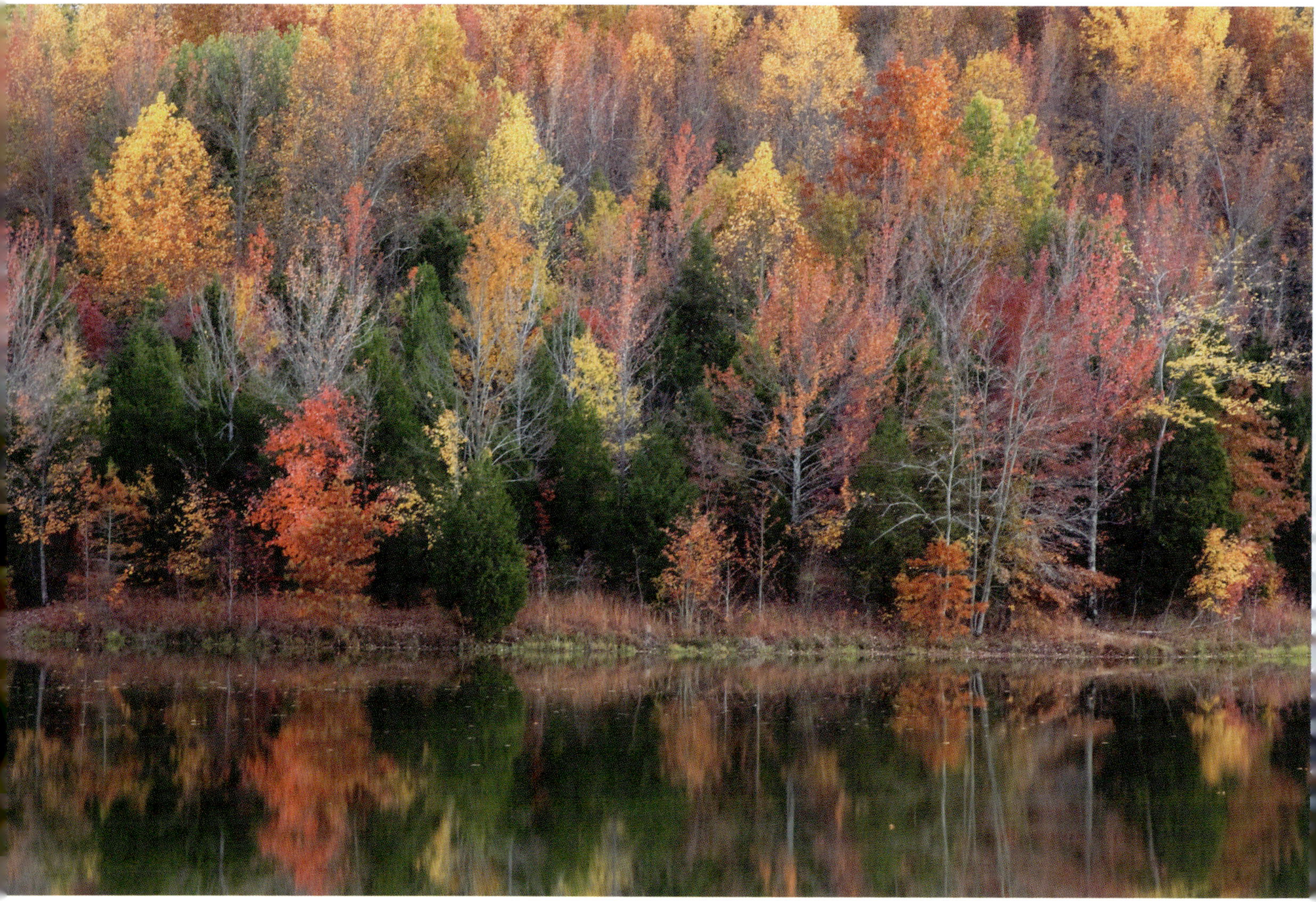

Fall colors at Ferne Clyffe State Park near Goreville. Photo courtesy of David Hammond

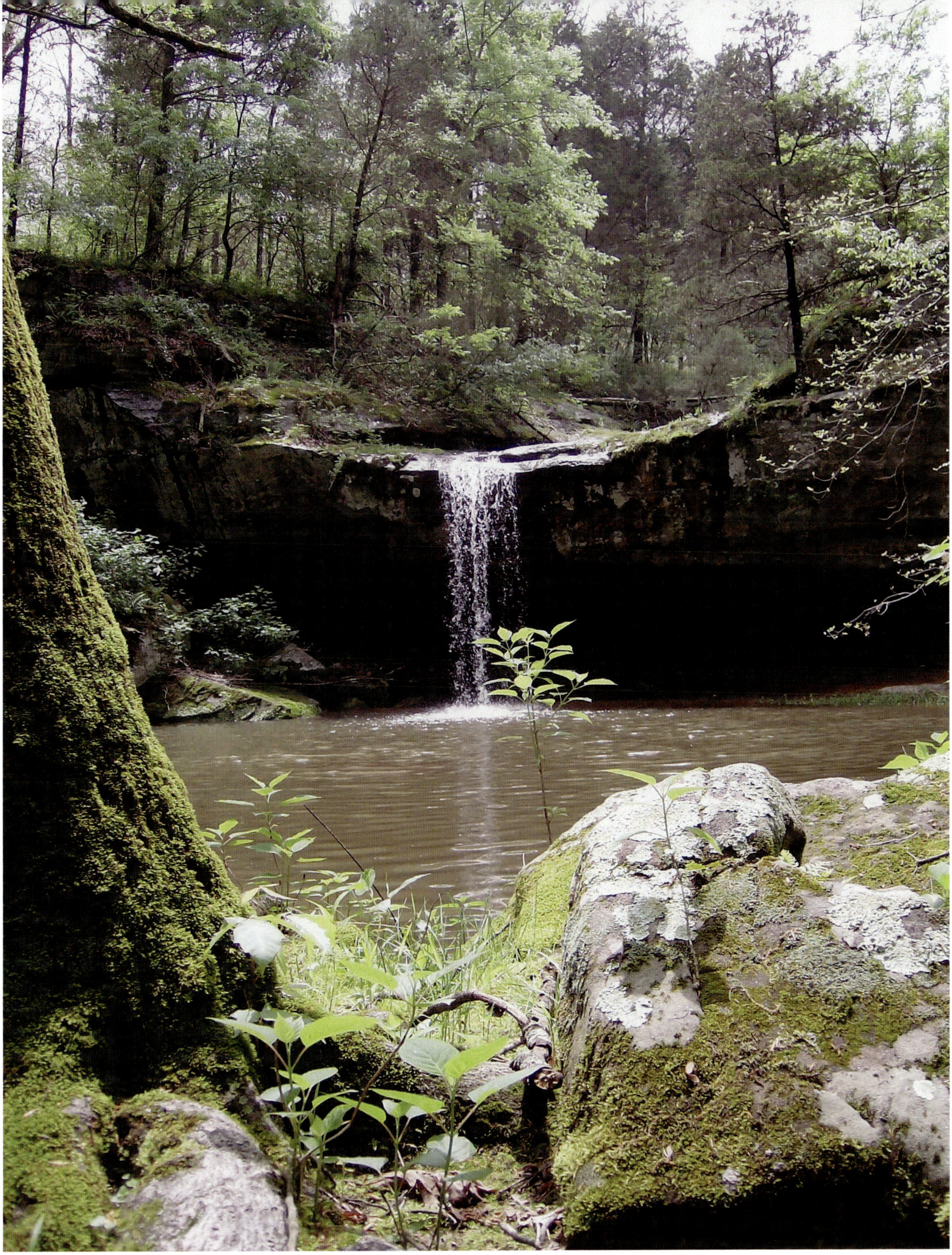

Falling water on Cedar Creek, Johnson County. Photo courtesy of Brian DeNeal

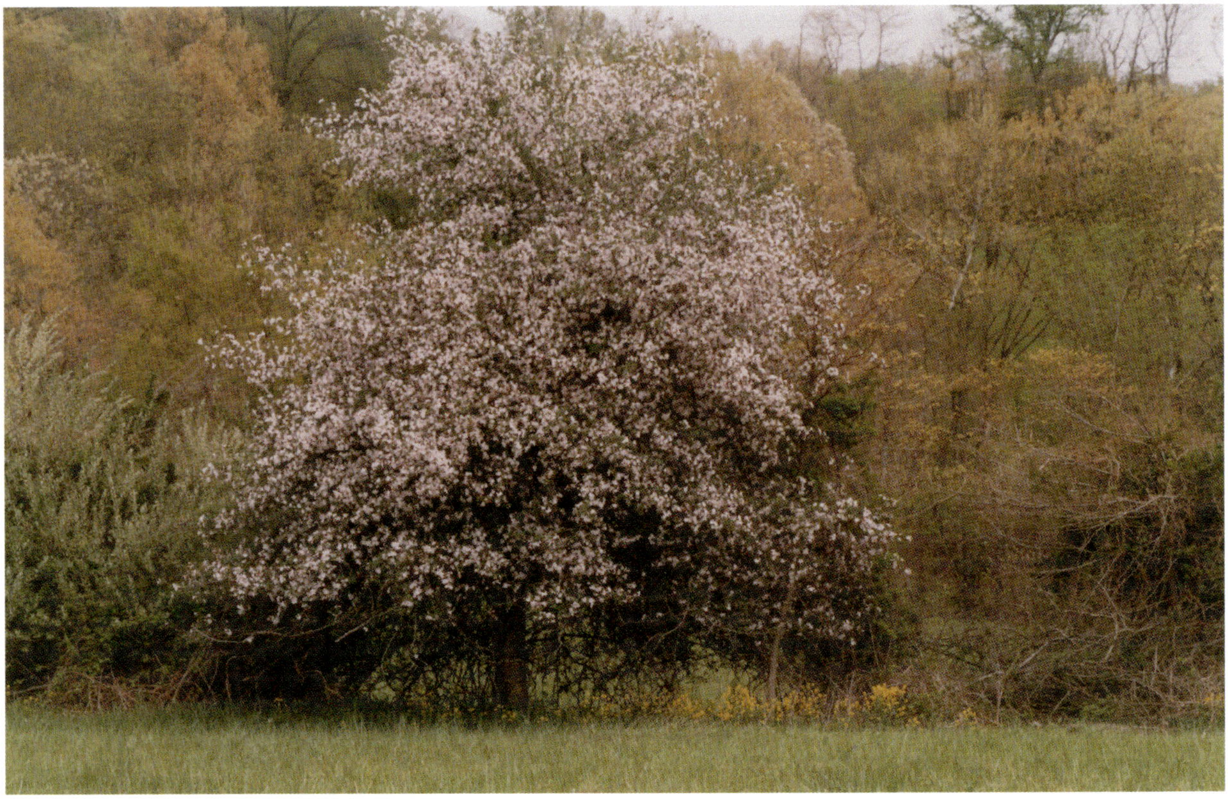

A wild flowering crab apple. Crab orchards flourished in nineteenth-century Williamson County and later lent their name to numerous places and things, including a creek, a lake, a town, a wildlife refuge, and a literary journal. Photo by Herbert K. Russell

Like horses, the country store lingered into the late 1940s and the 1950s. The convenience mart of its era and crossroads social center, the country store was a boar's nest of masculine opinions on township bridges, politics, crops, the inadequacies of the high school basketball coach (a truly hopeless fellow), and, invariably, the amount of money stolen from Egypt by Chicago. Most country stores owed their existence to poor roads, and when these were graveled after World War II, the stores' patrons abandoned them, driving away in the small pickup trucks then becoming popular and heading for the café or feed store in town.

But some feed stores with their animal feed and other rural necessities were also

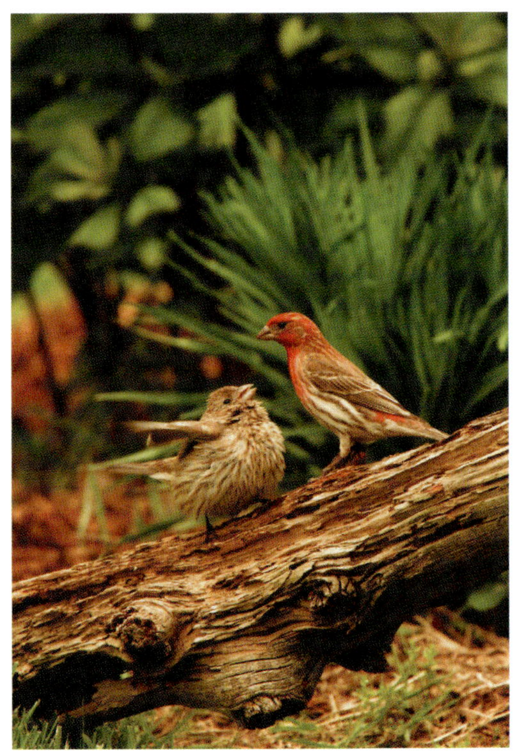

Finches on a weathered log seem to be discussing the day's events near the Shawnee National Forest. Photo courtesy of David Hammond

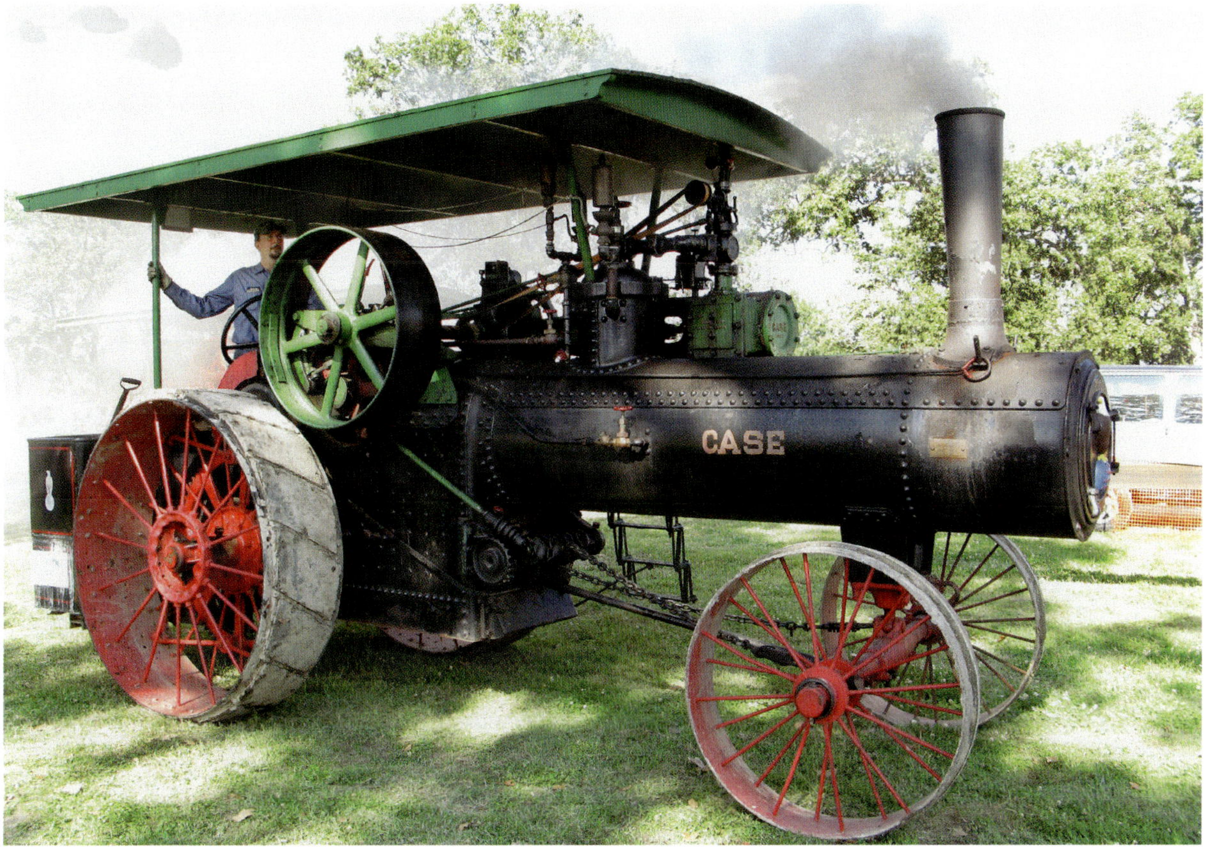

A forerunner of modern tractors, a steam-driven Case shows its stuff at the Threshermen's Reunion in Pinckneyville. Photo courtesy of David Hammond

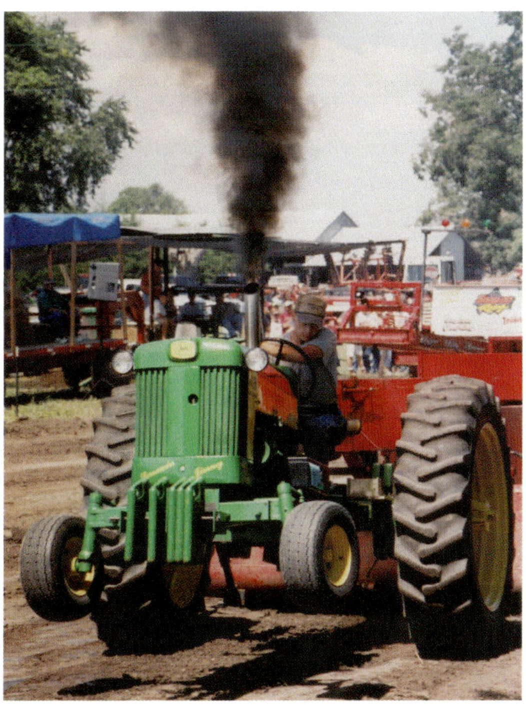

A tractor pull on Kaskaskia Island. The dark exhaust and elevated front wheels show this driver is getting the most from his machine. Photo by Herbert K. Russell

goods came from outside the area along with a handsome price tag. Egypt's farmers and other blue collar workers always knew that the raw materials they handled paid pennies but cost them dollars after northern Illinois middlemen processed them and sold them back. Even when the north-running freights carried their loads no farther than the Metro East Area of Granite City, Wood River, and East St. Louis, the old north-south duality lived on, along with bad feelings and some envy, and this remained the case for years.

The Great Depression's effects on Southern Illinois were so pervasive that five of President Franklin Roosevelt's public relations photographers came to Egypt, taking photos of the human misery and using the pictures to win support for his social programs. Photos taken in January 1939 by Arthur Rothstein (later the photo director for *Look* magazine) are shown here, two of many coal-country images used to define Southern Illinois. "Miner's Home" in Carrier Mills near Harrisburg is one of the bleakest of Depression pictures and a pictorial summary of the economic status of many miners that year.

"Unemployed Mine Worker" was taken in the coal town of Bush in Williamson County and became one of the region's most widely distributed photographs. The flowery wallpaper, the linoleum on the floor, a full scuttle of coal, and a second pair of shoes drying behind the stove suggest this worker is better off than some. But it is daytime, as a slit in the curtain shows, and he is sitting idly on a kitchen chair in a drafty house with his coat on and collar up. He seems intended for better things, this man with the thoughtful look and artistic hands, but not even his little dog can lift his spirits on this day. Perhaps he, like others, found employment when World War II began.

The war years of 1941–45 brought an influx of federal money into Southern Illinois along with many jobs. A 1930s conservation project on Crab Orchard Creek west of Marion grew into Crab Orchard Lake, and after the war began, a large ammunition plant was sited on its shores. The hamlet of Wolf Lake near Anna made explosives, and Cairo a component used in explosives. Murphysboro made army shoes, Mt. Carmel, electronics parts, and Centralia provided soldiers with candy. Alton made cartridges, Wood River processed chemicals, and Granite City provided steel. Fluorspar (or "fluorite") mined in Hardin and Pope Counties helped in the production of both steel and aluminum, the latter a necessity in the Air Corps' new lightweight planes. Scott Field near Belleville specialized in military communications, Parks Air College near Cahokia trained pilots, and Southern Illinois University schooled new officers. The list of how Southern Illinoisans helped win the war could be extended to those who provided grain, oil, lumber, coal, fruit, and vegetables. Everyone recycled metal (for bombs, ships, and tanks), and schoolchildren gathered milkweed pods, the silky down of which was used for buoyancy in life preservers. But one of the most enduring legacies of World War II had less to do with war than peace: the G.I. Bill. This guaranteed postwar financial benefits for military veterans, including what Southern Illinoisans needed most of all, education.

> There was an isolation . . . as if the area had been ringed with the mountains of Appalachia. Southern Illinois University was a gap in those mountains.
>
> —Robert Hastings, *A Nickel's Worth of Skim Milk*

It should be recalled that Egypt's image in the Bible was that of a land of darkness coupled with a despair so deep that only a man such as Moses could lead the children of Israel from it. The man who would lead the children of Illinois' Egypt out of their despair was not named Moses but Morris,

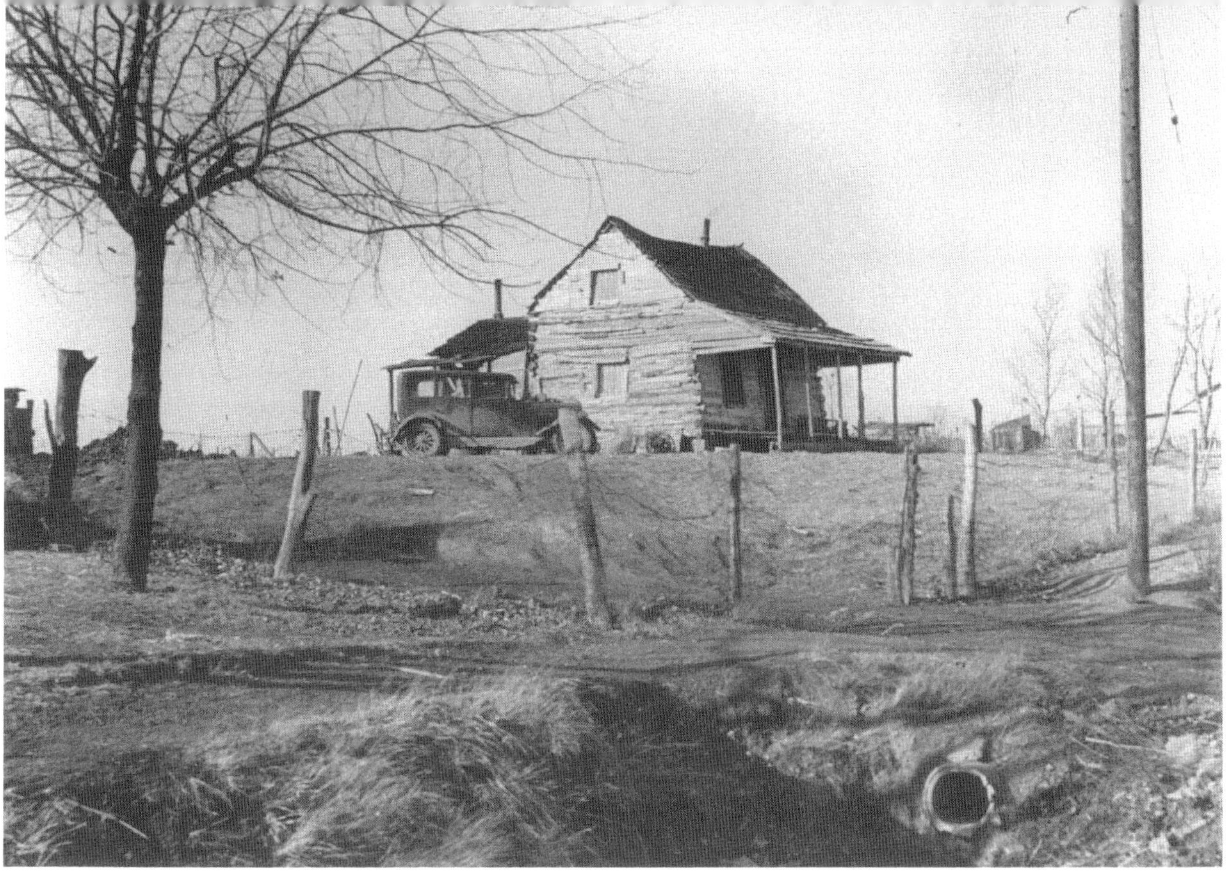

Miner's home in Carrier Mills. Saline County, January 1939. Photo by Arthur Rothstein, Farm Security Administration

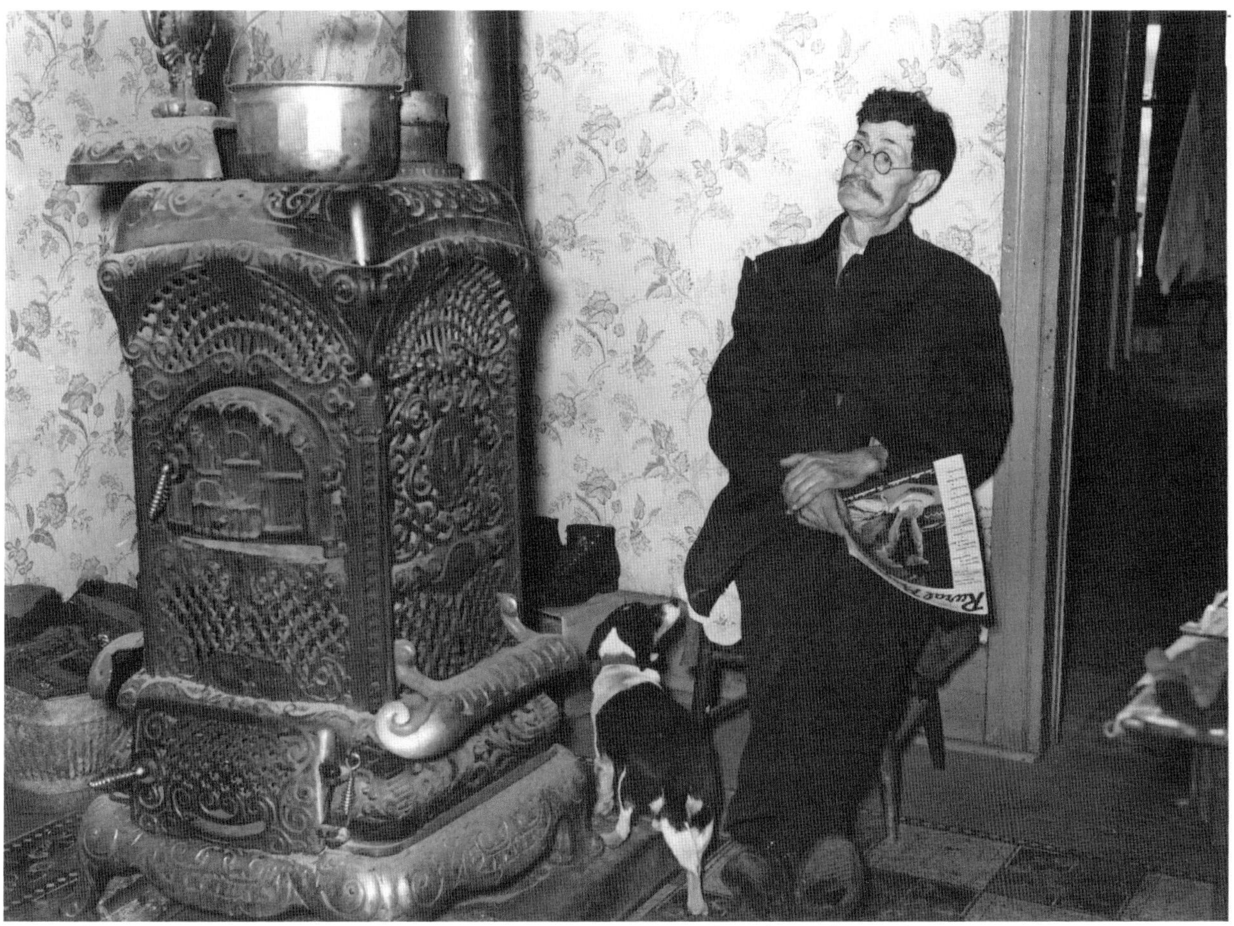

Unemployed mine worker in Bush. Williamson County, January 1939. Photo by Arthur Rothstein, Farm Security Administration

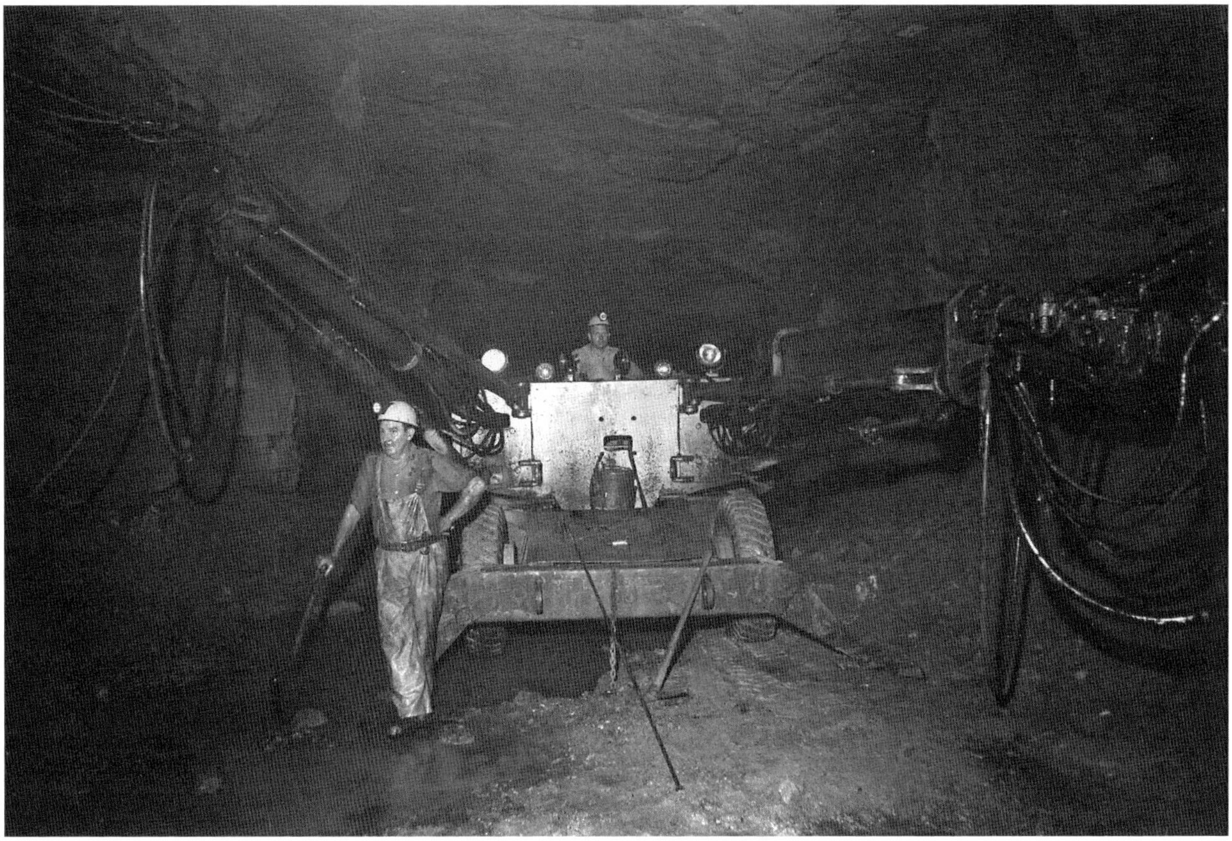

Fluorspar miners with a drilling machine in Hardin County in the 1950s. Though the mineral is no longer mined in the region, fluorspar's local history is summarized in Rosiclare's American Fluorite Museum in Hardin County. Photo courtesy of Fred Anderson

and he would require only twenty years, not forty. That Southern Illinois was regarded as a poor broken rib of Appalachia would work to the advantage of Delyte Morris, president of Southern Illinois University from 1948 to 1970.

Reared east of Salem on a farm near Xenia, Morris received his bachelor's degree from Park College in Missouri and served at several universities before discovering that his life work was to turn Carbondale's university of 3,000 into a multicampus student body of 35,000. Morris had the constitution of a mule, a handsome and capable first lady, and a doctorate in speech, a component of which is acting. Some said he acted during his presidency too, but if so, he usually played his part well.

One of Morris' first needs was for "Southern" to have its own board of trustees, an act of independence that was fought by tax-supported schools to the north, by the University of Illinois, accustomed to being the state's major public university, and by jealous teachers colleges in Charleston, Normal, Macomb, and DeKalb. These blocked Morris' efforts until a former mayor and restaurant owner from the sloping square of Vienna entered the scene. Democrat Paul Powell was then speaker of the Illinois House of Representatives and a member of the Legislative Budgetary Commission. Never one to let trifles

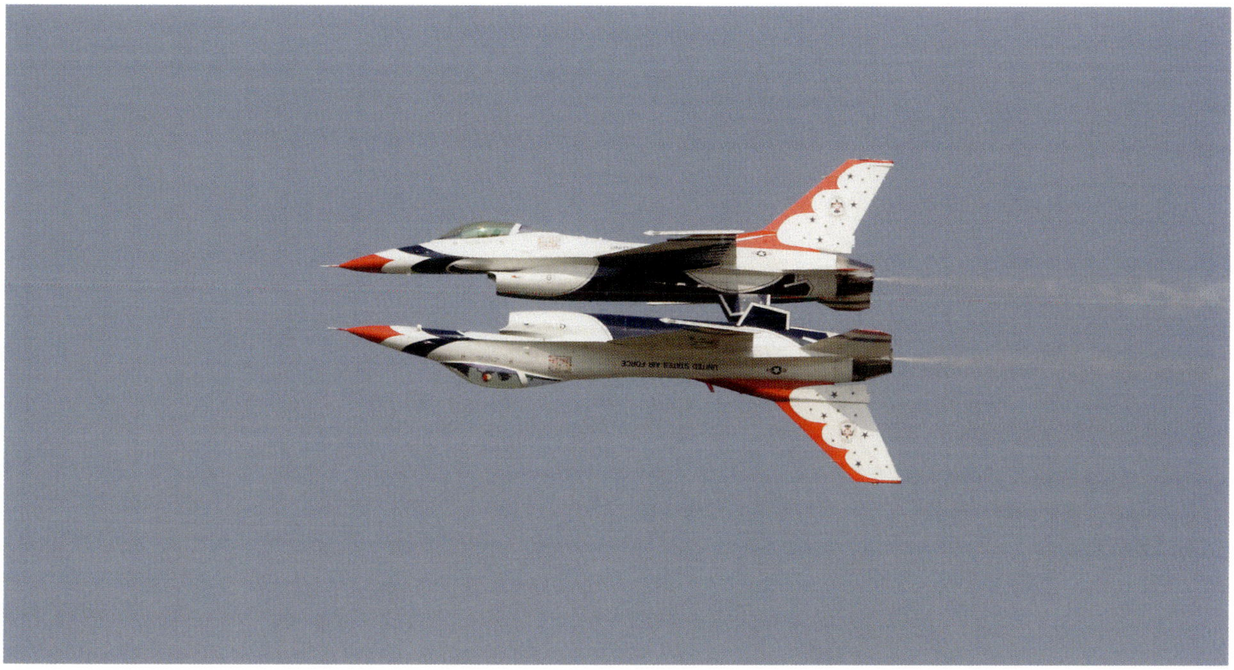

Precision flying at Scott Air Force Base near Belleville and O'Fallon. Photo courtesy of David Hammond

stand in his way, Powell shook his fist in the faces of University of Illinois officials and said (swear word) that he would not bring the U of I (swear word) budget request to a vote in the legislature unless Southern got its own board and money enough to run a first-class university. The Illini chiefs backed off as did the others, and Southern Illinois University began its ascendancy.

The South had finally defeated the North.

In the 1950s and early 1960s, SIU students returning to their central and northern Illinois homes were sometimes asked by older folks where this obscure place called "Carbondale" was in relation to places they knew—the state fair in Du Quoin, the restaurant called Tom's Place in DeSoto, and, occasionally, Colp, home of the best little whorehouse in Egypt. Articles in local, state, and national news outlets soon informed them, and record numbers enrolled at the university. Delyte Morris became the most popular Southern Illinoisan since John A. Logan, and taxpayers enthusiastically supported him, especially after 1950 when he established a Vocational-Technical Institute for blue collar and secretarial students. Minority students and students with disabilities were well treated, and the hiring of faculty such as technology visionary Buckminster Fuller and Shakespeare scholar T. W. Baldwin brought more attention.

By the early 1960s it was virtually impossible to find SIU students who were not enthusiastic about the university even when some of them lived in rented garages with dirt floors and in World War II barracks. The creation of a second campus in Edwardsville, the offering of advanced degrees, and plans for schools of nursing, dentistry, and law enhanced the university's reputation. State approval for an SIU medical school in Springfield in 1968 added new

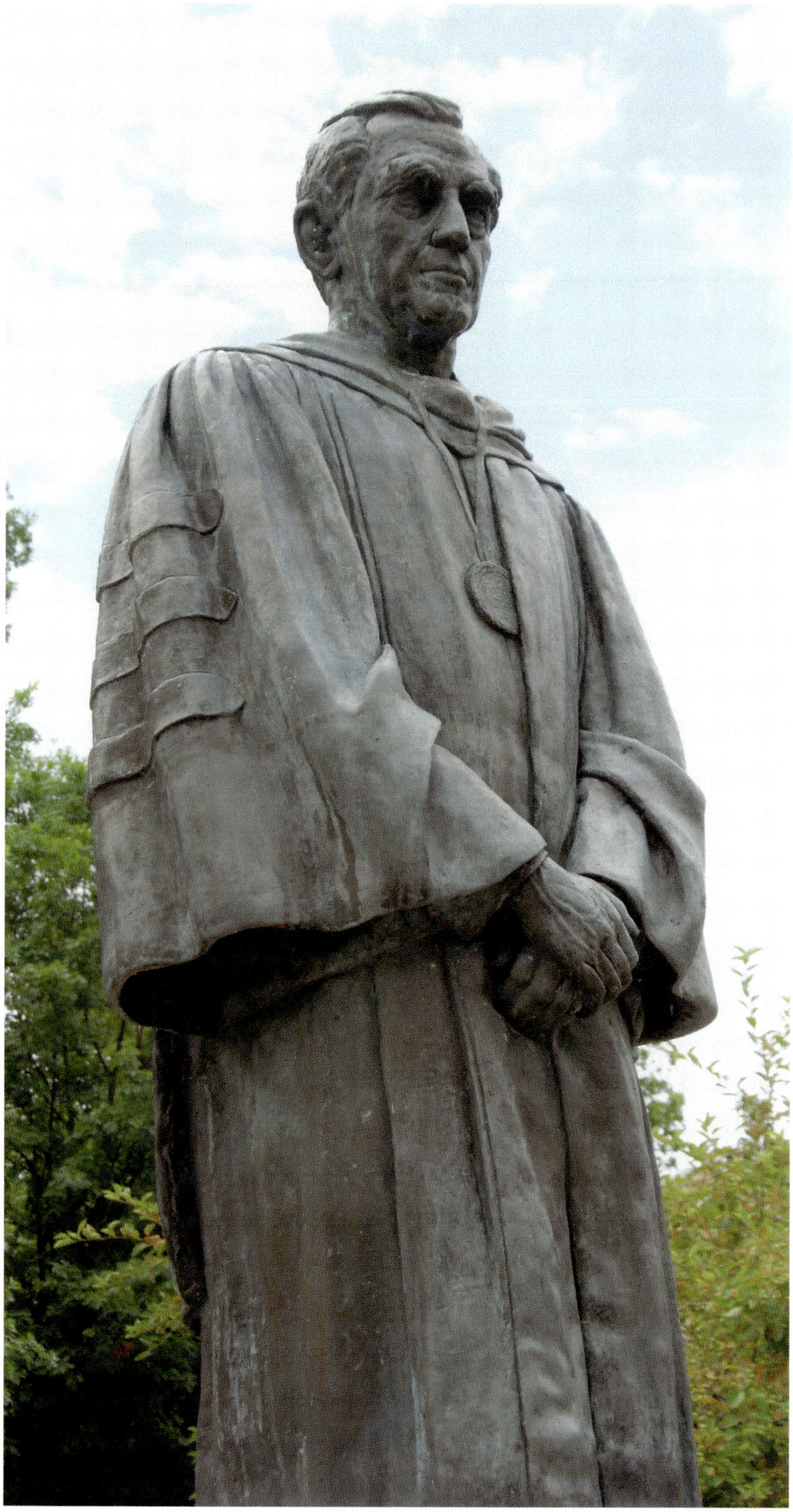

Fredda Brilliant's statue of Delyte Morris stands where Southern Illinois University began in 1869. Photo courtesy of Shannon Woodworth

responsibilities, but campus unrest over American involvement in the Vietnam War introduced special tensions.

It was Morris' misfortune that he encountered in the late 1960s a new generation of students who were more political, demanded a greater voice in campus affairs, and questioned everything (were curfew hours for female students legal?). This generation distrusted authority and scorned what they called "the establishment," the older generation who had led the country into the war in Vietnam. The war was their special symbol of protest, and they used it as leverage whenever it worked to their advantage. When the university opened a Center for Vietnamese Studies in 1969, its mission of academic instruction was obscured by the tear gas and riots generated by its presence.

The presiding father figure on two campuses, Delyte Morris was part of the older establishment whose values were being reevaluated. No matter that he could not alter the war in Vietnam, end the military draft, legalize marijuana, or address a dozen other issues alternately serious or silly, some 150–300 individuals now behaved as though he should. Worse, they tended to destroy things when frustrated. Imitating what they saw happening at dozens of other colleges, the war protestors—some were students, and some were not—burned, bombed, and bullied the campus and community for two years, always with the conviction that their own political opinions were more important than the rights of others. It was in this atmosphere that someone burned the school's Old Main building, a symbol of the university shown on the school seal. Rally numbers sometimes grew from hundreds to thousands, and after one window-breaking spree a future judge named Richard Richman likened the mostly white rioters to "Hitler youth."

In May 1970 rioters trashed portions of Carbondale, the local newspaper reporting damage to seventy-eight businesses. On South Illinois Avenue only one window remained unbroken, or so it was said at the barbershop. There was talk of getting even, of other towns that would be vandalized, and so the campus was closed, its students sent home, examinations and graduation canceled for spring 1970. Some of the rioters later said that closing SIU showed support for the antiwar movement and helped bring the Vietnam War to an end; others said the rioters had simply moved the war zone from Vietnam to Carbondale. The university eventually quieted down, but these turbulent times marked the end of Delyte Morris' presidency, as well as SIU's years of easy ascendency into the ranks of major state universities.

The rest of Southern Illinois also would end one era and begin another. The old image of Egypt defined by coal, gangsters, and isolation began its decline in the 1970s. The 1976 federal Clean Air Act was one of several progressively stringent laws that associated the burning of Egypt's high-sulfur coal with poor air quality. The coal could still be mined, but its major impurities would have to be removed or reduced before, during, or after burning; alternately, it could be blended with low-sulfur coal from other states and then burned. Either way, Southern Illinois coal became less competitive in the marketplace. Many mines had reduced production or closed by the 1990s, and the day came

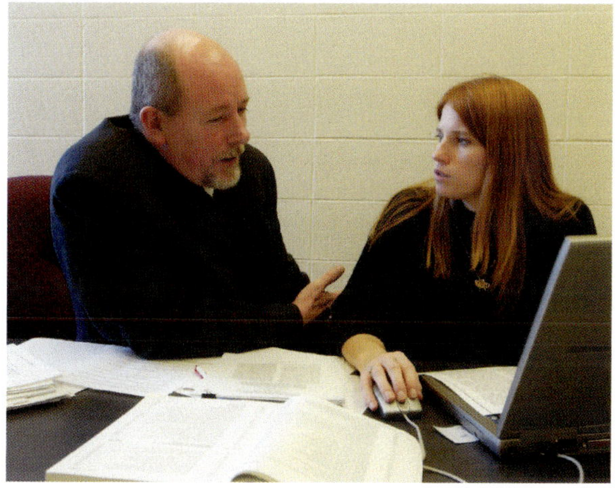

The College of Business at Southern Illinois University Carbondale is one of the finest in the nation. Departments include marketing, represented above, accounting, finance, and management. Courtesy of Office of the Provost and Vice Chancellor, Southern Illinois University Carbondale

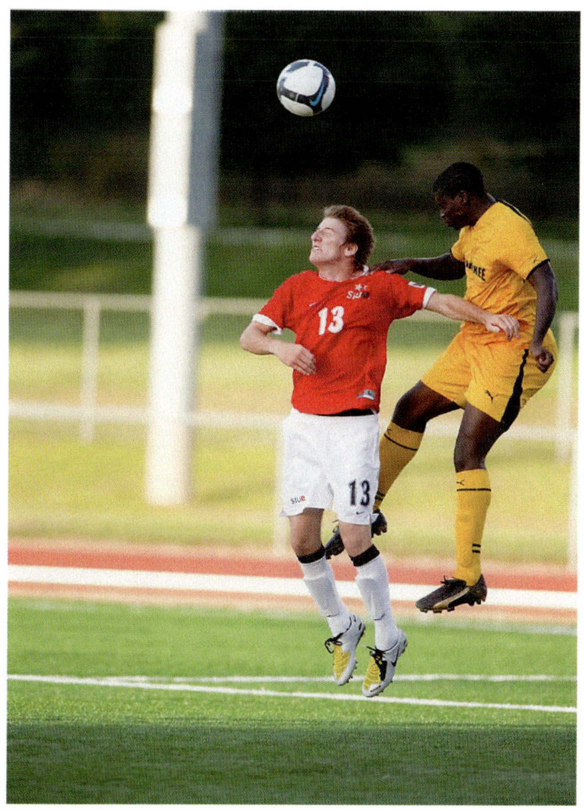

Soccer is a major sport at SIU Edwardsville. Photo courtesy of Denise MacDonald

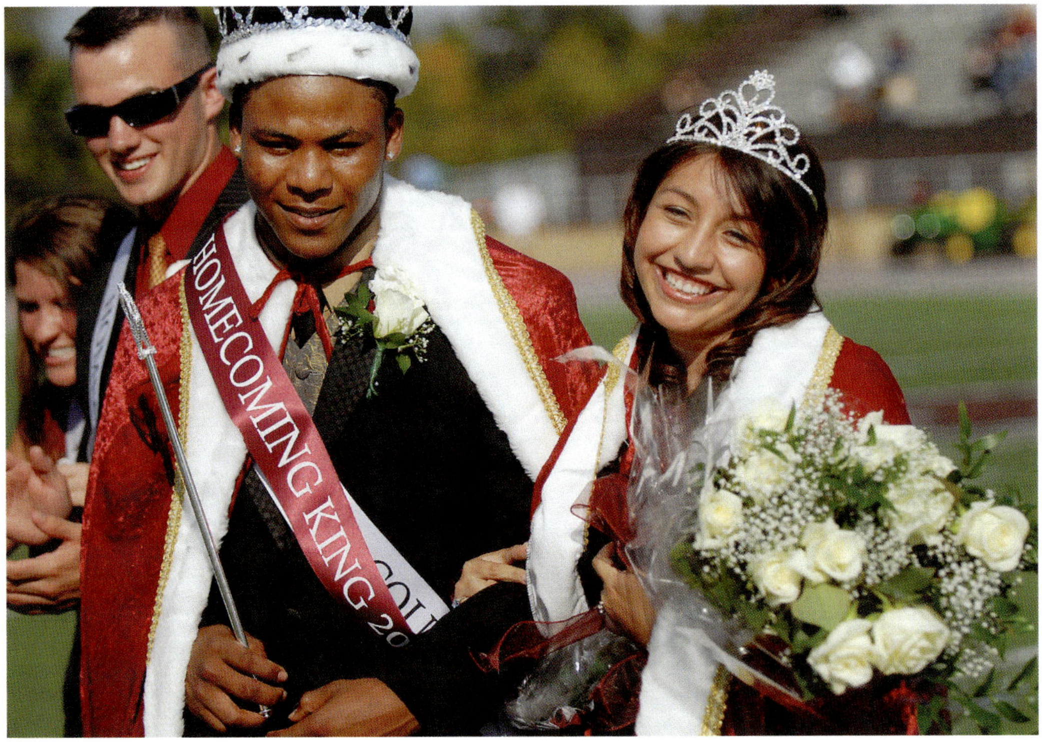

A homecoming king and queen try on new crowns and capes on the Carbondale campus. Photo by Steve Jahnke; courtesy of the *Southern Illinoisan*

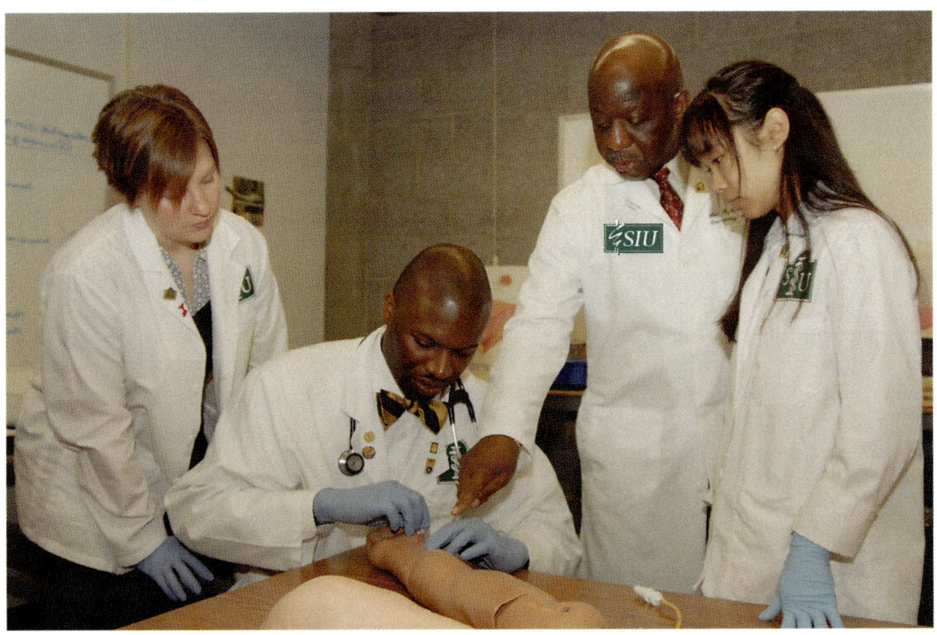

Southern Illinois University prepares health specialists at its School of Medicine in Springfield (*above*) and in Carbondale. The School of Nursing is in Edwardsville and Carbondale; the School of Dental Medicine, in Alton; and the School of Pharmacy, at Edwardsville. Photo by Michael Meyer; courtesy of SIU School of Medicine

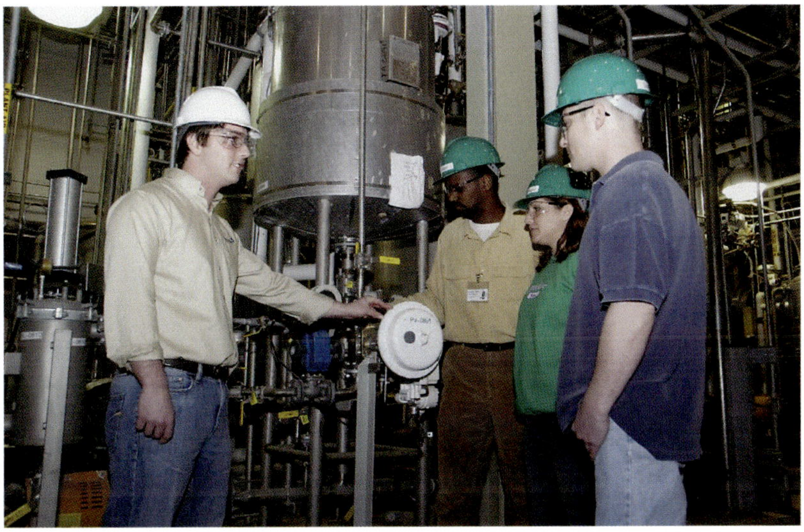

SIU's many research capabilities include the National Corn-to-Ethanol Research Center on the Edwardsville campus. Other energy and agriculture research facilities are on the Carbondale campus. Photo courtesy of Denise MacDonald

when not one mine was open in Franklin County, a name synonymous with Illinois coal for over a century.

The federal Surface Mining Control and Reclamation Act of 1977 governing surface or strip mining added other costs but also initiated desirable environmental changes. The process of surface mining had always yielded one positive environmental result: it broke up the stubborn layer of hardpan clay that lies under most of the region's topsoil. Unfortunately, traditional strip mining usually buried these two upper layers on the bottom of a strip pile. With the new law, coal companies had to put up a cash bond guaranteeing that they would return surface-mined land to its original configurations layer by layer after coal was removed. The topsoil would be returned to its uppermost position, and the layer of hard clay, now fragmented, would allow for greater penetration of plant roots, water, and nutrients.

Mining guidelines of the 1970s and later also affected the miners' union, the United Mine Workers of America, and the Southern Illinois towns in which they lived. The UMWA was a social and political force, as well as the miners' bargaining agency, but the union lost much of its clout during these years, and a large nonunion mine was being planned as early as 1981. Labor-management disagreements still occurred, along with strikes and vandalism, but the murderous behaviors of the old days had ended. Traditional coal towns such as Herrin and West Frankfort and smaller ones such as Zeigler, Royalton, Valier, and Orient bore the brunt of mining's cutbacks. Coal mining continued on a limited scale, but as the twentieth century ended, a generation of miners in

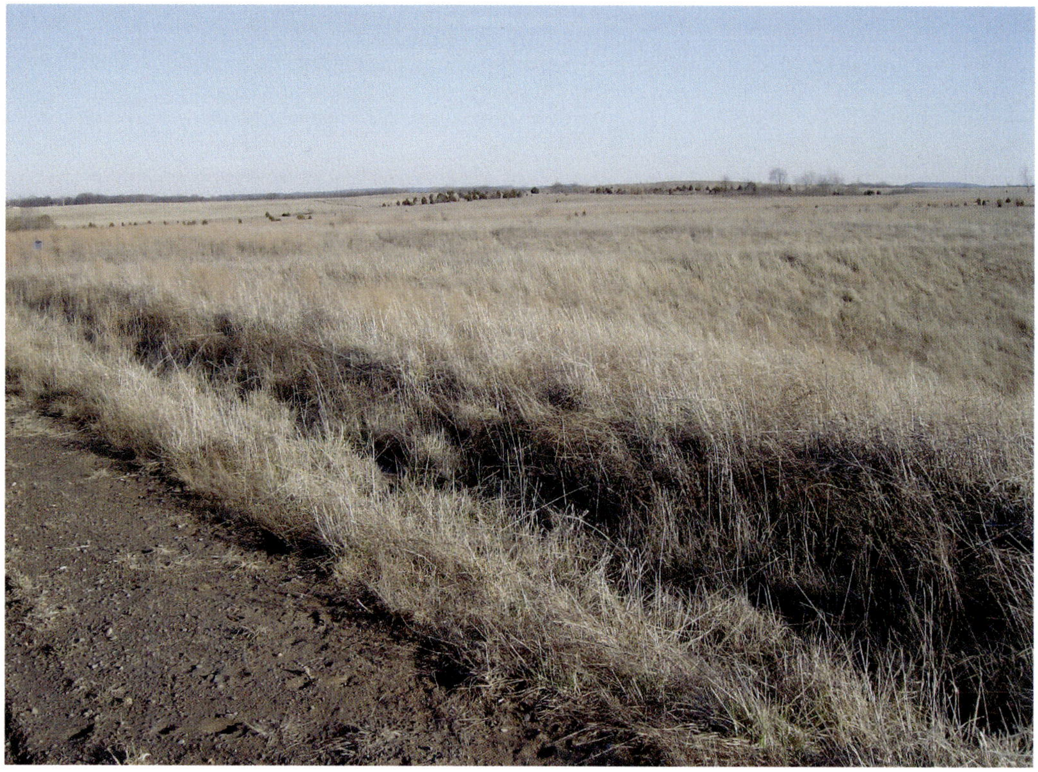

Near Harrisburg, thousands of acres of strip-mined land have been returned to grasslands and productive farm fields. Photo courtesy of Brian DeNeal

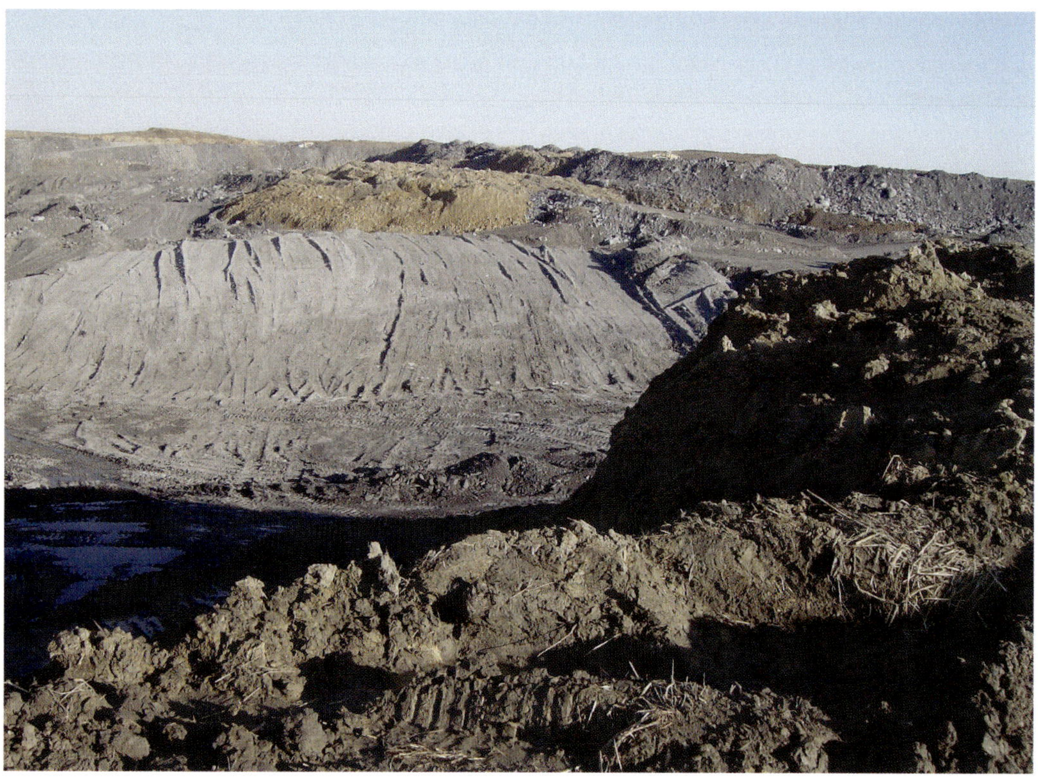

Strip-mined lands before reclamation. Photo courtesy of Brian DeNeal

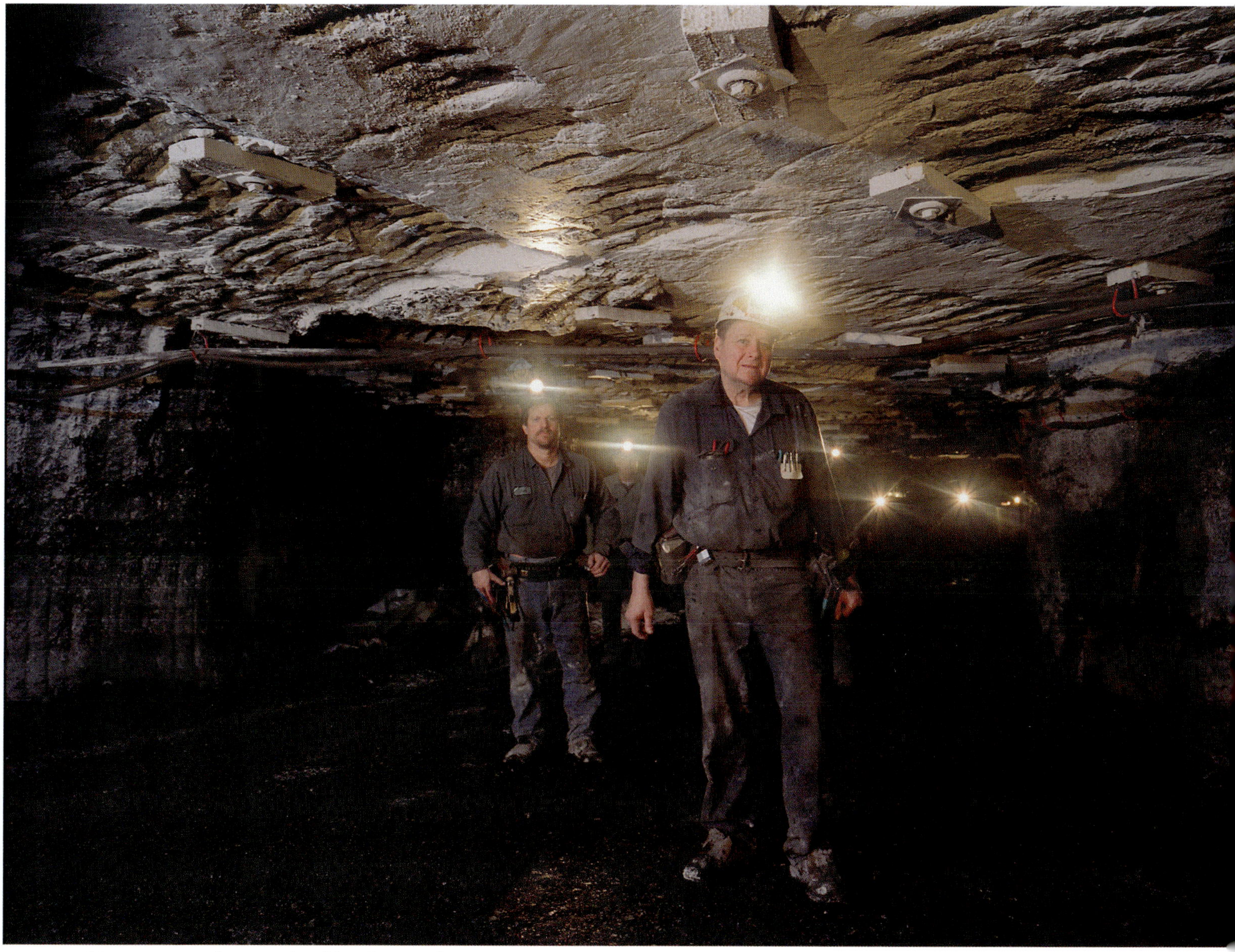

Miners in an underground or "deep" mine. Photo courtesy of Lee M. Buchsbaum

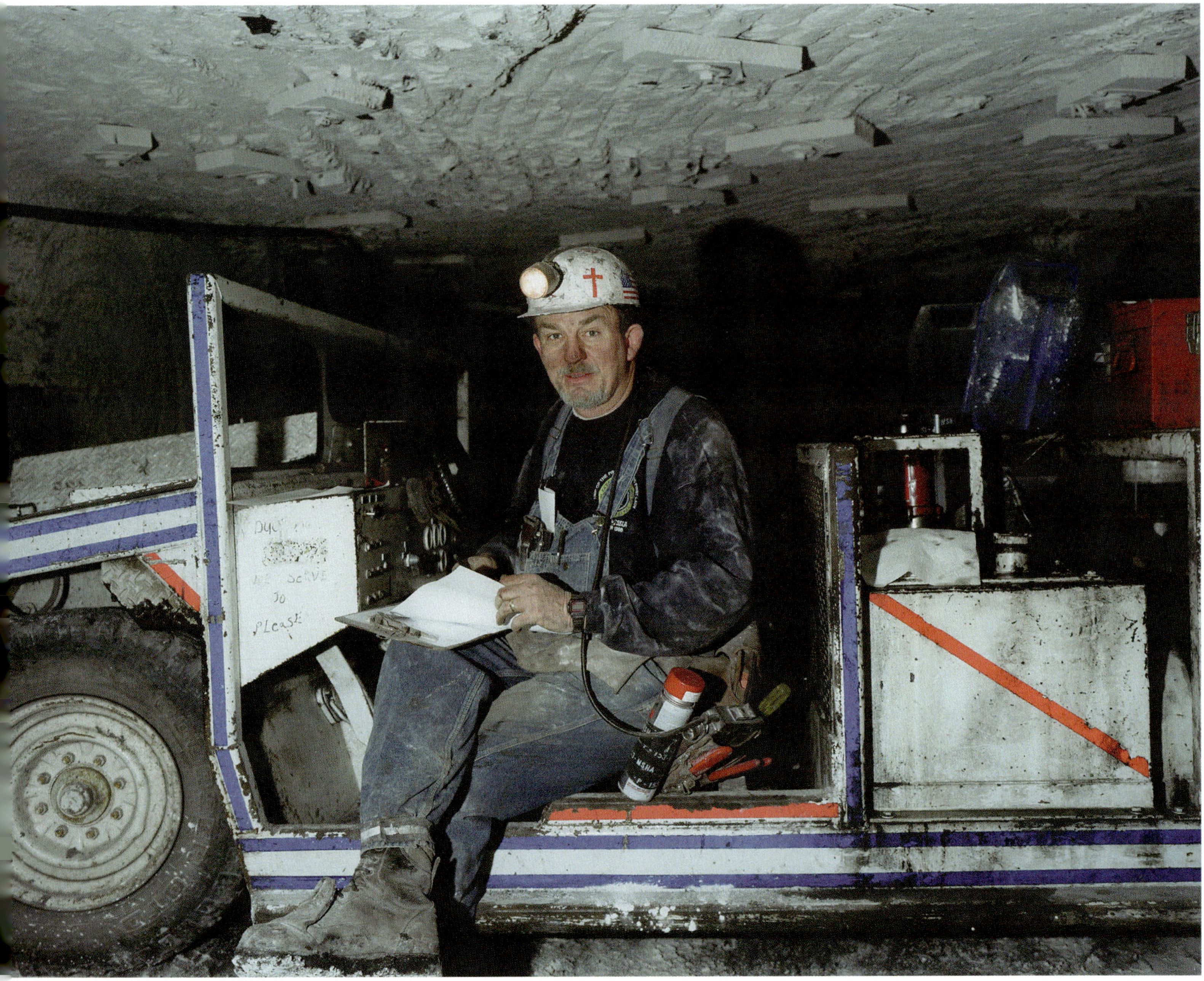

Miner on a utility vehicle. Photo courtesy of Lee M. Buchsbaum

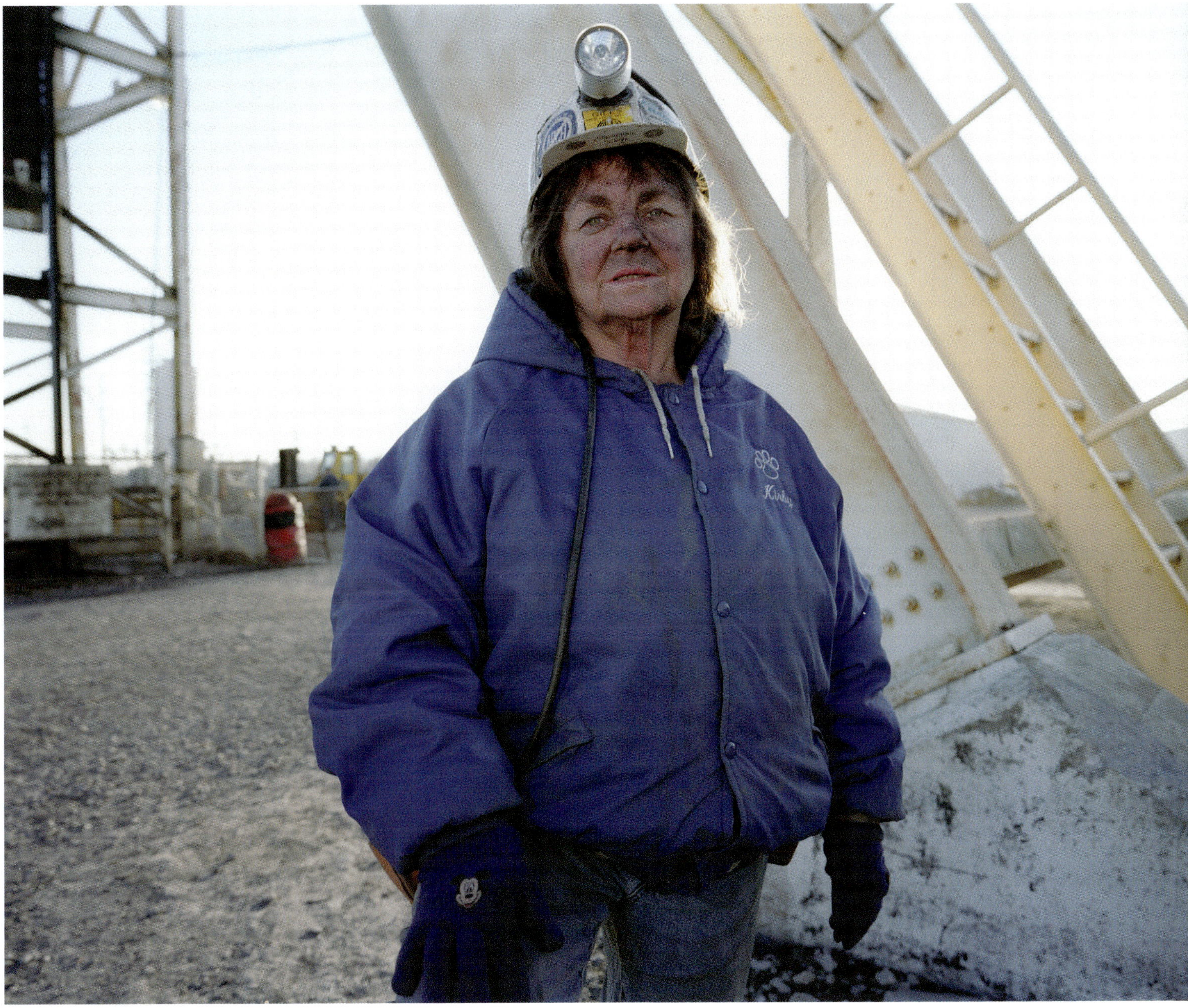

A coal miner ends her workday. Photo courtesy of Lee M. Buchsbaum

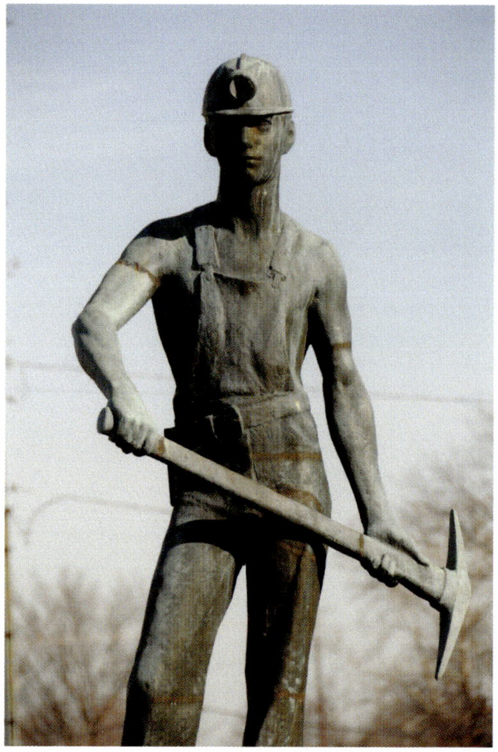

The miner's statue in Zeigler (*above*) once defined Southern Illinois' image, but government regulations have left some miners on the outside looking in (*below*). Franklin County. Photo of miner's statue courtesy of Shannon Woodworth; photo of miner courtesy of Lee M. Buchsbaum

their middle years faced an uncertain future. New "clean coal" technologies aimed at removing coal's impurities guaranteed that some mining would continue, but it was clear too that fewer miners would be required.

The era of old-time gangsters ended quietly in the late 1960s and '70s as one of the most dangerous of these spent his golden years in prison. Charles "Blackie" Harris had been a Wayne County associate of the Shelton Brothers in Prohibition days of the 1920s but had gone to prison for ten years for counterfeiting. The Sheltons had not allowed Harris to rejoin their circle after he was freed, and this slight and others came back to haunt them during their semiretirement from crime near Fairfield in the 1940s. Harris, a man with an ugly temper, began exacting revenge. He was probably respon-

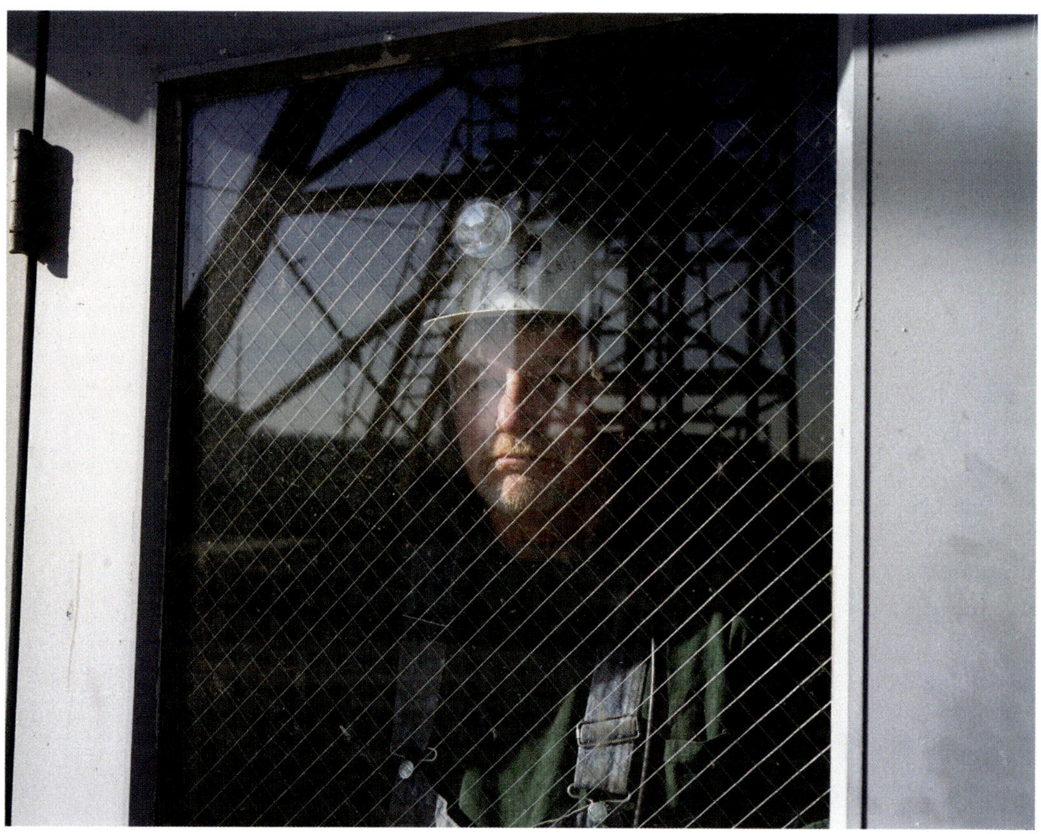

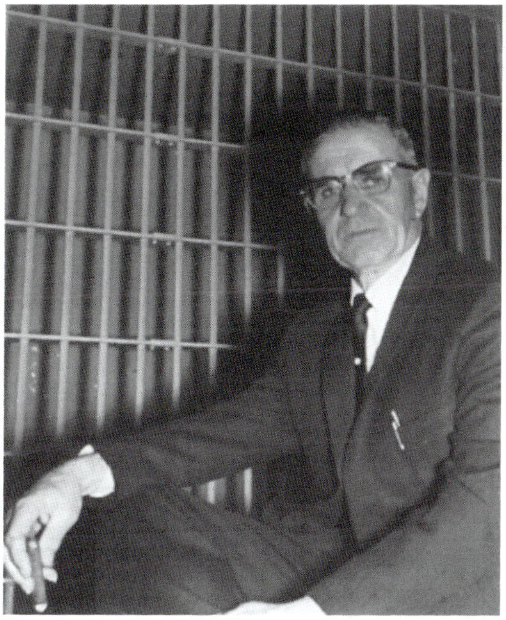

Small, polite, meticulous, and mean, a well-dressed Charles "Blackie" Harris awaits trial for murder in the Wayne County Jail, Fairfield. Photo by T. O. Mathews; courtesy of Tom Mathews Jr.

sible for murdering two of the Sheltons and scaring two more to Florida before attacking their family, friends, and business associates. Convicted of double murder and arson in 1965, Blackie Harris spent many of his final years in prisons at Chester and Vienna and died in the mid-1980s.

The completion of a national interstate highway system during the 1970s and '80s alleviated the isolation traditionally associated with Egypt, but it also diminished the importance of railroads as trucks carried more of the nation's goods. The slowdown in regional coal production began during these same years and contributed not only to the railroads' decline but also to the changing face of the Southern Illinois landscape. Some small towns lost businesses as rail tracks were taken up and century-old rights-of-way returned to woods or farmland. A few of the old rights-of-way became hiking and biking paths, such as the forty-seven-mile route between Harrisburg and the Cache River Wetlands Center on Route 37. The last vestige of railroading's old days ended in the 1980s and '90s, when union agreements and computers banished the railroader's home on wheels, the red caboose. The computer's ally, the Internet, brought the rest of the world to Southern Illinois.

The traditional small farm with a mix of livestock and grain would also change during these years. Many Southern Illinois farms had always operated at subsistence levels, producing enough to get by on but not much more. Widespread modernization began in the late 1940s when tractors became common and many rural areas received electricity, both of which decreased the need for laborers. During the next two decades, many in the younger generation moved away, the old folks died, and their farms of eighty to a hundred acres were absorbed by larger ones. Empty houses and barns on desirable farmland were often bulldozed, burned, and buried—the past swept away so cleanly that only a well and a pump remained, and sometimes not even those. By the mid-1970s the new slogan for successful farming was clear: "Get big or get out."

This new generation of farmers usually had limited interest in livestock operations and a greater interest in scientific farming: soil conservation, soil testing, the use of chemicals, and on-farm storage of harvests in large metal bins, which allowed them to market the grain when the price was right. They followed research on plant genetics and diseases, and planted the new soybean varieties that sometimes brought yields approaching those in central Illinois. They

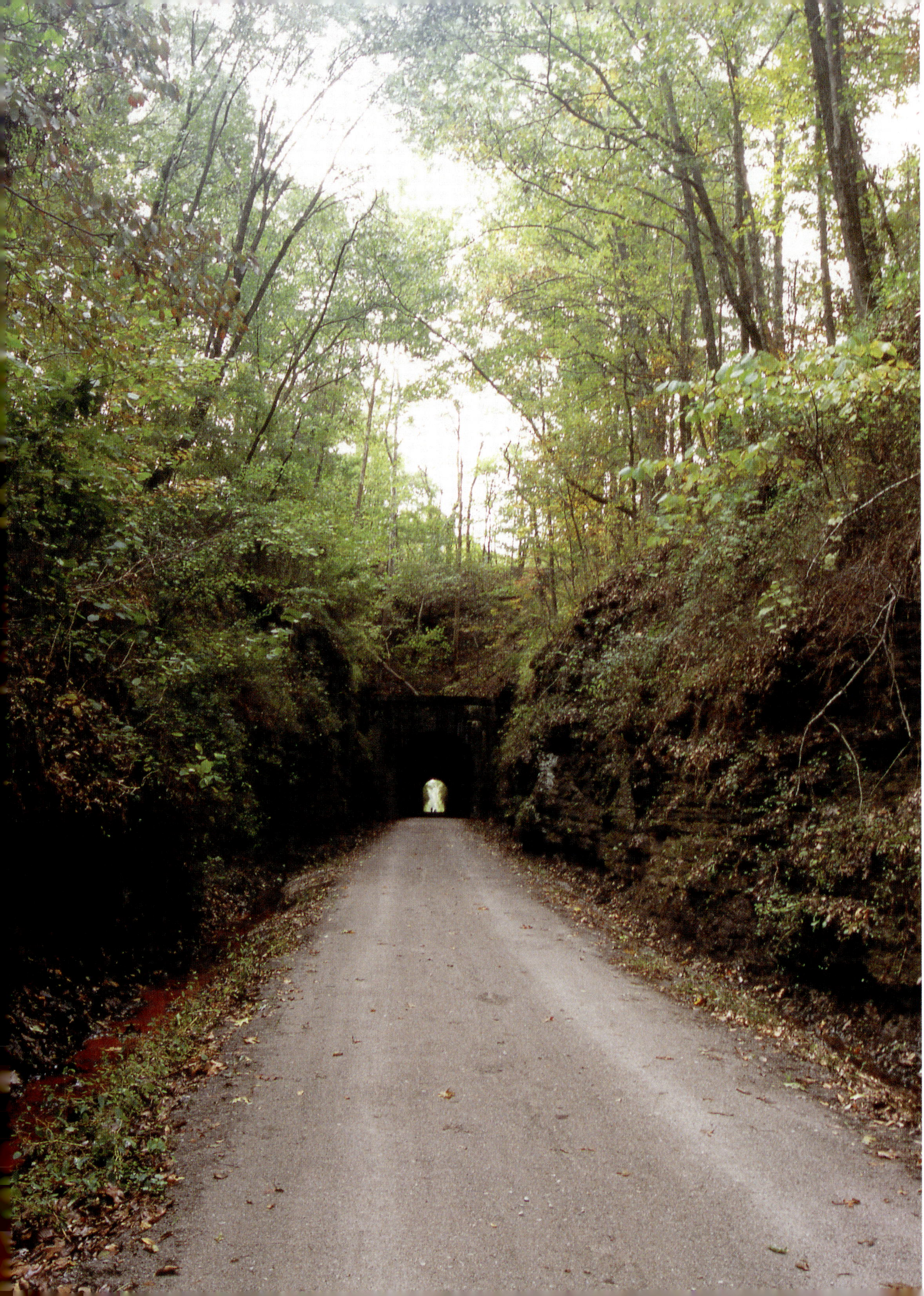

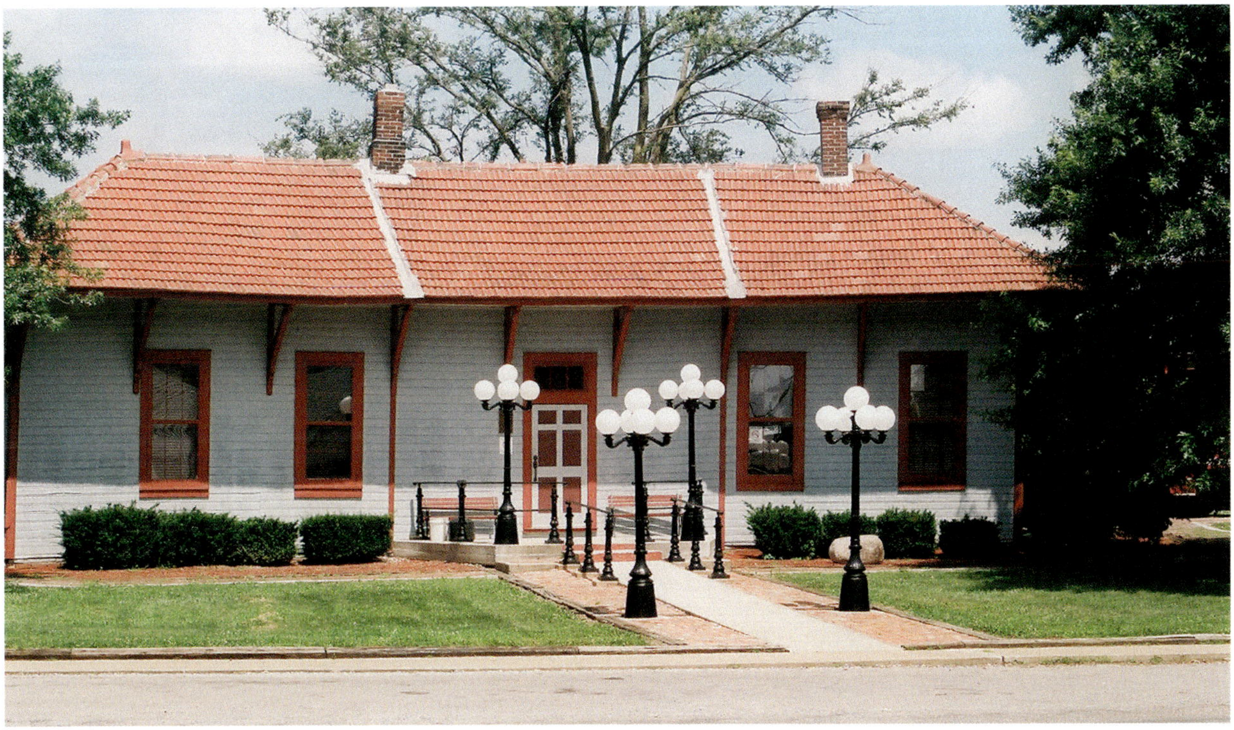

(Above) This 1899 Tamms depot served two rail lines before becoming the village hall. Photo by Herbert K. Russell

(Left) A portion of the nineteenth-century Cairo and Vincennes Railroad is now a bike path. Tunnel Hill, Johnson County. Photo courtesy of David Hammond

were willing to experiment with nontraditional crops such as milo and sunflowers, and had a continuing interest in the use of grains and grasses as energy sources. Some small swine operations survived through the 1990s, but here too the trend was toward production on a large scale or not at all. The few remaining poultry spent their lives indoors on acres of concrete before heading to market; a few large dairy herds remained near the Metro East market. By the beginning of the twenty-first century, only two of Southern Illinois' traditional farm animals were found in substantial numbers: feeder cattle grown for beef, which still grazed the region's grassy slopes, and, surprisingly, horses. These were not the workhorses that grandpa had used to cultivate his wide-spaced corn rows but riding horses for trails and rodeos, and, increasingly, their sleek equine cousins, the jumpers.

The 1970s would also be a pivotal decade for the region's fruit and vegetable growers as Illinois land prices escalated and a new group of migrant workers arrived. The first migrants had been out-of-work coal miners from Franklin County and poor whites from Missouri and Arkansas, followed by

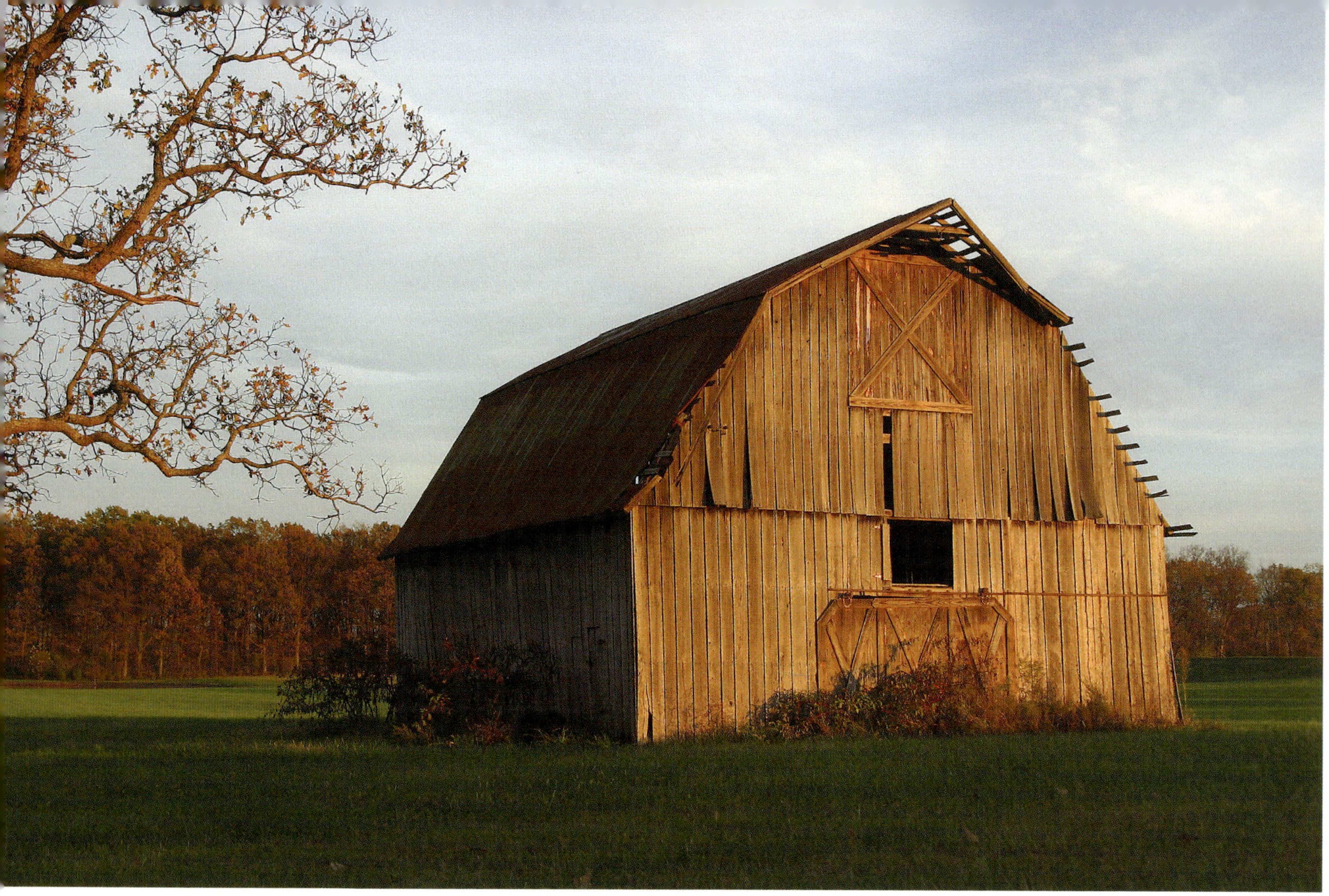
Spring sunlight warms a deserted barn from the era of small farms. Photo courtesy of Tom Kane

imported Jamaican laborers during the war years of the 1940s. There followed a decade or more in which area African Americans worked in the fields and orchards, after which Mexican migrant workers arrived in the 1970s. The latter demonstrated an excellent work ethic, and some remained to pursue citizenship and open their own businesses. The fruit and vegetable industry flourished because it produced tasty products in a timely manner, because owners and laborers got along, and because many farms were large enough to achieve cost efficiencies.

Some other farm and garden products contributing to the contemporary economy include pumpkins, horseradish, popcorn, and flowers such as daffodils, peonies, and iris. Southern Illinois has numerous farmers markets, where fresh produce is sold, as well as organic farms. The latter typically avoid the use of insecticides and other chemicals in favor of natural fertilizers. One must also mention the Amish, who work their land with horses much as they did in the nineteenth century and seem to get the most from their attractive farms, whatever their size.

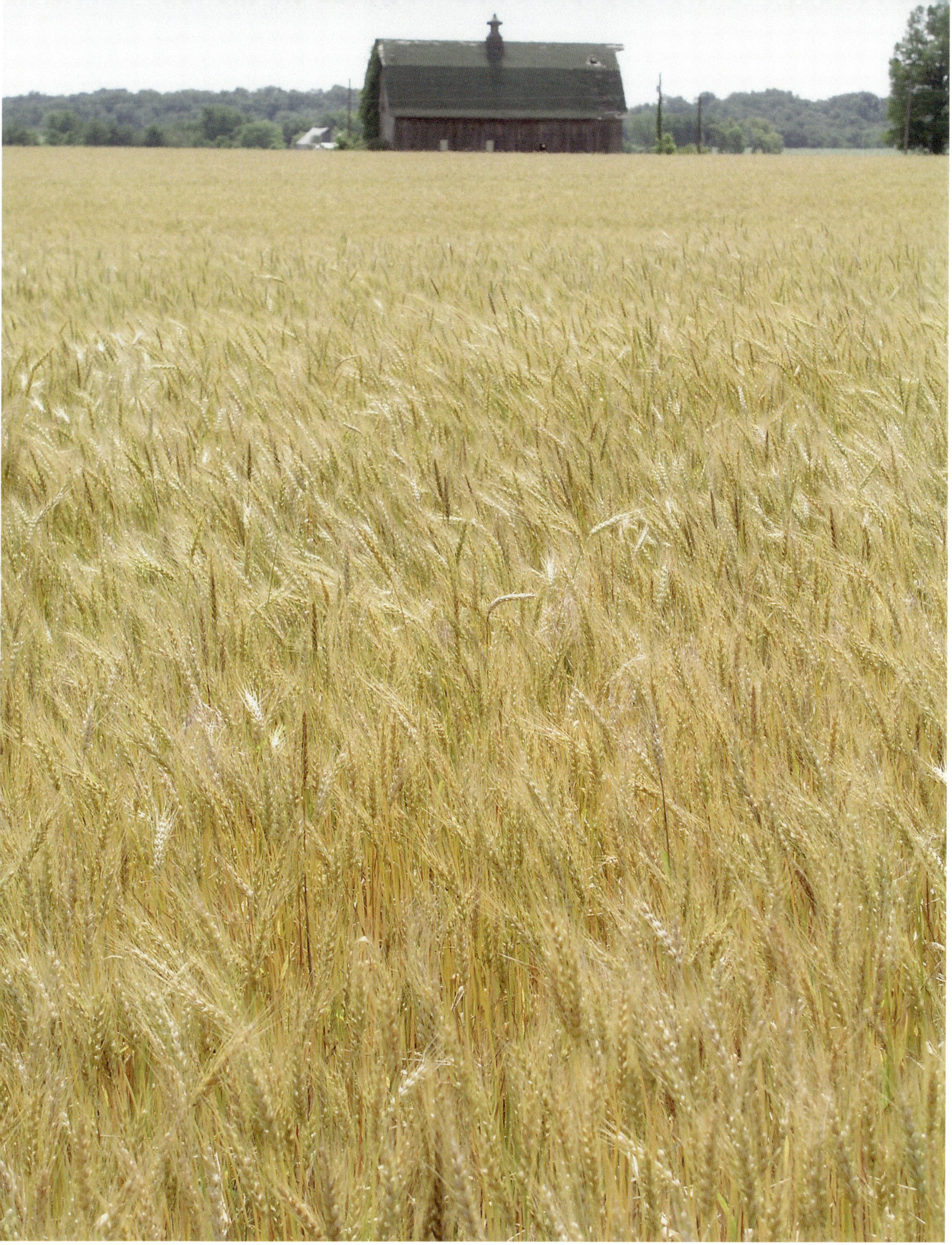

A field of wheat and a tattered barn affirm the ascendency of grain farming over small-scale livestock operations. Photo courtesy of Shannon Woodworth

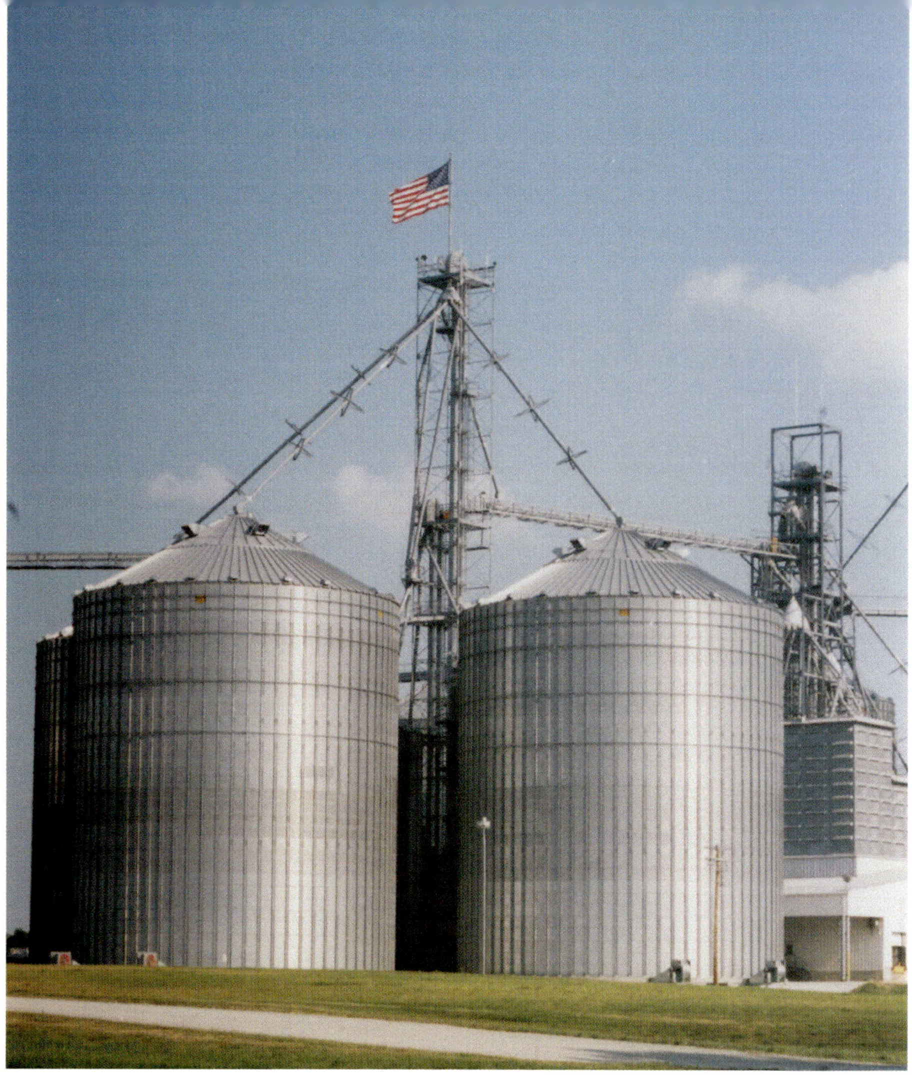

These massive grain bins at Carlyle help support one of the largest swine operations in the nation. Photo by Herbert K. Russell

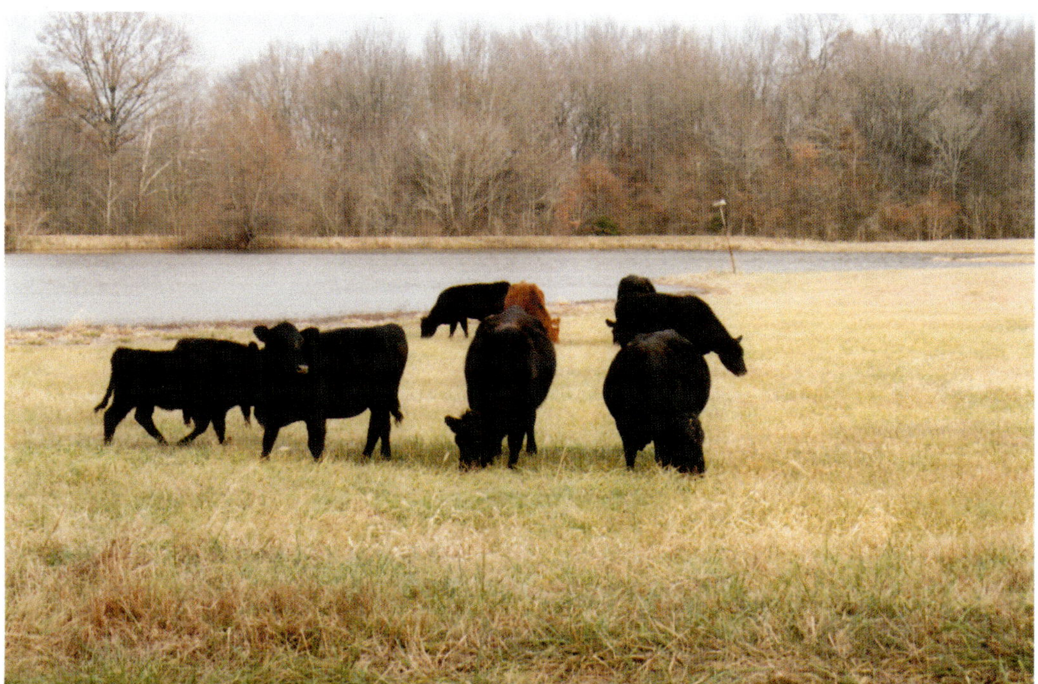

Feeder cattle graze before going to market. Photo by Herbert K. Russell

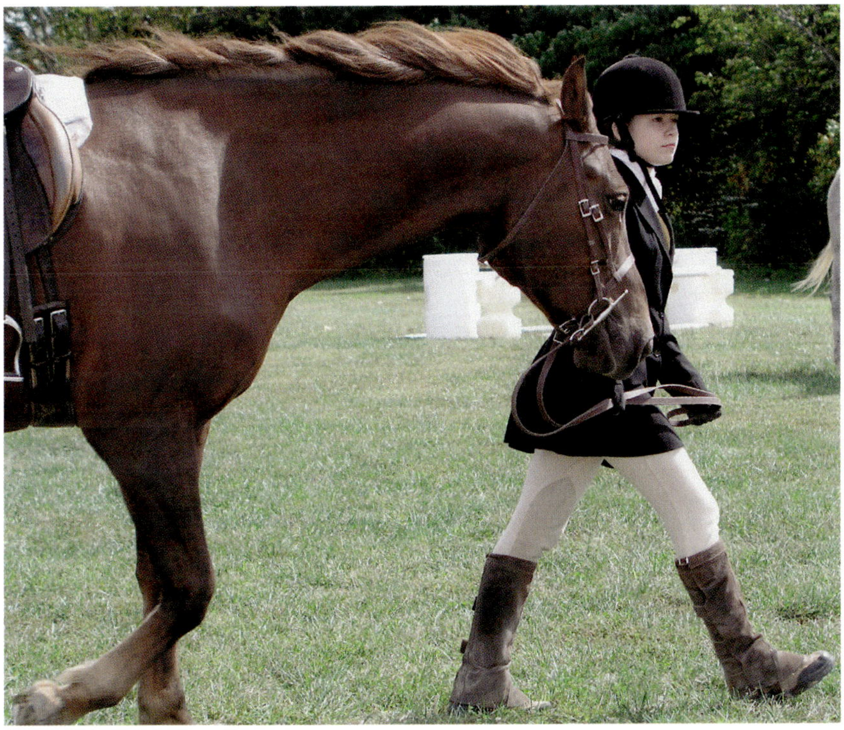

Equestrians and their mounts illustrate two different types of horse competitions. Photos courtesy of Shannon Woodworth

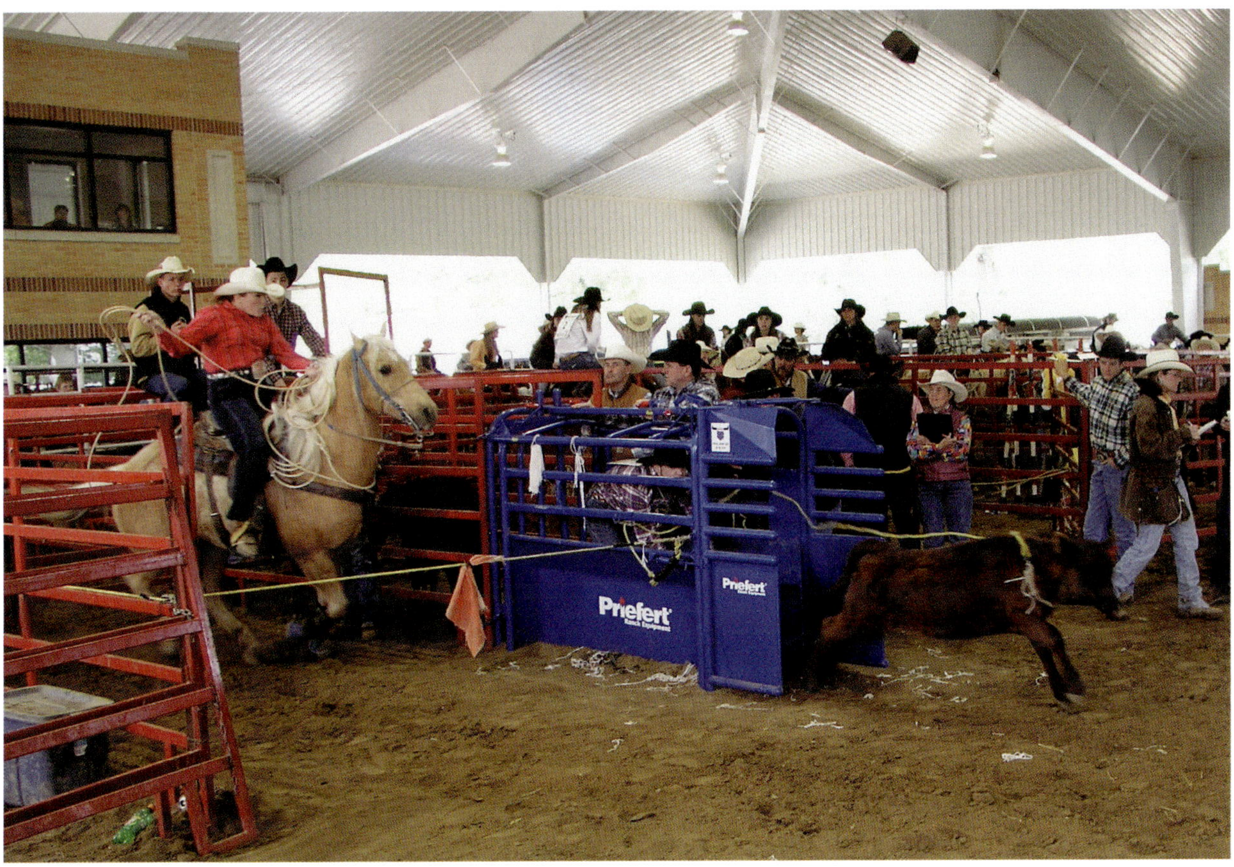

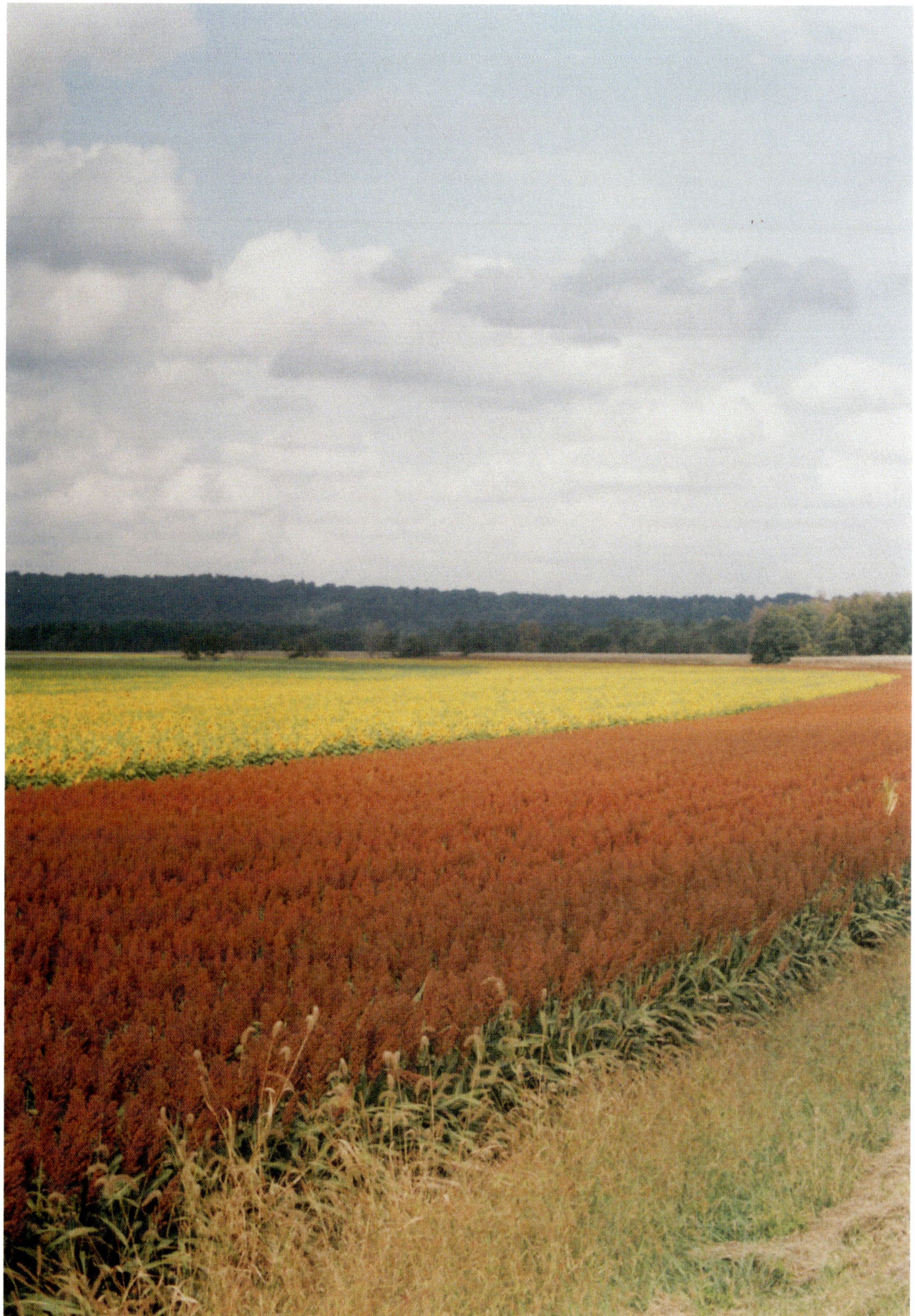

Bands of brown milo and yellow sunflowers follow a road out of Gorham in Jackson County. Photo by Herbert K. Russell

A major new market, the wine industry, has also come of age. In earlier days, some Southern Illinoisans made wine for personal use, but it was not until the mid-1980s that Alto Vineyards in Alto Pass demonstrated that quality wines could be produced and marketed on a commercial scale. During the 1990s and into the twenty-first century, Southern Illinois vineyards enjoyed spectacular growth when hillsides that had proved uncongenial for other crops proved just right for grapes. Wineries, tasting rooms, wine festivals, and wine trails soon followed, along with a refreshing new image of Southern Illinois as the state's principal (and prettiest) wine region.

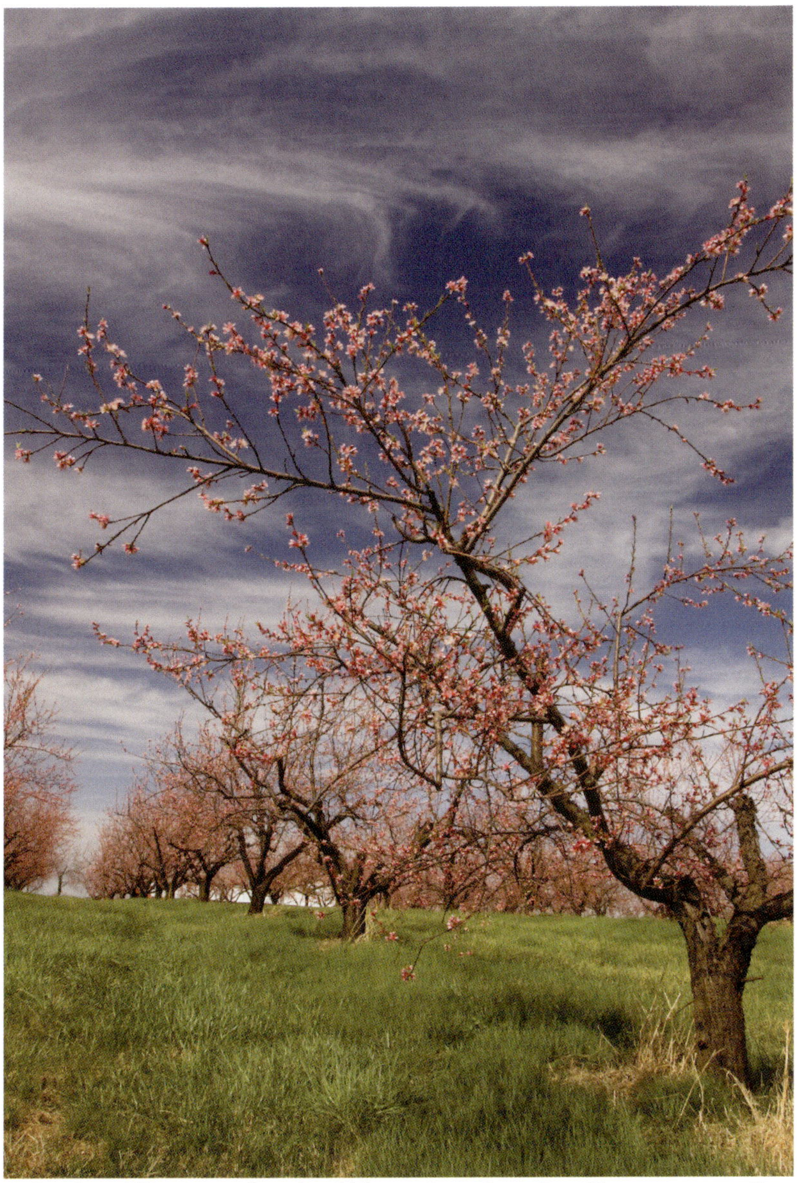

A Southern Illinois peach orchard blooms in early spring. Photo courtesy of David Hammond

This 1988 photo of Alto Vineyard's Guy Renzaglia captures the beginnings of Southern Illinois' commercial wine industry. Alto Pass, Union County. Photo by Joe Jines; courtesy of the *Southern Illinoisan*

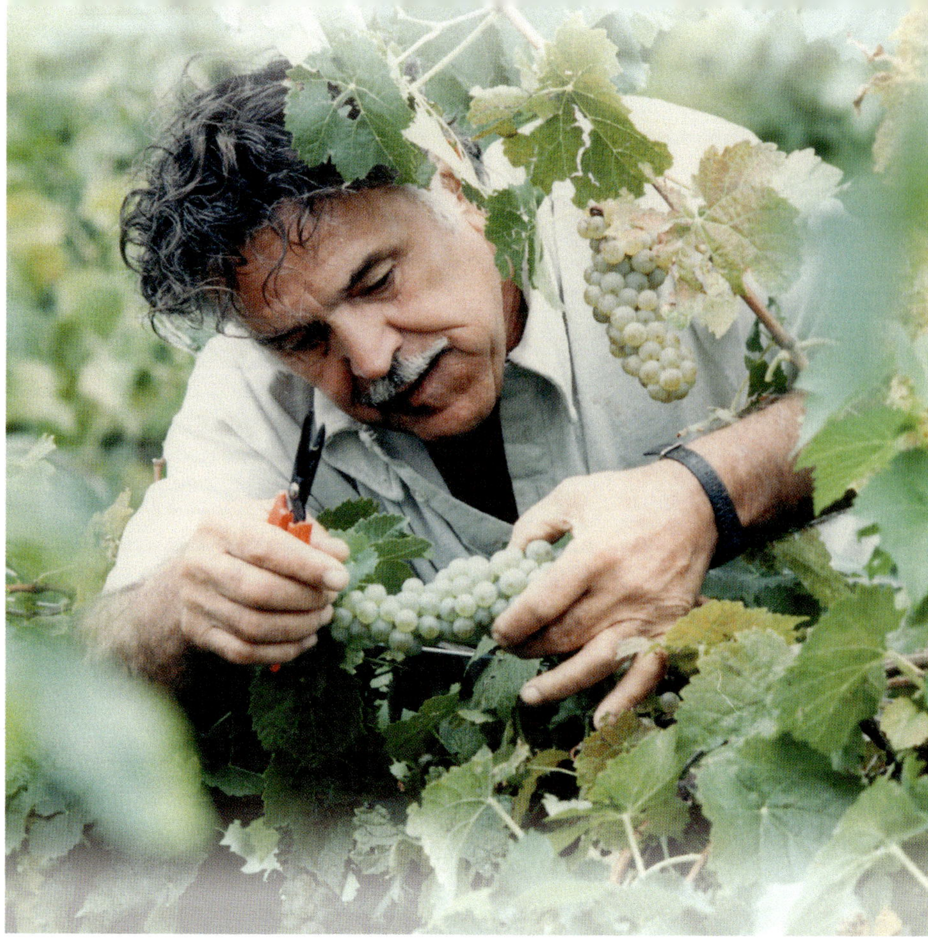

A wine festival offers tastes and tee shirts in the hill country town of Cobden in Union County, the state's chief wine-producing county. Photo by Herbert K. Russell

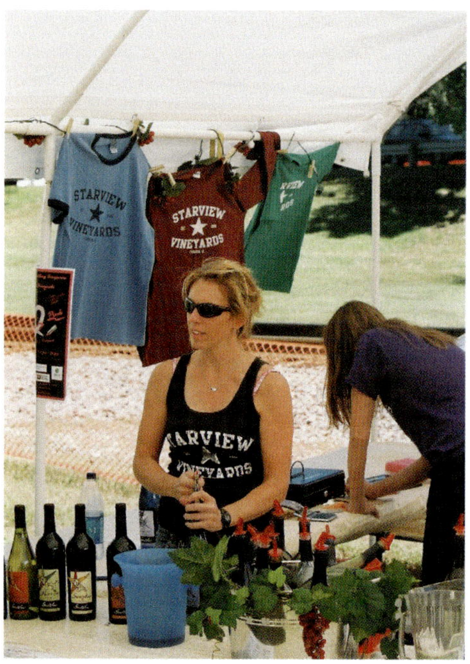

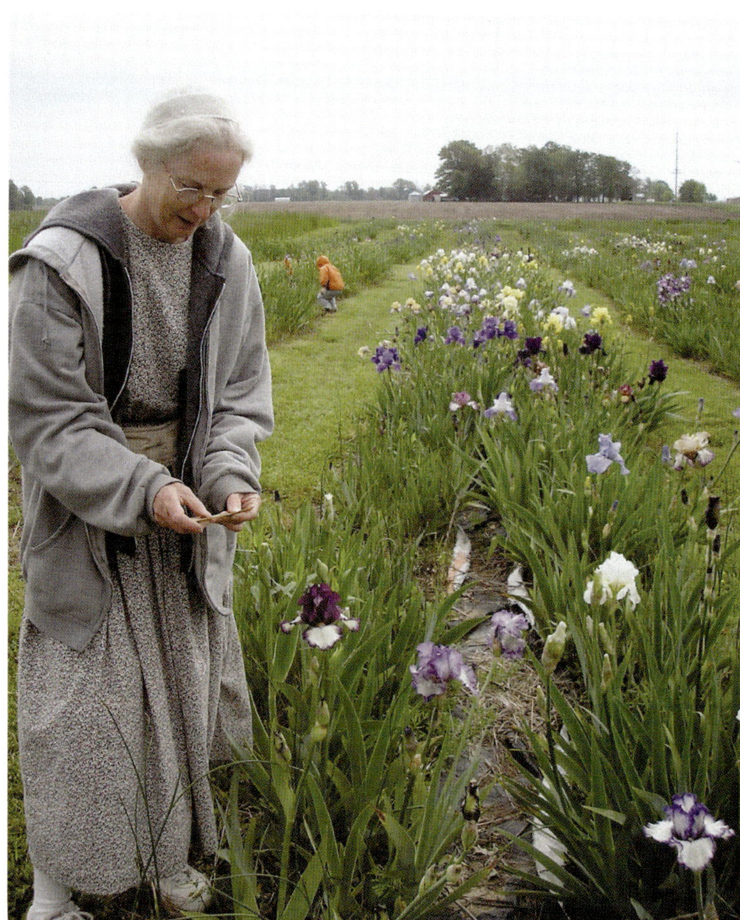

Early iris from this Wayne County flower farm will be shipped to major cities. Photo by Becky Malkovich; courtesy of the *Southern Illinoisan*

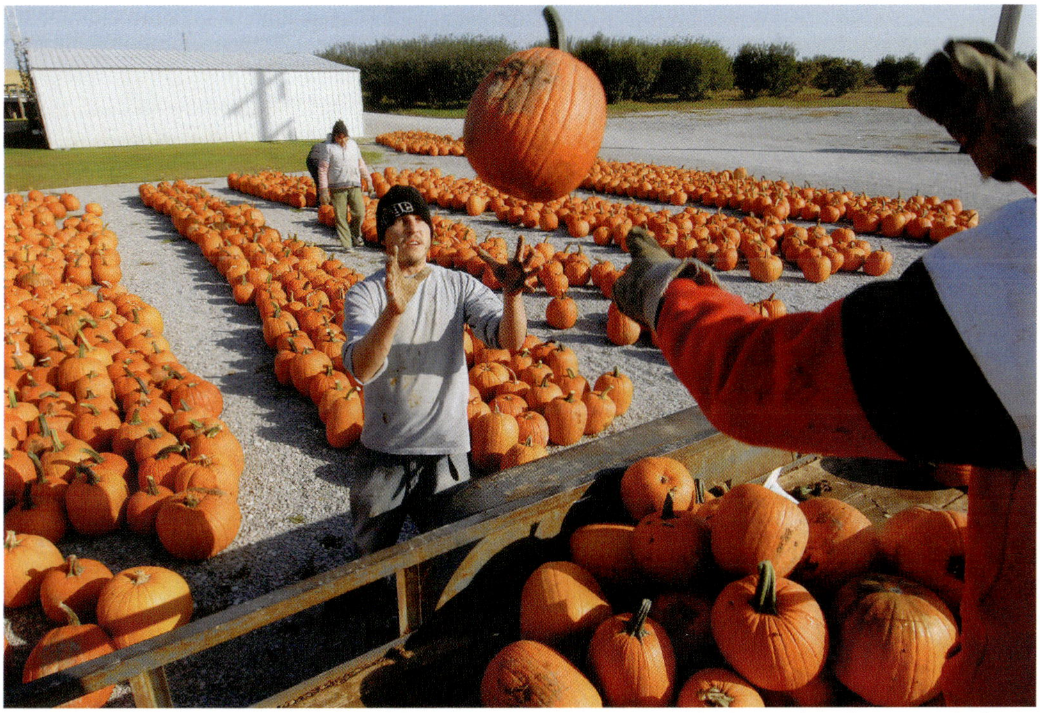

The pumpkin harvest marks the end of the growing season near Murphysboro. Photo by Steve Jahnke; courtesy of the *Southern Illinoisan*

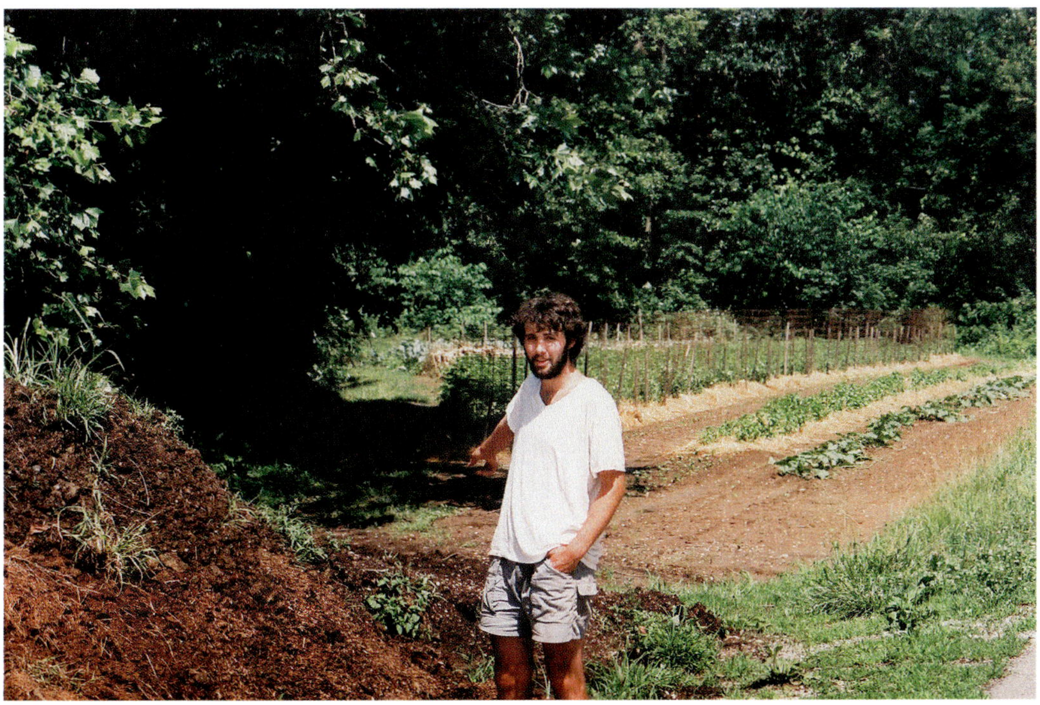

An organic gardener has a stack of compost as tall as he is. Green Ridge Road, Jackson County. Photo by Herbert K. Russell

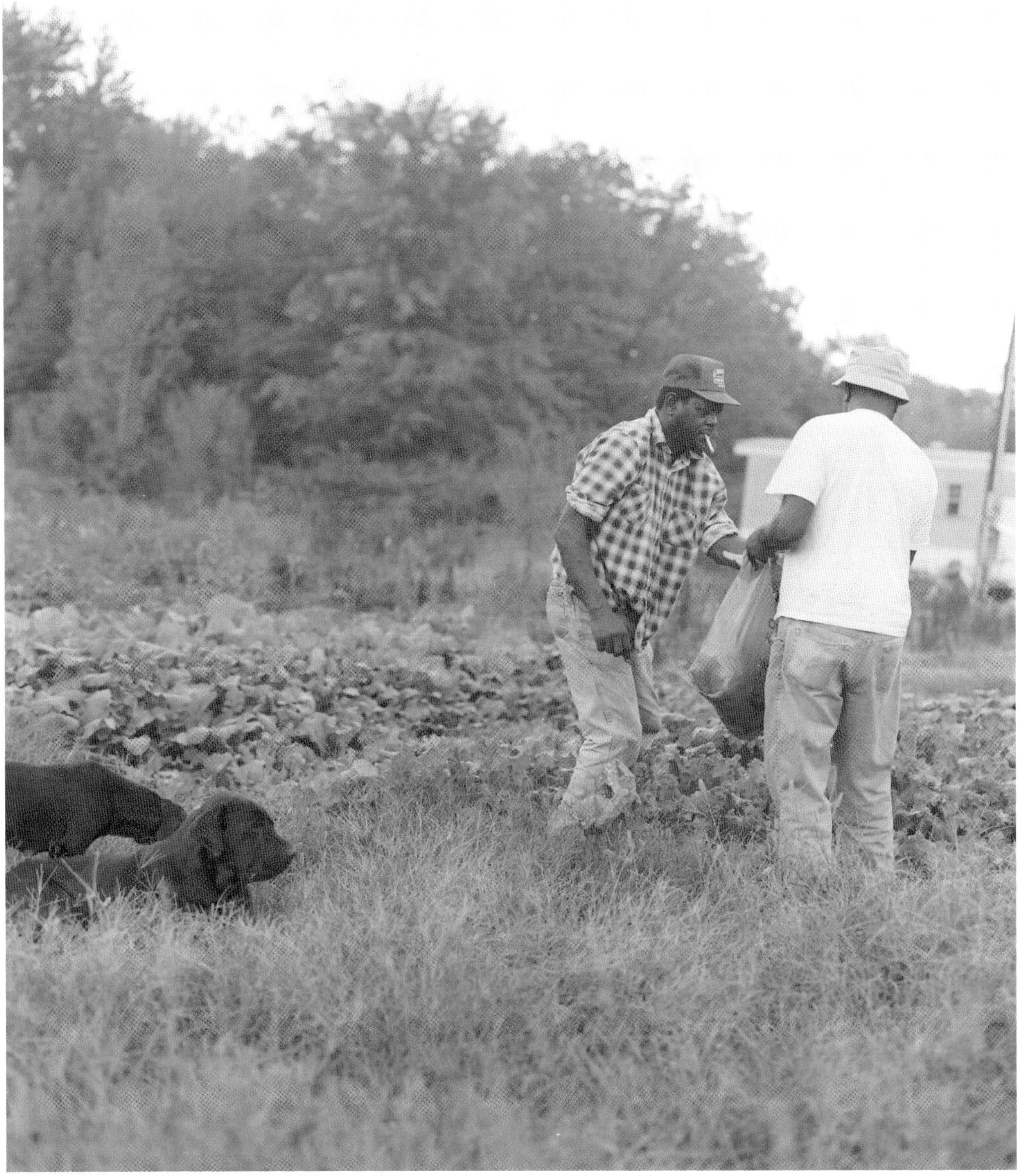

Picking greens in the hamlet of #9, Williamson County. Photo courtesy of Eric Robinson

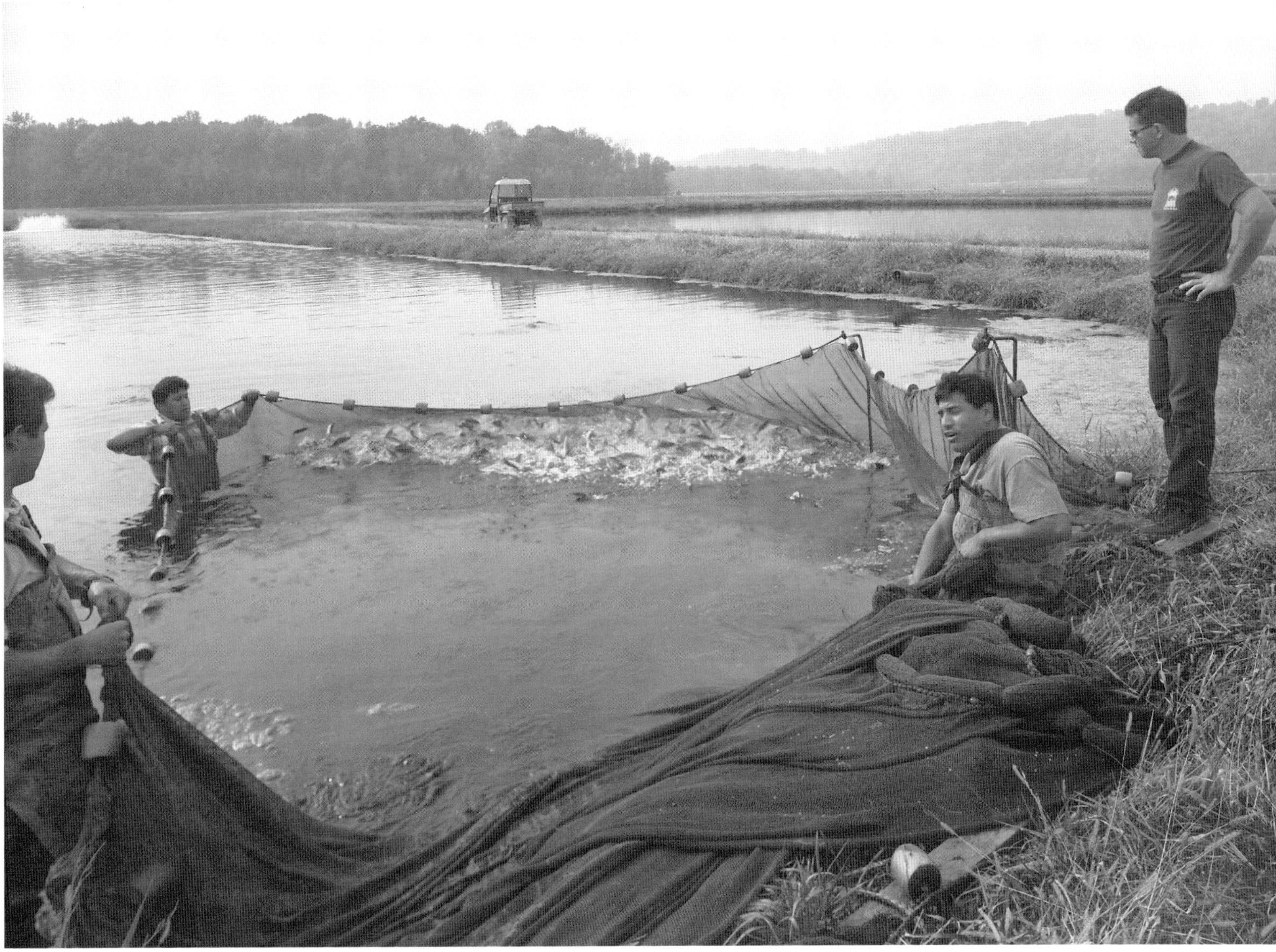

Alternative agriculture: a fish farm harvests bass in the Mississippi bottoms. Photo courtesy of Chris Walker

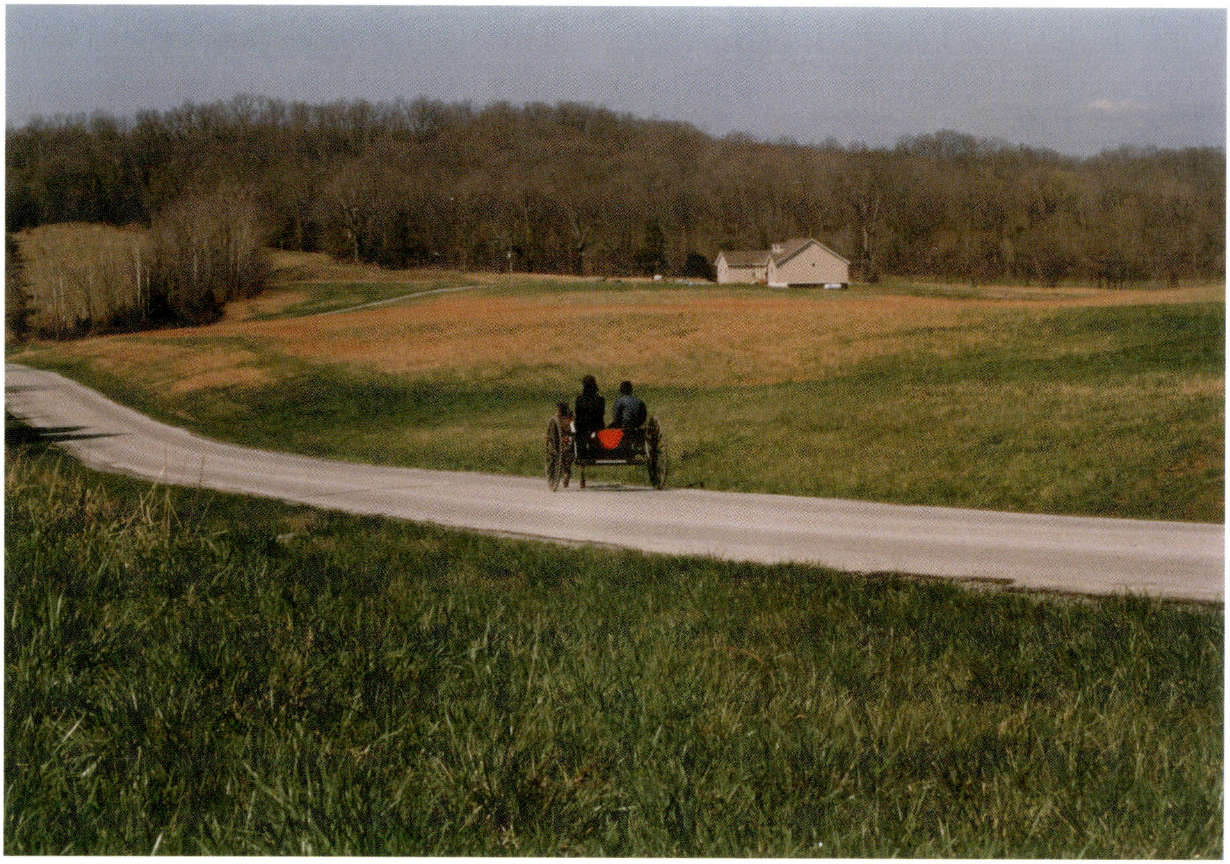

The road less traveled: Amish youngsters in a two-wheeled cart trot their horse down a hill in sparsely populated Johnson County. Photo by Herbert K. Russell

Community colleges would form an important part of the new Southern Illinois. The state's first junior college opened at Joliet in 1901, the first in Egypt as Centralia Township Junior College in 1940. In the 1960s other community colleges (as they prefer to be called) came into being, first at Harrisburg and then at Belleville, Carterville, East St. Louis, Ina, Mt. Carmel, Olney, and Ullin. All were two-year commuter colleges with low tuition, small classes, and a variety of traditional college and technical programs. All of them tailored their degree and certificate programs to meet the needs of local taxpayers, whose tax bills reflected their financial involvement.

Every square mile of Southern Illinois—and thus every person—is part of a community college district, and virtually anyone who wishes to pursue a low-cost education may do so. Low-income areas such as Cairo and East St. Louis have their own attendance centers, as do some towns that are distant from main campuses. As the twentieth century closed, two-thirds of those attending colleges in Illinois were enrolled at community colleges. A few years later, some Southern Illinois high schools reported that more than 50 percent of their graduating seniors were enrolling at community colleges.

The community colleges, Southern Illinois University, and private training schools

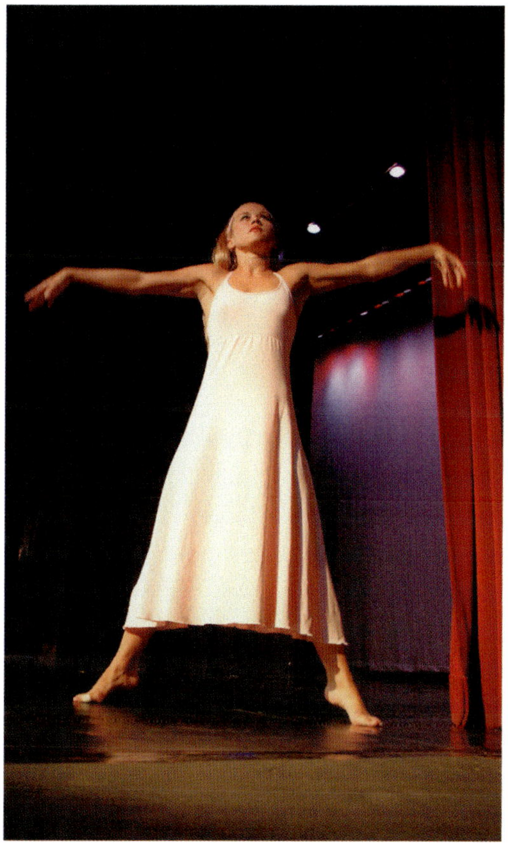

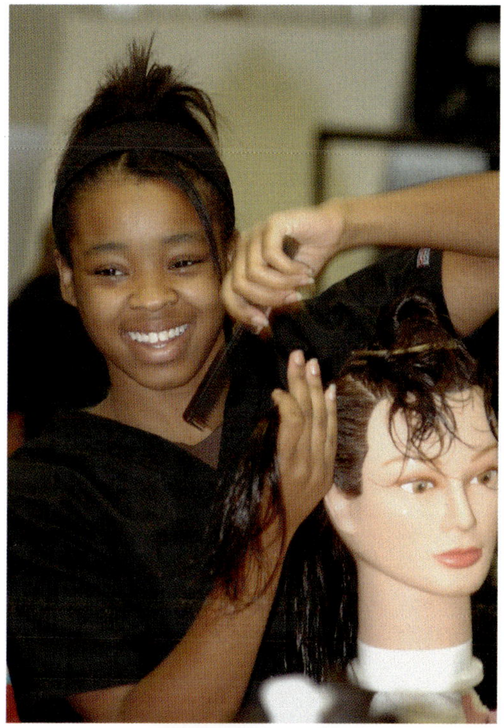

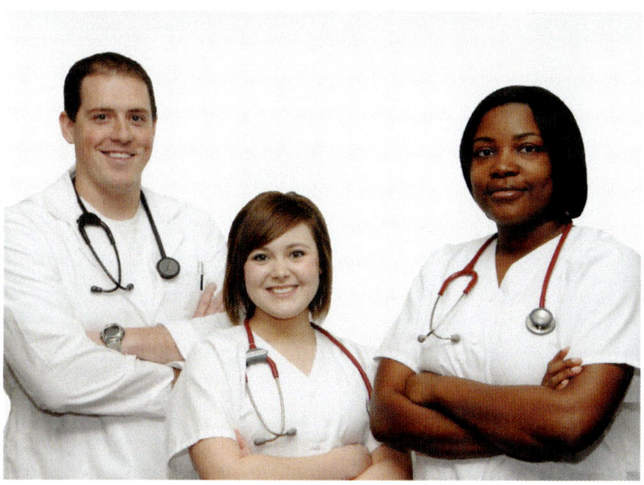

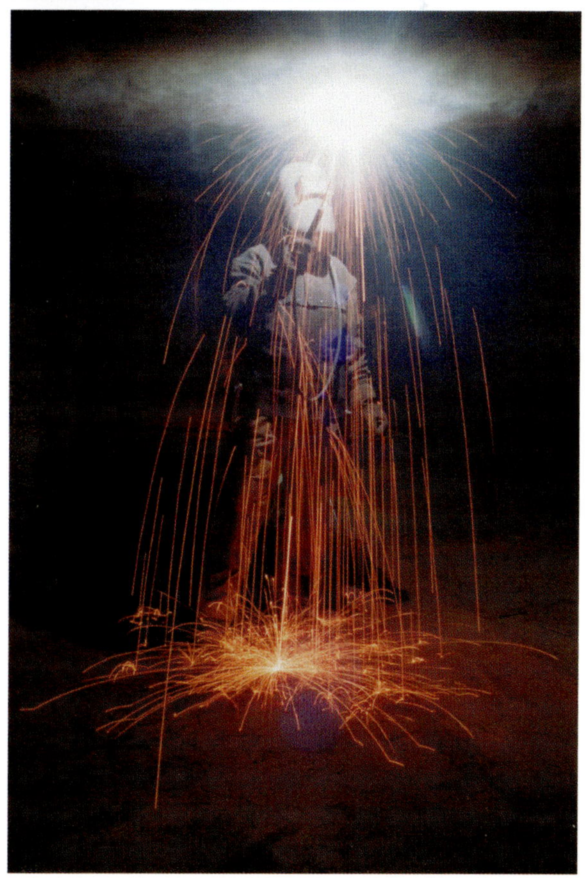

Community colleges offer hundreds of traditional college programs and technical training—from interpretive dance and cosmetology to nursing, welding, computer-assisted studies, and more. Photos courtesy of Shannon Woodworth

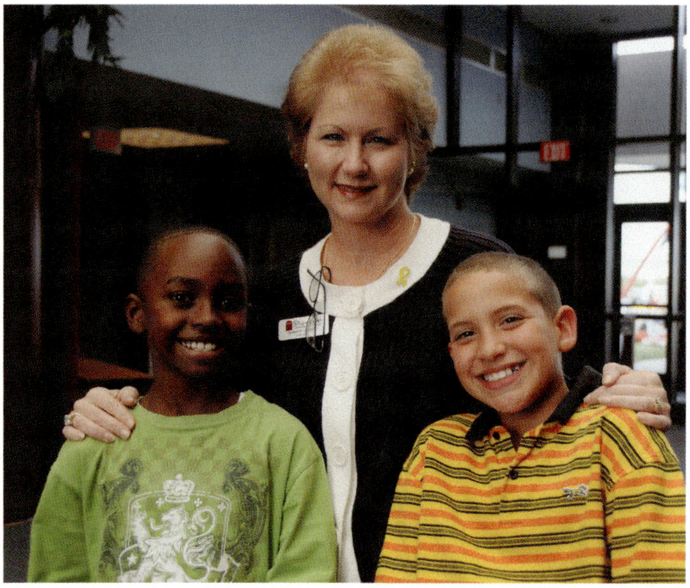

Community college outreach programs are especially successful: two future scientists from Cairo enjoy a science program. Photo courtesy of Shannon Woodworth

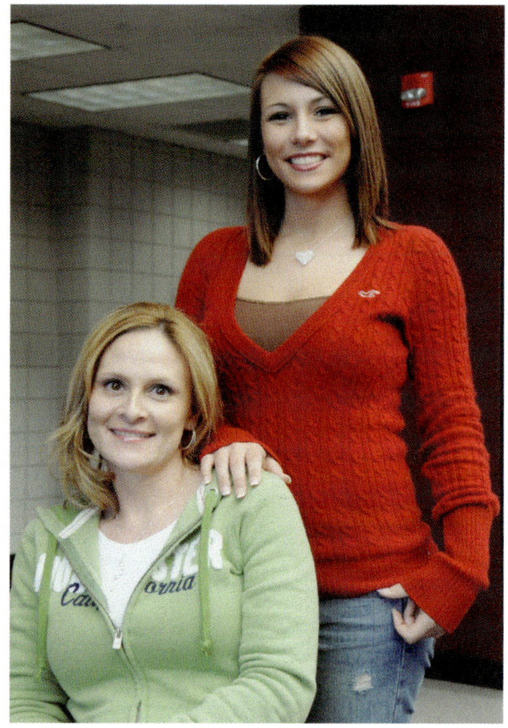

Second chances: a student trustee stands next to her mother, who is enrolled at the same community college. Photo courtesy of Shannon Woodworth

provide a professional and technical workforce for the area. Some Southern Illinois hospitals offer the same services found in large cities, and specialized health services are readily available. State-supported correctional and mental health facilities also dot the region and provide welcome sources of income in areas where much of the land has been removed from tax rolls to create forests, parks, lakes, and wildlife refuges. Manufacturing opportunities have developed on or near interstate highways at Nashville, Mt. Vernon, Marion, the Metro East Area, and elsewhere along with attractive shopping malls and other businesses.

Religion enjoys a stable place in Southern Illinois, and scores of one-room country churches still exist, many in the same locations if not the same buildings that they occupied in the late 1820s. The variety of denominations increased in the early twentieth century with the importation of foreign labor to mining towns, and was further enlarged by Southern Illinois University's drive for international diversity among students and staff. The church's old-fashioned ice cream social still flourishes, although it competes with church-sponsored road races, faith-based motorcycle groups, and ministerial alliances that work for the common good. Several faith-based organizations are complemented by high technology. Near West Frankfort, for example, Three Angels Broad-

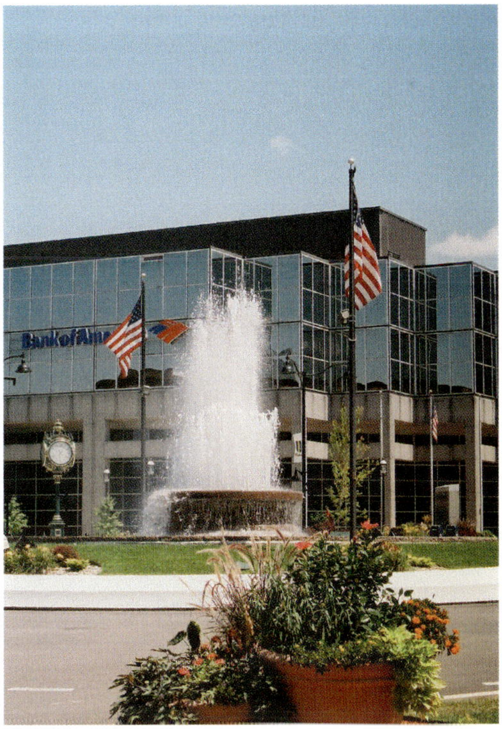

Belleville's attractive fountain marks its downtown in the Metro East Area. Photo by Herbert K. Russell

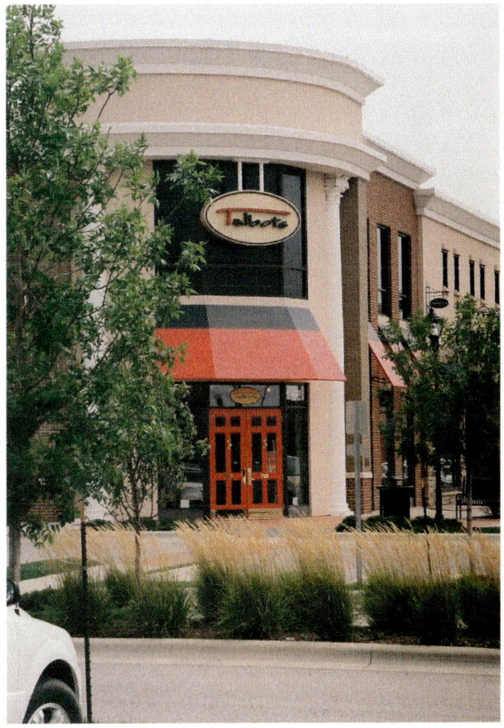

A shop in Fairview Heights, St. Clair County. Photo by Herbert K. Russell

casting, an independent satellite television and radio ministry, sends religious and family-oriented programming around the world in two languages twenty-four hours a day.

The arts are increasingly visible in Southern Illinois. Local musical offerings range from the Southern Illinois Symphony Orchestra to bluegrass and country. Theatrical presentations, along with a variety of museums and art outlets, are available at private and public venues. Former movie theatres such as those in Murphysboro, Sesser, Carbondale, and Centralia have become community cultural centers, and numerous historic and genealogy groups work to preserve the past. Marion enjoys a Cultural and Civic Center on the old courthouse square where John A. Logan made his famous Civil War speech. The rural crafts remain popular, and several festivals feature handcrafted items, some of which illustrate skills passed down from Appalachian forebears. The Cedarhurst Center for the Arts at Mt. Vernon and the Southern Illinois Art and Artisans Center at nearby Whittington feature the works of internationally known artists, as well as those with ties to Illinois. The two SIUs, community colleges, and local business groups also showcase many artists.

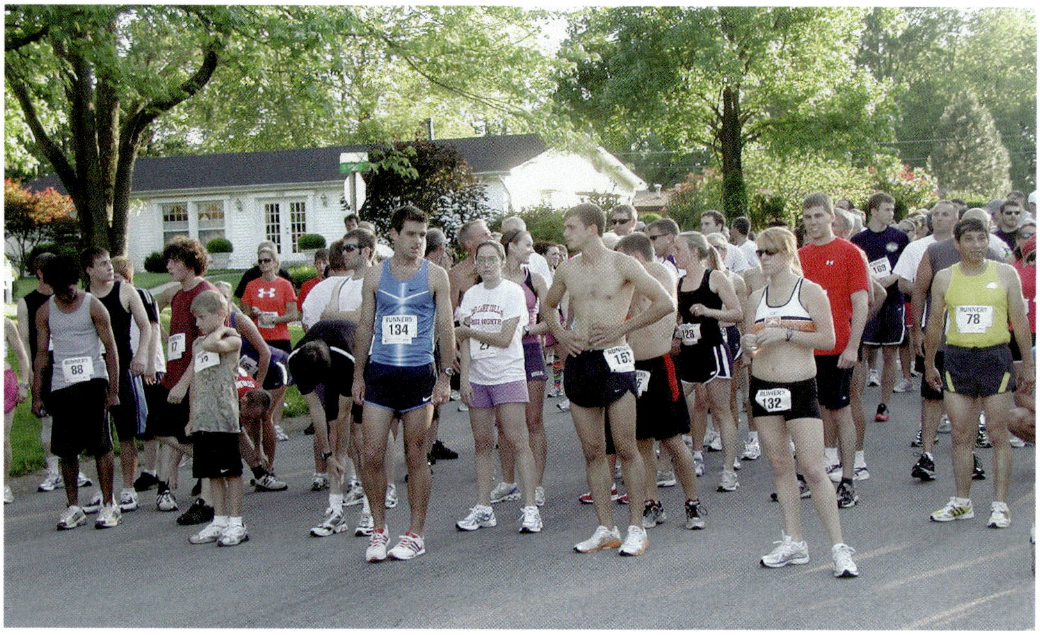

Runners line up for the church-sponsored Grace Race in Carbondale. Photo courtesy of Gregory Kupiec

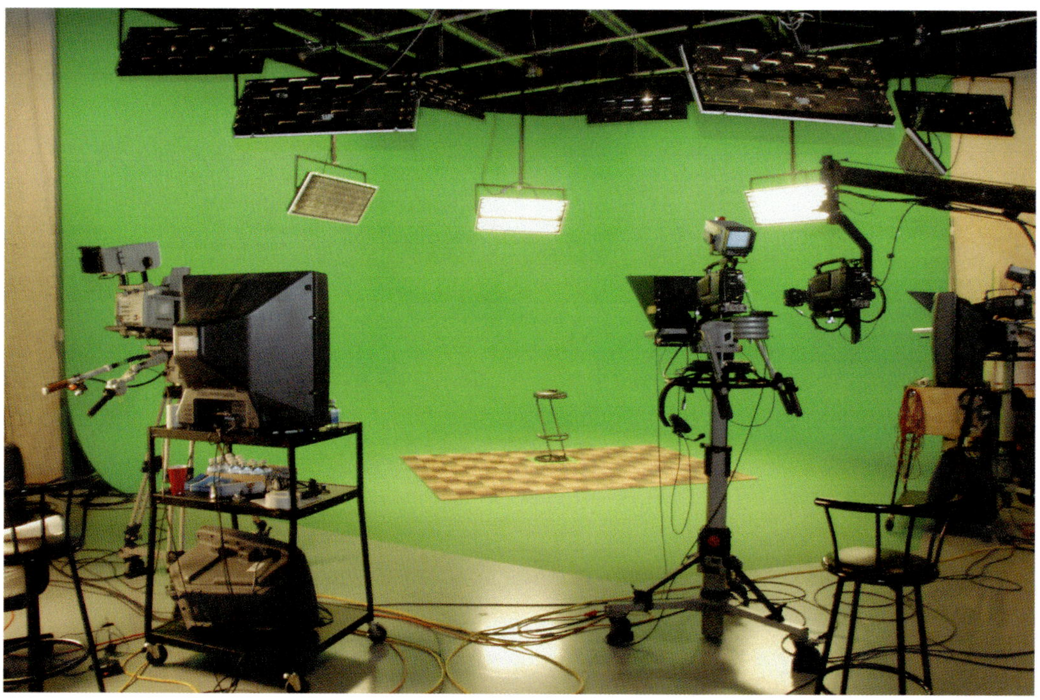

Three Angels Broadcasting uses a variety of studios and satellite equipment to send multilanguage religious and family programming around the globe. Rural West Frankfort. Photo courtesy of Shannon Woodworth

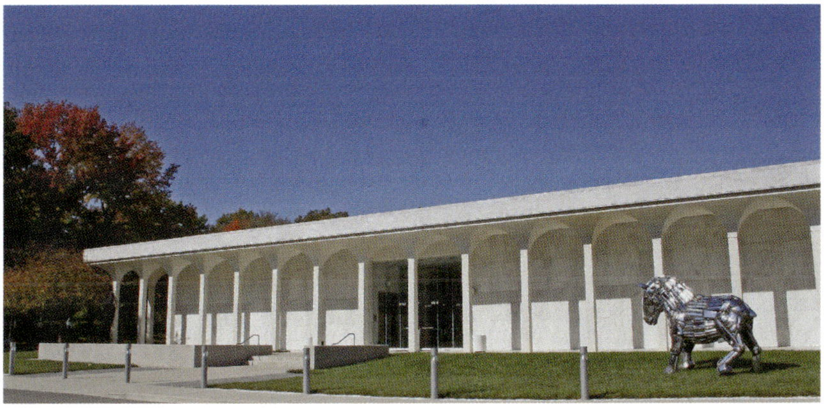

The graceful columns of the Mitchell Museum serve as introduction to the beautiful paintings within. Over sixty large-scale sculptures are on display in the outdoor sculpture park. Cedarhurst Center for the Arts, Mt. Vernon

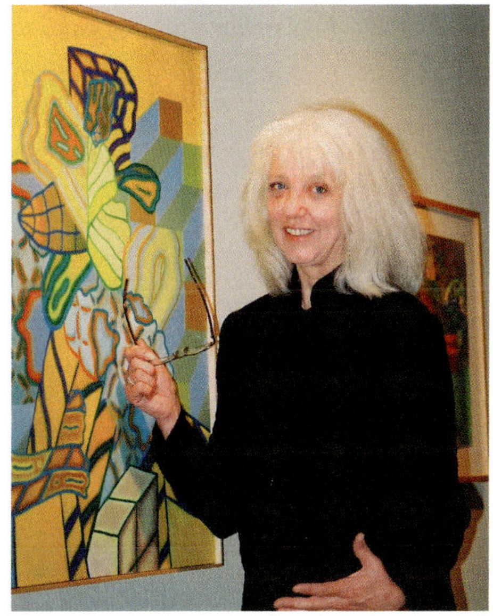

Associate Curator of Art Debra Tayes makes a point at the Southern Illinois Art and Artisans Center. Interstate 57 at Route 154, Whittington. Photo by Herbert K. Russell. Courtesy of the Illinois State Museum

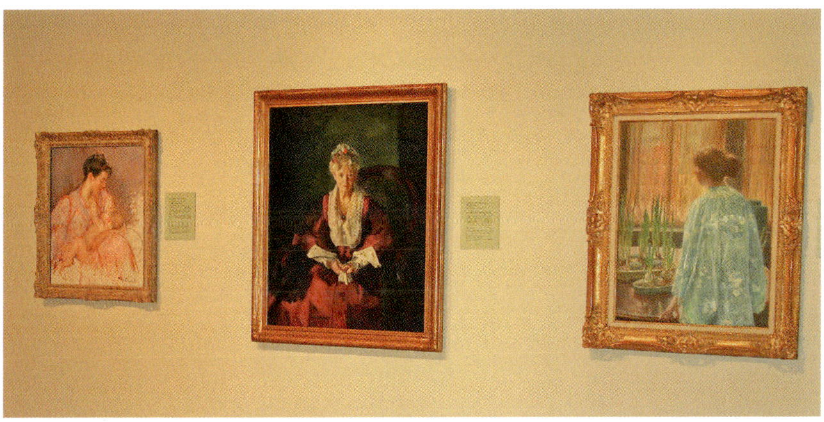

The permanent collection of the Mitchell Museum includes works by prominent American artists (*left to right*) Mary Cassatt, George Bellows, and Childe Hassam. Cedarhurst Center for the Arts, Mt. Vernon.

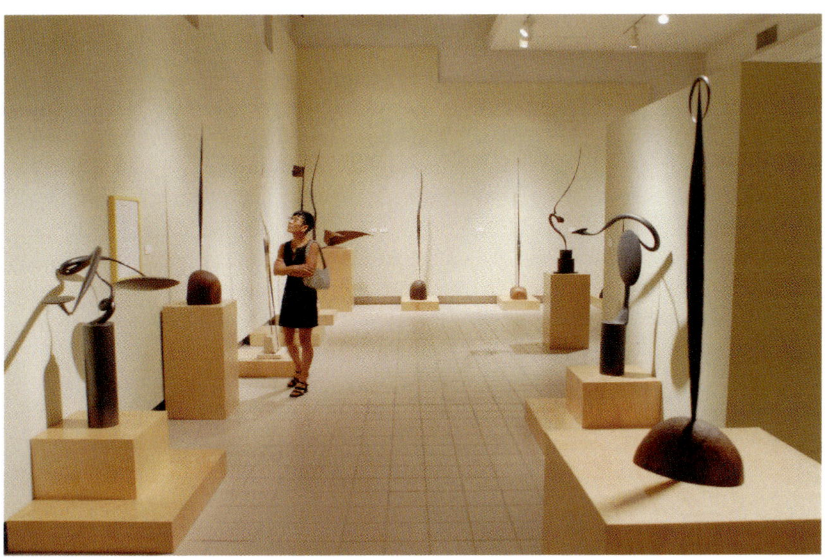

A visitor studies the work of L. Brent Kington, SIU professor emeritus, one of many artists whose work has appeared at the Southern Illinois Art and Artisans Center. Interstate 57 at Route 154, Whittington. Photo by Douglas Carr; courtesy of the Illinois State Museum

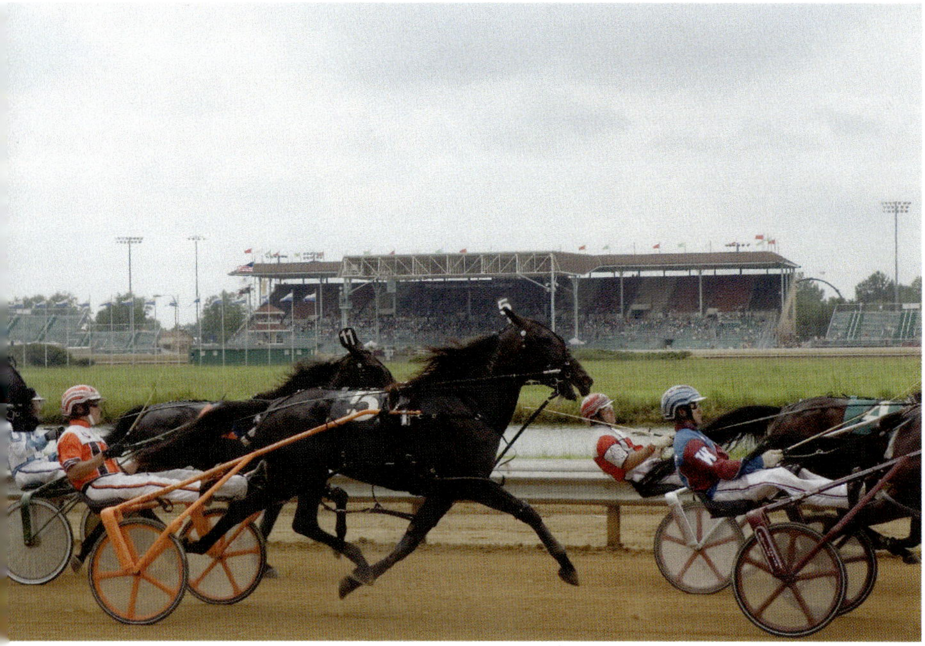

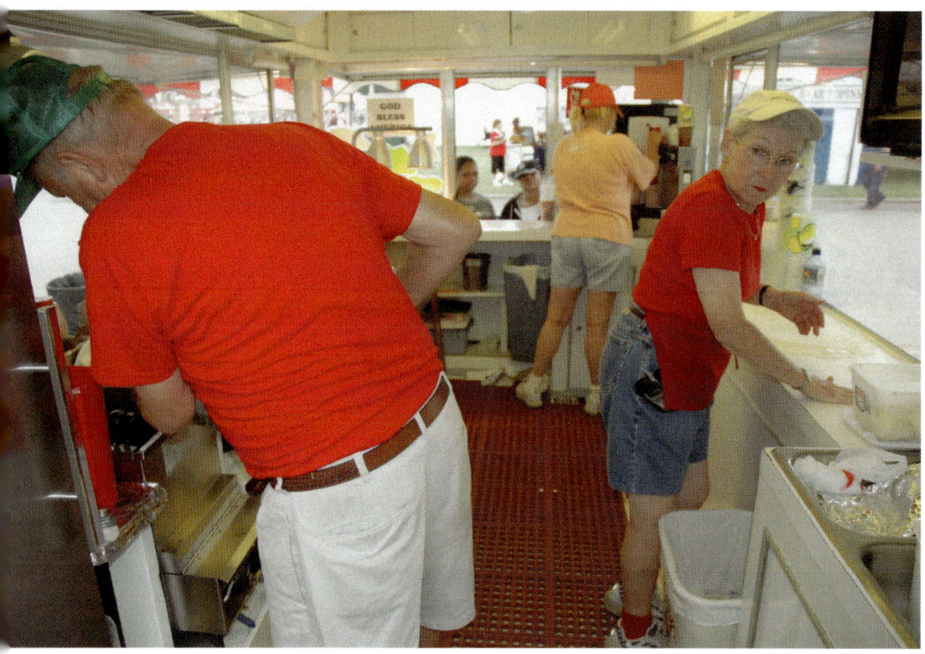

Southern Illinois tourism began soon after the arrival of steamboats in 1811, grew with the railroads in the 1850s, and matured with excursion trains in the 1880s and '90s. But it was not until the 1920s and '30s that paved highways and automobiles permitted large numbers of outsiders to enjoy Southern Illinois' interior. Newspaper publisher L. O. Trigg of Eldorado led tours of southernmost Illinois during the 1930s and '40s, and Makanda's Wayman Presley sponsored hikes, auto caravans, and excursion trains from the 1940s through the '60s. Du Quoin's William Hayes' dream was to create his own state fair. Beginning in the 1920s, he and others turned the Old Black Gold strip mine into 1,200 acres of fairgrounds and parklike settings of trees and lakes. Livestock exhibitions, Indianapolis-style racing cars, the Hambletonian harness race, and the World Trotting Derby made the Du Quoin State Fair a top tourism attraction. Entertainers from New York, Las Vegas, and Nashville gave it name recognition from coast to coast.

(*This page and next*) Scenes from the Du Quoin State Fair suggest reasons for its popularity. Photos of harness horse race and merry-go-round courtesy of Beth Alongi; other photos courtesy of Shannon Woodworth

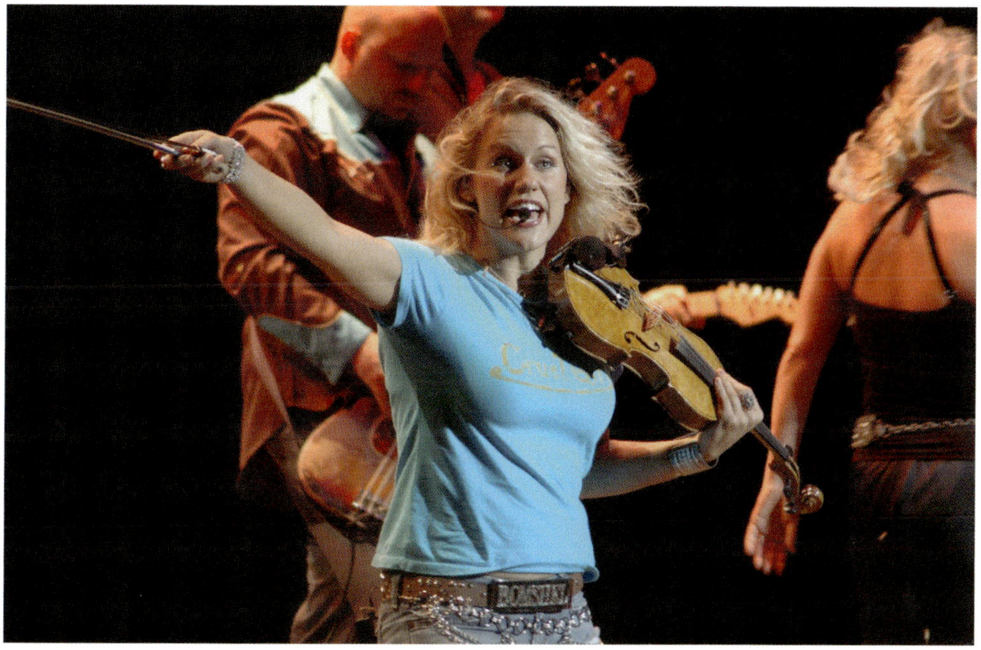

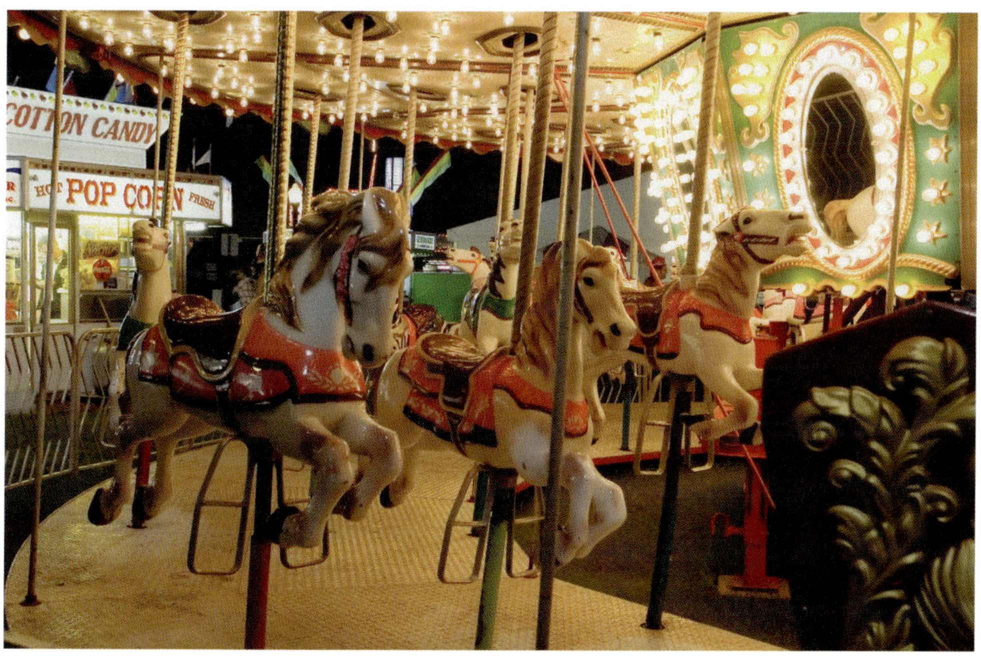
COTTON CANDY

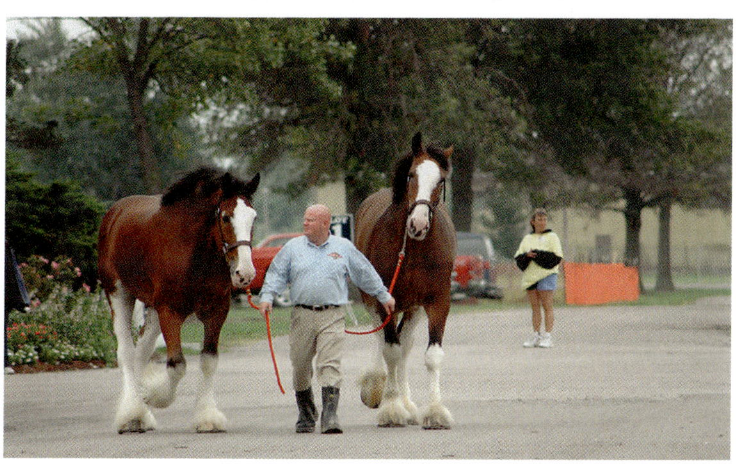

Some visitors simply follow the great rivers to scenic overlooks—or seek out the golf courses. Antique stores are found throughout the region, often in close association with tea rooms, coffee houses, or small cafés. Sportsmen enjoy hunting at clubs and in designated public areas at designated times, and can sharpen their reflexes at private ranges and at Sparta's World Shooting and Recreational Complex, 1,600 acres of shooting ranges. Southern Illinois also offers thousands of acres of lakes and water sports of all kinds. Popular restaurants, abundant motels, modern cabins in the woods, guest ranches, and bed-and-breakfasts offer rest and relaxation. The presence of a minor league baseball team, the Southern Illinois Miners, provides an evening of family entertainment, and numerous cultural and recreational activities are available for children.

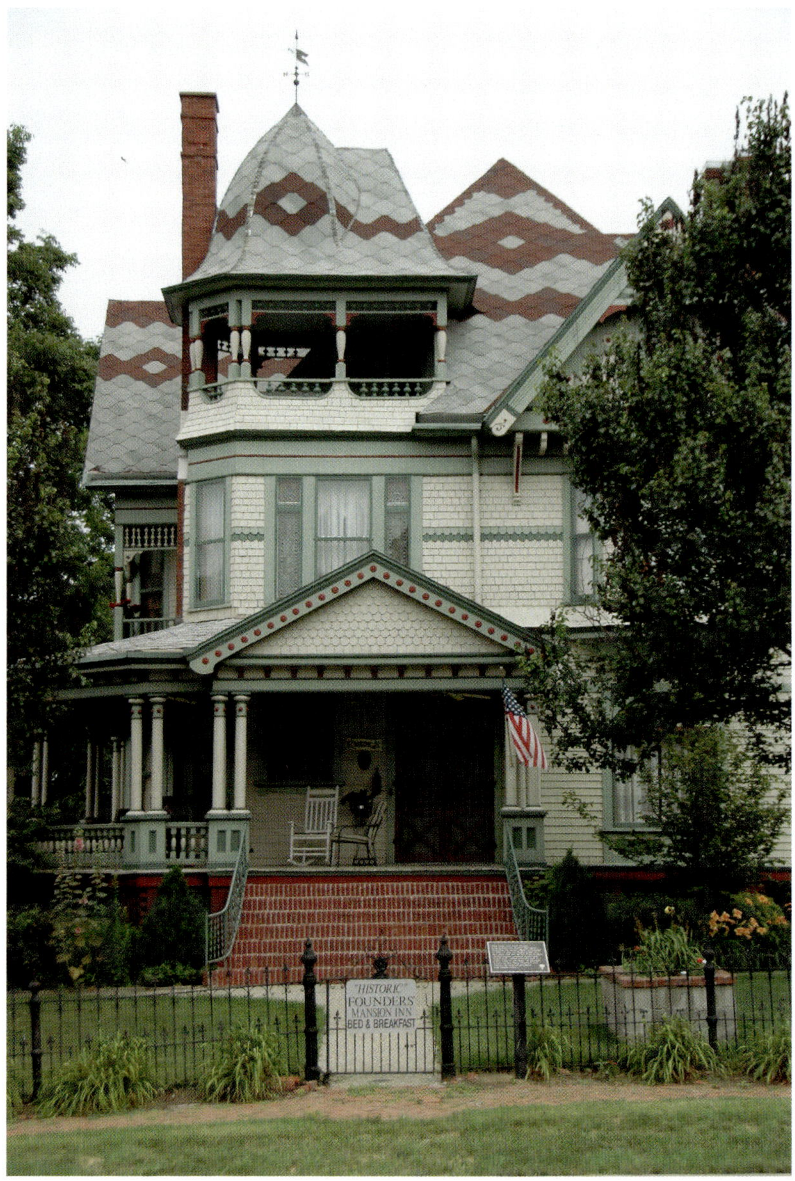

This nineteenth-century bed-and-breakfast near the Wabash River offers both history and hospitality. Grayville. Photo by Herbert K. Russell

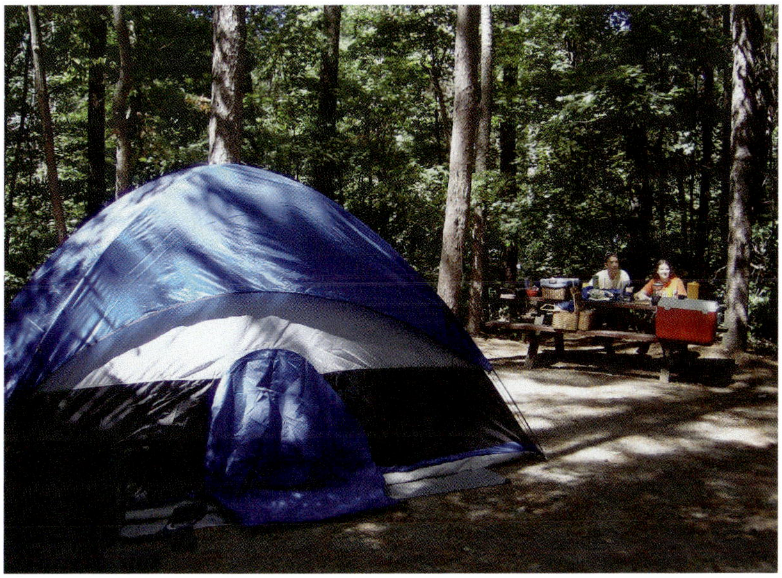

The Shawnee National Forest stretches from the Ohio to the Mississippi River, offering abundant opportunities for camping, fishing, bird watching, trail riding, and other recreational activities. Photo courtesy of Brian DeNeal

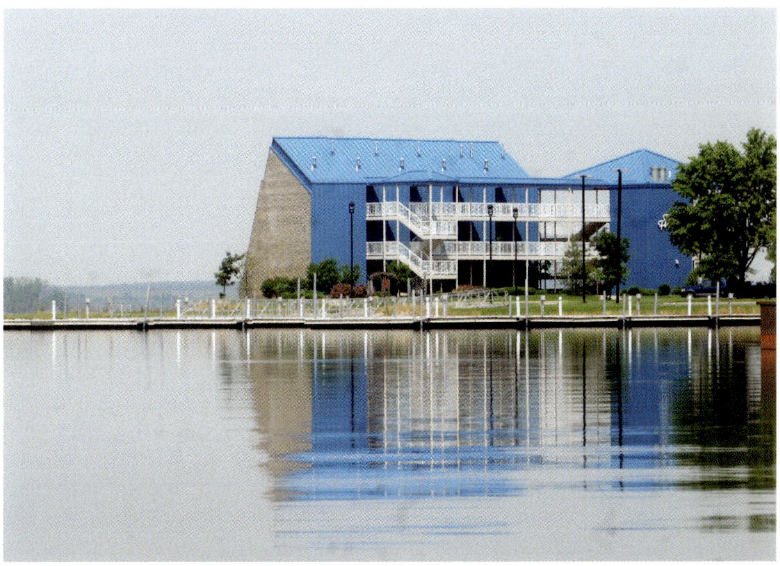

Lodging at Rend Lake shows a futuristic flair. Photo by Paul Newton; courtesy of the *Southern Illinoisan*

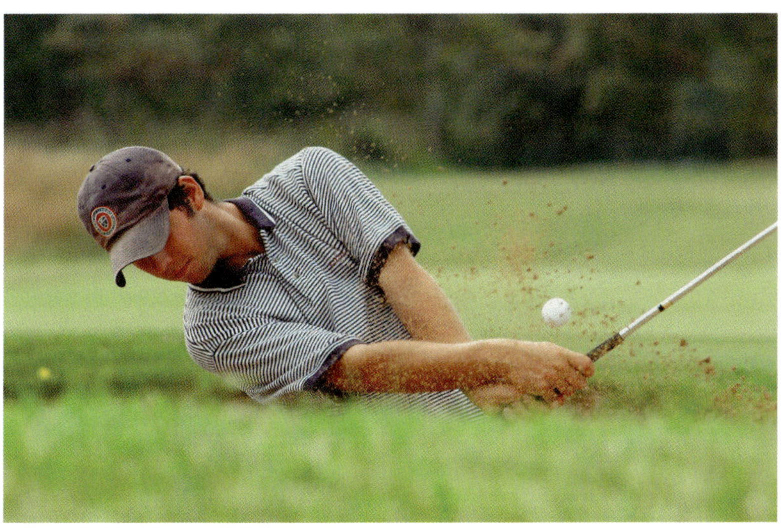

A golfer hits a shot from a sand trap on one of the many challenging courses in Southern Illinois. Photo courtesy of Shannon Woodworth

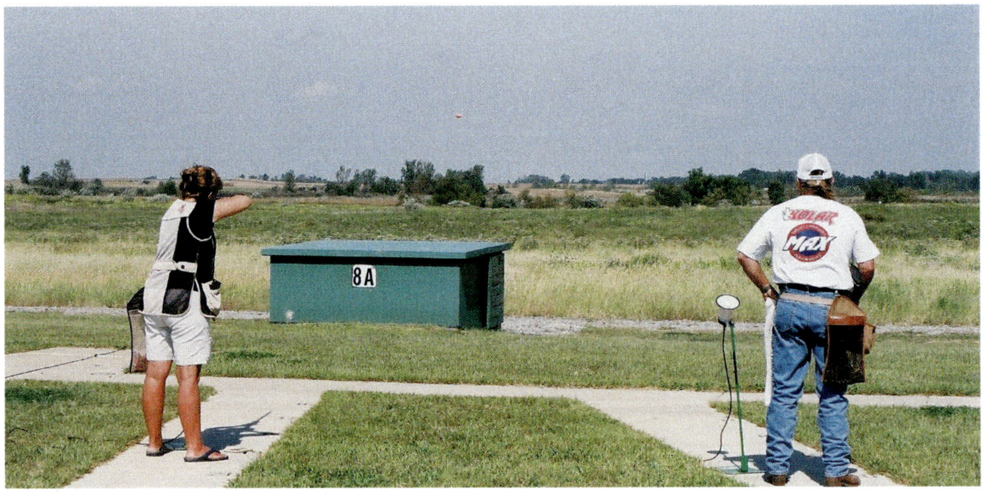

The World Shooting and Recreational Complex at Sparta offers a wide variety of courses and competitions, including the Grand American, a major trapshooting event. Photo by Herbert K. Russell

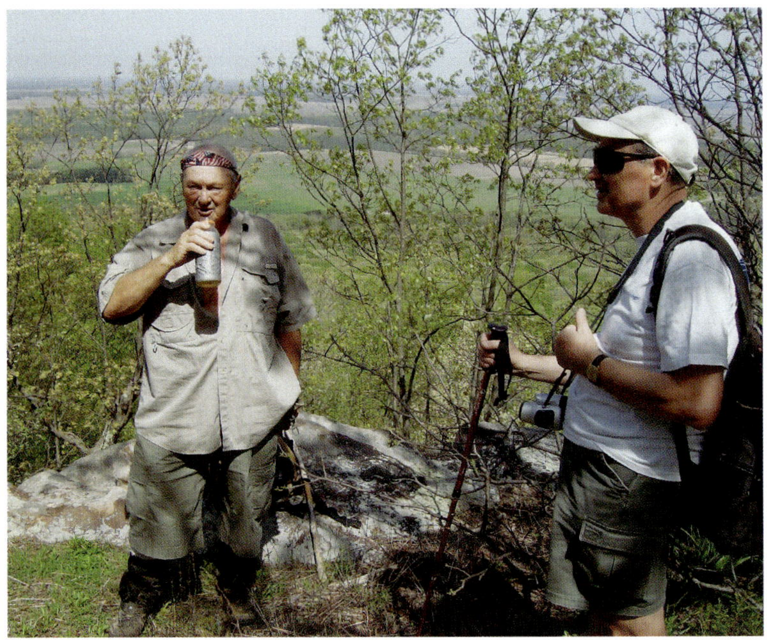

Hikers take a break on the Crest Trail from Glen O. Jones Lake to Old Stone Face. Saline County. Photo courtesy of Brian DeNeal

Overall, the "state" or condition of Southern Illinois is quite different from what it was only a few decades ago. Of course the most important component is a healthier and better-educated public that has the ability to deal with the present and the affluence and opportunity to learn of its past—perhaps in a book published by the Southern Illinois University Press, of which this is one.

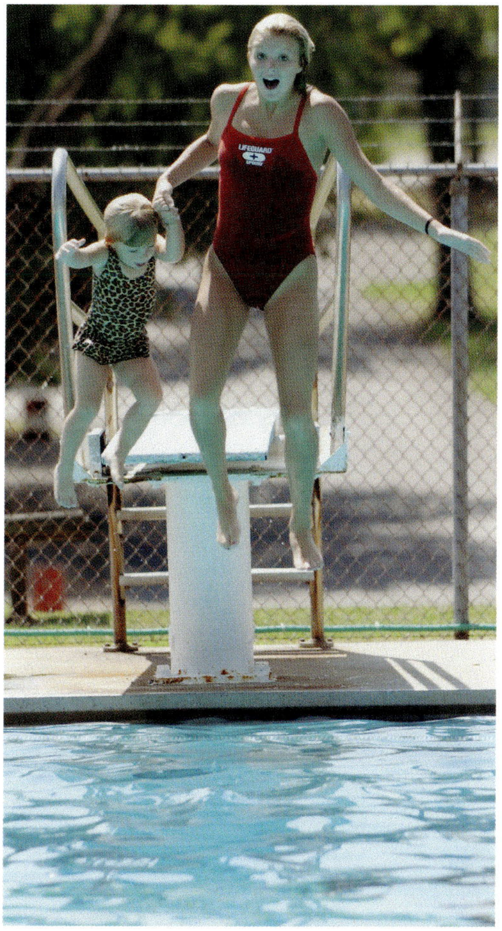

Cooling off with a friend. Photo by Paul Newton; courtesy of the *Southern Illinoisan*

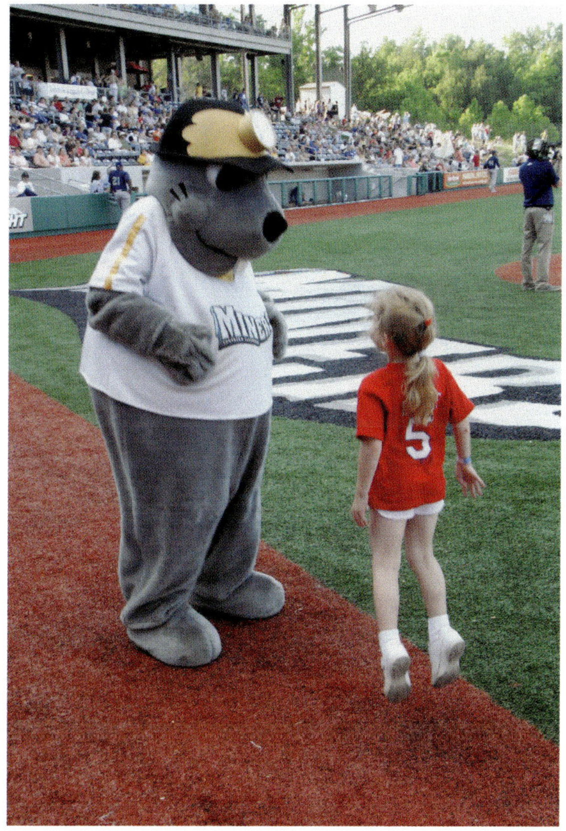

A team mascot and fan see who can jump the highest before a Miners baseball game in Marion. Photo courtesy of Shannon Woodworth

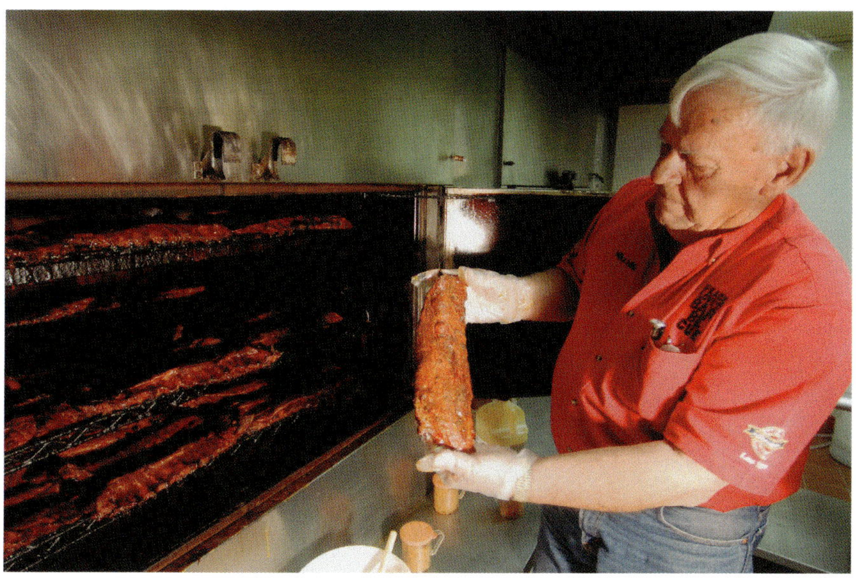

Mike Mills' 17th Street Bar and Grill in Murphysboro has the best barbecue in the nation, according to the Food Channel and *Bon Appétit* magazine. Photo by Thomas Barker; courtesy of the *Southern Illinoisan*

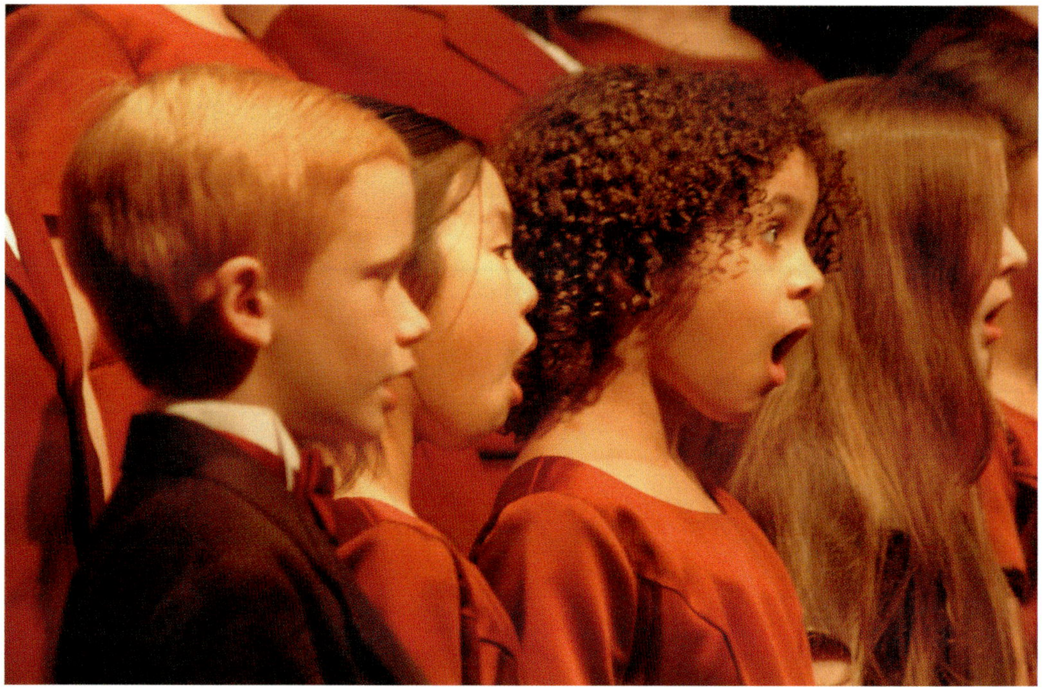

The Southern Illinois Children's Choir performs at a fund-raiser for needy children. Photo courtesy of Shannon Woodworth

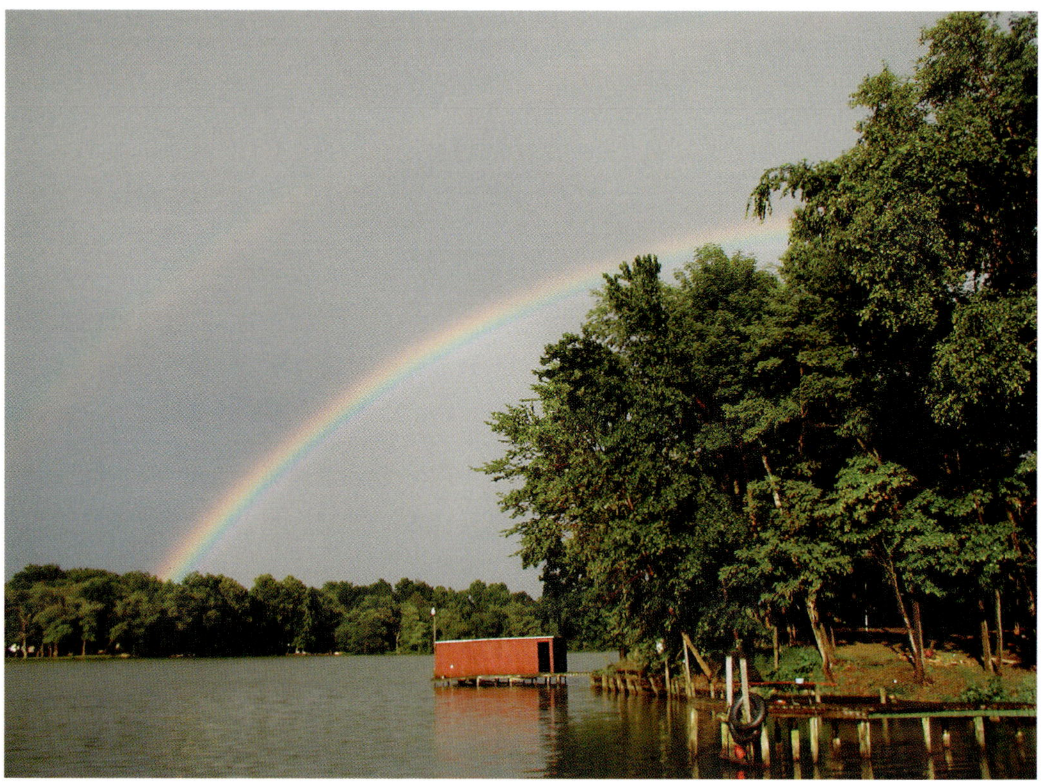

Double rainbows begin and end in Southern Illinois. Photo courtesy of Shannon Woodworth

Sources

Bibliography

Index

Sources

Sources are shown in full for their first use and in short form for second and subsequent uses. Also provided are complete sources for certain informative photo captions and epigraphs. A complete bibliography follows.

Sources for the Introduction

History of Gallatin, Saline, Hamilton, Franklin, and Williamson Counties, Illinois (Chicago: Goodspeed Publishing Company, 1887; rpt. Winnetka Public Library, 1973), p. 31, some southerners free slaves upon arriving in Gallatin County. *Combined History [of] Edwards, Lawrence, and Wabash Counties, Illinois* (Philadelphia: J. L. McDonough, 1883), p. 72, some newcomers to Illinois free their slaves.

Jasper W. Cross, "The Civil War Comes to 'Egypt,'" *Journal of the Illinois State Historical Society* 44 (summer 1951), pp. 160–69, about 40 percent of eligible men enlist in sixteen southernmost counties, about 28 percent elsewhere. Cross' information is from Schedule D, *Annual Report of the Adjutant General of the State of Illinois* (Springfield: Baker and Phillips, 1863), pp. 78–80.

Bluford Wilson, "Southern Illinois in the Civil War," *Transactions of the Illinois State Historical Society* 16 (1911), pp. 93–103; p. 98, myth that "thousands" of Southern Illinoisans fought for the Confederacy; p. 99, "not a half company" of men left Marion for the South. A Civil War company at full strength was about 100 men plus officers. Wilson's expression of "not a half company" may explain the figure of "about forty-five" secessionists that has sometimes been used to describe the number of men who left Marion to join the Confederate Army.

Ed Gleeson, *Illinois Rebels: A Civil War Unit History of G Company Fifteenth Tennessee Regiment Volunteer Infantry* (Carmel: Guild Press of Indiana, 1996), pp. 10–13, thirty-four secessionists, most leave Marion on May 25, 1861; pp. 10 and 125, one born in Southern Illinois; pp. 85–126, details on individual soldiers, states of birth, hometowns, desertions, and other data, much of it derived from military service records; p. 119, names of thirty-four men from Jackson and Williamson counties; additional source information is on pp. xi–xvi and pp. 127–44.

Gary Ecelbarger, *Black Jack Logan: An Extraordinary Life in Peace and War* (Guilford, Connecticut: Lyons Press, 2005), p. 73, shows thirty-five secessionists. John Y. Simon, "Disloyalty in Southern Illinois during the Civil War," Southern Illinois Learning in Retirement public lecture, Southern Illinois University Carbondale, August 17, 2005, thirty-five secessionists, some returned home to protect families. The figure of thirty-four secessionists is used in this study per their identities in *Illinois Rebels* above.

Robert Mize Sutton, *The Illinois Central Railroad in Peace and War, 1858–1868* (New York: Arno Press, 1981), p. 107, Cairo had nearly 3,000 Union soldiers by May 1, 1861. James Pickett Jones, *Black Jack: John A. Logan and Southern Illinois in the Civil War Era* (Tallahassee: Florida State University, 1967; rpt., foreword by John Y. Simon, Carbondale: Southern Illinois University Press, 1995), p. xiv, "about thirty-five" secessionists; p. 83, Cairo had about 4,000 Union soldiers by May 6, 1861; pp. xiv–xv, Brush's two speeches, Captain Ulysses S. Grant and Anna regiment. [Daniel Harmon Brush,] *Growing Up with Southern Illinois, 1820 to 1861, from the Memoirs of Daniel Harmon Brush*, ed. Milo Milton Quaife (Chicago: R. R. Donnelley, 1944; rpt., foreword by John Y. Simon, Herrin, Illinois: Crossfire Press, 1992), pp. I–III, Brush's two speeches.

Linda Jeanne Evans, "Abolitionism in the Illinois Churches, 1830–1865" (dissertation; Evanston, Illinois: Northwestern University, 1981), pp. 282–83, Emancipation Baptists work actively with coalition organized by governor Edward Coles to prevent Illinois from becoming a slave state. Myron D. Dillow, *Harvest-time on the Prairie: A History of Baptists in Illinois, 1796–1996* (Franklin, Tennessee:

Providence House Publishers, 1996), p. 82, Emancipation Baptists' opposition to slavery becomes religious doctrine; pp. 137–39, circulars oppose making Illinois a slave state. Ronald L. Nelson et al., *History of Liberty Baptist Church, Saline County, IL, 1832–1996* (Utica, Kentucky: McDowell Publications, 1996), p. 4, James Lemen founds Emancipation Baptists in 1809; pp. 1–57 summarizes people, churches, and important dates of Emancipation Baptists in Southern Illinois.

Robert J. Conley, *The Cherokee Nation: A History* (Albuquerque: University of New Mexico Press, 2005), p. 157, records show 182 Cherokee escaped or slipped away from the Trail of Tears; author notes that these records are incomplete and that the true number may be higher.

Sources for the Text

Notes to pages 1–19

Christopher J. Schuberth, *A View of the Past: An Introduction to Illinois Geology* (Springfield: Illinois State Museum, 1986). "Study Ties 1811, 1812 Quakes to Illinois Fault," *Southern Illinoisan*, June 9, 2010, p. 5B, Wabash Valley quakes related to New Madrid fault. Robert H. Mohlenbrock, "A New Geography of Illinois: Johnson County," *Outdoor Illinois* 14 (January 1975), pp. 29–30, "Great blocks of stone." Charles Colby, *Pilot Study of Southern Illinois* (Carbondale: Southern Illinois University Press, 1956), p. 21, Wisconsinan glacier and Kaskaskia, Little Wabash, and Embarras Rivers.

Notes to pages 19–21

Sally A. Kitt Chappell, *Cahokia: Mirror of the Cosmos* (Chicago: University of Chicago Press, 2002), p. 29, humans arrive about 9500 B.C. William Iseminger, *Cahokia Mounds: America's First City* (Charleston, South Carolina: The History Press, 2010), pp. 20–23, first humans about 9500 B.C. Timothy R. Pauketat, *Ancient Cahokia and the Mississippians* (New York: Cambridge University Press, 2004), pp. 152–53, decline and end by 1350; p. 139, Illinois uninhabited during large parts of fourteenth and fifteenth centuries; p. 143, images may reflect heaven, earth, and underworld. Mark J. Wagner, public lecture, Cultural and Natural Heritage Symposium, Southern Illinois University Carbondale, April 8, 2009, interpretation of Pope County cave-top painting, animal hides, and circle with four suns.

Fay-Cooper Cole et al., *Kincaid: A Prehistoric Illinois Metropolis* (Chicago: University of Chicago Press, 1951). Charles R. Cobb and Brian M. Butler, "The Vacant Quarter Revisited: Late Mississippian Abandonment of the Lower Ohio Valley," *American Antiquity* 67, no. 4 (2002), p. 625, Illinois largely uninhabited by 1450; p. 638, Old World diseases probably not a factor. Irvin M. Peithmann, *Indians of Southern Illinois* (Springfield, Illinois: Charles C. Thomas, 1964), p. 104, stone's throw.

Notes to pages 25–28

Natalia Maree Belting, *Kaskaskia under the French Regime* (Urbana: University of Illinois Press, 1948; rpt. Carbondale: Southern Illinois University Press, 2003), pp. 66–67, animal skins; pp. 74–75, marriage and children. Robert P. Howard, *Illinois: A History of the Prairie State* (Grand Rapids: Eerdmans, 1972), p. 38, tannery near Mound City. Margaret Kimball Brown and Lawrie Cena Dean, *The French Colony in the Mid-Mississippi Valley* (Carbondale, Illinois: American Kestrel Books, 1995), overview of French presence. Margaret Kimball Brown, *History as They Lived It: A Social History of Prairie du Rocher, Illinois* (Tucson: Patrice Press, 2005).

Notes to page 30

Herbert S. Klein, *The Atlantic Slave Trade* (New York: Cambridge University Press, 1999), pp. 9, 67, 90–92, 98, 103, 105–06, 117, Africans sell fellow Africans into slavery; p. 46, 95 percent of African slaves sent to New World went to Central and South America and Caribbean while 5 percent went to North America. Clayborne Carson et al., *The Struggle for Freedom: A History of African Americans* (New York: Pearson Longman, 2007), pp. 31–32, blacks sell fellow blacks into slavery, Muslim slavers purchase about half of all black slaves, tax on slaves.

Carl J. Ekberg, *French Roots in the Illinois Country: The Mississippi Frontier in Colonial Times* (Urbana: University of Illinois Press, 1998), pp. 146–47, slaves to Biloxi. James E. Davis, *Frontier Illinois* (Bloomington: Indiana

University Press, 1998), p. 54, Illinois slave numbers in 1732. George Washington Smith, *History of Illinois and Her People*, vol. 1 (Chicago: American Historical Society, 1927), p. 126, first college in Illinois.

Notes to pages 33–37

Davis, *Frontier Illinois*, pp. 69–79, details on George Rogers Clark; p. 91, Virginia relinquishes Illinois, slavery maintained. Richard Kuenneke, *The Search for Cantonment Wilkinsonville: The Archaeology of an 1801 American Military Post in Pulaski County, Illinois* (Oakview Road Media, 2006), DVD, interview with Southern Illinois University Carbondale staff archaeologist Mark J. Wagner. Brent Stewart, "For the Record," *Southern Illinoisan*, January 21, 2007, p. 1E+, summary of research at Cantonment Wilkinson.

Notes to pages 37–40

Robert E. Hartley, *Lewis and Clark in the Illinois Country: The Little-Told Story* (Westminster, Colorado: Sniktau Publications, 2002), pp. 65–73, some men recruited from Massac and Kaskaskia. Howard, *Illinois*, p. 62, Polypotamia, Illinoia, and Assenisipia. Solon J. Buck, *Illinois in 1818* (Springfield: Illinois Centennial Commission, 1917; rpt. Urbana: University of Illinois Press, 1967), p. 188, 1805 proposal to form a single state from southern parts of Indiana and Illinois.

Notes to pages 41–45

M. J. Morgan, *Land of Big Rivers: French and Indian Illinois, 1699–1778* (Carbondale: Southern Illinois University Press, 2010), pp. 25–26, Indians at Modoc shelter by 8000 B.C.; p. 94, Fox raid the Kaskaskia. Margaret Kimball Brown, "The Search for the Michigamea Indian Village," *Outdoor Illinois* 11 (March 1972), p. 19, locations of Illini Indians. Peithmann, *Indians of Southern Illinois*, p. 76, Indian trail through Bone Gap. Barbara Burr Hubbs, *Pioneer Folks and Places: An Historic Gazetteer of Williamson County, Illinois* (Herrin, Illinois: Herrin Daily Journal, 1939; rpt. Marion, Illinois: Williamson County Historical Society, 1979), p. 192, Tecumseh reportedly near Marion.

John Ehle, *Trail of Tears: The Rise and Fall of the Cherokee Nation* (New York: Doubleday, 1988), p. 348, estimate of 11,000 Cherokee removed from homeland; pp. 386–96, Indians who remained behind, death counts, popular but fabricated story of removal by John G. Burnett, daily life on the Trail of Tears. Conley, *The Cherokee Nation*, p. 154, author says 17,000 Cherokee removed from homeland, 5,000 by water, 12,000 by land; pp. 141–57, details leading up to removal, daily life on the Trail of Tears, dates of departure, routes, deaths, births, number who escaped or slipped away from Trail of Tears, incomplete records, winter of 1838–39 in Southern Illinois. Darrel Dexter to Herbert Russell, conversation, March 1, 2008, estimate of eight thousand Cherokee on Trail of Tears. Rowena McClinton to Herbert Russell, conversation, November 19, 2009, route through Southern Illinois would accommodate wagons, John G. Burnett discredited as witness, estimate that fewer than 300 Indians left Trail of Tears. Mary McCorvie to Herbert Russell, conversation, December 10, 2009, east-west trail through Southern Illinois was superior to roads farther south.

Notes to pages 45–46

James Webb, *Born Fighting: How the Scots-Irish Shaped America* (New York: Broadway Books, 2004), pp. 14, 119, 129, 134, 139, 214, 230. David Hackett Fischer, *Albion's Seed: Four British Folkways in America* (New York: Oxford University Press, 1989), pp. 618–21, "Scots Irish" composed of several ancestral groups; p. 633, encouraged to leave the East.

Arthur Singleton, *Letters from the South and West* (Boston: Richardson and Lord, 1824), p. 96, a "Letter from Kentucky" refers to Kentucky as "Egypt," as a source of grain, "From the poorer states." Richard M. Dorson, *Buying the Wind: Regional Folklore in the United States* (Chicago: University of Chicago Press, 1964), pp. 298–99, several areas named "Egypt," including those in New Hampshire and New Jersey.

Notes to pages 46–48

Smith, *History of Illinois and Her People*, vol. 1, p. 232, Egypt settled by poor whites. Nicole

Etcheson, *The Emerging Midwest: Upland Southerners and the Political Culture of the Old Northwest, 1787–1861* (Bloomington: Indiana University Press, 1996), p. 5, most upland southerners had no slaves or money to buy them. N. Dwight Harris, *The History of Negro Servitude in Illinois and of the Slavery Agitation in That State, 1719–1864* (Chicago: McClurg, 1904), p. 11, "most of the settlers." *Illinois Census Returns, 1810, 1818*, ed. with intro. and notes by Margaret Cross Norton (Springfield: Illinois State Historical Library, 1935), pp. x and 1, details of the 1810 federal census of Illinois exist for a fragment of one county. Darrel Dexter, *Bondage in Egypt: Slavery and Indentured Servitude in Southern Illinois, 1720–1865* (Cape Girardeau: Southeast Missouri State University Center for Regional History, 2011), appendix B shows haphazard methods of census takers through 1820. John Y. Simon, "Union County in 1858 and the Lincoln-Douglas Debate," *Journal of the Illinois State Historical Society* 62 (autumn 1969), p. 291, Southern Illinois settlers seldom descended from slaveholding families.

William Oliver, *Eight Months in Illinois, with Information to Immigrants* (William Andrew Mitchell, 1843; rpt. Walter M. Hill, 1924; rpt. Carbondale: Southern Illinois University Press, 2002), pp. 173–74, "On asking him." Buck, *Illinois in 1818*, p. 109, "good land dog-cheap"; p. 72, salt springs had black and white laborers. Mark J. Wagner and Mary R. McCorvie, "The Pirates of Cave-in-Rock in Myth and Legend," *Springhouse* 28, no. 1 [2011], pp. 9–14.

Notes to pages 52–56

H. Donald Winkler, *Lincoln's Ladies: The Women in the Life of the Sixteenth President* (Nashville: Cumberland House, 2004), pp. 25–36, Ann Rutledge lived in Enfield Township. John W. Allen, *Legends and Lore of Southern Illinois* (Carbondale: Southern Illinois University, 1963), pp. 26–27, Ann Rutledge spends over half her life in Enfield Township. *History of White County Illinois* (Chicago: Inter-State Publishing Company, 1883; rpt. White County Historical Society, 1966), pp. 699–702, Rutledge family, Seven Mile Prairie. R. Carlyle Buley, *The Old Northwest Pioneer Period, 1815–1840*, vol. 1 (Indianapolis: Indiana Historical Society, 1950), p. 326, "The Weev'ly Wheat."

Notes to page 60

Hubbs, *Pioneer Folks and Places*, p. 139, family with twenty-two children; p. 41, log schoolhouses.

Notes to pages 61–64

The Illinois Fact Book and Historical Almanac, 1673–1968, comp. John Clayton (Carbondale: Southern Illinois University Press, 1970), p. 15, Pope moves boundary 62.5 miles north. Paul E. Stroble Jr., *High on the Okaw's Western Bank: Vandalia, Illinois, 1819–39* (Urbana: University of Illinois Press, 1992), pp. 13–14, colony of Vandalia. Davis, *Frontier Illinois*, pp. 160–61, Nathaniel Pope and statehood; p. 306, about 70 percent of Illinoisans are nonsoutherners by 1850. *An Illinois Reader*, comp. and ed. Clyde C. Walton (DeKalb: Northern Illinois University Press, 1970), p. 92, over 75 percent of northern Illinoisans have roots in North and East.

The National Road, ed. Karl Raitz (Baltimore: Johns Hopkins University Press, 1996), p. 425, National Road reaches Vandalia in 1839; p. xi, is completed in 1850. John Hudson, *Making the Corn Belt* (Bloomington: Indiana University Press, 1994), p. 130, canal commissioners lay out Chicago. Michael McCafferty, "A Fresh Look at the Place Name *Chicago*," *Journal of the Illinois State Historical Society* 96 (summer 2003), pp. 116–24, skunk and wild onion or garlic.

Notes to pages 64–67

Carlton J. Corliss, *Main Line of Mid-America: The Story of the Illinois Central* (New York: Creative Age Press, 1950), p. 3, Alexander Jenkins; p. 6, John S. Hacker. Howard, *Illinois*, p. 251, private railroad hauling coal on wooden rails. Walter Havighurst, *The Heartland: Ohio, Indiana, Illinois* (New York: Harper and Row, 1962), pp. 154–55, "don't care shucks," Sam Slick. Davis, *Frontier Illinois*, pp. 247–68, Yankees scorn southern cultures, slavery, and low-life behavior; p. 254, "A Northern State." Thomas Beer, *The Mauve Decade: American Life at the End of the Nineteenth Century* (New York: Knopf, 1926; rpt. New York: Carroll and Graf, 1997), p. 103, "the odd blending." *Springhouse* magazine, inside cover, December 1992, "I sleep fine." Fred W. Kohlmeyer, "Illinois Agriculture in Retrospect," in *Illinois: Its History and Legacy*, ed. Roger D. Bridges and Rodney

O. Davis (St. Louis: River City Publishers, 1984), p. 2, "coon and catfish" society.

Notes to pages 67–70

Davis, *Frontier Illinois*, p. 96, "There shall be neither slavery"; p. 101, St. Clair maintains slavery; pp. 166–67, Illinoisans vote down slavery. Edgar J. McManus, *Black Bondage in the North* (Syracuse: Syracuse University Press, 1973), p. 6, Indian slaves; p. 10, Newport and Providence slave ports; p. 52, New England slavery; p. 19, New York slave markets; p. 181, indenture for ninety-nine years. Barnet Schecter, *The Devil's Own Work: The Civil War Draft Riots and the Fight to Reconstruct America* (New York: Walker and Company, 2005), p. 372, slave burial ground in New York City. "Remains of Colonial-Era Blacks Reach Resting Place," *Southern Illinoisan*, October 5, 2003, p. 4A, five-acre black graveyard dating to 1794 discovered in 1991 near Manhattan slave market. Brent Staples, "Wrestling with the Legacy of Slavery at Yale," *New York Times*, August 14, 2001, p. A16, Yale's founders, early presidents, and campus facilities benefited from slave trade. "Brown University's Debt to Slavery," *New York Times*, October 23, 2006, p. A18, thirty of Brown's governing board members owned or captained slave ships, donors provided slaves for some construction. Wood Gray, *The Hidden Civil War: The Story of the Copperheads* (New York: Viking, 1942), pp. 211–13, laborers and abolition, Connecticut carriages, Massachusetts mills, New York businesses. Paul Simon, *Freedom's Champion: Elijah Lovejoy* (Carbondale: Southern Illinois University Press, 1994), p. 72, abolitionist Garrison nearly killed in Boston, proslavery mobs and antiabolition riots in the North, including Connecticut, Maine, New Hampshire, proslavery mobs in numerous other cities. Roland H. Woodwell, *John Greenleaf Whittier: A Biography* (Haverhill, Massachusetts: Trustees of the John Greenleaf Whittier Homestead, 1985), pp. 75–76, abolitionist Whittier attacked.

Notes to pages 70–71

Simon, *Freedom's Champion*, p. 16, William; p. 72, proslavery mobs and antiabolition riots in the North; p. 82, "more than half"; p. 113, "you may hang me"; p. 140, shot. Missouri slave numbers are from the Missouri Department of Natural Resources' Missouri State Museum (access via Internet). Newton N. Newborn, "Judicial Decision Making and the End of Slavery in Illinois," *Journal of the Illinois State Historical Society* 98 (spring-summer 2005), pp. 7–33, circuit and state courts end indentures and slavery. Mrs. P. T. Chapman, *A History of Johnson County Illinois* (1925; rpt. Johnson County Genealogical and Historical Society, 2003), pp. 266–74, Johnson County circuit court frees runaway slaves after one year, freedom certificates from county officials. McManus, *Black Bondage in the North*, p. 179, over 17,000 slaves in New York, New Jersey, and Pennsylvania. Dana E. Weiner, "Anti-Abolition Violence and Freedom of Speech in Peoria, Illinois, 1843–1848," *Journal of Illinois History* 11 (autumn 2008), pp. 179–204, opposition to public discussions of abolition of slavery.

Notes to page 72–73

Jones, *Black Jack: John A. Logan and Southern Illinois*, p. 33, Southern Illinois predominantly Democratic; p. 20, some say black migration law not consistently enforced. Schecter, *The Devil's Own Work*, pp. 4–7, 32, 44, 52, 64, 74, 75, 86, 94, 107, 114, Democrats use race and white supremacy to maintain party loyalty. McManus, *Black Bondage in the North*, p. 183, Massachusetts flogging bill, New Jersey prohibits blacks; p. 181, no state freed slaves immediately. Richard Wormser, *The Rise and Fall of Jim Crow* (New York: St. Martin's Press, 2003), p. xi, first Jim Crow laws passed in the North. V. Jacque Voegeli, *Free but Not Equal: The Midwest and the Negro during the Civil War* (Chicago: University of Chicago Press, 1967), p. 2, Iowa bars blacks in 1851, Indiana in 1852, Illinois in 1853.

Edgar F. Raines Jr., "The American Missionary Association in Southern Illinois, 1856–1862: A Case History in the Abolition Movement," *Journal of the Illinois State Historical Society* 65 (autumn 1972), p. 252, shows 3,202 free African Americans by county in state's twenty-eight southernmost counties. Benjamin Quarles, *The Negro in the American Revolution* (Chapel Hill: University of North Carolina, 1961), p.

ix, about 5,000 free blacks and slaves fought on the American side in the Revolutionary War. Darrel Dexter, "Entries of Free Negroes 1814, 1822–1844, 1846–1863, St. Clair County, Illinois," *The Saga of Southern Illinois* 33 (July–September 2006), p. 19, free African Americans in Illinois Territory in 1813.

Paul Heinegg, *Free African Americans of North Carolina, Virginia, and South Carolina from the Colonial Period to about 1820*, vol. 1 (Baltimore: Clearfield, 2001), pp. 1–29, mingled black-white blood lines shown by deeds, court cases, land transfers, marriage and tax records, baptismal records, registries of free Negroes, references to mulatto children; p. 17, loss of right to vote, carry gun without license. Lerone Bennett Jr., *Before the Mayflower: A History of the Negro in America, 1619–1966* (Chicago: Johnson Publishing Company, 1966), pp. 249–56, African American historian discusses white female and black male sexual relations. Kenneth M. Stampp, *The Peculiar Institution* (New York: Knopf, 1956), pp. 21–22 and 351–53, white female and black male sexual relations.

Notes to pages 74–75

Raines, "The American Missionary Association in Southern Illinois, 1856–1862," p. 257, friendly relations between blacks and whites in Pope and Massac Counties. Smith, *History of Illinois and Her People*, vol. 1, p. 473, friends of kidnapped free blacks pursue and rescue. Jon Musgrave, *Slaves, Salt, Sex, and Mr. Crenshaw: The Real Story of the Old Slave House and America's Reverse Underground R.R.* (Marion, Illinois: IllinoisHistory.com, 2004–05), pp. 303–07, Pope County (Golconda) sheriff traces four kidnapped free black children to Arkansas and returns them to their home, Pope County citizens raise reward to rescue free mulatto children kidnapped to Missouri and Mississippi and return them to their home; pp. 335–36, Eddy requests governor to free imprisoned African Americans; p. 229, Shawneetown Colored Emancipation Baptist Church lists fifteen members.

History of Gallatin, Saline, Hamilton, Franklin, and Williamson Counties, Illinois, p. 31, some southerners free slaves upon arriving in Illinois, Lawler defends civil liberties of African Americans; p. 349, Franklin County man buys freedom for black acquaintances; p. 139, Pros Robinson. Darrel Dexter, "Harry: From Illinois Slave to Illinois Landowner," Illinois State Historical Society Symposium, Southern Illinois University Carbondale, April 14, 2011, Harry Dougherty, Vienna, Christmas day, becomes landowner in Pin Oak, Madison County.

Buley, *The Old Northwest Pioneer Period, 1815–1840*, vol. 2, pp. 467–68, Friends of Humanity ("Emancipation Baptists"), antislavery church. Nelson, *History of Liberty Baptist Church*, pp. 1–56, summarizes principal people, churches, beliefs, and locations of Illinois' Emancipation Baptists. *Handbook of Old Gallatin County*, ed. Jon Musgrave (Marion, Illinois: IllinoisHistory.com, 2002), p. 129, Shawneetown's Colored Emancipation Baptist Church may have met in African Methodist Episcopal Church; p. 84 note, "An old colored man."

Notes to pages 75–76

Darrel Dexter, *Free and American: A Study of Eleven Families of Color* (access via Internet at http://www.freeafricanamericans.com/Illinois.htm), chap. 8, p. 11, white groom marries Negro or mulatto bride circa 1833 (the couple and the justice of the peace are found not guilty of violating state law against mixed marriages); chap. 4, pp. 11–12, white groom marries black or mulatto bride in 1867; chap. 4, p. 13, mixed-race groom marries white bride; chap. 8 shows various legal cases in which African Americans are found not guilty in Union County court; chap. 9, p. 1, and chap. 10, p. 1, African Americans carry cases to court and win in Jackson and Union Counties. (The African American who won the Jackson County case, Cain Bracken, mentioned his case when he filed his freedom papers in Union County, as recorded in Union County Negro Book A, pp. 18–20—per Union County historian Darrel Dexter to Herbert Russell, March 1, 2010.) Darrel Dexter to Herbert Russell, May 18, 2011, runaway slave notices supposed to be printed in newspapers.

Notes to pages 76–77

Combined History [of] Edwards, Lawrence, and Wabash Counties, Illinois, pp. 69–72, fort at

Russellville, settlements of Pinkstaff, Lackey. Robert H. Mohlenbrock, "A New Geography of Illinois: Saline County," *Illinois* 16 (December 1977), p. 40, Grayson and Neal Elliott. [Gary DeNeal, editorial response to reader letter], *Springhouse* 16 (June 1999), p. 7, Grayson and Cornelius Elliott. Allen, *Legends and Lore of Southern Illinois*, pp. 132–33, settlement of Nigger Spring. Portions of summaries of pre–Civil War settlements of South America, Grayson, Nigger Spring, Pond/Lakeview, Miller Grove, and Africa are from the brochure *African American Settlements in Southern Illinois*, [2001], research and text compiled by Vickie Devenport through a cooperative agreement between the Shawnee National Forest, Mary McCorvie, forest archaeologist, and the General John A. Logan Museum, Michael Jones, director, Murphysboro.

W. S. Blackman, *The Boy of Battle Ford and the Man* (Marion, Illinois: Egyptian Press Printing, 1906), pp. 19, 43, Joseph and Ann Cole; p. 42, integrated baptism at Pond/Lakeview. Raines, "The American Missionary Association in Southern Illinois, 1856–1862," p. 257, pre–Civil War black-and-white relations in Miller Grove. Lowell A. Dearinger, "Miller Grove," *Outdoor Illinois* 4 (November 1965), pp. 7–12, post–Civil War black-and-white relations.

Notes to pages 77–78

Combined History [of] Edwards, Lawrence, and Wabash Counties, Illinois, p. 159, "The pioneers were so few." Chloe McNeill, "Africa, Illinois," *The Egyptian Key* 2 (March 1947), pp. 34–35, white neighbors encourage residents of Africa to remain.

Clay Roots [Louisville, Illinois: Clay County Genealogical Society,] (winter 1993), pp. 3, 17, 18, 25, 26, Higginbotham, Nigger Settlement, soldier reportedly in Union Army. Clay County General Index, Book A (Grantee), Clay County Courthouse, Louisville, Illinois, shows Higginbotham family land purchases, 1840s to at least 1861. *Clay County Census of 1860* (Louisville, Illinois: Clay County Genealogical Society, 1992), p. 138, shows seven Higginbothams with "B" (for black) by their names living in the neighborhood known locally as "Nigger Settlement."

Dexter, *Free and American*, chap. 8, p. 1, "free persons of color" and Joseph Ivey; chap. 8, p. 4, neither Joseph Ivey nor Arthur Allen registered certificates of freedom; chap. 1, pp. 1–22, Arthur Allen family, black-white relations, activities in Union County; chap. 1, p. 21, "the only regular negro settlement." Darrel Dexter to Herbert Russell, conversation, March 1, 2008, existence of "Negro Book A," two friends of Ivey indicted, charges dropped. Chapman, *A History of Johnson County Illinois*, p. 157, "proved themselves substantial."

Notes to pages 79–80

Carol Pirtle, *Escape Betwixt Two Suns: A True Tale of the Underground Railroad in Illinois* (Carbondale: Southern Illinois University Press, 2000), pp. 44–45, Covenanters in Eden area by 1819; pp. 50–57, court case involving runaway slave and children; map following p. 42, UGRR route passes through Covenanter settlements. Darrel Dexter to Herbert Russell, conversation, March 1, 2008, Covenanters likely force behind UGRR in southwestern Illinois. Allen, *Legends and Lore of Southern Illinois*, pp. 262–63, Eden on UGRR.

Michael McClay to Herbert Russell, conversations, March 26, 29, 2009, community lore places house near Oakdale on UGRR. Sundiata Keita Cha-Jua, *America's First Black Town: Brooklyn, Illinois, 1830–1915* (Urbana: University of Illinois Press, 2000), p. 32, Brooklyn settled in 1829; p. ix, Brooklyn established in 1830. Irving Dilliard, "John W. Allen: A Personal Word," in John W. Allen, *It Happened in Southern Illinois* (Carbondale: University Graphics, 1968), p. viii, Bethel Church on UGRR.

Notes to pages 80–81

Larry Gara, *The Liberty Line: The Legend of the Underground Railroad* (Lexington: University of Kentucky Press, 1967), pp. 17, 90, 142–43, 164, 179–82, much published information about UGRR is unconfirmed legend or folklore; pp. 2, 54–55, 93–94, 107–12, free Negroes aid runaways. Keith P. Griffler, *Frontier Line of Freedom: African Americans and the Forging of the Underground Railroad in the Ohio Valley* (Lexington: University Press of Kentucky,

2004), shows free black settlements instrumental to success of UGRR in the Midwest. Darrel Dexter to Herbert Russell, conversation, February 10, 2009, free black woman from Cairo (in *Rodney v. Illinois Central Railroad*) and Illinois Central porter George J. L. Burroughs each assist one runaway. Chapman, *A History of Johnson County Illinois*, p. 156, "Patrick" inquires of hamlet of South America.

Notes to pages 81–83

Musgrave, *Slaves, Salt, Sex, and Mr. Crenshaw*, describes research on Crenshaw and his mansion; pp. 556–58, several owners between Crenshaw and house tours; pp. 31–33, "Old Slave House" name not used until mid-1930s; pp. 175–77, 263, 553, and many other pages allege Crenshaw was a kidnapper of African Americans and warehoused victims on the third floor; pp. 442–59, "Uncle Bob" Wilson; pp. 24, 32–34, Underground Railroad. Darrel Dexter, *A Trot Down to Egypt: The Lincoln-Douglas Debate in Jonesboro, Illinois* (Jonesboro Lincoln-Douglas Debate Sesquicentennial Committee, 2008), p. 37, Cairo site of black kidnappings.

Ronald L. Nelson to Herbert Russell, conversation, March 25, 2008, "Crenshaw Mansion," "Hickory Hill." Allen, *Legends and Lore of Southern Illinois*, p. 268, historian remarks on alleged torture devices ("it is not easy to see the manner of their use").

Ronald L. Nelson and Gary DeNeal, "A Mystery Solved," *Springhouse* 14 (February 1997), p. 23, Crenshaw attorney Henry Eddy lines out "Granger," writes "Crenshaw." Gary DeNeal, "Crenshaw-Granger Update," *Springhouse* 14 (April 1997), p. 32, DeNeal–Ronald L. Nelson research shows Crenshaw pronounced as "Granger." Fischer, *Albion's Seed*, p. 259, Crenshaw name pronounced as "Granger" in eighteenth century Virginia and elsewhere. Musgrave, *Slaves, Salt, Sex, and Mr. Crenshaw*, p. 51, fellow Methodists know Crenshaw by nickname of "Granger." John Metzger, "The Old Slave House," *Outdoor Illinois* 12 (January 1973), p. 33, "See the breeding room."

James M. Cornelius, *John Hart Crenshaw and Hickory Hill: Final Report* (Springfield: Illinois Historic Preservation Agency, 2002), p. 4, suggests some unspecified stories about Crenshaw may be true. William Furry, "Historic Hullabaloo," *Illinois Times*, May 8–14, 1997; rpt. *Springhouse* 14 (June 1997), p. 36, Lincoln alleged to have spent night at house. Michael Tow, Review of *Slaves, Salt, Sex, and Mr. Crenshaw* by Jon Musgrave in *Journal of the Illinois State Historical Society* 101 (spring 2008), pp. 91–95, book fails to prove that any slaves were kidnapped.

Notes to pages 84–85

Simon, "Union County in 1858 and the Lincoln-Douglas Debate," p. 285, "trot him down to lower Egypt," "I know this people." Donald F. Tingley, "The Clingman Raid," *Journal of the Illinois State Historical Society* 56 (summer 1963), pp. 362–63, "Peace Democrats," "War Democrats," and those in between. *Cairo City Gazette*, December 6, 1860, "the sympathies of our people," as quoted in Ecelbarger, *Black Jack Logan*, p. 65. T. K. Kionka, *Key Command: Ulysses S. Grant's District of Cairo* (Columbia: University of Missouri Press, 2006), p. 31, *Cairo City Weekly Gazette* urges support for Union on February 21, 1861. *Cairo City Weekly Gazette*, February 28, 1861, [p. 1], paper prints John A. Logan's remarks against secession; April 18, 1861, [p. 2], paper prints article calling for reconciliation and maintenance of the Union (this newspaper printed a mix of articles, some supporting secession, some opposing it).

Notes to pages 86–87

Robert W. Johannsen, *Stephen A. Douglas* (New York: Oxford University Press, 1973), p. 868, "every man must be for." Jones, *Black Jack: John A. Logan and Southern Illinois*, p. 100, Logan's Marion speech echoed Douglas' speech. Ecelbarger, *Black Jack Logan*, p. 87, Logan's Marion speech relied on Douglas' ideas and words. Buck, *Illinois in 1818*, pp. 169–70, first public library. Charles Boewe, *Prairie Albion: An English Settlement in Pioneer Illinois* (Carbondale: Southern Illinois University Press, 1962; rpt. 1999), p. 227, drainage makes prairies productive.

Notes to pages 87–88

David Benedict, *A General History of the Baptist Denomination in America and Other Parts of the World* (New York: Lewis Copeland, 1848), pp. 850–51, Emancipation Baptists in early Illinois. Ralph S. Harrelson, *Pioneer Baptist Ministers: Voices in the Wilderness of the Illinois Country* (McLeansboro, Illinois: Ralph S. Harrelson, 1987), pp. 18–20, influence of Dodge on Lemen. Dillow, *Harvesttime on the Prairie*, p. 82, opposition to slavery as religious doctrine in 1796; pp. 137–39, circulars against slavery, Baptists unite against slavery, sixty-four churches, 2,400 members by 1845; pp. 30–32, Lemen's five sons, James Lemen Jr.; pp. 118, 128–29, black churches in St. Clair and Madison Counties.

Nelson, *History of Liberty Baptist Church*, p. 52, "Being opposed to slavery," "We believe it to be"; pp. 1–57, summarizes people, churches, beliefs, numbers, and locations of Illinois' Emancipation Baptists. Evans, "Abolitionism in the Illinois Churches, 1830–1865," pp. 282–83, Lemen, sons, and other Emancipation Baptists work actively with Governor Coles to prevent Illinois from becoming a slave state, "could not be property." Ronald L. Nelson to Herbert Russell, conversation, March 25, 2008, black and white ministers occasionally exchange churches.

Notes to pages 88–89

Cross, "The Civil War Comes to 'Egypt,'" pp. 160–69, about 40 percent of eligible men enlist in sixteen southernmost counties, about 28 percent elsewhere—from Schedule D, *Annual Report of the Adjutant General of the State of Illinois*, 1863, pp. 78–80. Milo Erwin, *History of Williamson County Illinois* (Marion, Illinois, 1876; rpt. Herrin, Illinois: The Herrin News, 1914), pp. 170–71, "The interest of the citizens"; "ten or fifteen men." Ecelbarger, *Black Jack Logan*, p. 70, eleven of twelve men support resolution. Gleeson, *Illinois Rebels* , p. 127, sources of names of secessionists at Marion meeting; pp. 1–13, Thorndike Brooks, John M. Cunningham, Henry C. Hopper, eleven of twelve men identified by name support resolution for secession, resolution to secede rescinded, thirty-four men in all, most leave May 25; pp. 85–126, additional information about thirty-four men. Cross, "The Civil War Comes to 'Egypt,'" p. 160, *Tribune* reprints stories; p. 166, Republican newspaper biased against Democrat-dominated Southern Illinois. [William Camm,] "Diary of Colonel William Camm, 1861 to 1865," comp. Fritz Haskell, *Journal of the Illinois State Historical Society* 18 (January 1926), p. 873, "What a wonderful and stupid nonsense." Ulysses S. Grant to Julia [Dent Grant], May 21, 1861, in *Ulysses S. Grant, Memoirs and Selected Letters* (New York: Library of America, 1990), p. 964, refutes reports of Egypt's disloyalty.

Notes to pages 89–91

An Illinois Reader, ed. Walton, p. 224, 2,800 miles of track. Sutton, *The Illinois Central Railroad in Peace and War*, p. 44, 112 miles of track, 6-mile short line; pp. 105–7, Northern troops guard Big Muddy bridge; pp. 194–98, cotton seed to farmers, tobacco, sorghum.

[Brush,] *Growing Up with Southern Illinois*, pp. 246–49, telegraph office, secessionists hold meeting in Carbondale, "the rampant rebels"; pp. I–III, Brush speaks twice; p. XX and XXII, twenty-four secessionists identified by name, including Thorndike Brooks, John M. Cunningham, and Henry C. Hopper, as well as southern sympathizers Israel Blanchard, Anderson Corder, and William Joshua Allen. Jones, *Black Jack: John A. Logan and Southern Illinois*, pp. xvi–xvii, Blanchard and Allen. "Cortos," "Apprehensions of an attack . . . ," *Chicago Tribune*, April 26, 1861, front page, "Williamson County passed resolutions." Long-time Southern Illinois historian John Allen also noticed that "the same names appear in the accounts of [secessionist] meetings at several places." See *It Happened in Southern Illinois*, p. 301.

John W. D. Wright, *A History of Early Carbondale, Illinois, 1852–1905* (Carbondale: Southern Illinois University Press, 1977), p. 23, Carbondale population 1,147; p. 168, Brush raises flag; p. 18, Brush business on southwest corner. Kionka, *Key Command*, p. 40, secessionists successful in giving impression that Carbondale wishes to secede.

Notes to page 92

Jane E. Schultz, *Women at the Front: Hospital Workers in Civil War America* (Chapel Hill: University of North Carolina Press, 2004), p. 176, Safford, Bickerdyke, Belmont, Donelson, Shiloh. Emmet F. Pearson, "The Historic Hospitals of Cairo," *Journal of the Illinois State Historical Society* 77 (1984), pp. 21–28, Safford, Bickerdyke, Catholic nuns, Confederates, and freed African Americans treated at Cairo hospitals.

Notes to page 93

Ezra J. Warner, *Generals in Gray: Lives of the Confederate Commanders* (Baton Rouge: Louisiana State University Press, 1959), p. 156, Adam "Stovepipe" Johnson wounded August 21, 1864, Caldwell County, near Princeton, Kentucky. "The Invasion of Illinois," *New York Times*, August 19, 1864, p. 2. "Guerillas in Illinois," *Louisville Journal*, September 3, 1864, p. 1, August 19, "ten miles above Smithland," "at Bayfield," "Adam Johnson's command," McCormick Store. "Riding a Raid" lyrics, access via Internet; some Civil War song collections show variations in wording.

Adam R. Johnson, *The Partisan Rangers of the Confederate States Army* (Louisville: George G. Fetter Company, 1904; rpt. Evansville, Indiana: Unigraphic, Inc., 1971), pp. 282–83, details preceding "Stovepipe" Johnson's wounding on August 21, 1864, in Caldwell County, Kentucky. *Handbook of Old Gallatin County*, ed. Musgrave, pp. 518–19, summarizes raid near Shawneetown and raid on McCormick Store.

Mildred McCormick, "Raiders on the Ohio," *Springhouse* 1, no. 7 (November-December 1984), pp. 6, 46, family lore and background of receipt, 1976 letter from William E. Metzler to Mildred McCormick, raider Johnson in area, raiders cross into Illinois, Johnson wounded August 21, 1864. Mildred McCormick to Herbert Russell, fall 2008 and September 30, 2009, conversations regarding family lore and receipt. *Confederate Soldiers of Kentucky: A Roster of the Veterans 1861–1865*, ed. Stephen Douglas Lynn (Dexter, Michigan: Thomson-Shore, 2002), p. 190, Henry Johnson in 3rd Cavalry.

Notes to pages 93–95

Roger Biles, *Illinois: A History of the Land and Its People* (DeKalb: Northern Illinois University Press, 2005), pp. 114–15, Knights of the Golden Circle, Charleston shootout leaves nine dead. Gleeson, *Illinois Rebels*, p. 10, depart May 25–26; pp. 11 and 119, thirty-four men; pp. 85–118, biographical sketches, places of birth; pp. 10, 104, only one of thirty-four born in Southern Illinois; pp. 4, 37, 80–81, Hibert Cunningham. Ecelbarger, *Black Jack Logan*, p. 73, Hibert to South; p. 158, Hibert deserts to Union.

Jones, *Black Jack: John A. Logan and Southern Illinois*, p. 107, counties in the 31st; p. 166, "boys," "Thirty-Onesters," "remember the blood." William F. Fox, *Regimental Losses in the American Civil War, 1861–1865* (Albany: Brandow Printing, 1898; rpt. Morningside Bookshop, 1974), p. 506, 31st Illinois and 11th Illinois each lost 471 men. Ecelbarger, *Black Jack Logan*, p. 230, Slasher.

Notes to page 97

Schecter, *The Devil's Own Work*, pp. 4–5, 87, 107, 113–14, Democrat propaganda aimed at lower class; pp. 143–223, deaths of free African Americans, soldiers, and rioters, burning of Colored Orphan Asylum; p. 251, twenty-three black deaths, seventy missing. James M. McPherson, *The Illustrated Battle Cry of Freedom: The Civil War Era* (New York: Oxford University Press, 2003), p. 526, "worst riot in American history." Darrel Dexter, "Desertion from the 109th Regiment Illinois Volunteer Infantry," *Saga of Southern Illinois* 33, no. 2 (April–June 2006), p. 30, Democrats in Jonesboro.

[James Evans,] *Letters to the Editor of the Jonesboro Gazette, 1862–1863, from James Evans, Adjutant, 109th Illinois Volunteer Infantry Regiment, Union Army*, ed. Patrick Brumleve et al. (Union County Historical and Genealogy Society, 2006), p. 42, white veterans will have to compete for wages with ex-slaves. Voegeli, *Free but Not Equal*, pp. 60–61, Chicago, Quincy, Olney refuse to help ex-slaves. Wright, *A History of Early Carbondale*, pp. 44, 285, ex-slaves with smallpox; pp. 216–17, white Carbondale resident remembers how he received meals in a bucket on the end of a pole when he was quarantined with smallpox in 1858.

Notes to pages 97–98

Frederick Douglass: Selected Speeches and Writings, ed. Philip S. Foner (Chicago: Lawrence Hill Books, 1999), p. 527, "the iron gate." John Y. Simon, foreword, in Howard C. Westwood, *Black Troops, White Commanders, and Freedmen during the Civil War* (Carbondale: Southern Illinois University Press, 1992), p. viii, 10 percent. Victor Hicken, *Illinois in the Civil War*, 2nd ed. (Urbana: University of Illinois Press, 1991), pp. 134–36, 1,811 African Americans in infantry, artillery, cavalry, some drafted into service, 54th Massachusetts. Dexter, *Free and American: A Study of Eleven Families of Color*, chap. 3, p. 13, ten Gallatin County men in the 29th U.S. Colored Infantry; chap. 2, p. 6, two Saline County men in the 28th U.S. Colored Infantry; others not noted here also served.

Edward A. Miller Jr., *The Black Civil War Soldiers of Illinois: The Story of the Twenty-Ninth U.S. Colored Infantry* (Columbia: University of South Carolina Press, 1998), p. 30, O'Fallon man in 29th U.S. Colored Infantry. Brown, *History as They Lived It*, pp. 254–55, at least seven African Americans from Prairie du Rocher area in colored infantry units. Victor Hicken, "The Record of Illinois' Negro Soldiers in the Civil War," *Journal of the Illinois State Historical Society* 56 (autumn 1963), pp. 529–51.

Bryce A. Suderow, "The Battle of the Crater: The Civil War's Worst Massacre," in *Black Flag over Dixie: Racial Atrocities and Reprisals in the Civil War*, ed. Gregory J. W. Urwin (Carbondale: Southern Illinois University Press, 2004), p. 208, war's worst massacre of African Americans. George S. Burkhardt, *Confederate Rage, Yankee Wrath: No Quarter in the Civil War* (Carbondale: Southern Illinois University Press, 2007), pp. 2, 121, 237–39, African American soldiers murder white prisoners at Fort Blakely near Mobile and elsewhere.

Notes to pages 99–103

Corliss, *Main Line of Mid-America*, photo of Logan Day in Chicago follows p. 302. Allen, *Legends and Lore of Southern Illinois*, pp. 269–71, Emancipation Day observed in Elizabethtown, Brookport, Carbondale, Metropolis. *1866–1966 National Memorial Day Centennial, Carbondale, Illinois*, pamphlet dated May 30, 1966, shows the program for the centennial observance, the 1866 note of caretaker John Green ("Decration, Was held here"), and discusses local events leading up to the 1868 observance nationwide.

Woodlawn Cemetery, informational flyer dated 2001, grave of freed slaves, Mrs. J. W. Landrum. *Atlas of the State of Illinois* (Chicago: Union Atlas Co., 1876; rpt. Indianapolis: Ye Olde Genealogie Shoppe, 2000), p. 102, shows J. W. Landrum was large landowner two miles east of Woodlawn Cemetery. Wright, *A History of Early Carbondale*, p. 44, freed slaves; p. 285, about thirty freed slaves.

Notes to pages 103–8

Elizabeth McNulty, *Chicago Then and Now* (San Diego: Thunder Bay Press, 2000), p. 5, "Boss City." For accounts of how railroads shaped Illinois, see three books: Corliss, *Main Line of Mid-America: The Story of the Illinois Central*; Sutton, *The Illinois Central Railroad in Peace and War, 1858–1868*; and Albro Martin, *Railroads Triumphant* (New York: Oxford University Press, 1992). Stanley A. Changnon, *The Triangle—Busy Railroading in Southern Illinois* (Champaign, Illinois: Printec Press, 1991), rail traffic in Centralia, Salem, Mt. Vernon, and related areas; p. 38, indicates Centralia was nation's largest maker of freight cars; p. 39, Sandoval was busy railroad junction.

Judith Joy, "When the Railroad Car was King in Mt. Vernon," *Illinois Magazine* 19 (January-February 1980), p. 14, 2,300 workers; pp. 8–19, history of freight car manufacturing plant. Douglas C. Ridgley, *The Geography of Illinois* (Chicago: University of Chicago Press, 1921), detailed information on agriculture and many other economic activities in Southern Illinois and northward circa 1900 to 1910.

Donald F. Tingley, *The Structuring of a State: The History of Illinois, 1899–1928*, Sesquicentennial History of Illinois, vol. 5 (Urbana: University of Illinois Press, 1980), p. 230, Centralia as railroad center; p. 46, soybeans. William Goins to Herbert Russell, conversations, 2005, 2006, Stumptown. Town and county histories show dozens of sawmill settlements in Egypt, as does Glenn J. Sneed in his *Ghost Towns of Southern Illinois* (Johnston City, Illinois: A.E.R.P. Publisher, 1977): sawmill settlements in Delta, pp. 4–5, and Aden, p. 46.

Notes to pages 108–12

My discussion of the region's agriculture and raw materials relies heavily on Ridgley, *The Geography of Illinois*. Edmund Newsome, *Historical Sketches of Jackson County, Illinois* (Carbondale: E. Newsome Publisher, 1894; rpt. Jackson County Historical Society, 1997), p. 119, Boskydell stone used for SIU building. Corliss, *Main Line of Mid-America*, p. 295, Earle experiments with fruit.

The Changing Face of Farmwork in Union County, Illinois: A History of Fruits and Vegetables and the People Who Worked in the Industry, ed. Judy Travelstead et al. (Union County Historical and Genealogy Society, 2008), p. 67, quotes *Illinois Central Magazine* for October 1928: Cobden is "birthplace of railway refrigeration as applied to perishable fruit shipments." Robert H. Mohlenbrock, *Forest Trees of Illinois* (Illinois Department of Natural Resources, 1996), uses of different trees.

Notes to pages 113–15

Doyne A. Horsley, *Illinois: A Geography* (Boulder: Westview Press, 1986), pp. 134–35, railroads and industries in or near East St. Louis. Elliott M. Rudwick, *Race Riot at East St. Louis, July 2, 1917* (Carbondale: Southern Illinois University Press, 1964), p. 5, twenty-seven railroads.

Eli G. Lentz, *Seventy-Five Years in Retrospect: Southern Illinois University, 1874–1949* (Carbondale: Southern Illinois University Publications, 1955), pp. 7–12, siting requirements, possible sites for the university, Carbondale selected, first state agricultural college at Irvington; p. 18, Mrs. Sanders' strawberry patch. Accounts of early Southern Illinois academies and colleges may be found in their respective town and county histories.

Notes to pages 115–17

Tombstone of George Mitchell Miller, Oakland Cemetery, Petersburg, Illinois, downstate boy "killed by the cars." Allen, *It Happened in Southern Illinois*, p. 109, Fountain Bluff excursion trains. Sol Bloom, *The Autobiography of Sol Bloom* (New York: G. P. Putnam's Sons, 1948), p. 136, midway director Sol Bloom says no woman danced as Little Egypt at 1893 fair.

Donna Carlton, *Looking for Little Egypt* (Bloomington, Indiana: IDD Books, 1995), pp. ix–xi, 51–52, 65, 71, 75, no woman danced as Little Egypt at the 1893 Chicago fair; Ashea Wabe made the name "Little Egypt" famous at an 1896 gentleman's club in New York City; Fahreda Mahzar at 1933 Chicago World's Fair. Mrs. Elizabeth Lowe Parsons with William J. Brinkley, "Shawneetown," *Springhouse* 6 (December 1989), p. 41, Joseph Street, Westwood.

Notes to pages 118–29

Corliss, *Main Line of Mid-America*, IC's role in Illinois history and involvement with coal; p. 74, successful experiments with Du Quoin area coal; p. 275, first train in Franklin County in 1879; p. 371, Edgewood Cutoff; pp. 301–11, Casey Jones. Changnon, *The Triangle*, pp. 18–19, C&EI in 1895. George Kimball Plochmann, *The Ordeal of Southern Illinois University* (Carbondale: Southern Illinois University Press, [1959]), p. 35, 16,000 miners in Franklin County.

Several overlapping books discuss Coal Belt violence, murders, Prohibition, the Ku Klux Klan, or gangsters during the 1920s and '30s: Paul M. Angle, *Bloody Williamson: A Chapter in American Lawlessness* (New York: Knopf, 1952). *Life and Exploits of S. Glenn Young: World-Famous Law Enforcement Officer* (Herrin, Illinois: Mrs. S. Glenn Young, 1924; rpt. Herrin, Illinois: Crossfire Press, 1989). Gary DeNeal, *A Knight of Another Sort: Prohibition Days and Charlie Birger* (Danville, Illinois: Interstate Printers, 1981; 2nd ed. Carbondale: Southern Illinois University Press, 1998). Taylor Pensoneau, *Brothers Notorious: The Sheltons, Southern Illinois' Legendary Gangsters* (New Berlin, Illinois: Downstate Publications, 2002). Taylor Pensoneau, *Dapper and Deadly: The True Story of Black Charlie Harris* (New Berlin, Illinois: Downstate Publications, 2010).

C. William Horrell, Henry Dan Piper, John W. Voigt, *Land between the Rivers: The Southern Illinois Country* (Carbondale: Southern Illinois

University Press, 1973), p. 41, Billy Bryan. Sneed, *Ghost Towns of Southern Illinois*, p. 251, repeats story that some customers boycotted Southern Illinois coal after the Herrin Massacre. Brocton Lockwood, "Delos L. Duty: Williamson County's Bravest Man," *Springhouse* 18, no. 6 (December 2001), pp. 14–15, jury possibly bribed.

Notes to pages 118, 124, 129–31

Robert E. Hartley and David Kenney, *Death Underground: The Centralia and West Frankfort Mine Disasters* (Carbondale: Southern Illinois University Press, 2006), pp. 1–20, overview of all aspects of Coal Belt through 1951, including strikes, union violence, decrease in mine employment after mid-1920s, use of other sources of energy; pp. 114–15, Centralia explosion caused by improper materials used in blasting; pp. 162–65, West Frankfort explosion sparked by miners smoking cigarettes.

Notes to page 131

Melvyn Dubofsky and Warren Van Tine, *John L. Lewis: A Biography* (New York: Quadrangle/New York Times, 1977), numerous pages describe union violence, including pp. 8, 85, 165; p. 84, "Representatives of our organization." Hartley and Kenney, *Death Underground*, p. 18, Lewis hits opponent in face.

Joy, "When the Railroad Car was King in Mount Vernon," p. 17, labor disputes. Changnon, *The Triangle*, pp. 38, 40, strong labor unions limit freight car production in Centralia. Herman R. Lantz, *A Community in Search of Itself: A Case History of Cairo, Illinois* (Carbondale: Southern Illinois University Press, 1972), p. 197, strikes in Cairo. Baker Brownell, *The Other Illinois* (New York: Duell, Sloan, and Pearce, 1958), pp. 41–42, strikes in Joppa. Willadene Brown, *You Will Never Know What You Can Do Until You Try* (Springfield, Illinois: Phillips Brothers, 1977), pp. 100–02, labor racketeering, dozens of strikes in Joppa.

Notes to pages 131–32

Rudwick, *Race Riot at East St. Louis*, p. 172, labor shortage existed in East St. Louis in 1917, union leaders claim white laborers replaced by African Americans. Neal R. Peirce, *The Megastates of America: People, Politics, and Power in the Ten Great States* (New York: W. W. Norton, 1972), p. 401, railroads and meat packers import southern blacks as strikebreakers, East St. Louis employers leave in 1940s and '50s. Tingley, *The Structuring of a State*, p. 296, 1917 race riot occurs after Aluminum Ore company imports southern blacks as strikebreakers.

Janice Petterchak, *Historic Illinois: An Illustrated History* (San Antonio: Historical Publishing Network, 2005), p. 55, labor shortage existed in East St. Louis. Howard, *Illinois*, p. 445, unions often deny membership to African Americans. Horsley, *Illinois: A Geography*, pp. 136–37, East St. Louis' corruption, strong local unions, high labor costs. Robert A. Harper, *The University That Shouldn't Have Happened, but Did: Southern Illinois University during the Morris Years, 1948–1970* (Carbondale, Illinois: Devil's Kitchen Press, 1998), p. 9, nonunion sweatshops staffed by women.

DeNeal, *A Knight of Another Sort*, pp. 183–95, Phil Hanna. "Gunfire Lays Low One More Shelton," *Life*, June 19, 1950, p. 39+. Harry B. Wilson, "Terror in Southern Illinois," *Esquire*, February 1951, p. 61+. John Bartlow Martin, "The Sheltons: America's Bloodiest Gang," *Saturday Evening Post*, March 18, 1950, p. 24+.

Notes to pages 132–34

Ron Powers, *Far from Home: Life and Loss in Two American Towns* (New York: Random House, 1991), analyzes Cairo's problems. Marva Nelson, "Memory's Lessons," in *Let My People Go: Cairo, Illinois, 1967–1973*, ed. Preston Ewing Jr., and Jan Peterson Roddy (Carbondale: Southern Illinois University Press, 1996), p. xvi, some restaurants served African Americans, some did not; pool filled with concrete; photo captions, pp. 66–68, fire bomb, black-owned and white-owned stores burned in suspected arsons. Lantz, *A Community in Search of Itself*, p. 76, 1909 lynching of black and white men; p. 54, welfare creates dependency; p. 80, Cairo murder rate.

Biles, *Illinois*, p. 196, south side Black Belt, Chicago one of country's most segregated cities during second decade of the 1900s, black homes bombed; p. 242, Chicago maintains segregation in 1940s; p. 257, white mobs attack and kill blacks encroaching on white neighborhoods in 1940s and 1950s, white mobs sometimes number in the thousands, Chicago press downplays racial incidents, Cicero riots; pp. 181–82, Oak Park fire bombs, in year 2000 most of Chicago's suburbs remained all white or all black; p. 271, zoning makes Chicago largest segregated city in Illinois.

Notes to pages 134–35

Shirley Motley Portwood, *Tell Us a Story: An African American Family in the Heartland* (Carbondale: Southern Illinois University Press, 2000), personal and family stories of segregation in and around Mounds, Illinois, and elsewhere. Charles E. Koen, *The Cairo Story: And the Round-up of Black Leadership* (Cairo, Illinois: Koen Press, [1988?]), African American activist tells of Cairo in the 1960s. H. B. Koplowitz, *Carbondale after Dark and Other Stories* (Hollywood: Dome Publications, 1982; rpt. 2007), pp. 22–23, Black Panthers. Peirce, *The Megastates of America*, p. 401, by 1969 white and black residents of East St. Louis fear murder and strong-arm robbery, outsiders warned not to go to East St. Louis.

Colby, *Pilot Study of Southern Illinois*, pp. 64, 82, frequent strikes, picket lines, and violence scare outside industries. Harper, *The University That Shouldn't Have Happened, but Did*, p. 9, militant unions frighten prospective employers. Hartley and Kenney, *Death Underground*, p. 15, United Mine Workers of America union frightens prospective businesses. Gordon Pruett to Herbert Russell, conversation, summer 2008, Herrin overcomes labor turmoil and achieves balance of strong unions and stable employers for decades.

Notes to page 135–37

Valerie Glidehaus et al., "The End of the Steamboat Era in Jackson County," *Illinois Heritage* 7 (March-April 2004), p. 6, *Golden Eagle*. Stefano Fermi, "A National Historic Landmark Preserves America's Past" (1998; rpt. *Delta Queen* Steamboat Company, access via Internet).

Notes to pages 137, 139

Birth of the Shawnee National Forest—1933–Present; written in 1938, this nine-page summary of the establishment of the forest shows the involvement of Harrisburg area citizens and their goals in 1930 (access by Internet). "Out of the Past," *Hardin County Independent*, May 18, 2006, p. 8, "from forest reserves to National Forests"; this reprint from a May 1955 *Hardin County Independent* tells of the fiftieth anniversary of the U.S. forest service and its early goals. Kay Rippelmeyer, *Giant City State Park and the Civilian Conservation Corps: A History in Words and Pictures* (Carbondale: Southern Illinois University Press, 2010). The CCC statue at Giant City is one of several identical statues produced by Elliott Ganz Foundry, New York, for former CCC sites—per Internet information.

Notes to pages 139, 142–43

Petterchak, *Historic Illinois*, p. 57, early paved roads. Tingley, *The Structuring of a State*, pp. 47–56, tractors and farming. Corliss, *Main Line of Mid-America*, p. 412, trains are major consumer of Illinois coal.

Notes to pages 143, 145–46

John H. Keiser, *Building for the Centuries: Illinois, 1865 to 1898*, Sesquicentennial History of Illinois, vol. 4 (Urbana: University of Illinois Press, 1977), p. 289, rural, blue-collar handlers of raw materials resent urban middlemen. Herbert K. Russell, *A Southern Illinois Album: Farm Security Administration Photographs, 1936–1943* (Carbondale: Southern Illinois University Press, 1990), p. 40, "Unemployed mine worker"; p. 53, "Miner's home." Mary Watters, *Illinois in the Second World War*, 2 vols. (Springfield: Illinois State Historical Library, 1951–52).

Notes to pages 146, 148–51

Three overlapping sources deal in detail with President Delyte Morris: Harper, *The University That Shouldn't Have Happened, but Did*.

Plochmann, *The Ordeal of Southern Illinois University*, which emphasizes years 1943–55. Betty Mitchell, *Delyte Morris of SIU* (Carbondale: Southern Illinois University Press, 1988). Robert E. Hartley, *Paul Powell of Illinois: A Lifelong Democrat* (Carbondale: Southern Illinois University Press, 1999), pp. 78–79, Powell confronts University of Illinois officials.

Koplowitz, *Carbondale after Dark*, p. 20, Center for Vietnamese Studies; p. 52, Richard Richman, "Hitler youth," seventy-eight businesses damaged; pp. 9–63, protests, riot details, crowd numbers, destruction. Herman R. Lantz, *People of Coal Town* (Carbondale: Southern Illinois University Press, 1958; rpt. Arcturus Books, 1971), p. xv, rumors of taking revenge on those who vandalized Carbondale. Codell Rodriguez, "Former SIU Students Recount 1970 Protests," *Southern Illinoisan*, March 25, 2010, p. 2B, a former student leader of protests says SIU's shutdown helped end Vietnam War.

Notes to pages 153–59

Lee Griggs, "In Illinois: Deep-Shaft Trouble," *Time*, September 28, 1981, p. 16, nonunion mine. Pensoneau, *Dapper and Deadly*. Pensoneau, *Brothers Notorious*, pp. 222–78, Harris and the Shelton Brothers. Among the old-time gangsters whose careers came to an end in the late 1960s was Frank "Buster" Wortman, East St. Louis and Collinsville hoodlum who died in 1968, per *Brothers Notorious*, pp. 281–82.

Notes to pages 159–71

Changnon, *The Triangle*, p. 85, 1982 union agreement curtails cabooses by 1990s. J. L. Anderson, *Industrializing the Corn Belt: Agriculture, Technology, and Environment, 1945–1972* (DeKalb: Northern Illinois University Press, 2009), pp. 188–95, the late 1960s and early '70s marked a new era in farming. *The Changing Face of Farmwork in Union County*, ed. Travelstead, history of produce and migrant workers.

Notes to pages 172–74

The Illinois Community College Board, Springfield, maintains enrollment records. Teri Campbell, John A. Logan College, to Herbert Russell, conversations, September 2008, over 50 percent of senior classes from Johnston City and Carterville, Illinois, attend the local community college.

Notes to pages 178, 183

"The 47th Ozark Tour," *Outdoor Illinois* 15 (June-July 1976), p. 6, L. O. Trigg's tourism work. Brown, *You Will Never Know What You Can Do Until You Try*, pp. 130, 140, Wayman Presley's tours. Dianne Throgmorton, "W. R. Hayes Did It His Way When He Established the Du Quoin State Fair," in *Concerning Coal: An Anthology*, ed. Magdalen Mayer et al. (Carbondale: Coal Research Center, 1997), pp. 34–35. Bethany Krajelis, "17th Street Ribs Receive Top Honor from Food Network," *Southern Illinoisan*, August 19, 2007, p. 1+, *Bon Appétit* choice announced on the Food Network.

Bibliography

African American Settlements in Southern Illinois, brochure comp. Vickie Devenport ([Harrisburg, Illinois:] Shawnee National Forest; Murphysboro, Illinois: General John A. Logan Museum, [2001]).

Allen, John W. *It Happened in Southern Illinois* (Carbondale: University Graphics, 1968; rpt. Carbondale: Southern Illinois University Press, 2010).

———. *Legends and Lore of Southern Illinois* (Carbondale: Southern Illinois University, 1963; rpt. Carbondale: Southern Illinois University Press, 2010).

Anderson, J. L. *Industrializing the Corn Belt: Agriculture, Technology, and Environment, 1945–1972*. (DeKalb: Northern Illinois University Press, 2009).

Angle, Paul M. *Bloody Williamson: A Chapter in American Lawlessness* (New York: Knopf, 1952; rpt. Urbana: University of Illinois Press, 1992).

Annual Report of the Adjutant General of the State of Illinois (Springfield: Baker and Phillips, 1863).

Atlas of the State of Illinois (Chicago: Union Atlas Co., 1876; rpt. Indianapolis: Ye Olde Genealogie Shoppe, 2000).

Beer, Thomas. *The Mauve Decade: American Life at the End of the Nineteenth Century* (New York: Knopf, 1926; rpt. New York: Carroll and Graf, 1997).

Belting, Natalia Maree. *Kaskaskia under the French Regime* (Urbana: University of Illinois Press, 1948; rpt. Carbondale: Southern Illinois University Press, 2003).

Benedict, David. *A General History of the Baptist Denomination in America and Other Parts of the World* (New York: Lewis Copeland, 1848).

Bennett, Lerone, Jr. *Before the Mayflower: A History of the Negro in America, 1619–1966* (Chicago: Johnson Publishing Company, 1966).

Biles, Roger. *Illinois: A History of the Land and Its People* (DeKalb: Northern Illinois University Press, 2005).

Birth of the Shawnee National Forest—1933–Present [1938]. Access via Internet.

Blackman, W. S. *The Boy of Battle Ford and the Man* (Marion, Illinois: Egyptian Press Printing, 1906).

Bloom, Sol. *The Autobiography of Sol Bloom* (New York: G. P. Putnam's Sons, 1948).

Boewe, Charles. *Prairie Albion: An English Settlement in Pioneer Illinois* (Carbondale: Southern Illinois University Press, 1962; rpt. 1999).

Bond, David. "Temporary Work Stoppage," *Colors* (greatunpublished.com, 2001).

Brown, Margaret Kimball. *History as They Lived It: A Social History of Prairie du Rocher, Illinois* (Tucson: Patrice Press, 2005).

———. "The Search for the Michigamea Indian Village," *Outdoor Illinois* 11 (March 1972).

Brown, Margaret Kimball, and Lawrie Cena Dean. *The French Colony in the Mid-Mississippi Valley* (Carbondale, Illinois: American Kestrel Books, 1995).

Brown, Willadene. *You Will Never Know What You Can Do Until You Try* (Springfield, Illinois: Phillips Brothers, 1977).

"Brown University's Debt to Slavery," *New York Times*, October 23, 2006.

Brownell, Baker. *The Other Illinois* (New York: Duell, Sloan, and Pearce, 1958).

[Brush, Daniel Harmon.] *Growing Up with Southern Illinois, 1820 to 1861, from the Memoirs of Daniel Harmon Brush*, ed. Milo Milton Quaife (Chicago: R.R. Donnelley, 1944; rpt., foreword by John Y. Simon, Herrin, Illinois: Crossfire Press, 1992).

Buck, Solon J. *Illinois in 1818* (Springfield: Illinois Centennial Commission, 1917; rpt. Urbana: University of Illinois Press, 1967).

Buley, R. Carlyle. *The Old Northwest Pioneer Period, 1815–1840*. 2 vols. (Indianapolis: Indiana Historical Society, 1950).

Burkhardt, George S. *Confederate Rage, Yankee Wrath: No Quarter in the Civil War* (Carbondale: Southern Illinois University Press, 2007).

Cairo City Gazette / Cairo City Weekly Gazette, December 6, 1860–April 18, 1861.

[Camm, William.] "Diary of Colonel William Camm, 1861–1865," comp. Fritz Haskell, *Journal of the Illinois State Historical Society* 18 (January 1926).

Campbell, Teri. Conversations re community college enrollments, September 2008.

Carlton, Donna. *Looking for Little Egypt* (Bloomington, Indiana: IDD Books, 1995).

Carson, Clayborne, Emma J. Lapsansky-Werner, and Gary B. Nash. *The Struggle for Freedom: A History of African Americans* (New York: Pearson Longman, 2007).

Cha-Jua, Sundiata Keita. *America's First Black Town: Brooklyn, Illinois, 1830–1915* (Urbana: University of Illinois Press, 2000).

Changing Face of Farmwork in Union County, Illinois, The: A History of Fruits and Vegetables and the People Who Worked in the Industry, ed. Judy Travelstead, Bonnie Heidinger, and Pat Meller (Union County Historical and Genealogy Society, 2008).

Changnon, Stanley A. *The Triangle—Busy Railroading in Southern Illinois* (Champaign, Illinois: Printec Press, 1991).

Chapman, Mrs. P. T. *A History of Johnson County Illinois* (1925; rpt. Johnson County Genealogical and Historical Society, 2003).

Chappell, Sally A. Kitt. *Cahokia: Mirror of the Cosmos* (Chicago: University of Chicago Press, 2002).

Clay County Census of 1860 (Louisville, Illinois: Clay County Genealogical Society, 1992).

Clay County General Index, Book A (Grantee), Clay County, Illinois, Courthouse, Louisville.

Clay Roots [Louisville, Illinois: Clay County Genealogical Society] (winter 1993).

Cobb, Charles R., and Brian M. Butler. "The Vacant Quarter Revisited: Late Mississippian Abandonment of the Lower Ohio Valley," *American Antiquity* 67, no. 4 (2002).

Colby, Charles. *Pilot Study of Southern Illinois* (Carbondale: Southern Illinois University Press, 1956).

Cole, Fay-Cooper, et al. *Kincaid: A Prehistoric Illinois Metropolis* (Chicago: University of Chicago Press, 1951).

Combined History [of] Edwards, Lawrence, and Wabash Counties, Illinois (Philadelphia: J. L. McDonough, 1883).

Confederate Soldiers of Kentucky: A Roster of the Veterans 1861–1865, ed. Stephen Douglas Lynn (Dexter, Michigan: Thomson-Shore, 2002).

Conley, Robert J. *The Cherokee Nation: A History* (Albuquerque: University of New Mexico Press, 2005).

Corliss, Carlton J. *Main Line of Mid-America: The Story of the Illinois Central* (New York: Creative Age Press, 1950).

Cornelius, James M. *John Hart Crenshaw and Hickory Hill: Final Report* (Springfield: Illinois Historic Preservation Agency, 2002).

"Cortos." "Apprehensions of an attack . . . ," *Chicago Tribune*, April 26, 1861, re Williamson County secession.

Cross, Jasper W. "The Civil War Comes to 'Egypt,'" *Journal of the Illinois State Historical Society* 44 (summer 1951).

Davis, James E. *Frontier Illinois* (Bloomington: Indiana University Press, 1998).

Dearinger, Lowell A. "Miller Grove," *Outdoor Illinois* 4 (November 1965).

DeNeal, Gary. Conversations with Herbert Russell re Southern Illinois history and books, 2003–10.

———. "Crenshaw-Granger Update," *Springhouse* 14 (April 1997).

———. *A Knight of Another Sort: Prohibition Days and Charlie Birger* (Danville, Illinois: Interstate Printers, 1981; 2nd ed. Carbondale: Southern Illinois University Press, 1998).

———. [Editorial response to reader letter.] *Springhouse* 16 (June 1999), p. 7 note on Cornelius Elliott.

———. ["These hills impound archaic silence,"] *Blue Hills, Blue Shadows* (privately circulated, 1995).

Dexter, Darrel. *Bondage in Egypt: Slavery and Indentured Servitude in Southern Illinois, 1720–1865* (Cape Girardeau: Southeast Missouri State Center for Regional History, 2011).

———. Conversations with Herbert Russell re race relations and slavery in Southern Illinois, March 1, 2008, February 10, 2009; and correspondence, March 1, 2010, May 18, 2011.

———. "Desertion from the 109th Regiment Illinois Volunteer Infantry," *Saga of Southern Illinois* 33, no. 2 (April–June 2006).

———. "Entries of Free Negroes 1814, 1822–1844, 1846–1863, St. Clair County, Illinois," *Saga of Southern Illinois* 33, no. 3 (July–September 2006).

———. *Free and American: A Study of Eleven Families of Color* (access via Internet at http://www.freeafricanamericans.com/Illinois.htm).

———. "Harry: From Illinois Slave to Illinois Landowner," Illinois State Historical Society Symposium, Southern Illinois University Carbondale, April 14, 2011.

———. *A Trot Down to Egypt: The Lincoln-Douglas Debate in Jonesboro, Illinois* (Jonesboro Lincoln-Douglas Debate Sesquicentennial Committee, 2008).

Dilliard, Irving. "John W. Allen: A Personal Word," in John W. Allen, *It Happened in Southern Illinois* (Carbondale: University Graphics, 1968; rpt. Carbondale: Southern Illinois University Press, 2010).

Dillow, Myron D. *Harvesttime on the Prairie: A History of Baptists in Illinois, 1796–1996* (Franklin, Tennessee: Providence House Publishers, 1996).

Dorson, Richard M. *Buying the Wind: Regional Folklore in the United States* (Chicago: University of Chicago Press, 1964).

Douglass, Frederick. "'Men of Color, to Arms!'" in *Frederick Douglass: Selected Speeches and Writings*, ed. Philip S. Foner (Chicago: Lawrence Hill Books, 1999).

Dubofsky, Melvyn, and Warren Van Tine. *John L. Lewis: A Biography* (New York: Quadrangle/New York Times, 1977).

Ecelbarger, Gary. *Black Jack Logan: An Extraordinary Life in Peace and War* (Guilford, Connecticut: Lyons Press, 2005).

Ehle, John. *Trail of Tears: The Rise and Fall of the Cherokee Nation* (New York: Doubleday, 1988).

1866–1966 National Memorial Day Centennial, Carbondale, Illinois (pamphlet, May 30, 1966).

Ekberg, Carl J. *French Roots in the Illinois Country: The Mississippi Frontier in Colonial Times* (Urbana: University of Illinois Press, 1998).

Erwin, Milo. *History of Williamson County Illinois* (Marion, Illinois, 1876; rpt. Herrin, Illinois: The Herrin News, 1914).

Etcheson, Nicole. *The Emerging Midwest: Upland Southerners and the Political Culture of the Old Northwest, 1787–1861* (Bloomington: Indiana University Press, 1996).

[Evans, James.] *Letters to the Editor of the Jonesboro Gazette, 1862–1863, from James Evans, Adjutant, 109th Illinois Volunteer Infantry Regiment, Union Army*, ed. Patrick Brumleve, Bonnie Heidinger, and Judy Travelstead (Union County Historical and Genealogy Society, 2006).

Evans, Linda Jeanne. "Abolitionism in the Illinois Churches, 1830–1865" (dissertation; Evanston, Illinois: Northwestern University, 1981).

Fermi, Stefano. "A National Historic Landmark Preserves America's Past" (1998; rpt. *Delta Queen* Steamboat Company, access via Internet).

Fischer, David Hackett. *Albion's Seed: Four British Folkways in America* (New York: Oxford University Press, 1989).

"47th Ozark Tour, The," *Outdoor Illinois* 15 (June-July 1976).

Fox, William F. *Regimental Losses in the American Civil War, 1861–1865* (Albany: Brandow Printing, 1898; rpt. Morningside Bookshop, 1974).

Furry, William. "Historic Hullabaloo," *Illinois Times*, May 8–14, 1997; rpt. *Springhouse* 14 (June 1997).

Gara, Larry. *The Liberty Line: The Legend of the Underground Railroad* (Lexington: University of Kentucky Press, 1967).

Gleeson, Ed. *Illinois Rebels: A Civil War Unit History of G Company Fifteenth Tennessee Regiment Volunteer Infantry* (Carmel: Guild Press of Indiana, 1996).

Glidehaus, Valerie, Robert Morefield, and Cliff Swafford. "The End of the Steamboat Era in Jackson County," *Illinois Heritage* 7 (March-April 2004).

Goins, William. Conversations with Herbert Russell re Stumptown, 2005, 2006.

Grant, Ulysses S., to Julia [Dent Grant], May 21, 1861, in *Ulysses S. Grant, Memoirs and Selected Letters* (New York: Library of America, 1990).

Gray, Wood. *The Hidden Civil War: The Story of the Copperheads* (New York: Viking, 1942).

Griffler, Keith P. *Frontier Line of Freedom: African Americans and the Forging of the Underground Railroad in the Ohio Valley* (Lexington: University Press of Kentucky, 2004).

Griggs, Lee. "In Illinois: Deep-Shaft Trouble," *Time*, September 28, 1981.

"Guerillas in Illinois," *Louisville Journal*, September 3, 1864.

"Gunfire Lays Low One More Shelton," *Life*, June 19, 1950.

Handbook of Old Gallatin County, ed. Jon Musgrave (Marion, Illinois: IllinoisHistory.com, 2002).

Harper, Robert A. *The University That Shouldn't Have Happened, but Did: Southern Illinois University during the Morris Years, 1948–1970* (Carbondale, Illinois: Devil's Kitchen Press, 1998).

Harrelson, Ralph S. *Pioneer Baptist Ministers: Voices in the Wilderness of the Illinois Country* (McLeansboro, Illinois: Ralph S. Harrelson, 1987).

Harris, N. Dwight. *The History of Negro Servitude in Illinois and of the Slavery Agitation in That State, 1719–1864* (Chicago: McClurg, 1904).

Hartley, Robert E. *Lewis and Clark in the Illinois Country: The Little-Told Story* (Westminster, Colorado: Sniktau Publications, 2002).

———. *Paul Powell of Illinois: A Lifelong Democrat* (Carbondale: Southern Illinois University Press, 1999).

Hartley, Robert E., and David Kenney. *Death Underground: The Centralia and West Frankfort Mine Disasters* (Carbondale: Southern Illinois University Press, 2006).

Hastings, Robert J. *A Nickel's Worth of Skim Milk: A Boy's View of the Great Depression* (Carbondale: Southern Illinois University Press, 1972).

Havighurst, Walter. *The Heartland: Ohio, Indiana, Illinois* (New York: Harper and Row, 1962).

Heinegg, Paul. *Free African Americans of North Carolina, Virginia, and South Carolina from the Colonial Period to about 1820*, vol. 1 (Baltimore: Clearfield, 2001).

Hicken, Victor. *Illinois in the Civil War,* 2nd ed. (Urbana: University of Illinois Press, 1991).

———. "The Record of Illinois' Negro Soldiers in the Civil War," *Journal of the Illinois State Historical Society* 56 (autumn 1963).

History of Gallatin, Saline, Hamilton, Franklin, and Williamson Counties, Illinois (Chicago: Goodspeed Publishing Company, 1887; rpt. Winnetka Public Library, 1973).

History of White County Illinois (Chicago: Inter-State Publishing Company, 1883; rpt. White County Historical Society, 1966).

Horrell, C. William, Henry Dan Piper, and John W. Voigt. *Land between the Rivers: The Southern Illinois Country* (Carbondale: Southern Illinois University Press, 1973).

Horsley, Doyne A. *Illinois: A Geography* (Boulder: Westview Press, 1986).

Howard, Robert P. *Illinois: A History of the Prairie State* (Grand Rapids: Eerdmans, 1972).

Hubbs, Barbara Burr. *Pioneer Folks and Places: An Historic Gazetteer of Williamson County, Illinois* (Herrin, Illinois: Herrin Daily Journal, 1939; rpt. Marion, Illinois: Williamson County Historical Society, 1979).

Hudson, John. *Making the Corn Belt* (Bloomington: Indiana University Press, 1994).

Illinois Census Returns, 1810, 1818, ed. with intro. and notes by Margaret Cross Norton (Springfield: Illinois State Historical Library, 1935).

Illinois Fact Book and Historical Almanac, 1673–1968, The, comp. John Clayton (Carbondale: Southern Illinois University Press, 1970).

Illinois Reader, An, comp. and ed. Clyde C. Walton (DeKalb: Northern Illinois University Press, 1970).

"Invasion of Illinois, The," *New York Times*, August 19, 1864.

Iseminger, William. *Cahokia Mounds: America's First City* (Charleston, South Carolina: The History Press, 2010).

Johannsen, Robert W. *Stephen A. Douglas* (New York: Oxford University Press, 1973).

Johnson, Adam R. *The Partisan Rangers of the Confederate States Army* (Louisville: George G. Fetter Company, 1904; rpt. Evansville, Indiana: Unigraphic, Inc., 1971).

Jones, James Pickett. *Black Jack: John A. Logan and Southern Illinois in the Civil War Era* (Tallahassee: Florida State University, 1967; rpt., foreword by John Y. Simon, Carbondale: Southern Illinois University Press, 1995).

Joy, Judith. "When the Railroad Car was King in Mt. Vernon," *Illinois Magazine* 19 (January-February 1980).

Keiser, John H. *Building for the Centuries: Illinois, 1865 to 1898*, Sesquicentennial History of Illinois, vol. 4 (Urbana: University of Illinois Press, 1977).

Kimmel, Stanley. "Du Quoin," *The Kingdom of Smoke: Sketches of My People* (New York: Nicholas L. Brown, 1932).

Kionka, T. K. *Key Command: Ulysses S. Grant's District of Cairo* (Columbia: University of Missouri Press, 2006).

Klein, Herbert S. *The Atlantic Slave Trade* (New York: Cambridge University Press, 1999).

Koen, Charles E. *The Cairo Story: And the Round-up of Black Leadership* (Cairo, Illinois: Koen Press, [1988?]).

Kohlmeyer, Fred W. "Illinois Agriculture in Retrospect," in *Illinois: Its History and Legacy*, ed. Roger D. Bridges and Rodney O. Davis (St. Louis: River City Publishers, 1984).

Koplowitz, H. B. *Carbondale after Dark and Other Stories* (Hollywood: Dome Publications, 1982; rpt. 2007).

Krajelis, Bethany. "17th Street Ribs Receive Top Honor from Food Network," *Southern Illinoisan*, August 19, 2007.

Kuenneke, Richard. *The Search for Cantonment Wilkinsonville: The Archaeology of an 1801 Military Post in Pulaski County, Illinois* (Oakview Road Media, 2006), DVD.

Lantz, Herman R. *A Community in Search of Itself: A Case History of Cairo, Illinois* (Carbondale: Southern Illinois University Press, 1972).

———. *People of Coal Town* (Carbondale: Southern Illinois University Press, 1958; rpt. Arcturus Books, 1971).

Lentz, Eli G. *Seventy-Five Years in Retrospect: Southern Illinois University, 1874–1949* (Carbondale: Southern Illinois University Publications, 1955).

Let My People Go: Cairo, Illinois, 1967–1973, ed. Preston Ewing Jr. and Jan Peterson Roddy (Carbondale: Southern Illinois University Press, 1996).

Life and Exploits of S. Glenn Young: World-Famous Law Enforcement Officer (Herrin, Illinois: Mrs. S. Glenn Young, 1924; rpt. Herrin, Illinois: Crossfire Press, 1989).

Lockwood, Brocton. "Delos L. Duty: Williamson County's Bravest Man," *Springhouse* 18, no. 6 (December 2001).

McCafferty, Michael. "A Fresh Look at the Place Name *Chicago*," *Journal of the Illinois State Historical Society* 96 (summer 2003).

McClay, Michael. Conversations with Herbert Russell re Oakdale, Illinois, March 26, 29, 2009.

McClinton, Rowena. Conversation with Herbert Russell re Trail of Tears through Southern Illinois, November 19, 2009.

McCormick, Mildred. Conversations with Herbert Russell re Confederate raid at Bayfield, fall 2008, September 30, 2009.

———. "Raiders on the Ohio," *Springhouse* 1, no. 7 (November-December 1984).

McCorvie, Mary. Conversation with Herbert Russell re Trail of Tears through Southern Illinois, December 10, 2009.

McManus, Edgar J. *Black Bondage in the North* (Syracuse: Syracuse University Press, 1973).

McNeill, Chloe. "Africa, Illinois," *The Egyptian Key* 2 (March 1947).

McNulty, Elizabeth. *Chicago Then and Now* (San Diego: Thunder Bay Press, 2000).

McPherson, James M. *The Illustrated Battle Cry of Freedom: The Civil War Era* (New York: Oxford University Press, 2003).

Martin, Albro. *Railroads Triumphant* (New York: Oxford University Press, 1992).

Martin, John Bartlow. "The Sheltons: America's Bloodiest Gang," *Saturday Evening Post*, March 18, 1950.

"'Men of Color, to Arms!'" in *Frederick Douglass: Selected Speeches and Writings*, ed. Philip S. Foner (Chicago: Lawrence Hill Books, 1999).

Metzger, John. "The Old Slave House," *Outdoor Illinois* 12 (January 1973).

Miller, Edward A., Jr. *The Black Civil War Soldiers of Illinois: The Story of the Twenty-Ninth U.S. Colored Infantry* (Columbia: University of South Carolina Press, 1998).

Missouri Department of Natural Resources' Missouri State Museum re slave numbers (access via Internet).

Mitchell, Betty. *Delyte Morris of SIU* (Carbondale: Southern Illinois University Press, 1988).

Mohlenbrock, Robert H. *Forest Trees of Illinois* (Illinois Department of Natural Resources, 1996).

———. "A New Geography of Illinois: Johnson County," *Outdoor Illinois* 14 (January 1975).

———. "A New Geography of Illinois: Saline County," *Illinois* 16 (December 1977).

Morgan, M. J. *Land of Big Rivers: French and Indian Illinois, 1699–1778* (Carbondale: Southern Illinois University Press, 2010).

Musgrave, Jon. *Slaves, Salt, Sex, and Mr. Crenshaw: The Real Story of the Old Slave House and America's Reverse Underground R.R.* (Marion, Illinois: IllinoisHistory.com, 2004–2005).

National Road, The, ed. Karl Raitz (Baltimore: Johns Hopkins University Press, 1996).

Nelson, Marva. "Memory's Lessons," in *Let My People Go: Cairo, Illinois, 1967–1973*, ed. Preston Ewing Jr. and Jan Peterson Roddy (Carbondale: Southern Illinois University Press, 1996).

Nelson, Ronald L. Conversation with Herbert Russell re Emancipation Baptists, research on Old Slave House, March 25, 2008.

Nelson, Ronald L., Doris Nelson, and Ralph S. Harrelson. *History of Liberty Baptist Church, Saline County, IL, 1832–1996* (Utica, Kentucky: McDowell Publications, 1996).

Nelson, Ronald L., and Gary DeNeal. "A Mystery Solved," *Springhouse* 14 (February 1997).

Newborn, Newton N. "Judicial Decision Making and the End of Slavery in Illinois," *Journal of the Illinois State Historical Society* 98 (spring-summer 2005).

Newsome, Edmund. *Historical Sketches of Jackson County, Illinois* (Carbondale: E. Newsome Publisher, 1894; rpt. Jackson County Historical Society, 1997).

Oliver, William. *Eight Months in Illinois, with Information to Immigrants* (William Andrew Mitchell, 1843; rpt. Walter M. Hill, 1924; rpt. Carbondale: Southern Illinois University Press, 2002).

"Out of the Past," *Hardin County Independent*, May 18, 2006, re national forests.

Parsons, Mrs. Elizabeth Lowe, with William J. Brinkley. "Shawneetown," *Springhouse* 6 (December 1989).

Pauketat, Timothy R. *Ancient Cahokia and the Mississippians* (New York: Cambridge University Press, 2004).

Pearson, Emmet F. "The Historic Hospitals of Cairo," *Journal of the Illinois State Historical Society* 77 (1984).

Peirce, Neal R. *The Megastates of America: People, Politics, and Power in the Ten Great States* (New York: W.W. Norton, 1972).

Peithmann, Irvin M. *Indians of Southern Illinois* (Springfield, Illinois: Charles C. Thomas, 1964).

Pensoneau, Taylor. *Brothers Notorious: The Sheltons, Southern Illinois' Legendary Gangsters* (New Berlin, Illinois: Downstate Publications, 2002).

———. *Dapper and Deadly: The True Story of Black Charlie Harris* (New Berlin, Illinois: Downstate Publications, 2010).

Petterchak, Janice. *Historic Illinois: An Illustrated History* (San Antonio: Historical Publishing Network, 2005).

Pirtle, Carol. *Escape Betwixt Two Suns: A True Tale of the Underground Railroad in Illinois* (Carbondale: Southern Illinois University Press, 2000).

Plochmann, George Kimball. *The Ordeal of Southern Illinois University* (Carbondale: Southern Illinois University Press, [1959]).

Portwood, Shirley Motley. *Tell Us a Story: An African American Family in the Heartland* (Carbondale: Southern Illinois University Press, 2000).

Powers, Ron. *Far from Home: Life and Loss in Two American Towns* (New York: Random House, 1991).

Pruett, Gordon. Conversations with Herbert Russell re Herrin, Illinois, summer 2008.

Quarles, Benjamin. *The Negro in the American Revolution* (Chapel Hill: University of North Carolina Press, 1961).

Raines, Edgar F., Jr. "The American Missionary Association in Southern Illinois, 1856–1862: A Case History in the Abolition Movement," *Journal of the Illinois State Historical Society* 65 (autumn 1972).

"Remains of Colonial-Era Blacks Reach Resting Place," *Southern Illinoisan*, October 5, 2003.

Ridgley, Douglas C. *The Geography of Illinois* (Chicago: University of Chicago Press, 1921).

"Riding a Raid" lyrics. Access via Internet.

Rippelmeyer, Kay. *Giant City State Park and the Civilian Conservation Corps: A History in Words and Pictures* (Carbondale: Southern Illinois University Press, 2010).

Rodriguez, Codell. "Former SIU Students Recount 1970 Protests," *Southern Illinoisan*, March 25, 2010.

Rudwick, Elliott M. *Race Riot at East St. Louis, July 2, 1917* (Carbondale: Southern Illinois University Press, 1964; rpt. Urbana: University of Illinois Press, 1982).

Russell, Herbert K. *A Southern Illinois Album: Farm Security Administration Photographs, 1936–1943* (Carbondale: Southern Illinois University Press, 1990).

Schecter, Barnet. *The Devil's Own Work: The Civil War Draft Riots and the Fight to Reconstruct America* (New York: Walker and Company, 2005).

Schuberth, Christopher J. *A View of the Past: An Introduction to Illinois Geology* (Springfield: Illinois State Museum, 1986).

Schultz, Jane E. *Women at the Front: Hospital Workers in Civil War America* (Chapel Hill: University of North Carolina Press, 2004).

Simon, John Y. "Disloyalty in Southern Illinois during the Civil War," Southern Illinois Learning in Retirement public lecture, Southern Illinois University Carbondale, August 17, 2005.

———. Foreword in Howard C. Westwood, *Black Troops, White Commanders, and Freedmen during the Civil War* (Carbondale: Southern Illinois University Press, 1992).

———. "Union County in 1858 and the Lincoln-Douglas Debate," *Journal of the Illinois State Historical Society* 62 (autumn 1969).

Simon, Paul. *Freedom's Champion: Elijah Lovejoy* (Carbondale: Southern Illinois University Press, 1994).

Singleton, Arthur. *Letters from the South and West* (Boston: Richardson and Lord, 1824).

Smith, George Washington. *History of Illinois and Her People*, vol. 1 (Chicago: American Historical Society, 1927).

Sneed, Glenn J. *Ghost Towns of Southern Illinois* (Johnston City, Illinois: A.E.R.P. Publisher, 1977).

Springhouse magazine inside cover showing hillbilly saying, December 1992.

Stampp, Kenneth M. *The Peculiar Institution* (New York: Knopf, 1956).

Staples, Brent. "Wrestling with the Legacy of Slavery at Yale," *New York Times*, August 14, 2001.

Stewart, Brent. "For the Record," *Southern Illinoisan*, January 21, 2007, re Cantonment Wilkinson.

Stroble, Paul E., Jr. *High on the Okaw's Western Bank: Vandalia, Illinois, 1819–39* (Urbana: University of Illinois Press, 1992).

"Study Ties 1811, 1812 Quakes to Illinois Fault," *Southern Illinoisan*, June 9, 2010.

Suderow, Bryce A. "The Battle of the Crater: The Civil War's Worst Massacre" in *Black Flag over Dixie: Racial Atrocities and Reprisals in the Civil War*, ed. Gregory J. W. Urwin (Carbondale: Southern Illinois University Press, 2004).

Sutton, Robert Mize. *The Illinois Central Railroad in Peace and War, 1858–1868* (New York: Arno Press, 1981).

Throgmorton, Dianne. "W. R. Hayes Did It His Way When He Established the Du Quoin State Fair" in *Concerning Coal: An Anthology*, ed. Magdalen Mayer, Mara Lou Hawse, and Paula J. Maloney (Carbondale: Coal Research Center, 1997).

Tingley, Donald F. "The Clingman Raid," *Journal of the Illinois State Historical Society* 56 (summer 1963).

———. *The Structuring of a State: The History of Illinois, 1899–1928*, Sesquicentennial History of Illinois, vol. 5 (Urbana: University of Illinois Press, 1980).

Tombstone of George Mitchell Miller, Oakland Cemetery, Petersburg, Illinois.

Tow, Michael. Review of *Slaves, Salt, Sex, and Mr. Crenshaw* by Jon Musgrave in *Journal of the Illinois State Historical Society* 101 (spring 2008).

Voegeli, V. Jacque. *Free but Not Equal: The Midwest and the Negro during the Civil War* (Chicago: University of Chicago Press, 1967).

Wagner, Mark J. Public lecture re Southern Illinois Indian art, Cultural and Natural Heritage Symposium, Southern Illinois University Carbondale, April 8, 2009.

Wagner, Mark J., and Mary R. McCorvie. "The Pirates of Cave-in-Rock in Myth and Legend," *Springhouse* 28, no. 1, [2011].

Warner, Ezra J. *Generals in Gray: Lives of the Confederate Commanders* (Baton Rouge: Louisiana State University Press, 1959).

Watters, Mary. *Illinois in the Second World War.* 2 vols. (Springfield: Illinois State Historical Library, 1951–52).

Webb, James. *Born Fighting: How the Scots-Irish Shaped America* (New York: Broadway Books, 2004).

Weiner, Dana E. "Anti-Abolition Violence and Freedom of Speech in Peoria, Illinois, 1843–1848," *Journal of Illinois History* 11 (autumn 2008).

Wilson, Bluford. "Southern Illinois in the Civil War," *Transactions of the Illinois State Historical Society* 16 (1911).

Wilson, Harry B. "Terror in Southern Illinois," *Esquire*, February 1951.

Winkler, H. Donald. *Lincoln's Ladies: The Women in the Life of the Sixteenth President* (Nashville: Cumberland House, 2004).

Woodlawn Cemetery, informational flyer, 2001.

Woodwell, Roland H. *John Greenleaf Whittier: A Biography* (Haverhill, Massachusetts: Trustees of the John Greenleaf Whittier Homestead, 1985).

Wormser, Richard. *The Rise and Fall of Jim Crow* (New York: St. Martin's Press, 2003).

Wright, John W. D. *A History of Early Carbondale, Illinois 1852–1905* (Carbondale: Southern Illinois University Press, 1977).

Index

Maps are indicated by page numbers in ***boldface italics***.

Herbert K. Russell earned the Ph.D. in English from Southern Illinois University Carbondale. The author of *Edgar Lee Masters: A Biography* and scholarly articles in journals and reference works, he has edited and written introductions for several Southern Illinois University Press books, including *A Southern Illinois Album: Farm Security Administration Photographs, 1936–1943* and *Southern Illinois Coal: A Portfolio.*

A Shawnee Book

Also available in this series . . .

The Next New Madrid Earthquake: A Survival Guide for the Midwest
WILLIAM ATKINSON

Forgetting and the Forgotten: A Thousand Years of Contested Histories in the Heartland
MICHAEL C. BATINSKI

Reckoning at Eagle Creek: The Secret Legacy of Coal in the Heartland
JEFF BIGGERS

History as They Lived It: A Social History of Prairie du Rocher, Illinois
MARGARET KIMBALL BROWN

Foothold on a Hillside: Memories of a Southern Illinoisan
CHARLESS CARAWAY

Growing Up in a Land Called Egypt: A Southern Illinois Family Biography
CLEO CARAWAY

Colonial Ste. Genevieve: An Adventure on the Mississippi Frontier
CARL J. EKBERG

A Nickel's Worth of Skim Milk: A Boy's View of the Great Depression
ROBERT J. HASTINGS

A Penny's Worth of Minced Ham: Another Look at the Great Depression
ROBERT J. HASTINGS

Southern Illinois Coal: A Portfolio
C. WILLIAM HORRELL

Always of Home: A Southern Illinois Childhood
EDGAR ALLEN IMHOFF

Lives of Fort de Chartres: Commandants, Soldiers, and Civilians in French Illinois, 1720–1770
DAVID MACDONALD

Kaskaskia: The Lost Capital of Illinois
DAVID MACDONALD AND RAINE WATERS

20 Day Trips in and around the Shawnee National Forest
LARRY P. AND DONNA J. MAHAN

Land of Big Rivers: French and Indian Illinois, 1699–1778
M. J. MORGAN

America's Deadliest Twister: The Tri-State Tornado of 1925
GEOFF PARTLOW

Escape Betwixt Two Suns: A True Tale of the Underground Railroad in Illinois
CAROL PIRTLE

Fishing Southern Illinois
ART REID

All Anybody Ever Wanted of Me Was to Work: The Memoirs of Edith Bradley Rendleman
EDITH BRADLEY RENDLEMAN
EDITED BY JANE ADAMS

The Civilian Conservation Corps in Southern Illinois, 1933–1942
KAY RIPPELMEYER

Giant City State Park and the Civilian Conservation Corps: A History in Words and Pictures
KAY RIPPELMEYER

Fluorspar Mining: Photos from Illinois and Kentucky, 1905–1995
HERBERT K. RUSSELL

A Southern Illinois Album: Farm Security Administration Photographs, 1936–1943
HERBERT K. RUSSELL

Snake Road: A Field Guide to the Snakes of LaRue–Pine Hills
JOSHUA J. VOSSLER